Absentee Ownership

Business Enterprise in Recent Times: The Case of America

Thorstein Veblen

With a new introduction by **Marion J. Levy, Jr.**

Transaction Publishers

New Brunswick (U.S.A.) and London (U.K.)

New material this edition copyright © 1997 by Transaction Publishers, New Brunswick, New Jersey 08903. Originally published in 1923 by B.W. Huebsch, Inc./Viking Press.

Library of Congress Catalog Number: 96-2795
ISBN: 1-56000-922-5
Printed in the United States of America

Library of Congress Cataloging-in-Publication Data

Veblen, Thorstein, 1857–1929.
    [Absentee ownership and business enterprise in recent times]
    Absentee ownership : business enterprise in recent times : the case of America / Thorstein Veblen ; with a new introduction by Marion Levy.
        p.   cm.
    Originally published: New York : B.W. Heubsch, 1923.
    ISBN 1-56000-922-5 (pbk.)
    1. Economic history—1918–1945. 2. Industries—United States. I. Title.
HC106.V4   1996
338.0973—dc20   96-2795
                                                          CIP

CONTENTS

INTRODUCTION TO THE TRANSACTION EDITION

THE title of *Absentee Ownership* is itself typical of Veblen's use of language. True, on the title page of the original book the full title is given: Absentee Ownership (in large caps) and Business Enterprise in Recent Times (in smaller caps) and The Case of America (in smaller caps yet), but the title on the cover of the original book is *Absentee Ownership,* and I confess that not until I turned to this introduction did I realize that the title technically included the words cited here. For me, and I would wager that for 99 percent of its readers, the book was *Absentee Ownership*. Even in this Veblen is peculiar. For ordinary folk *Absentee Ownership* is two words but for Veblen the two really constituted one word, "Absenteeownership." Veblen was extraordinarily concerned with the precise use of words. J. Dorfman states (*Thorstein Veblen and His America,* Viking Press, p. 324), "He was so meticulous in this respect that he declared that there are no synonyms in the English language." Veblen did not actually create words de nouveau, but he did create neologisms out of words lying about. These neologisms were a major base for his claim to be the number one prose stylist of American social analysts—or for that matter of the English-speaking world after the eighteenth century. These new words were almost all composed of two perfectly well-known words lying about. It is easy to list some: leisure class, conspicuous consumption, ostentatious display, business enterprise, putative profits, parental bent, idle curiosity (defined by four words, the propensity to pry), higher learning, and, of course, absentee ownership. His works built around these "words" made so powerful an impression that people who never read or even heard of Veblen use them as single words.

Absentee Ownership was not the least of these, and Veblen used it with telling effect. Even in Veblen's day, the vast majority of people were farmers of one sort or another. They lived out their lives on a localized basis with an ideal of as much self-sufficiency as possible. The absentee landlord or his equivalent, the feudal landlord, was and is a figure of dark connotations. He not only represents an intrusion on desired levels of self-sufficiency, but he is usually a person who neither knows nor cares about the local community *if* the members of that community do not thwart his desire to get as much as possible out of the land and out of the people whom he may or may not own as well. He is not only a frustration of desired levels of self-sufficiency; he is an outsider to boot. It is, alas, not true that people have always placed a high value on personal freedom. Throughout history high levels of hierarchy have generally been taken for granted as normal and natural. People have not generally felt that he or she governs best, who governs least—but almost to a person they have felt that he or she governs best who governs most locally. Even though the absentee landlord is technically defined by economic ownership, such allocations of goods (in this case property rights) and services can never be irrelevant to governance—and vice versa. The absentee landlord is thus not only an absentee owner of land; he is simultaneously an absentee source of governance. General governance at great distance may have been a rarity until modern history—high levels of local self-sufficiency were both ideally and actually taken for granted, but high levels of absentee landlordism were not. It is not the role of *landlord* or *ownership* that casts a pall on these relationships, it is the qualifier, *absentee.*

It is safe to say that *absentee* as a term before Veblen was applied most often to landlordism and the holding of political roles, and it always cast the pall of outsiderism and hence an overwhelming probability of lack of empathy with the locals. Hoi polloi never had the luxury of absentee roles. And what does Veblen do with the term, "absentee?" He applies it to virtually the whole of the economic system of any modernized state, although he is presumably only referring to "America." The 1933 edition of and the 1982 supplement to the *Oxford English Dictionary* contain no reference to "absentee ownership." The second edition of *Webster's New International Dictionary* (1954) does not have it, but the third edition (1966) does. It may do an injustice, but I attribute the term's current currency to its use by Veblen.

And how does Veblen use it? He uses it to cast a pall over the whole current system of economic ownership. Years later the *Modern Corporation and Private Property,* by Berle and Means (1934) picked up Veblen's themes of the concentration of power and control and above all of the separation of ownership and control which Veblen certainly attributed to the larger use of loan credit. In the earlier days, the giants of business enterprise had faces—Rockefeller, Vanderbilt, Ford, Edison—but they all turned into faceless bureaucracies. The giants may not have been nice, and they weren't noted for their empathy, but they had faces and human traits. Absentee ownership wiped that out for the common man. He or she had to deal with bureaucratic representatives of huge and distant entities. If your business with them covered more then one visit, you couldn't even count on dealing with the same person. In effect, when absentee ownership became generalized, it become the fate of the common man always to have to deal with a "bastard from out of town." You couldn't know what he was doing or often what ends he sought, but they weren't likely to be your own.

And so *Absentee Ownership* introduces alienation as a characteristic of the system. Veblen sees that, furthered by his distinction between technology and material output on the one hand and the use of credit and the pursuit of profit, however obtained, on the other. The whole of *Absentee Ownership* depicts the common man as a helpless pawn. Sometimes Veblen thinks of the common man as mentally deficient; he is clearly impatient that the common person doesn't do something about the state of affairs. He predicts instability if the present system continues. Veblen died on August 3, 1929. The 1929 crash and the Great Depression were just down the road Veblen delineated. He was another Cassandra; nobody was listening.

I was first given Veblen to read by Professor Clarence E. Ayres at the University of Texas when I was a sixteen-year-old sophomore. I was given *The Theory of Business Enterprise,* and I decided within the first ten pages that Veblen was the best thing since Voltaire. I didn't realize until much later that this was a peculiar introduction to economics in general. It seems even more odd today. I am, as far as I know, the only academic left who got interested in economics through Thorstein Veblen. I didn't realize the virtues of such an introduction at the time. But it gave me perspective and a place to stand that I still appreciate. It was an alternative to what we then referred to as classical economics, and more importantly for a young person like myself, it was an alternative to Marxism. Veblen had an unusual perspective on practically everything, mostly because he was reared in a Norse farmer setting in a rapidly changing American society. He had the same kind of comparative critical advantage that he discussed in his essay "The Intellectual Preeminence of the Jews in Europe." We never met, but reading Veblen gave this comparative advantage to me, in a sense. The economics of my days as a young student was classical economics. Paul Samuelson had yet to work his wonders on the study of economics in the United States. And although American economists could have gotten much from Walras and Pareto, they clearly didn't. On the other side was Marx, who despite his enormous importance, wasn't a very good economist.

I lived at the time in a peculiar intellectual world based on three premises: (1) intellectual matters were more important than anything else; (2) if two people disagreed on an intellectual matter, one of them was right and the other was wrong; and (3) the one who was right was brighter than the one who was wrong. It seemed to me that Veblen had the better of lots of arguments, so I felt he was brighter than any of the other economists around. Although the basis of my position was ridiculous, my conclusion probably wasn't very far off the mark.

Veblen didn't write like anybody else. I was intrigued by his style. When he thought officials were corrupt, dishonest, and so forth, he didn't waste any words. He simply referred to them as *kept* officials. In those days "kept" was a derogatory participle used to stigmatize women. It somehow lent a salacious tone to Veblen's description of those officials. At the same time he could bring to bear the vocabulary of several different fields to make his points about economics. The most famous of these began, "If we are getting restless under the taxonomy of a monocotyledonous wage doctrine and a cryptogamic theory of interest...." And yet he wasn't fooling around. He wrote, "The physical properties of the materials accessible to man are constant; it is the human agent that changes,—his insight and his appreciation of what these things can be used for is what develops" (Veblen, *The Place of Science in Modern Civilization,* p. 71).

Someone, I can't now remember who, referred to Veblen's technique of writing as "inverse normalization." This first caught people's attention in his first book, *The Theory of the Leisure Class,* where he has a famous passage on how college football is viewed and how he sees it to be. He simply refused to write about economic analysis in the language of the economists of his day. But then he was trying to jog them out of writing that way too. Therefore, many of the things that he wrote, which anticipated the classical or the neoclassical literature in economics, got into the fields of economics through entirely different avenues. Perhaps the most conspicuous of these was the theory of monopolistic competition, the essence of which was published in "The Use of Loan Credit in Modern Business" (1903), later incorporated in *The Theory of Business Enterprise* (1904). In this essay Veblen maintained that the use of credit that would have given a comparative advantage to a single entrepreneur became a competitive necessity for all, adding to the cost of doing business without conferring comparative advantage. Costs were higher and output lower than would have been the case under pure and perfect competition. This didn't get into the general economic literature until the 1930s with the publication of Professor E. A. Chamberlain's book *The Theory of Monopolistic Competition.*

The Theory of Business Enterprise contained a theory of business cycles very close to what came into the general literature with the work of Keynes three decades later. Veblen's concept of putative profits, which he regards as the basis for the decisions of businessmen, is remarkably close to what came to be very much better known as the unknown elements in the schedule of the marginal efficiency of capital.

The heart of the distinction between Veblen's work and the economics he disdained was the distinction between production for output and production for profit on the one hand, and developmental process versus equilibrium situations on the other. There is, as far as I know, no reason to believe that

Veblen knew of the work of Walras and Pareto; he died long before their work was known to economists in general in the United States.

Perhaps one of Veblen's most startling insights was that at a time when people saw either capitalism as continuing indefinitely into the future, substantially without change, or socialism as the only alternative outcome, in *The Theory of Business Enterprise* Veblen scouted another alternative. We would call it fascism today, but we didn't have the term then. Remember, this was 1904. But he saw the predatory search for national profits leading to a militaristic state with an emphasis on pomp and ceremony and an accent on national glory.

He carefully distinguished between "modern Socialism," a scheme of society under democratic organization, and what he referred to as "state, church, or monarchical Socialism" (see J. Dorfman, *Thorstein Veblen and His America,* 1934, p. 241). He apparently didn't consider the Russian experiment to be "modern socialism." He assumed that modern socialism would arise under the direction of engineers. He may not have been "right." He wasn't, but his argument sidestepped the available ideologies. Technocracy may have developed out of Veblen, but certainly not vice versa.

For Veblen markets washed out the intrinsic qualities of commodities and services and reduced them all to financial reckoning. Because the analysis of rational action was so little studied or developed in his time, he seems not to have been aware of a function of markets, even less than pure and perfect ones, as one, perhaps the only one, of the few devices mankind ever invented that offset the effects of differing degrees and kinds of ignorance. Markets aren't nice, but they grind exceedingly fine. Veblen was also perhaps the last major American social analyst who really felt that humankind would be benefitted if all major decisions regarding allocation were in the hands of engineers who in a modern democratic socialist state would manage everything for output rather than for profits or war. For him, nationalism was not one whit different from chauvinism in general, and he saw surcease from war as only possible with an international organization, not oriented to or determined by local sovereignties.

Veblen really was unusual. He was the quintessential outsider about whom he wrote in one sense in every book he ever turned out. His initial learning was that of a Norse farmhand transported to the wilds of the United States. He was our indigenous Norse pragmatist. It is interesting that there were two great outsiders who viewed America (it is not quite correct to talk about the United States in either case) as a very special setting. The first, of course, was Tocqueville whose primary point of view was that of an elite representative of the enlightenment of France. He was overwhelmingly preoccupied with what he viewed as our political inventions. We wanted to read what Tocqueville wrote. We remember him not least because what he said about us very much appealed to us. Veblen, on the other hand, viewed us from an economic point of view, but always taking the economic results as a function for the setting and types of social action in which we engage. Tocqueville viewed us as a miraculously open class elite system, whereas Veblen viewed us as an anthropologist from another planet or better as a biologist observing termites. But we were a set of termites who all wanted to be queens. We always felt that his values had more to do with his analysis than he let on, but it was very difficult to catch him at it because his most biting revelations were always presented as careful statements of fact "with no intention to disparage"—and they were statements of fact inversely normalized. What he said of religious organizations was in one sense factual, but Veblen alone saw them as sales organizations carried to perfection.

Veblen made another contribution that got lost. More than any other social analyst of his time economic analysis was for him a part of general social analysis. This is clear in all his books, especially so in *Absentee Ownership*. He railed against the general economic concern with materials and things other than with people and their plans and motivations and actions. One searches far in his first volume, *The Theory of the Leisure Class,* for anything that smacks of an ordinary economist's analysis of the allocation of goods and services. And yet he gives us an explanation of why wealthy people cultivate green lawns and elaborate weddings. He uses terms like "conspicuous consumption" and "invidious displays," but those concepts are used to elucidate the allocation of goods and services. It is just that even now, when interdisciplinary approaches are so taken for granted as to duck intellectual responsibility, we regard *The Theory of the Leisure Class* as satire rather than economics. As Veblen said, "people were inclined to giggle." (Dorfman, p. 197)

In Veblen's day the first comers to modernization were just getting their acts and facades in place. The whole panoply of the problems of latecomers to modernization was not on his plate. He saw the structures of modernization being put in place as importantly pathological. He did not see modernization as a kind of universal social solvent. And yet again, there is that strong hint of one of the major still overlooked aspects of all that, the long-term exponentially increasing level of interdependency—the relentless increase of what he referred to as the "delicacy of interstitial adjustments amongst the closely concatenated processes." Had the concept of modernization been available to him, *Absentee Ownership* might have been subtitled, "The Pathological Development of Modernization." Veblen grew up and lived in a period of our increasing confidence and self-assurance. He was awed by the material welfare that could be achieved by the industrial revolution and infuriated by human institutions that thwarted and frustrated the possibilities of material productivity. People who should have paid closer attention to what he had to say let him live out his life on very short rations as a kind of ornament and verification of their own tolerance. If another Veblen appears in our world, liberals and conservatives alike will stone him.

All sorts of people saw the system; Veblen saw through the system. Remember, it was a day when investment bankers were like God Almighty as far as the economic system was concerned. But now there are a whole group of operators in the economic system who have investment bankers jumping through hoops. This is the day of the raider and merger, and we've fallen back to thinking of investment bankers as useful handmaidens to real economic operators. Never mind how unrealistic that is. *Absentee Ownership* is a dividing line book. It can be rightly claimed, I believe, that Veblen did more than foresee the crash of 1929. He was bathed in wonderment that it hadn't happened already. He died, of course, before it happened, albeit by only a few months. But that was the crash par excellence that wiped out what a Norse farm boy economist thought of as the unrealities of the system. And that crash was a dividing line in history. There had and has been no other like it. There is not only the magnitude of that crash and its implications, but also the way it changed the system. Before that crash we thought of government as the ordinary negligible, non-acting part of the system. It wasn't supposed to do much. It was to provide a few public goods, but not too many. Political bosses and their political machines, not the official government, provided what welfare system there was. Only during wars did government become the biggest player in the game. But something happened with the 1929 crash. For awhile people simply dithered, sold apples, and wrung their hands as unemployment took off. And then in 1932, with the election of Franklin Delano Roosevelt, a man who really made a difference in history, the government became the biggest player in the game. It wasn't exactly like Veblen's view of the engineers and the technologists, but business and banking never again became the factor they were before the 1929 crash. There is increasing talk today of taking the government out of the picture, but even the people who are most in favor of that don't really think it is possible. This makes a big difference for people who read *Absentee Ownership* and other books by Veblen now. It is very hard to put ourselves back into the position of looking at the players as Veblen saw them.

Absentee Ownership seems old-fashioned as I reread it now. Of course, Veblen didn't see things the way most people saw them in his day, and that's why he was so hard to take in *Absentee Ownership* and in every other book he wrote. But ever since Franklin Delano Roosevelt and the New Deal came in, the government has been the *big player,* and the accessibility of credit for the government was never in question. Indeed, by our accounting (fictions?), the government doesn't hold any assets of any sort. So there the absentee ownership stands. The crash that Veblen could have claimed to have predicted because what counted as credit and what counted as material objects were quite different, flushed out the system and created a revolution that nobody seemed to be aware of except perhaps for some 12 million unemployed (of a total labor force of 50 million), who weren't very articulate.

The new world of America that came into existence after the Great Crash followed by the Great Depression (Not a "recession," a *depression!*) was a wholly different world, and that fact alone makes it difficult to give credence to the world of America as described by Veblen in *Absentee Ownership.* It's a very worrisome book to read because Veblen obviously takes as real things that just don't seem real to us anymore. Mind you, again, he saw those realities as very different from what other people of his age and generation saw. And much of the value that he contributed to knowledge lay in the fact that he saw them peculiarly. In his time he was regarded as quixotic because he viewed the world differently. Yet, even when you disagreed with what he said, there was a disturbing reality about what he wrote. Even his outrageously funny note about the Propaganda of the Faith (*Absentee Ownership*, pp. 319–25) has a realism about it that shines through all the shock. There is certainly, for example, no other book describing America in the two decades after the twentieth century began that bears any resemblance to the way in which Veblen described it. We can still read that sort of quixotic view, but for us he's doubly quixotic because it's hard to believe that that world he described was ever the world of America. Nevertheless, while it was the world of America that was looked at differently than other people looked at it, it certainly was in some sense the world of America.

There is another aspect of the America described in *Absentee Ownership*. The current faithful, who call themselves Libertarians, along with those who oppose them, don't seem to realize they had their wished for lack of governance from at least 1900 to 1932. Except for the Federal Reserve Board and times of war, there was little governance to give the business community let or hindrance. What government there was more often plundered then prohibiting. Few "public goods" were offered, and the concept of "public bads" (pollution, unemployment, etc.) as a governmental responsibility was unheard of. The absentee owners against whom Veblen railed, though he claimed merely to describe them, had things pretty much their own way. And their ways led directly to 1929 and by 1932 to 12 million unemployed (24.1

percent of the civilian labor force; 36.3 percent of the non-farm labor force) out of a 50 million labor force and a total population of a 125 million people! Veblen would surely be the first to say that the Libertarians have had their shot at U.S. history. They have had their shot at acting as though interdependency had no relevance, as though Veblen's increasing delicacy of the interstitial adjustments of the closely concatenated processes were irrelevancies that would take care of themselves or at least could be ignored by the movers and shakers of absentee ownership, that is, the bankers and business lords.

Had Veblen survived until now, he could have written an *Absentee Ownership, Done and Redone*. How would he see us now? One thing is sure, he would have had a field day with *junk bonds*. He could place Michael Milken alongside the Propaganda of the Faith as an unabashed triumph of salesmanship—of *suppressio veri, suggestio falsi*. Milken and those who took up the junk bond with a whoop and a holler carried the larger use of loan credit to an extreme even a Norse farm boy economist simply couldn't imagine. He thought the absentee owners would protect themselves whilst they plundered the laymen. Even Veblen couldn't predict a feeding frenzy of junk bonds. But in *Absentee Ownership* he descries better than anyone else the road to 1929—no matter how much he relishes flaying the system. Our interdependencies are mounting exponentially. We may be sorely in need of another Veblen to cry havoc.

As each day brings us further along toward the next millennium, our increasing libertarianism tugs the shrill warnings of *Absentee Ownership* back into focus—back into style. There is a new dark cloud to be coped with, exponentially increasing interdependency. Veblen correctly caught its beginnings, but it has gone on nearly seventy years and a Second World War since then. The public bads of libertarianism are far more potent now than they were in Veblen's day, though they brought about the Great Depression even then. While most people saw only onward and upward, Veblen predicted a slippery slope whose angle of inclination steepened. Veblen thought, the more the new lords of business enterprise paid attention to maximizing profits rather than to maximizing material output and its increasingly unimodal distribution to the general public on whom in some sense economic welfare had, in the long run, to be based—the greater would be the reaping of woe.

If we could have Veblen back now, he need not point out the slippery slope. The government is now a major player even though the thought of governmental dismantlement is so popular among articulate political power players. But anyone as perspicacious as Veblen might now be able to devise a system of holding responsible the creators of public bads whether they be government officials or "private players." In the long run the slippery slope does not threaten life as much as a level plane of operation threatens it. The slippery slope invites everyone to seek again the increasing slope of material productivity. The level plane can destroy hope, and our great material productivity is based on reasonable hope. Continually increasing horizons of the possibility of material development have created our dangerous new world of interdependency. Veblen was so preoccupied with calling our attention to the pitfalls we were digging that he didn't show us how to fill them in. His one naivete was his faith in engineers. We could all do with a rereading of *Absentee Ownership;* we are not out of the reach of the horrors of libertarianism. That rereading with the new roles we take too much for granted of the government as a major player in the game might lead us to a solution of the problem of how to keep the "absentee owners" of both the economic and political spheres responsible. We need the energy and the imagination of business and governmental leaders, but we seem at a loss to inculcate responsibility on absentee owners. Disillusionment with the government as a major player undermines a governmental balance wheel for business enterprise. The popularity of politics as a zero sum game makes statesmanship vulnerable to politics. The market can destroy reckless players, but Veblen showed how that could go awry. Competition in the flesh is neither pure nor perfect though its record in the last century has been preferable to overall state planning. Tocqueville told us how good our system could be. Veblen described how bollixed up we could get it. We must now add to our marvelous political system of checks and balances, which has preserved our liberties, a set of checks and balances for economic allocation. We must set absentee ownership a new task in addition to individual enrichment. Politics as a set of checks and balances is one thing. Politics as a zero sum game is quite another. We need an *Absentee Governance* to alert us to the lack of participation and statesmanship that becomes ever more critical as we become ever more interdependent.

MARION J. LEVY, JR.
Woodrow Wilson School
Princeton University
June 1996

PREFACE

The following essay is an inquiry into the economic situation as it has taken shape during this (twentieth) century, particularly as exemplified in the case of America. Its aim is an objective, theoretical analysis and formulation of the main drift, as determined by the material circumstances of the case, including the industrial arts, and by the dominant institution of absentee ownership, including the use of credit. This analysis and formulation occupies Part II of the essay. It makes little use of the received theories of Political Economy; not as departing from the received theories or discrediting them, but because the inquiry is concerned chiefly with economic forces and phenomena which are of later date than the received doctrines.

Part I of the essay is occupied with a summary description of that range of economic circumstances and that sequence of economic growth and change which have led up through the nineteenth century and have come to a head in the situation of the past two decades; regard being had chiefly to the case of England for the earlier decades of the century and chiefly to the case of America for the later years. It makes no use of recondite information and makes no attempt to penetrate beyond the workday facts which are already familiar to students of these matters.

March 1923

ABSENTEE OWNERSHIP AND BUSINESS ENTERPRISE IN RECENT TIMES

PART I

CHAPTER I

Introductory

In recent times absentee ownership has come to be the main and immediate controlling interest in the life of civilised men. It is the paramount issue between the civilised nations, and guides the conduct of their affairs at home and abroad. The Great War arose out of a conflict of absentee interests and the Peace was negotiated with a view to stabilise them.

This state of things is not precisely new, nor has it come on suddenly. It is a growth out of the past, but it has reached something like a culmination during these opening decades of the century; and it is an outcome of cumulative changes which have been directed to no such end. The years of the Great War and the Armistice have brought many things to a head, and among other things they have also thrown this factor into the foreground of the situation. And the experience of the War and after has stirred men to a crude and uneasy realisation of this state of things. Under one form of words or another, issues which arise out of the sovereign rights of absentee ownership are stirring the popular sentiment and engaging the attention of the officials with an ever increasing urgency. These issues are the substance of all those desperate perplexities that beset the constituted authorities and they underlie all those dissensions that continually trouble the nation's industry and business. With the result that popular attention and sentiment are gathering about the issues of absentee ownership more and more directly and consciously with each further move,—questions of its aims and uses, its necessary limitations, its continued security, its rightful claims, and its possible eventual abridgment or disallowance.

It is true, this particular form of words—"Absentee Ownership"—has not been commonly employed to describe this peculiar institution which now engrosses public policy and about which controversy is beginning to gather. But that only marks a deficiency of speech. It is only within the last few decades, and only by degrees, that the facts in the case have been changing in such a way as to call for the habitual use of such a phrase as "absentee ownership." It is only within the last few decades, and only by degrees, that absentee ownership has visibly come to be the main controlling factor in the established order of things. Yet it is no less true that this peculiar institution which this form of words is fit to describe has now plainly come to be the prime institutional factor that underlies and governs the established order of society. At the same time and in the same degree it has, as a matter of course, become the chief concern of the constituted authorities in all the civilised nations to safeguard the security and gainfulness of absentee ownership. This state of things is now plain to be seen, and it is therefore beginning to cloud the sentiments of the underlying population at whose cost this security and gainfulness are maintained.

So, by degrees the drift of changing conditions has been heading up in a new alignment of economic forces and of economic classes. So that the dominant considerations which now govern the material fortunes of the community are no longer the same as they have been in the recent past; nor indeed such as they are alleged to be in the present. These matters are still spoken of in terms handed down from the past, and law and custom still run in terms that are fit to describe a past situation and conform to the logic of a bygone alignment of forces. As always, the language employed and the principles acted on lag behind the facts. But when, as now, the facts have been changing at an unexampled rate the language and the principles will lag behind the facts by an unexampled interval. Yet under the urgent pressure of new material conditions some degree of adjustment or derangement of these ancient principles is due to follow. Continued "lag, leak and friction" is bound to count for something in the outcome. Continued irritation and defeat begot of a system of law and custom that no longer fits the material conditions of life will necessarily be an agency of unrest, particularly as touches the frame of mind of that fraction of the community on whom the irritation and defeat continue chiefly to fall.

Therefore these time-worn principles of ownership and control, which are now coming to a head in a system of absentee ownership and control, are beginning to come in for an uneasy and reluctant reconsideration; particularly at the hands of that underlying population who have no absentee ownership to safeguard. Their questioning of these matters habitually takes the shape of personal recrimination and special pleading, but the drift of it all is no less evident. Those traditions that underlie the established order and that guide legal and administrative policy, proceed on an assumed community of class interests, a national solidarity of interests, and an international conflict of interests; none of which is borne out by material facts. Therefore these traditional policies that still govern the conduct of affairs, civil and political, legal and administrative, are also falling under suspicion of being incompetent, irrelevant and impertinent, if not downright mischievous. The losers under these rules of the game are beginning to see that law and politics, too, serve the needs of the absentee owners at the cost of the underlying population.

So, popular interest and sentiment no longer cluster about these respectable heirlooms of civil liberty and national rivalry with the same enthusiastic bigotry as in the recent past. Among these unblest classes who have to pay its cost, patriotic animosity is no longer so unreflectingly self-sufficient as it once was, and as perhaps it always should be. Among these classes of the underlying population the new alignment of material interests is beginning to threaten the continued life of the patriotic spirit. The effectual division of interest and sentiment is beginning visibly to run on class lines, between the absentee owners and the underlying population. In material effect, the national frontiers no longer divide anything but national groups of special interests, and these special interests are quite uniformly interests of absentee owners. National rivalries are useful to these special interests; hence the feverish urgency with which the constituted authorities and the substantial citizens are concerned to foment national animosity and to penalise backsliders.

Of course these matters are not currently spoken of in these terms. The new alignment of interest and sentiment is not formally recognised, not yet. A decent respect for the obsolete amenities of Natural Liberty forbids it, and there is always the human propensity to hold fast that which once was good. And more particularly, the bygone issues of national ambition still continue to hold the affections of the substantial citizens, and the spirit of national rivalry still continues to serve the needs of the special interests. Therefore national ambitions must and shall be preserved and all conflict of class interests must and shall be ignored.

But all the while the drift of circumstances goes forward and cuts the lines of the new cleavage of interest and sentiment no less deep and with no less intractable ill-will on both sides, for all their being decently covered over with patriotic invective and authentic verbiage about the common good. And all the while, under one form of words or another, men's everyday interest and attention gathers more and more consciously about this ill-defined and shifty issue of absentee ownership, and about its place and value in the country's industry, to the slowly increasing neglect of obsolete political ambitions. And all the while it is increasingly evident that patriotic sentiment and national ambitions are no longer of any material consequence, except as ways and means by which the statesmen are enabled to further the material interests of the substantial citizens. A "substantial citizen" is an absentee owner of much property.

This summary description of things as they are may seem overdrawn. But it is intended to describe the present drift of things, rather than the accomplished facts hitherto. It is drawn from current observation rather than from the historical records; so that it aims to describe the current facts rather than the current talk about these facts. Of course there is no intention to intimate that the ancient and honorable habits of national conceit and patriotic intolerance have been forgotten or even that they are by way of becoming inoperative; nor is it that the rightful claims of absentee ownership are being neglected or being formally questioned and required to show cause why. Those cardinal realities of the established order have not gone out of date or out of mind, neither the one

nor the other. Nor is there an effectual resolution anywhere being taken to put either of them away; not yet.
But these ancient and honorable pillars of the old order
are by way of becoming holdovers, both the one and the
other; and the spokesmen of both are beginning to find
themselves on the defensive. As witness the Treaty
of Peace, which foots up to little if anything else than a
plan of defense for the vested interests, concerted between the several custodians of the old order, at any cost
to the world's peace or to the underlying population.
As witness also the later conferences of the Powers at
Genoa, at The Hague, and at Lausanne, which have turned
on little else than measures designed to stabilise the rightful claims of absentee owners as against the defection
of the Russians and other recusants, together with the
equitable distribution of absentee perquisites among the
several groups of vested interests represented by the several governments concerned.

In effect, and notoriously, it has been the chief and
engrossing business of all the statesmen of the Armistice
and the Treaty, on the winning and the losing side alike,
to safeguard these two essential holdovers that go to make
up the *status quo ante*. National rivalry is a necessary
means of making things safe and profitable for the absentee owners, as will appear more in detail in the further
argument. All this is a traditional matter of course and
has consequently aroused no particular discussion. Indeed, it is so much a matter of course as to be taken for
granted. But the defensive measures concerted by these
statesmen, and their continued manœuvres for the stabilisation of absentee interests, go to show which way the
cleavage of interests runs. Statesmen do not resort to
counsels of desperation, such as underlie the Treaty and
the later negotiations concerning partition of colonies and

military establishments, except to save a precarious situation. And the same defensive purpose, it must be admitted, runs through that desperate recourse to the strong arm of repression which today engages the energies of the civilised governments, all and several, with the clamorous approval of their substantial citizens whose pecuniary interests are sought to be safeguarded by these measures.

Now, this red line of cleavage, in material interest and in sentiment, runs not between those who own something and those who own nothing, as has habitually been set out in the formulas of the doctrinaires, but between those who own more than they personally can use and those who have urgent use for more than they own. The issue now is turning not on a question of ownership, as such, but on absentee ownership. The standard formalities of "Socialism" and "Anti-socialism" are obsolete in face of the new alignment of economic forces. It is now not so much a question of equity in the distribution of incomes, but rather a question of expediency as regards the absentee management of productive industry, at large and in detail. It is not a matter of moral revulsion. It may be said, of course, and perhaps truthfully, that the absentee owners of the country's industrial equipment come in for a disproportionate share of the "national dividend," and that they and their folks habitually consume their share in superfluities; but no urgent moral indignation appears to be aroused by all that. All that has long been a familiar matter of course, and no substantial question as to the merits of that arrangement has yet been seriously entertained. Efforts to capitalise such a sentiment for purposes of disturbance have uniformly failed.

What the material circumstances are bringing to men's attention is a question of how to get the work done rather than of what to do with the output. It is a question of the effectual use of the country's industrial resources, man-power, and equipment.[1] Investment and corporation finance have taken such a turn and reached such a growth that, between them, the absentee owners large and small have come to control the ways and means of production and distribution, at large and in detail, in what is to be done and what is to be left undone. And the business interests of these absentee owners no longer coincide in any passable degree with the material interests of the underlying population, whose livelihood is bound up with the due working of this industrial system, at large and in detail. The material interest of the underlying population is best served by a maximum output at a low cost, while the business interests of the industry's owners may best be served by a moderate output at an enhanced price.

[1] Cf., e. g., Walther Rathenau, "Die neue Wirtschaft," *Schriften,* vol. V.

CHAPTER II

THE GROWTH AND VALUE OF NATIONAL INTEGRITY

THERE is no question of the legality of absentee ownership, nor of its moral right. It is a settled institution of civilised life, embedded in law and morals, and its roots run through the foundations of European civilisation. Legality and morality are a matter of statute, precedent, and usage; and absentee ownership is quite securely grounded in the Common Law and deeply ingrained in the moral sense of civilised men. In the American commonwealth such ownership is also covered by the constitutional provision which declares that men must not be deprived of their property except by due process of law. And the legal precedents, interpretations and refinements which have been set up and worked out by jurists under this constitutional provision have in the main been concerned with fortifying and extending the security and implied rights of absentee ownership in one bearing and another; with the result that these rights are, legally and morally, more secure and more extensive today than ever before. Indirectly too, the provision for "due process of law" has greatly reënforced the dominant position of absentee ownership as against any claims of another kind or against claimants of any other class. Litigation as conducted according to the rules and precedents which govern the "due process" has in recent times become too costly to be carried to a conclusion by any litigant who is not an absentee owner of large means. This will hold true in America perhaps in a more conclusive fashion than in any other civilised nation.[1] In effect, due process of law as it concerns property has become an appliance for the regulation of relations between absentee owners.

Legally, the dominant position of absentee ownership is not to be questioned or shaken. And as regards its moral foundations in current common sense, in the habits of thought of this people, the institution is in a similarly strong position. It remains true that absentee ownership is still the idol of every true American heart. Indeed, chief among the civic virtues of this people is that steadfast cupidity that drives its citizens, each and several, under pain of moral turpitude, to acquire a "competence," and then unremittingly to augment any competence already acquired. The high ideal which of moral right animates these good citizens in this pursuit of a "competence" is to get something for nothing, to get legal possession of some source of income at a less cost than its capitalisable value. Invariably a "competence" signifies the ownership of means in excess of what the owner can make use of, personally and without help; which is also a convenient definition of "absentee ownership." By so coming into the possession of an unearned increase of wealth a man becomes a "substantial citizen." And according to the sturdy common sense of a population trained to this pursuit of something for nothing, failure

---

[1] American law and procedure have taken shape under the hand of legislatures and courts which have habitually and as a matter of course been made up of investors and lawyers, with no control from outside these classes; and the upshot of it has been an arrangement such as to serve the convenience and profit of these two classes of persons,—such as to increase the cost, volume, uncertainty and intricacy of litigation.—Cf., e. g., Charles A. Beard, *Contemporary American History*, especially ch. III and IX.

to acquire such a competence is visited with unsparing moral reprobation. Any person who falls short in this pursuit of something for nothing, and so fails to avoid work in some useful occupation, is a shiftless ne'er-do-well; he loses self-respect as well as the respect of his neighbors and is in a fair way to be rated as an undesirable citizen. By and large, the line of moral demarkation runs between the substantial citizen and the undesirable citizen. These ideals of propriety and morality are not peculiarly American, of course; although the Americans may perhaps be able to claim some slight peculiar degree of certitude and moral sufficiency on this head.

The established order of law and custom which safeguards absentee ownership in recent times and among civilised nations is, in the main, a modern creation; being, in effect, an outgrowth of usages and principles (habits of thought) which were induced by the conditions of life during early-modern times. The type-form of organised control by which this modern law and custom is upheld and enabled to function is that of the Nation—a politically self-determining body of people, legally and morally competent to make war.[2]

[2] There appears to be no other or further attribute or capacity that can be specified as a universally essential characteristic of the modern nation except this moral and legal license to resort to violence at will. A nation is a (*de jure*) self-determining body in respect of its hostilities. Other attributes and capacities may be taken away without thereby terminating any given nation's existence as such, but if this formally authentic competency for self-determining hostility be surrendered the nation, *qua* nation, is *functa officio*. It will accordingly be remarked, of course, that in respect of its authentic legal and moral type-form the modern nation is essentially of a predatory nature. And such is necessarily the case in view of its deri-

Not that this modern system of law and order embodies nothing that is of older date than early-modern times. Indeed, embedded in this early-modern system are large remnants which have stood over from antiquity and from the Middle Ages; as how should it not, since it is in all its constituents a creature of habit and tradition? The experience of life in early-modern times and since has not broken at all points—nor indeed in the main—with what had gone before. At the same time there have been substantial though minor changes brought into the system in the course of later experience and habituation. But apart from interpretations and refinements instituted *ad hoc,* and in so far as it bears directly on the security, rights and powers of absentee ownership, this current system of law and custom is grounded in the principles of law and morals that were worked up and stabilised in the course of the sixteenth, seventeenth, and eighteenth centuries.

The system as it now stands comprises elements of older date, but the scheme was rounded out and stabilised in that time and in response to the impact of the conditions which prevailed then, and the resulting structure of law and moralities has not been seriously disturbed since then. By and large, the system is a holdover out of the early-modern centuries, and its period of growth was formally closed during the later half of the eighteenth century. Later experience has fluttered against the stable framework of Natural Rights set up in the eighteenth century and has, on the whole, brought no substantial change of principles; assuredly nothing that amounts to a break with the eighteenth-century point of

vation. The same state of the case will also be evident on first-hand reflection, to any person who may be passably informed as to the run of events during the past few years.

departure. Meanwhile an industrial revolution has passed over the European peoples and has brought on an unexampled change in the material conditions of life.

It has consistently been the pride and boast of civilised men that the laws and customs which govern their conduct and regulate their behavior in all their civic and industrial relations are grounded in a system of time-worn principles—immutable principles of immemorial antiquity which are fundamentally and eternally right and good. That is to say, in this particular instance, these principles of law and morals have been "immemorially ancient" and "eternally right and good" ever since they became ingrained by habit and presently reduced to documentary statement in modern times. As regards those principles of right conduct which specifically cover the just rights and powers of absentee ownership, their immemorial antiquity and immutable validity came on by degrees during the transition from feudalism and canon law to the handicraft era and the common law; when the petty trade of that time expanded to such dimensions as enabled it to change from peddling for a livelihood to investment for a profit. In America specifically, the immutable validity which so invests the law and morals of absentee ownership dates from A. D. 1776 or 1787, according as one may prefer to see it.

Meantime, while these immutable principles of law and morals have continued to embody the habits of thought of a bygone age, the industrial system within which and in control of which absentee ownership exercises these its ancient and immutable rights and powers is of the twentieth century and is in no respect and in no degree immutable; quite the contrary, in fact. While modern men continue to boast and laud the changeless antiquity and stability of the rules which govern their industrial relations, it is at the same time their pride and boast that the industrial arts which condition their behavior under these rules are forever changing, progressively and at an ever-accelerating rate. In time, immutable rules of conduct enforced under progressively changing conditions should logically result in a muddle.

There is, of course, nothing particularly new or peculiarly civilised about this obstinate assumption that the main specifications of the legal and moral code are ancient and immutable. Indeed, it is quite the usual thing among the common run of barbarians and savages, ancient and contemporary. But all the while, in point of fact and as a matter of course, any system of law and custom, being a product of habituation, is necessarily subject to continued change, even in respect of its underlying principles. An underlying principle is, after all, little else than a personalised and stabilised blend of the overlying details that go to make up everyday behavior. The chain of responses to the impact of changing circumstances runs on as a course of progressive habituation, and the resulting average run of blended habits will necessarily shift and bend its course to follow the progressive displacement of its constituent elements. It follows that the upshot of this progressive habituation, which goes to create the standards of conduct, will change cumulatively from day to day by fluctuating variations.[3] But always and everywhere men like to believe that their own particular standards of conduct are fixed in the nature of things, so that to each people their own established scheme of usages, in law and morals, is immutably right and good, in principle.

But habituation follows after experience and works

[3] Cf. Dewey, *Human Nature and Conduct.*

against the side-draft of previous habituation. With the result that any deliberate change which is sought to be worked into the accepted scheme of use and wont will take effect only tardily, reluctantly, and sparingly. And it is a trait of human nature that any unavoidable minimum of change which so is perforce infused into the scheme of conduct will be covered in with an apologetic appeal to even more ancient and immutable principles erected out of painstaking subtleties and evasions, such as go to make up the consistency of the jurists and theologians. The new effectual factors in the case, those altered material circumstances that enforce a change in the established scheme of usage and law, are not allowed to come in openly as being in themselves conclusive grounds for the changes of principle which they enforce. Such is human nature. Any unavoidable move of this nature must be vouched for by make-believe. Authenticity must be found in underlying principles and immemorial usage, to be discovered by sophistical dialectics.

In the long run, of course, the pressure of changing material circumstances will have to shape the lines of human conduct, on pain of extinction. And this "long run" will necessarily have to be a shorter run when, as in the present, these relentless material circumstances are changing swiftly and at an ever accelerated rate. But always this running adaptation of the legal and moral conventions, if it is allowed at all, will be allowed to take effect only in the long run and sparingly, with an apparatus of make-believe and under cover of metaphysically immutable principles discovered *ad hoc*. But it does not follow that the pressure of material necessity, visibly enforced by the death penalty, will ensure such a change in the legal and moral punctilios as will save the nation from the death penalty. Witness the case of the civilised nations during the past few years and the immediate present (1923).

Whether any given people is to come through any given period of such enforced change alive and fit to live, appears to be a matter of chance in which human insight plays a minor part and human foresight no part at all. As has already been spoken of above and as is well known to students of these things, any established scheme of law and morals is an outgrowth of custom, of past habituation, and is bound to change incontinently in the course of further habituation. It is an empirical creation, a system of habits of thought induced by past habits of life, which have been induced by the drive of those material circumstances under which these human generations have been living in the past. And this system of habits of thought (law and custom) is, at the best, in a state of moving equilibrium, forever subject to readjustment and derangement by further habituation induced by further changes in those material circumstances that condition the community's habits of life.

In the nature of things the growth of custom follows after the facts of experience which give rise to it, and any systematic change in the substance or direction of this growth of custom follows after the material changes which entail it. In this sense, therefore, any established order of law and custom is always out of date, in some degree. The code of right and honest living is always in arrears, by more or less; more so in the case of any people for whom the material conditions of life are in rapid process of change, as in America and the civilised countries of Europe.

Any large and persistent change in the material conditions—such, e. g., as has been taking effect in the scale and methods of industry during the past one hundred years—will necessarily be followed in due course by more or less pronounced changes in the established order of human relations and principles of conduct; but it need not follow that the resulting changes in law and morals will be of such a nature as to enhance the facility of life under the new order of material conditions which has induced these changes. Habituation affects the aptitudes of the individual as such, and comprises no collective bent. It is in the nature of a *vis a tergo,* which may drive many persons in the same general direction, but which looks to no end. In effect, any resulting revision of the principles of conduct will come in as a drift of habituation rather than a dispassionately reasoned adaptation of conduct to the circumstances of the case. It appears always to be a matter of "forced movements" rather than an outcome of shrewd initiative and logical design—even though much argument may be spent in the course of it all. As witness the helplessly evil case of the civilised nations since the War and the Armistice, and the solicitous fluttering of all the shrewd statesmen and the responsible men of affairs.[4] When seen in a

[4] By ingrained habit stabilised with precept and example the statesmen and men of affairs, together with the substantial part of their underlying constituencies, conceive the situation in terms of national intrigue and absentee ownership, and they endeavor to deal with it all along those lines. National rapacities are to be balanced and absentee property-claims are to be made secure; and there is at least a make-believe of hope that all that will help some, at least for the time being. Whereas the hardships of the situation effectually run in terms of population, foot-loose man-power, idle equipment, under-production. These are material facts that can be handled only by recourse to material science, technical organisation, industrial allocation of resources, quantity production of useful goods. But in effect, in so far as touches any action on their part in these premises, they know nothing and take no cognisance of the material sciences, the mechanical technology, or the growth of population. In the present disarray of these material ways and means, na-

longer historical perspective and with a consequent greater detachment of observation any deliberate revision of the received scheme of law and morals will appear all the more patently to be a work of casual drift and an outcome of fortuitous habituation—Forced Movements, Tropisms, and Animal Conduct.[5] Such in effect has been the growth of nationalism in recent times, as well as of the progressively expanded rights of absentee ownership during the same period.[6]

So in the passage from mediæval to modern times certain profound and enduring changes took effect in the civil and political institutions of Europe. But all that had gone before was not lost, of course. Many things were carried over. As a matter of course very much of the institutional furniture of the Middle Ages has stood over and has continued to govern men's conduct

tional interests and absentee claims can serve only to obstruct the work that is to be done. National interests after all are essentially predatory interests and the rightful claims of absentee ownership are essentially claims to unearned income; and the singleminded concern of the statesmen and men of affairs with these endeavours to get something for nothing has in effect resulted in unremitting sabotage on the work that is waiting to be done. So they have hitherto achieved nothing more to the point than a passably complete stultification.

[5] It is evident now that such has been the nature of those revolutionary constitutional transactions that have marked the history of modern Europe and given its special character to the present established order of law and politics; as, e. g., the English revolution of 1688 or the French and the American transactions in the late eighteenth century.—Cf., e. g., Robinson and Beard, *Outlines of European History,* Part II.

The form of words made use of above will be recognised as taken from the title of a volume published by Jacques Loeb under that caption.

[6] In all this it remains true, of course, that interested parties have shrewdly turned these forced movements of popular sentiment to account, and so have exercised something of a selective guidance over the growth of institutions.

and convictions very nicely in one bearing and another through the modern era,—as, e. g., the Church and the Gentry. Articles of institutional furniture of this spiritual order, being somewhat out of touch with those material changes that make for change, stand a better chance of survival, with less derangement. The mechanically enforced behavior of workday life does not impinge so directly and intimately on those habits of thought that make up the verities and proprieties of religion and gentility. However intrinsic to the due balance of human affairs, these things of the spirit are after all, in their material bearing, of less immediate and less concrete effect, and they are therefore less rudely touched by innovations in the industrial arts. Regard being had to the very respectable body of such institutional holdovers, it will be seen that the established order of law and custom is, after all, modern only in the sense that it has been modernised out of the past, and that its modernisation has necessarily been incomplete, in the nature of things.

It is this modernisation of European institutions that is in question here, and only in so far as it bears directly on ownership and industry; and therefore on the material fortunes of the civilised peoples, including America. The rest of the institutional furniture that goes to make up Western civilisation, those other articles of usage and belief that are comprised in the spiritual heritage, may be no less interesting and no less admirable in their own right, but a discussion of these other things does not belong here.

In so far as bears on latterday questions of ownership and industry, there are two main articles of modern law and custom that call for consideration,—the system of Natural Rights, and the growth of National Integrity.

The two are closely in touch with one another, indeed they are bound up together, inasmuch as it is the national establishment that gives effect to the code of natural rights in this modern scheme of things. The two together make the framework of democratic institutions. Of these two pillars of the house of democracy, the national establishment may conveniently be spoken of first.

The growth of national integrity has run a fairly unbroken course since the close of the Middle Ages. It has all the while gathered vigor and momentum, on the whole, and has grown gradually more definite in its aims and motives; and this course of growth and ripening appears by no means to be concluded yet. As it bears on the questions involved in the present inquiry the spirit (or habit) of national integrity may be said to have taken its rise and assumed much of its distinctive character in those princely adventures in "state-making" that fill the political history of early modern times.

State-making was a competitive enterprise of war and politics, in which the rival princely or dynastic establishments, all and several, each sought its own advantage at the cost of any whom it might concern. Being essentially a predatory enterprise, its ways and means were fraud and force. The several princely and dynastic establishments took on a corporate existence, with a corporate interest, policy, and organisation; and each of them worked consistently at cross purposes with all other similar corporations engaged in the same line of adventure. Among them were also principalities of the Faith, including the Holy See. The aim of it all centered in princely dominion and prestige, and in unearned incomes for the civil, military, and ecclesiastical personnel by whose concerted efforts the traffic in state-making was carried on.

Any one of these dynastic corporations could gain further dominion and prestige only at the expense of others of their kind, and only at the cost of their underlying population. It is a matter of course that the loss, damage, decay or discomfort of any one counted as gain for the rest; all gains being differential gains. The traffic was carried on then as now by warfare and warlike diplomacy;[7] which always resolves itself into an expenditure of life and substance on the part of the underlying population of all contending parties. It was always, as it has always continued to be, an enterprise of intimidation which counted on an eventual recourse to arms—*ultima ratio principum*—and the business was always, then as now, worked out in terms of mutual damage and discomfort, the outcome being decided by the balance of damage and loss; the cost in life and substance falling, then as now, on the underlying population, and the gains in dominion, prestige and goods going to the princely establishment and the kept classes.

This whole traffic in state-making is of a singularly unambiguous character and makes a sufficiently notorious chapter of history. And the States which it made were such as it might be expected to make. It was an enterprise in mutual defeat, quite unashamed. To the end that these adventures in damage, debauch and discomfort might be carried to a fitting conclusion, as they commonly have been, the several dynastic corporations claimed, and enforced, an undivided usufruct of their underlying populations and all their ways and works. So this unqualified usufruct of the underlying population became a perpetual and unalienable asset of the

[7] The part of wise statecraft then as now was to "speak softly and carry a big stick," as the principle has been formulated by one of the greater democratic statesmen of a later time.

dynastic establishment, by Grace of God. In time, and indeed in a relatively short time, by force of strict and unremitting discipline and indoctrination the underlying population learned to believe that this princely usufruct of their persons and property by Grace of God was indispensably right and good, in the nature of things. By law and custom the underlying population came to owe, and to own, an unbounded and unquestioning allegiance of service to the princely establishment in whose usufruct they are held. Therefore servile allegiance has become not only a point of law but also a point of morals and honor. Such is the force of use and wont.

In the nature of things, these competitive princely corporations were always working at cross purposes and were imbued with an all-pervading spirit of enmity and distrust, suitable to that enterprise in mutual damage and discomfort for which they were organised and equipped; and in all this diligent pursuit of disaster it was recognised as a plain matter of course that there was no place for scruples of any kind. All is fair in war and politics. It is a game of force and fraud. There is said to be honor among thieves, but one does not look for such a thing among statesmen. And so this spirit of dynastic statecraft spread down and outward by diffusion, by precept and example, throughout the underlying population until presently they were, all and several, bound together in the service of their predacious masters by an inveterate and unreflecting solidarity of national conceit, fear, hate, contempt, and an enthusiastically slavish obedience to the constituted authorities. Such has been the force of use and wont, and such is its institutional residue.[8]

[8] Cf. e. g., Max Silvius Handman, "The Sentiment of Nationalism." *Political Science Quarterly*, March, 1921.—No peo-

By habituation through these bleak centuries of state-making this national integrity of hate, mischief and distrust has been ground into the texture of civilised life and thought, until it has become one of the sovereign facts in the established order of law and morals in all the civilised nations. So that when presently, under the pressure of altered material circumstances and consequent altered habits of life, a growth of democratic institutions set in, the ancient habitual solidarity of national conceit, fear, hate, contempt, and servility was carried over intact and unabated into the ideals of the democratic commonwealth, where it is still treasured as the essential substance of citizenship. It still remains the chief engine of dissension and distress at the hands of the national statesmen, whose chief end of endeavour still continues to be mutual defeat. It is only that the divine right of the prince has passed over into the divine right of the Nation. The democratic corporations of national statesmen continue to carry on the traffic in war and politics on the same lines and by use of the same means and methods as the dynastic statesmen of the era of state-making in their time. And the ways and means of it all is still the same dutiful usufruct of the underlying population, dedicated to this use by their corporate spirit of national vanity, fear, hate, contempt, and servility.

In the course of this era of state-making the prince became a "sovereign" by Grace of God, with tenure in perpetuity. His divine right to the usufruct of the underlying population was worked out and established by help of the interested connivance of the Church; and this appears to have been the only substantial contribution which the Church has made to the modern scheme of civil and

ple can be a *bona-fide* Nation so long as it falls short in respect of this overhead of futilities and turpitudes.

political institutions. The prince became a sovereign; that is to say, all men became subject and abjectly inferior to him, in the nature of things; and to him, for no reasoned cause, all men thereupon owed unquestioning and unqualified obedience and service, in the divine nature of things. This notion of "sovereignty" is essentially a proposition in theological metaphysics, according to which some sort of immaterial superiority is infused in the person of the sovereign by divine fiat; which invests him with an axiomatically authentic personal dominion over the underlying population and all their ways and works. The Freudians would presumably call it an inferiority complex with benefit of clergy.

When and in so far as the democratic commonwealth has displaced the monarchical State, this theologico-metaphysical attribute of sovereignty is conceived by the experts in political law and speculation to have passed over intact to the Nation; so that the Grace of God in this bearing now invests the national establishment, conceived as a corporate personality, instead of the person of the prince. The retention of this princely sovereignty in behalf of the "sovereign people" marks the Nation as a successor of the dynastic State, chartered to do business on the same lines and with the same powers; very much as a modern oil corporation will take over all the powers and liabilities of any individual promoters whom it has bought out. The democratic Nation, therefore, is a sovereign by Grace of God, whatever other blessings it may enjoy. But the democratic Nation has no personal existence except in the several persons of its citizens. So the experts in political speculation have drawn the logical consequence, to the effect that these democratic citizens are vested with this princely sovereignty, each and several, unalienably and in perpetuity. That is to say, these democratic citizens, each and several, by Grace of God hold sovereign dominion over the under-lying population of which they each and several are ab-jectly servile components.[9] So also it should apparently follow by force of the same metaphysics that each of these sovereign citizens, being at the same time a loyal member of the underlying population, by Grace of God owes un-qualified and unalienable allegiance to his own person in perpetuity.

All this seems foolish, of course. But it has the merit of consistency. And it was for a democracy of this complexion that the world once was to have been made safe. So also of course it is at least extremely doubtful if any stretch of human fantasy could have designed and embroidered such an extraordinary conception of citizen-sovereignty, if it had not been that the maggoty conceit of princely divine right was ready to hand,— an institutional heirloom handed down to the democratic commonwealth from the days of the Grace of God; the days of dynastic state-making and princely bishops; when the Lord's anointed "tore each other in the slime" of political intrigue, while they visited upon the underly-

[9] "Men jeg er denne Kong Apis,
Det ser jeg saa soleklart;
Og dersom du ikke forstaar det
Saa skal du forstaa det snart.

"Kong Apis var nemlig paa jagten,
Og steg af sin hest en stund," o. s. v.

"But I am that same King Apis,
I see it as clear as noon;
And if you don't understand it
You shall understand it soon.

"King Apis once rode out a-hunting,
And he went aside by himself," etc.
Peer Gynt, Act IV

ing population "the high justice, the middle, and the low."

When divested of this metaphysical figment of sover-eignty and divine right, any national pretensions on the part of any democratic commonwealth become footless nonsense. The commonwealth in such a case would no longer be a political engine to be turned to account for political traffic by the politicians. It would be nothing to bluster and give off fumes about; nothing better, in fact, than an unsanctified workday arrangement for the common use of industrial ways and means. In fact the democratic commonwealths would in such event be in a fair way to become what they profess to be,—neighborly fellowships of ungraded masterless men given over to "life, liberty and the pursuit of happiness" under the ancient and altogether human rule of Live and Let Live. In that event loyal subjection to the national establish-ment of politicians would have no sacramental value, and patriotic fervor would be no more meritorious than any other display of intolerance. Treason and sedition would accordingly fall from their high estate as the chief of crimes, and would take rank as nothing bet-ter than scandalous dissension about matters of taste and opinion. However, that is not the way things have been arranged by the blind drift of habituation out of that sorry past. And as things now stand, thanks to that parlous legacy of despotism and predation by Grace of God, patriotic inflation is the chief of the civic virtues, and failure to abet the government's political intrigues is "high crimes and misdemeanors."

By grace of this ingrained bias of predacious enmity toward the outside and voluntary servitude within the Nation the constituted authorities of these democratic commonwealths have fallen neatly into the place once oc-cupied by the dynastic statesmen, and so they have, quite as a matter of course, also fallen into the same lines of dreary traffic in competitive force and fraud, without material abatement. Therefore civilised mankind is still divided against itself in a predatory scramble to get something for nothing at the cost of any whom it may concern; which always foots up to mutual defeat at the cost of the underlying population.

This is the domain of External Politics; a domain created out of national animosities, by statecraft, for the pursuit of national prestige and unearned gain.

In internal affairs, on the other hand, it is loosely presumed that the statesmen will be actuated by principles of equity and fair dealing and will be occupied with a humane pursuit of the common good. But the more fully the commonwealth has come to realise its status as a Nation, the more does its external politics (war and diplomacy) take precedence of its domestic concerns. The exigencies of external politics are paramount, and the conduct of internal affairs therefore are, in effect, required to conform to the needs of the nation's external policies. And the administration of external politics, being in the nature of an enterprise in chicane and coercion, is necessarily furtive, runs forever on sharp practice, carefully withholds "information that might be useful to the enemy," and habitually gives out information with intent to deceive. In effect, external politics is a blend of war and business and combines the peculiar traits of both. So the shadow of external politics covers also the management of domestic affairs, with the result that the authorities of the democratic commonwealths habitually go about their work under a cover of reticence tempered with prevarication.

Now, this may seem a fault; but the strategy enforced by the paramount exigencies of national politics is a

furtive business, in the nature of things, and will have
to be accepted with the defects of its qualities, if the
Republic is to fulfil its destiny as a dignified and self-
respecting Nation. The needful screen of strategic
reticence serves also as a useful cover for many interested transactions that would not bear the light of un-
tempered publicity; and the reasonable officers who
thrive under the shade of the screen will presumably be
such as the circumstances call for. By selective elimination of artless persons the personnel of official life comes
to be made up, in the main, of such persons as will feel
at home in the resulting spiritual twilight of official life,
by native gift or by sedulous training.[10] So it has also
come about, under the stress of national strategy and
political business enterprise, that any effectual distinction between honest politics and corrupt politics is an
elusive difference of degree, not a difference in kind.[11]
Due to the same causes it also follows that patriotic devotion to the national establishment will, in effect, come to
much the same thing as partisan devotion to the fortunes
of some particular gang or clique of political hucksters
whose concern it is to make use of the national establishment for the profit of some particular group of special
business interests; which is called "party government" by
those who theorise in Political Science.

The practical outcome has been a comprehensive defeat
of democratic institutions in civilised Europe, at home
and over-seas. It seems not likely that national vanity

[10] This will ordinarily imply a degree of arrested development,
particularly of the moral faculty, such as goes to create what
is called a "moron." Still, sedulous training will also do much.

[11] As seen, e. g., in the late election of a United States Senator
from Michigan, where this question has been decided on a tech-
nicality.

and dissension alone and working at random could have brought the affairs of the democratic nations to this pass, but they have also not been left to work out their own qualities unguided and unblended. Since and so far as the anointed princes have ceased to provide an interested motive for fomenting and mobilising international jealousies, statesmen have found a substitute in the pursuit of business interests. So the propagation of special interests under the shelter of national policy has come into the case, and this intoxicating blend has brought the civilised nations to the place where they now stand, after the War that was fought for commercial dominion. When national inflation is compounded with business enterprise bent on getting something for nothing at any cost, the product is that democratic "Imperialism" that is now carrying on the ancient traffic of statecraft. As once at the call of the anointed princes, so now at the call of a businesslike imperialist policy, the nation's citizen has no rights which the nation's politicians are bound to respect, except such property rights as are identified with business transactions on a reasonably large scale. So, the democratic commonwealths have fallen back on the ancient footing of intolerance, coercion, and furtive jobbery, that belongs of right to the statecraft of despotism and predation by Grace of God.

But it is, after all, a relapse with a difference, at least by profession. So far as the dynastic State has formally passed out of use among the civilised nations, and wherever democratic forms have by degrees taken its place, it is formally assumed and professed that the material needs of the country at large have displaced the ambitions of the Crown in the counsels of the statesmen who manage the nation's affairs. All this has brought on a change in the sentiments and aims which it is now incumbent on the statesmen to profess in their public utterances.

The resulting change has affected their professions more profoundly than their policies. During the era of state-making, war-like enterprise was always the chief and abiding concern of the dynastic statesmen. But as a means to this end the politicians of the Crown were also bent on increasing the material resources of their State at the cost of their neighbors. In this endeavor, which included a "mercantile" policy, so called, they were guided by the axiomatic general principle that one nation's gain is another's loss, and conversely; which assumes that international hostility is a matter of course, in the nature of things; and which appears to be a sound axiom of national statecraft, in the nature of things national.

The main and abiding pursuit of mutual defeat was never lost sight of in the economic policy of the dynastic state-makers; and, indeed the same familiar principle still continues to govern the motions of the national statesmen and the sentiments of their democratic constituencies. This economic policy of dynastic and imperial statecraft is called Mercantilism. In practice it is always in the nature of sabotage. The ways and means of its strategy are obstruction of trade and interference with industry; as, e. g., by a protective tariff, a colonial policy, a subsidy to shipping or munitions, an injunction of trade-unions, etc.

With the rise of the democratic nations the divine right of international obstruction and chicane passed from the dead hand of the anointed princes into the hands of the constituted authorities in these commonwealths, and these have since then continued with singular consistency to pursue the same tactics of mutual hindrance and defeat;

well approved all the while by their patriotic constituencies. The only sensible departure from this course of policy occurred during the early half of the nineteenth century, before the special interests of business had conclusively displaced the material interest of the community at large in the counsels of the statesmen and in the affections of the underlying population.

America particularly, which is by all accounts the most democratic nation in Christendom, has reverted to the princely policy of mercantilism with the least abatement; or perhaps it should rather be said that America, the most democratic, has pushed the inherited kingly policy of economic obstruction and defeat to greater lengths than the others. America's unexampled resources have enabled this nation to carry a heavier handicap of artificial disabilities than the others. Presumably it is not that the Americans are endowed with a larger capacity for clannishness and self-deception.

Certain considerations bearing on the case of mercantilism in America may be called to mind to explain and exculpate the peculiarly shameless abandon with which that ancient policy of damage and defeat continues to be pursued by this nation. America has by nature been endowed with unexampled resources, which have hitherto enabled this people to find an easy livelihood in spite of their costly and vexatious tariffs and their equally thriftless land policy. At the same time this people has been subject to a somewhat special course of habituation, due to the peculiar position in which their resources have placed them. They have from the outset been engaged among themselves on a competitive pursuit of unearned gain to be got from taking over these resources and holding them out or trading in them. So that, by steady habituation, cupidity and sharp practice have been embedded in the common sense of this people as civic virtues of the first order, under the decent camouflage of thrift and self-help. A people whose workday ideal of self-help is unearned gain by legalised seizure at the cost of the community, who have been schooled in the practice of salesmanship until they believe that wealth is to be created by sharp practice, and that the perfect work of productive enterprise and initiative consists in "cornering the market" and "sitting tight,"—a body of men whose sense of the realities is palsied with this manner of hip-shotten logic is also fit to believe that "the foreigner pays the tax" imposed by a protective tariff or that a ship subsidy is of some benefit to someone else than the absentee owners of the ships. An illustrious politician has said that "you can not fool all the people all the time," but in a case where the people in question are sedulousy fooling themselves all the time the politicians can come near achieving that ideal result.

And all the while, being a new nation and of humble antecedents, this American people has ever been quite irritably beset with a felt need of national prestige; which has engendered a bitterly patriotic sentiment and a headlong protestation of national solidarity; such a spirit as will lend itself to all manner of dubious uses in the hands of astute politicians. And finally it is also to be noted that the more maturely vicious development of this policy of commercial sabotage in America coincides in point of time and degree with the rise and dominance of absentee ownership in this country, and that any gains to be derived from such restraint of trade always accrue to one and another of the vested interests of the absentee owners, at the cost of the underlying population.

This protectionist sabotage on trade is a piece of the nationalist politics called Imperialism. Imperialism is dynastic politics under a new name, carried on for the benefit of absentee owners instead of absentee princes; but so far as regards its bearing on the material fortunes of the underlying community it all comes to the same thing. All the civilised nations are beset with imperialistic ambitions, and so far as their limitations will permit them they are all occupied with imperialistic schemes; that is to say schemes for the benefit of their vested business interests, masked as schemes for the aggrandisement of the nation.

There is a growing need of such national aids to business. A business corporation as such is restricted by certain large formalities of common honesty, the observance of which is not contemplated when business is done in the name of the Nation. The Nation, being in effect a licenced predatory concern, is not bound by the decencies of that code of law and morals that governs private conduct. So the national pretensions make a convenient cover for such adventures in pursuit of gain as run beyond the pale. These adventures in business, as well as the national pretensions, unavoidably run at cross purposes with one another; the abiding purpose of all competitors being to get whatever may be got at the cost of their neighbors or at the cost of those industrially backward peoples who have something to lose. It is the foremost aim of the imperialistic statesmen to extend and enlarge the advantages of such of the nation's business men as are interested in gainful traffic in foreign parts; that is to say, it is designed to extend and enlarge the dominion of the nation's absentee owners beyond the national frontiers.

And by a curious twist of patriotic emotion the loyal citizens are enabled to believe that these extra-territorial gains of the country's business men will somehow benefit the community at large. The gains which the business men come in for in this way are their private gains, of course; but the illusions of national solidarity enable the loyal ones to believe that the gains which so come to these absentee owners at the cost of the taxpayers will benefit the taxpayers in some occult way,—in some obscure way which no loyal citizen should inquire into too closely.

So the loyal citizens loyally place their persons and their substance at the service of those absentee owners who aim to get something for nothing by lucrative traffic in foreign parts and among the helpless outlying peoples; the constituted authorities dutifully cover the traffic with the national honor, the national prestige, the national consular service, and the national armament; and the taxpayers faithfully pay the public cost of the armaments and the diplomatic and consular service by use of which their absentee owners are enabled to increase their private gains. Indeed, on occasion the same loyal taxpayers have been known gladly and proudly to risk life and limb in defense of this absentee trade that "follows the flag." Should any undistinguished citizen, not an absentee owner of large means, hesitate to throw in his life and substance at the call of the politicians in control, for the greater glory of the flag and the greater profit of absentee business in foreign parts, he becomes a "slacker."

By stress of this all-pervading patriotic bias and that fantastic bigotry which enables civilised men to believe in a national solidarity of material interests, it has come now to pass that the chief—virtually sole—concern of the constituted authorities in any democratic nation is a concern about the profitable business of the nation's substantial citizens.[12]

But business enterprise here and now, and particularly business done on so large a scale as to bring it under the favorable notice of the federal authorities, is quite invariably an enterprise in absentee ownership. Any "Business Administration" will be a "Big-Business Administration." So the constituted authorities of this democratic commonwealth come, in effect, to constitute a Soviet of Business Men's Delegates, whose dutiful privilege it is to safeguard and enlarge the special advantages of the country's absentee owners. And all the while the gains of the absentee owners are got at the cost of the underlying population,[13] whether with or without special countenance from the side of the democratic authorities.

It is perhaps needless to say that all this is said without malice. A description by simple enumeration will sometimes look like fault-finding. But in all that has been said there is no presumptuous aspiration to reprove,

[12] This is not a matter of reproach, of course; quite the contrary, in fact. Indeed it is the boast of the present, latest and presumably best, Federal Administration in this country that this is altogether a Business Administration; and this is no idle boast. Its legal findings as well as its legislative and administrative measures have run admirably true to the form so set up. Always, night and day, the peculiar care of the Administration is now and ever shall be the profitable activity of the nation's business concerns, more particularly the larger concerns with a large capitalisation and a substantial rate of earnings.

[13] "The essence of business success is not to make good goods. It is not to have a host of employees. It is *to have something left*. The biggest word in the language of Business is not gross but *net*. *To increase the net profits*—that is the one aim of Efficiency.—Decreasing net profit is to a company what pain is to a human body. It is a symptom of injury or disease."—Herbert Casson, in the *Sabean*, April, 1921.

amend, hinder, improve, or otherwise interfere with this appointed task of the constituted authorities at any point, or in any manner or degree to take exception to the very singular net residue in which democratic institutions have culminated at this point. Evidently with no such intention but simply as a matter of objective results, driven by the exigencies of national jealousies and absentee ownership, democratic institutions have worked out to such an outcome as is sketched above. By force of the unguarded drift of habituation democratic institutions, which once were designed to serve the ends of liberty, equality, and the brotherhood of man, have under these latterday conditions come to converge upon the security and free income of the absentee owners, at the cost of the underlying population.

That such a state of things has resulted is plainly due to the continued prevalence—and ever-increasing intolerance—of that unreasoning habit of national conceit, fear, hate, contempt, and servility, which the democratic peoples have inherited from the statecraft of dynastic politics, as it ran in the era of state-making; when the prelates and princes competitively bled their underlying populations in the royal sport of *realpolitik*. Diligent habituation makes all things right. Except for this mob-mind of national integrity it is conceivable that democratic institutions might have come to serve the common good; but because of this the rule of Live and Let Live has in effect gone in the moral discard.

Born in iniquity and conceived in sin, the spirit of nationalism has never ceased to bend human institutions to the service of dissension and distress. In its material effects it is altogether the most sinister as well as the most imbecile of all those institutional incumbrances that have come down out of the old order. The national mob-mind of vanity, fear, hate, contempt, and servility still continues to make the loyal citizen a convenient tool in the hands of the Adversary, whether these sentiments cluster about the anointed person of a sovereign or about the magic name of the Republic. Within a fraction of one per cent., the divine right of the Nation has the same size, shape, color, and density as the divine right of the Stuart kings once had, or as the divine right of Bourbons, Hapsburgers and Hohenzollern have continued to have at a later date; and it has also the same significance for "life, liberty, and the pursuit of happiness." [14]

[14] There is, of course, no intention to find fault with these facts of history, or in any way to question the moral value of this untoward frame of mind which by ancient habit besets civilised mankind. It is only that this habitual mob-mind is untoward in the material respect. Moral values are another matter, and many untoward usages are highly moral. Moral values are a matter of settled habit; and assuredly national animosity is a sufficiently settled habit. When all is said, it remains an unshaken axiom in the popular mind that these mob sentiments of national conceit, fear, hate, contempt, and servility are high qualities of manhood, and that they do greatly adorn the character of any person whose moral tissues they may infest. All of which remains a sacramental matter of course, about which there is no disputing.

See also *The Nature of Peace,* ch. II, "On the Nature and Uses of Patriotism"; Bertrand Russell, *Why Men Fight*; H. H. Powers, *What Men Fight For.*

CHAPTER III

LAW AND CUSTOM IN RECENT TIMES:
I. HANDICRAFT AND NATURAL RIGHT

As in what has just been said in the last few paragraphs, on the nature and growth of Nationalism, so also as regards the argument which here follows, on the grounds of Ownership, the discussion is designed to cover nothing more than the modern case,—Nationalism and Ownership as these two institutions have taken shape in later times, in the habits of life of the modern civilised peoples, and only in those respects in which these institutions are characteristically modern.

Of course, neither ownership nor nationalism are substantially new and peculiar to recent times and to the modern peoples. Both are ancient institutions, at least in their elements, and something of their kind, more or less effectual, is to be found among barbarians and civilised peoples generally; though both institutions are wanting or slightly developed among those peoples that are reasonably to be classed as savages. Ownership which has developed so far as to take the form of absentee ownership has also been freely practiced here and there in other times and other places, outside of the European circle of industrial peoples and under material circumstances of a character notably different from those which have prevailed in recent times within the sweep of that industrial civilisation which now dominates Europe and its colonies. So also an onset of nationalism has come up repeatedly in past times and among other peoples, and has in fact served much the same purpose as that sentiment of national integrity which now is at work to abridge and deflect the material fortunes of these civilised peoples. To all appearance, human nature is, by native bent, eminently prone to settle into some such habits of thought as are embodied in these two dominant institutions, and European human nature is no less prone to some such frame of mind than any other. Yet the case of these civilised peoples as it shows up in the immediate present is marked by certain special traits which it seems worth while to inquire into.

In this connection it is as well to recall that in point of native bent and capacities European mankind is still the same as the neolithic European population once was, some ten or twelve thousand years ago. The hybrid mixture of races that occupies the countries of Europe and its colonies is still the same as the European population was in prehistoric (post-glacial) times, so far as regards all hereditary traits, spiritual, mental, and physical. So that the native aptitudes and disposition of these European peoples, and therefore also the limits imposed on their institutional development by their native aptitudes and capacities, are still the same as they were in neolithic antiquity. It follows that the scheme of law and custom which now governs civilised life under modern industrial conditions is still made up out of the same human mentality and still leans on the same spiritual forces that have made the outcome in the past, early and late. It is only that the material circumstances which condition the growth and working of this established scheme of law and custom in recent times are different in certain notable respects from anything that has gone before. By force of habit these altered material circumstances have made some difference in the existing scheme of institutions; but the existing situation is, after all, a variation on an ancient theme, through which runs always the same human strain.

The national integrity of these civilised European peoples has come down from feudal antecedents, and it took on its modern shape during the era of state-making in early modern times, having come into its characteristic modern form through strict habituation under the exacting discipline to which the political traffic of that time subjected all these European populations. Minor agencies, excursions and refinements of the patriotic fancy, have contributed something in the way of elaboration of the theme in later times; but, by and large, the nationalism of later times is still such as it once took shape under the stern discipline of the era of state-making.

No doubt, in the last analysis it will be found that the political traffic of that time was brought on and conditioned by a profound change in the material circumstances which conditioned the life of the European peoples in that time.[1] The like is true for the modern system of ownership, which also took shape about the same time and driven by the same material forces. These driving forces, it is held, were such things as the growth of the handicraft industry, the growth of population, and the growth of trade and the consequent resort to credit.[2] The prime mover in the making of the new era, and therefore also in making over the principles of ownership, is evidently the change which was then going forward in the industrial arts, as embodied in the handicraft system of industry.[3]

[1] Cf. Edward Jenks, *Law and Politics in the Middle Ages.*
[2] Cf. Sombart, *Moderne Kapitalismus,* bk. i.
[3] Cf. *The Instinct of Workmanship,* ch. vi.—The literature

Modern ownership and nationalism have both come out of that period of profound change in the industrial arts that gave rise to the handicraft system and to the petty trade that ran along with the growth of handicraft; but all the while this growth of new ideas was conditioned by institutions and ideals that were standing over from an earlier state of things. Law and custom are a product of use and wont, but use and wont will enforce a closer degree of conformity to material circumstances in that range and manner of conduct that has most immediately and intimately to do with the material circumstances. In point of psychological incidence, law and custom in matters of political and civil usage were a degree farther removed from the touch of that disturbance that was set up by the growth of handicraft and the petty trade. So that the political establishment and the national spirit on which the State and its interests are borne up have remained farther in arrears; as contrasted with the new growth of ownership and its rights, powers, and immunities, which have been more intimately touched by the everyday facts of productive industry. Doubtless, as has already been spoken of above, law and custom in matters of ownership will also always be found somewhat in arrears, as compared with those driving forces of industrial change that bring on changes in law and custom. In the nature of things, the scheme of law and custom is always archaic, at all points, in some degree; always out of date more or less. But the law and custom that rules political relations and political ideals is, by the same token, always more archaic, out of date in a more pronounced degree, than the principles of such human conduct as is of more immediate consequence.[4]

dealing with this topic is excellent and very extensive, in all the modern languages.

[4] On the other hand, as a further term of comparison, the

Fons et origo of the era of handicraft and its new order was the Masterless Man. The handicraft industry took its rise in the interstices of the feudal (manorial) system, which was a settled order of mastery and service, orderly, standardised, and stabilised as fully as might be, resting on a population engaged in mixed farming and bound to the soil. The law and custom of the feudal régime was a balanced scheme of coercion and submission, dependence and fealty, in which all human values—rights and obligations, security of life and limb, equity and justice, neighborly respect and affection, religious profit and loss—were of right to be rated and apportioned according to a settled schedule of graded privilege, standardised superiority and inferiority. It was always and by settled principle a question of gradation in respect of mastery and service. In this scheme of human things there was no place and no room for the masterless man. In its terms he had no ratable human value and no rights which honest folks were bound to respect. In effect, the Masterless Man was not to be distinguished from the Sturdy

scheme of religious observances, e. g., is necessarily even more archaic, more widely out of date; since religious observances, after all, have little or no immediate industrial value and are not in any pronounced degree exposed to the direct and intimate impact of that habituation that is enforced by the state of the industrial arts. So that while the political institutions and ideals in vogue today may be said to date back a few hundred years for their main substance; the religious observances and ideals of the present still draw on dates and experience lying a few thousand years in the past, being in great part erected out of elements of habit supplied by the pastoral civilisations of remote antiquity. Yet even the divine and immutable verities of the Faith have not altogether escaped the corrosive touch of this later state of the industrial arts. But for all the impact of new habits to which it is exposed, there still hangs about the Faith and its reactionary adepts an air of hoary antiquity, compared with which the mediæval ideals of the statesmen are a recent growth.

Beggar. In terms of the nearest modern analogy he would be a tramp, a drifter, a hobo, a species of Industrial Worker of the World at large, taking that term in its simpler and more sinister meaning.

What lends a measure of interest to this masterless man when seen in the perspective of history is the fact that he was the appointed beginning of a new order of industry and the underlying factor of an eventual new dispensation in law and custom. But in his own time and in that institutional setting he was a graceless intruder and a good deal of a nuisance, as still is likely to be the case with any human material that does not fit into the framework of current use and wont. He was an institutional misfit. He owed no allegiance to any master according to the standard methods of allegiance current in that time, and therefore he was a social, industrial, civil, and political encumbrance; very much as is now the case with any I. W. W. who is endowed with no absentee ownership and who disclaims that standardised allegiance to the national establishment that is stipulated by the forms of law and custom in such cases made and provided. And, then as now, the whole duty of loyal citizens in dealing with these homebred aliens was that which is embodied in the watchword of the Legion—"Treat 'em rough!"

In much the same measure as the feudal régime matured into perfection and settled down to its work, it also grew progressively more irksome to the underlying population; as would naturally happen in the case of any system of absentee rights and powers, and as has happened more than once since then. Such a system of personal control runs on organised and standardised hardship, and the more efficiently it is organised for its work the greater will be the resulting hardship to the underlying population. Long and steady habituation will go far to make it all right and proper; but there is also always a limit of tolerance, beyond which an increasing net residue of popular hardship begins to work mischief to the system. So, when Knighthood was in Flower the mills of the gods ground out an ever increasing number of restless and graceless ones who turned away from the underpaid virtues of feudal allegiance and went out to seek a livelihood on their own. Feudal allegiance no longer brought any net material advantage to the common man, so soon as the feudal régime had come into full bearing; very much as national allegiance has ceased to offer any net material advantage to the common man in our own time; and so, an increasing number of the harder-headed, or hotter-headed, common men drifted loose from those ties of loyalty that so had come to signify nothing but material hardship overlaid with spiritual pomp and circumstance.

So, by drift of circumstance, these masterless men drew together to seek a livelihood by the work of their hands and without formal dependence on the absentee rights and powers of those who owned the material world in that time. Out of the resulting scattered parcels of industrial drifters there grew up in course of time and experience the industrial towns and the arts, principles and mysteries of the handicraft industry. By degrees a new order of life arose and gave rise presently to a new line of habits of thought, and so gave something of a new bent to the subsequent growth of institutions among the European peoples. The modernisation of mediæval Europe set in.

The denizens of the incipient towns were ungraded masterless men who worked for a living. That is the ground and beginning of the handicraft scheme of things; and the principles and ideals under shelter of which the handicraft system presently grew great and displaced the spiritual furniture of feudalism were such as emerged by habituation out of these facts of everyday life.

The denizens of these new towns drew together for a concerted defense against the constituted authorities of that time; and out of this experience in illicit manœuvring along the margin of tolerance, there presently emerged a commonwealth of ungraded masterless men bound together for the common defense and governed by self-imposed rules designed for the common good; with a jealous eye to the common material interests at home and a stiff defense toward the outside. The insistent need of a common defense kept alive, stabilised, and carried over that trained sense of partisan solidarity which the factional struggles of feudalism and the devout intolerance of the Church had already ground into the moral tissues of Christendom. So that when presently the militant princely State of the era of state-making began to give place to the democratic commonwealth of modern times, a jealous national sentiment of collective ill-will was ready to shift into the place once held by the habit of personal allegiance to a feudal overlord. That habit of bellicose loyalty to a personal superior, which was the most meritorious virtue of chivalry, blended with the popular devotion to the common defence, and so gave rise to that spirit of militant nationalism that pervades Christendom today. In time, under the fostering care of the statesmen who guard the vested interests, this national spirit has headed up in the profligate imperialism of more recent date; which makes a virtue of getting something for nothing by force and fraud at the cost of any whom it may concern.

But the craftsmen were, after all, masterless men working for a living; men on whose productive industry no absentee claimant had any claim which they felt bound to respect. Out of this workday experience appears to have arisen the common-sense notion that ownership is a "natural right"; in the sense that what a man has made, whatsoever "he hath mixed his labor with," that has thereby become his own, to do with it as he will. He has extended over and infused into the material of his work something of that discretionary force and control which, in the nature of things, the masterless man of right exercises in the movements of his own person. So the thing is his by virtue of his having made it. "Natural" ownership is workmanship wrought out and stabilised in a material object.[5] By this "natural" right of creative workmanship the masterless man is vested with full discretionary control and disposal over the work of his hands, and so he comes in for a natural right of free bargain and contract in all that concerns his labor and its product.

Trade—in this connection spoken of as the "Petty Trade"—is of the essence of the handicraft system of industry. The trade runs on this "natural right" of free bargain, and comes in on an equal footing with workmanship as an inalienable right of the masterless man. At the same time it is a necessary factor in the handicraft system, being the expedient without which the division of labor that makes the craftsman could not take effect. By force of this natural right of free bargain, ownership passes unimpaired to the party of the second part, who so comes in for the same secure tenure and disposal of the goods. Whatever so passes into the buyer's possession is his by warrant of the same natural right of free con-

[5] Cf. Locke, *Of Civil Government,* ch. v; See also *The Theory of Business Enterprise,* ch. iv., for a more extended discussion; also, Edward Jenks, *Law and Politics in the Middle Ages.*

tract, whether the goods in question continue to be held under his hand and eye or are held *in absentia*. And so absentee ownership comes into the case again, as a natural right tracing back to the workmanship of the owner or vendor.

Craftsmanship and the petty trade, the two creative factors in the handicraft system, call for free contract and secure tenure as a necessary condition of their carrying-on; which by force of circumstances entails ownership *in absentia,* more particularly when the petty trade presently develops beyond the scale of peddling, huckstering, or "itinerant merchandising," so called. At the same time ancient precedent is ready to hand, according to which ownership is a prescriptive right grounded in the feudalistic principle of Vested Interest. A vested interest is a prescriptive right to get something for nothing. Absentee ownership as it comes up in recent times, therefore, has all the legitimation given it by those principles of Natural Right that were induced by the workday experience of self-help during the era of handicraft, together with the reinforcement given it by immemorial usage. But the ground to which modern men—jurists, moralists, economists—have preferred to trace its derivation and on which they have preferred to rest its equitable claims has on the whole continued to be the natural right of workmanship, rather than the prescriptive right of vested interest,—that "whatsoever a man hath mixed his labor with," that is his by virtue of his having made it. According to the moral bias created by age-long experience during the era of handicraft, men are still inclined to justify property rights on the ground of productive industry, serviceable work, rather than prescriptive tenure.

II. The Natural Right of Investment

The "natural" right of property is grounded in the workmanship of the man who "hath mixed his labor with" the materials out of which a valuable article has been created. By this right of ownership the owner is vested with power to dispose of his property by bargain and sale. He may sell for cash or for deferred payment, and he may also lend. In so lending, the use of the valuable article passes to the borrower (debtor) while the usufruct remains with the owner (creditor) in the way of a stated or customary payment for the use of the property. This is the simplest form of absentee ownership that arises out of the "natural" right of property under the principles of the handicraft system. But the masterless men of the crafts had also the natural right to turn their workmanship to account for a valuable consideration in working up materials owned by another, without becoming owners of the resulting product; which gives rise to the wage relation and so brings on a second variant of absentee ownership, still securely guaranteed by the handicraft principle which derives ownership from workmanship and free contract. It was along these two lines —credit and hired labor—that absentee ownership chiefly found its way into the industrial system of recent times, until by degrees it has come to dominate the organisation of industry and has taken over the usufruct of the community's workmanship.

But included in the scheme of ownership as it stands in recent times there is also an alien strain, not warranted by the principles of Natural Right and not traceable to workmanship. Ownership of natural resources —lands, forests, mineral deposits, water-power, harbor rights, franchises, etc.—rests not on a natural right of workmanship but on the ancient feudalistic ground of privilege and prescriptive tenure, vested interest, which runs back to the right of seizure by force and collusion. The owners of these natural resources own them not by virtue of their having produced or earned them, nor on the workmanlike ground that they are making use of these useful things in productive work. These owners own these things because they own them. That is to say, title of ownership in these natural resources is traceable to an act of seizure, legalised by statute or confirmed by long undisturbed possession. All this is wholly foreign to the system of Natural Rights, altogether at cross purposes with the handicraft principle of workmanship, but quite securely incorporated in the established order of law and custom. It is, in effect, a remnant of feudalism; that is to say, absentee ownership without apology or after-thought.

Not that all ownership of natural resources is absentee ownership. Nor is it to be said that such ownership may not be grounded in the owner's workmanship. The small farmer, e. g., is not usually an absentee owner. The land owned and worked by the small farmer without hired help is raw material with which he mixes his labor in the work of producing crops, and so is to be counted in as a typical case of ownership based on workmanship. The like is true for other natural resources that are made use of in a similar way in other productive work. These things are not to be classed under the head of absentee ownership so long as these useful things are fully employed as ways and means of work by their owners alone. It is only when and in so far as such useful things are worked by the help of others than their owners, or so far as they are held out of productive use by their owners, that they are rightly to be classed under absentee ownership; only in so far as their productive use is disjoined from their usufruct, so that workmanship and ownership part company.

It follows that the small farmer's land-holding falls into the scheme of Natural Rights on an equal footing with the craftsmen's right to work for a living and to dispose of their product or their labor under the rule of free contract. It is not unusual to defend private property in land and other natural resources on the plea that the cultivator must have unhampered use of the land which is the raw material of his work. In the main, as things have turned in recent times, this plea is pettifoggery and subterfuge. It is not the small farmer's holding that needs apology or defense; and in the main the small farmer and his husbandry by self-help are already out of date in those communities where the machine system of industry has thoroughly taken effect. It is also to be noted that in the practical working-out of law and custom in all the civilised countries, absenteeism throws no cloud on the title to lands or other material resources. In this connection workmanship and the needs of productive work give no title, not even title to "improvements." Except by way of sophistication and *obiter dictum,* the tenure of lands and similar resources is not brought in under the "natural" principle of creative workmanship, but remains a tenure by prescription,—that is to say by legalized seizure. It might perhaps be argued that "squatter's rights" are a case of tenure arising out of workmanship, but closer attention to the question will show that the squatter's right, whatever it may amount to, rests on priority of seizure and possession.

Indeed, in the practical working-out of law and custom

during the era of Natural Rights, the cultivator's "natural" claim to the soil on grounds of workmanship has gone by default, even where a claim might have been sustained on that ground; for the reason, apparently, that there has been no sufficiently massive body of masterless men engaged in husbandry, such as would bend custom to its own habitual way of thinking about these things. On the other hand, the Landed Interest was vested with title by prescription and was a formidable spokesman for absentee ownership, tenacious of its prescriptive rights and full of an habitual conviction of the justice of its cause. So the feudalistic principle of absentee ownership by prescriptive right of seizure and possession still stands over as the accepted rule covering land and other natural resources.

As is well known, from the outset the handicraft system of industry included the petty trade, as a necessary factor in the work to be done. Therefore, that workday routine out of which the principles of Natural Right arose included also daily contact with the market and familiarity with the conduct of trade; so that all those preconceptions and usages of free contract and of bargain and sale which were involved in the conduct of the petty trade came to be worked into the texture of Natural Rights, by unbroken habit, and became a constituent part of the system. In the balanced order of the handicraft system, the trader, too, was counted in as a workman engaged in serviceable work and therefore entitled to a livelihood on the ground of work done. At the outset the petty trade runs along with handicraft as a traffic of give and take, a method of keeping the balance of work among the specialised workmen and between the body of these workmen and the world outside. It was a traffic in the nature of marketing, huckstering, or peddling, and much of it was not far removed from barter.

But the traffic presently grew greater in range, scale, and volume, and took on more of the character of "business," in that the necessary management of contracts, bargaining, and accounts became an occupation distinct from the handling and care of the merchandise in transit and in the market-place. The exigencies of the larger volume of traffic over longer distances and larger intervals of time necessarily removed the responsible merchant from personal contact with his merchantable goods; so that ever more and more he shifted from the footing of an itinerant huckster who handled his own wares in transit and in the market-place to that of an enterprising absentee investor who took care of the business; while agents, supercargoes, factors took over the handling, carriage, and even the buying and selling of the goods, which so passed under the merchant's ownership without passing under his hand. By degrees, instead of an itinerant merchant he grew to be a "merchant prince," and instead of being an industrial occupation the trade became a business enterprise.[6] But even the "merchant adventurer" of that time continued in close touch with the merchandising traffic from which his profits were drawn, as well as with the productive industry which supplied the merchantable goods.[7]

---

[6] Cf. Ehrenberg, *Das Zeitalter der Fugger,* where this transition is shown in syncopated form in the history of the House of Fugger, from the time when Jakob Fugger I came into Augsburg with a peddler's pack, to the great days of the third generation. A recent parallel may be found in the fortunes of the House of Guggenheim, which also shows the larger dimensions and swifter pace of the current facts in a felicitous way.

[7] Cf. Thomas Mun, *England's Treasure by Forraign Trade,*

The growth of absentee ownership out of the crafts-man's natural right grounded in his workmanship comes on first and most visibly in the merchandising trade. Investment, that is to say absentee ownership in the way of business enterprise, was commercial investment. It was in the shape of commercial enterprise that the modern world got used to the practice of investment for a profit and so learned to appreciate business principles and to value the investor and his work. But investment presently made its appearance also in industry proper, in the shape of ownership of industrial equipment and materials and the employment of hired labor.

By the time when the era of handicraft was drawing to a close and the transition to the machine industry and the factory system had set in, investment in industry was already a customary fact, particularly in certain of the leading industries, as, e. g., in textiles. It was absentee ownership, and would be recognised as such by anyone looking back to the facts of that time from the stand-point of the present; but it does not appear to have seemed so, at least not obtrusively so, to the men of that time, who had to do with the industrial situation as it then lay before them. Absenteeism was not the main and obvious feature of the case. It was still the tradition, and in great part the practical rule, that the owner of the works was on the ground in person and acted as overseer and director of the work in hand; although the work done was not the work of his own hands.[8]

But with the transition to the machine industry and the factory system the business organisation of industry

which shows the qualifications and daily occupation of a mer-chant of the larger sort at the middle of the sixteenth Century.

[8] Cf. Bücher, *Entstehung der Volkswirtschaft*, No. V, "Nie-dergang des Handwerks"; Ashley, *Economic History and Theory*, Part II.

gradually underwent such a change as to bring investment and absenteeism very practically into the foreground; so that since then, during the period which can properly be called "recent times" in the industrial respect, absentee ownership has been the rule in industry and investment has been the type-form of ownership and control. By a slight stretch it can be said that in the days of handicraft absentee ownership was an incidental or adventitious feature of the case, while since that time it will hold true that it is the ordinary and typical practice; it now is that which is expected, and anything else is regarded as exceptional and sporadic.

Very much as was the case in the petty trade of the Middle Ages, so also in the handicraft industry; by degrees but unavoidably, absentee ownership came in so soon and so far as the scale of operation advanced to such a point that trade or industry became a matter of team-work. With the advance of specialisation and division of labor the equipment required for carrying on any given line of work presently became larger than what a workman could ordinarily provide out of his own work as he went along, at the same time that the equipment took on more and more of the character of a "plant" designed for the joint use of a number of workmen. Such a plant would ordinarily be the property of a master workman or of a partnership of such masters, who thereby and in that degree became absentee owners of the plant. The like is true for the ownership of the materials employed and of the finished product.

Yet it was still the tradition in Adam Smith's time, at the close of the handicraft era in England, that the wealth so invested in trade and industry was, in the natural and normal run of things, an accumulation of useful goods saved out of the productive work of its owner, and it was likewise the tradition that the owner whose savings were so employed in production should "naturally" direct and oversee the work in which his savings were employed. What was "natural" in the Eighteenth Century was that which had the sanction of unbroken tradition; and so far as touches the economic life in that time, that was "natural" which was attested by unbroken habituation under the régime of handicraft.

Adam Smith spoke the language of what was to him the historical present, that is to say the recent past of his time, and he has left a luminous record of the state of things economic in his time as formulated in terms of the habits of thought with which the recent past had invested that generation of men. But in the historical sequence of things he stood at the critical point of transition to a new order in industry and in ownership, and what was "natural" in his view of things, therefore, ceased to be the common run of things from and after the date at which his luminous formulation of economic laws was drawn up. What had gone before was the era of handicraft and the petty trade, the habitual outlook of which had become (second) nature to the thoughtful men of that time; what has followed after is the era of the machine industry and business enterprise, in which the "natural" laws and rights handed on from the era of handicraft are playing the rôle of a "dead hand."

From and after Adam Smith's date (last quarter of the eighteenth century) a new era sets in in industry and business. As an incident of the new era there sets in also a visible and widening division between industrial work and business enterprise. The era of the machine industry opens in England in that time, and it opens presently after for the other civilised peoples also; at the same

time that the businesslike management of industrial concerns begins to shift from a footing of workday participation in the work done, to that of absentee ownership
and control. Instead of continuing to act as foreman of
the shop, according to the ancient tradition, the owner
began to withdraw more and more from personal contact and direction of the work in hand and to give his
attention to the financial end of the enterprise and to
control the work by taking care of the running balance
of bargains involved in procuring labor and materials and
disposing of the product. Instead of a master workman,
he became a business man engaged in a quest of profits,
very much after the pattern of business men engaged in
commercial enterprise. The result was that investment
and absentee ownership presently became the rule in the
mechanical industries, as it already was the rule in commerce and as it had long been the rule in husbandry.

This rearrangement of economic factors, and division
of economic activities, was brought on by the increasing
scale of the industrial plant and operations, wherever and
so far as the new technology of the machine process took
effect. And the characterisation just offered is intended
to apply only so far and so fast as the new mechanistic
technology gradually took over the industries of the country. There came on a progressive, but none the less
revolutionary, change in the standard type of industrial
business, as well as in the ways and means of industrial
work; and the same line of change has gone forward unremittingly from that time to the present, as it is also
visibly running on into the future.

If the word be defined to suit the case, "capitalism" in
industry may be said to have arisen in that time and out
of the circumstances described. Until the machine process had made serious inroads in the standard industries,

and until things had consequently begun to shift to the new scale, the business man in industry continued, in the typical case, to be personally concerned with the work in hand; and until this change took effect, therefore, the employer-owner answered quite reasonably to the character which Adam Smith assigned him, as a master workman who owned certain industrial appliances which he made use of with the help of hired workmen. But from this time on he became, in the typical case, an absentee manager with a funded interest in the works as a going business concern. The visible relation between the owner and the works shifted from a personal footing of workmanship to an impersonal footing of absentee ownership resting on an investment of funds. Under the new dispensation the owner's guiding interest centered on the earnings of the concern rather than on the workmen and their work. The works—mill, factory, or whatever word may be preferred—became a business concern, a "going concern" which was valued and capitalised on its earning-capacity; and the businesslike management of industry, accordingly, centered upon the net earnings to be derived in a competitive market,—earnings derived from the margin of the sale price of the product over the purchase price of the labor, materials, and equipment employed in its production. Industrial business became a commercial enterprise, and the industrial plant became a going concern capitalised on its earning-capacity.[9]

[9] The economists and others who discuss business and industry as carried on in that time—late eighteenth and early nineteenth century—do not speak of "capitalisation of earning-capacity"; but business practice at the time gives evidence of the fact. Then as always the theoretical discussions endeavored to formulate the new facts in terms derived from an earlier state of things. Indeed, it has taken something like a hundred years for the formulas of the economists to adapt themselves to the new run of facts in business and industry which set in in the

It is not that nothing of the kind is to be found in the practice of earlier times. Indeed it is quite easy so to analyse the facts of property-holding in any age as to show that the value of absentee ownership always and everywhere is necessarily a matter of the capitalisation of the earning-capacity of the property so held. It is more difficult, perhaps it would prove impracticable, to apply the same line of reasoning to the same end in the case of other than absentee ownership. At any rate the matter is fairly obvious in the case of absentee ownership, early or late, to anyone who has occasion to see it from that point of view. But with the advance into the new era, into what is properly to be called recent times in business and industry, the capitalisation of earning-capacity comes to be the standard practice in the conduct of business finance, and calls attention to itself as a dominant fact in the situation that has arisen. The value of any investment is measured by its capitalised earning-capacity, and the endeavors of any businesslike management therefore unavoidably center on net earnings.[10]

It should be worth while to take stock of this earning-capacity that underlies modern business enterprise, and see what it comes of and what it comes to. The earning-capacity of any given going concern is measured by the habitual excess of its income over its outlay. The net aggregate income, and therefore the net aggregate earn-

days of Adam Smith. Right lately the economists have begun to recognise that "capital" means "capitalisation of earning-capacity"; but when seen in the long perspective of history it is evident that the business men who had to do with these things were learning to do business on that footing something over a hundred years ago.

[10] Cf. *The Theory of Business Enterprise*, ch. vi; W. H. Lyon, *Capitalisation*, chs. ii and iii.

ings, of the business community taken as a whole is derived from the margin of product by which the output of the industrial system exceeds its cost—counting cost and output in physical terms. This may conveniently be called the net product of industry. So far as the country's industries have been placed on a business footing; that is to say, so far as the control of the industries has been taken over by business men on a basis of investment for a profit; so far the aggregate earnings of the business community will tend to coincide with the net product of the industrial system. This coincidence, or identity, between the net aggregate product of industry and the net aggregate earnings of business is by no means exact; but then, the whole system of absentee ownership and businesslike control is also not yet complete or altogether supreme, either in range or scope. Indeed, it is safe to affirm that the earnings of business come as near taking up the total net product of industry as one has a right to expect, regard being had to the present imperfect state of things.

It is this net product, counted in terms of its price, that makes up the earnings of business and so makes the basis of capitalisation; for earnings and capital, both, are counted in terms of price, and not otherwise. It is the ownership of materials and equipment that enables the capitalisation to be made; but ownership does not of itself create a net product, and so it does not give rise to earnings, but only to the legal claim by force of which the earnings go to the owners of the capitalised wealth. Production is a matter of workmanship, whereas earnings are a matter of business. And so the question returns: What are the circumstances by force of which industry yields a net product, which can be turned to account as earnings?

It will appear on analysis that there are two main circumstances which enable human industry to turn out a net product, and which govern its rate and volume: (a) the state of the industrial arts, and (b) the growth of population. Transiently, production will also be limited by the available stock of industrial appliances, materials, and means of subsistence; as well as by a variety of hindrances of a conventional or institutional nature, chief among them being a businesslike curtailment of production with a view to private gain. But always the state of the industrial arts and the state of man-power provided by the population will determine what will be the productive capacity of the industrial system; and in the absence of disturbing causes of an extraneous kind the effectual rate and volume of production will approach the limit so set by these two abiding factors of workmanship.

At the same time, by and large, the growth of population is governed by the state of the industrial arts, in such a way that the numbers of the population cannot exceed the carrying capacity of the industrial arts as known and practiced at the time, although the population may, and habitually does, fall somewhat short of that limit. It appears, therefore, that the prime creative factor in human industry is the state of the industrial arts; that is to say, the determining fact which enables human work to turn out a useful product is the accumulated knowledge, skill, and judgment that goes into the work,—also called technology or workmanship.

The dominant creative force of this accumulated industrial wisdom, within the sweep of which human workmanship lives and moves, has become evident more and more obtrusively since the era of the mechanical industry set in. The increasingly impersonal sweep of mechanical processes in industry during the past century has brought a realisation of the indispensably creative function of technology. But in the light of what the machine industry has made plain it is readily to be seen that the state of the industrial arts, the accumulated knowledge of ways and means, must in the nature of things always be the prime factor in human industry. So that in this respect the technology of this mechanistic era differs from what has gone before only in that the creative primacy of the state of the industrial arts is a more palpable fact today than ever before.

The state of the industrial arts determines what natural materials will be useful as well as how they will be made use of.[11] For the greater part the state of the industrial arts is a heritage out of the past, a knowledge of ways and means hit upon and tried out by past generations and from them handed on to their posterity; and for the greater part also any addition, extension, advance, or improve-

---

[11] E. g., in prehistoric times men (or more probably women) invented the domestication of certain crop-plants, and presently also of certain animals. By virtue of these technological discoveries in ancient times these products of nature came to be ways and means of human industry. And they have continued to hold their place in the industrial system since then; so that the life of the civilised peoples still depends on the continued use of these industrial appliances, and those lands and soils which lend themselves to use in the resulting system of husbandry are valuable natural resources in the precise measure in which the domestication of plants and animals has made them so. So, again, in later times, within the era of the machine industry, petroleum and rubber, e. g., which were of no account a hundred years ago, have come to be indispensable factors in the industrial situation today, because technology has made them so. There is no end to the number of instances that might be adduced in illustration of this thesis, because the same proposition applies to all natural materials or processes that are or have been turned to human use. It holds true throughout that "Invention is the mother of necessity" and that workmanship turns brute matter into natural resources, ways and means of productive industry.

ment in technology is a rearrangement of and a refinement upon the elements of such knowledge so handed down from the past. Industrial inventions and improvements invariably consist, in the main, of elements of knowledge drawn from common notoriety but turned to new and technologically unexpected uses. The novelties of today are a technologically later generation of the commonplaces of the day before yesterday.[12]

Evidently the state of the industrial arts is of the nature of a joint stock, worked out, held, carried forward, and made use of by those who live within the sweep of the industrial community. In this bearing the industrial community is a joint going-concern. And the "industrial community" does not mean the Nation; since no nation is or can be self-sufficient in this matter of technology. Of course, the patriotic spirit of nationalism drives men to imagine vain things of that kind; but all that is in the nature of a pathological make-believe, which has only a paranoiac relation to the facts of the case. And of course, the statesmen endeavor to hedge the nation about with restrictions designed to set up some sort of technological self-sufficiency and isolation; but all that is done in the service of technological sterilisation and decay, with a paranoiac view to the defeat of outsiders. It is only that the statesmen are running true to form. The industrial community as a technologically going concern is so much of mankind as is living in and by the industrial arts that go to make up the effectual system of technological knowledge and practice. And in this relation, as in most others, the national frontiers are the frontiers of the national futilities.

[12] Cf. *The Instinct of Workmanship,* chapter iii, especially pp. 103–112.

The state of the industrial arts is a joint stock of technological knowledge and practice worked out, accumulated, and carried forward by the industrial population which lives and moves within the sweep of this industrial system. As regards the modern mechanical industry this immaterial equipment of knowledge and training is held jointly by the peoples of Christendom. And the broad center of its diffusion still is that community of peoples that cluster about the North Sea, together with their colonial extensions into newer lands. It is this joint stock of industrial knowledge and practice that makes the nations of Christendom formidable, and it is this same joint stock of technology that gives to the modern world's tangible assets whatever use and value they have. Tangible assets, considered simply as material objects, are inert, transient and trivial, compared with the abiding efficiency of that living structure of technology that has created them and continues to turn them to account.

But for the transient time being the material appliances of industry, the natural resources and the material equipment in hand, are indispensable to the conduct of industry; since the current state of the industrial arts does its creative work only by use of suitable mechanical apparatus. Modern industry is a system of mechanical processes devised and directed by expert knowledge and carried out by means of mechanical apparatus and raw materials. For the transient time being, therefore, any person who has a legal right to withhold any part of the necessary industrial apparatus or materials from current use will be in a position to impose terms and exact obedience, on pain of rendering the community's joint stock of technology inoperative to that extent. Ownership of industrial equipment and natural resources confers such

a right legally to enforce unemployment, and so to make
the community's workmanship useless to that extent.
This is the Natural Right of Investment.

Ownership confers a legal right of sabotage, and absentee ownership vests the owner with the power of sabotage at a distance, by help of the constituted authorities
whose duty it is to enforce the legal rights of citizens.
This legal right of sabotage is commonly exercised only
to the extent of a partial and fluctuating unemployment
of the material equipment and therefore of the available
workmanship; only to such an extent as seems wise for
the enforcement of terms satisfactory to the owners,—
only so far "as the traffic will bear."   It is to the owner's
interest to derive an income from these his legal rights;
and in the long run there will be no income derivable
from equipment or natural resources that are wholly unemployed,[13] or from man-power which is not allowed to
work.

So the common practice has come to be partial employment of equipment and man-power on terms satisfactory
to the owners; often rising to something near full employment for a limited time, but always with the reservation that the owner retains his legal right to withhold his
property from productive use in whole or in part.
Plainly, ownership would be nothing better than an idle
gesture without this legal right of sabotage.   Without the
power of discretionary idleness, without the right to keep
the work out of the hands of the workmen and the product
out of the market, investment and business enterprise

[13] This does not overlook the case of speculative real estate
which is held quite idle for the time being with a view to a
lump gain in the future, in which case sabotage is carried to perfection for the time being.

would cease. This is the larger meaning of the Security of Property.

By virtue of this legal right of sabotage which inheres as a natural right in the ownership of industrially useful things, the owners are able to dictate satisfactory terms; so that they come in for the usufruct of the community's industrial knowledge and practice, with such deductions as are necessary to enforce their terms and such concessions as will induce the underlying population to go on with the work. This making of terms is called "Charging what the traffic will bear." It consists, on the one hand, in stopping down production to such a volume as will bring the largest net returns in terms of price, and in allowing so much of a livelihood to the working force of technicians and workmen, on the other hand, as will induce them to turn out this limited output. It evidently calls for a shrewd balancing of production against price, such as is best served by a hard head and a cool heart. In the ideal case, in so far as the "Law of Balanced Return" works out to a nicety, the output of production should be held to such a volume that the resulting price of the limited output will take up the entire purchasing power of the underlying population, at the same time that the livelihood which the owners allow their working force of technicians and workmen is held down to the "subsistence minimum." But such a precise balance is not commonly maintained in the practical management of affairs. The difficulties arising out of a very complex and fluctuating situation are very perplexing; so that in practice it is necessary to allow for a certain margin of error, which a businesslike (safe and sane) management will bring in on the conservative side, to the effect that the volume of production and the allowance of livelihood will commonly fall short of what the traffic would bear rather than exceed that amount.

It appears, therefore (a) that industrial appliances and materials (tangible assets), as well as the industrial man-power, are productive agencies because and so far as the accumulated industrial knowledge and practice make them so; (b) that investment in industrial plant and natural resources is worth while to the investor because and so far as his ownership of these useful things enables him to control and limit the operation of the industrial arts which make these things useful,—that is to say, because and so far as his ownership of these things confers on him the usufruct of the community's workmanship; (c) the earning-capacity of these assets, which gives them their value as property, is measured by the net returns— in terms of price—which come to their owner as usufructuary or pensioner on the community's workmanship; (d) these valuable assets are assets to the amount of their capitalised value, that is to say to the amount of their funded earning-capacity; (e) their earning-capacity is determined by what the traffic will bear, that is to say by curtailing production to such an amount that the output multiplied by the price per unit will yield the largest net aggregate return; so that (f) the natural right of investment becomes, in effect, a vested right of use and abuse over the current industrial knowledge and practice.[14]

[14] Cf. Two papers "On the Nature of Capital," in the *Quarterly Journal of Economics,* August and November, 1908; reprinted in *The Place of Science in Modern Civilisation and Other Essays,* pp. 324–386.

CHAPTER IV

THE ERA OF FREE COMPETITION

By a concourse of historical accidents, both the origins of the Machine Industry and the principles of Natural Right were first worked out in England.[1] Between them, these two factors of modern civilisation gave rise to that Competitive System that governed the conduct of industry through much of the nineteenth century and that has continued to dominate the speculations of the economists and the make-believe of the statesmen since that time.

In England, and in the other countries into which the mechanistic technology was then finding its way, the half or three-quarters century which saw the introduction of the machine industry was a period of extraordinary activity coupled with profound changes in the economic

[1] This does not overlook or question that tortuous documentary pedigree which legal learning has been at pains to find for the system of Natural Rights. It is not intended to cloud the priorities of the *jus naturale* or the *jus gentium* or Time Immemorial. It applies only *de facto*, not *de jure*. It is intended to speak only of the effectual emergence and diffusion of those habits of thought that have made the principles of Natural Liberty an effectual factor in the shaping of law and custom in recent times. And in this matter it was the fortune of the English-speaking people to take the lead; not by virtue of any peculiar gifts of character or insight, but only because of the accidental fact that the Industrial Revolution first took effect in that country; which, in its turn, was due to the partial isolation of the Island from the rest of Europe.

order.[1a]. It comprised the interval during which competition, as near as may be, has run free in recent times; and it is also the period during which investment for a profit established itself in civilised law and custom as the staple manner of ownership and control in industry. So also the latterday forms and uses of credit took settled shape and entered on their dominion in industrial business during the same period. Before that time indebtedness had been an ominous incumbrance, to be "lifted" as soon as might be. During this period indebtedness came into its own, as a staple means of gain for the debtor and an indispensable recourse in the ordinary conduct of business.

In effect, the Captain of Industry, too, emerged and grew into an institution in that time. In the course of these half-a-dozen decades or so the Captain of Industry —that is to say the absentee owner and controller of industrial equipment and resources—comes gradually into the foreground in the world of affairs and presently becomes the center of attention and deference as well as of policy and intrigue in all that concerns the ordinary conduct of affairs, political, civil, social, ecclesiastical. It is the era of personal business enterprise carried on under the immunities of impersonal investment. The course of things in that time inducted the Captain of Industry, the Substantial Business Man, into the Seats of the Mighty, where he presently took precedence of the Absentee Landlord and the Merchant Prince, who had recently been his betters.

It is not that Commercial Enterprise or the Landed Interest lost ground in any positive sense during that era of new growth; but only that investment in the mechanical

[1a] Cf., e. g., L. C. A. Knowles, *The Industrial and Commercial Revolutions in Great Britain during the Nineteenth Century.*

industries and in the trade which served the needs of those industries then became profitable and consequential beyond the rest; so that the industrial investments, and the captains of industry who were the personal upshot of such investments, presently outgrew those others who had ruled the road and set the pace of law and custom, usage and morals, before that time. During that era of new growth the civilised nations swiftly shifted to the ground of business interest and businesslike incentives in all that was to be done or to be left undone. Those nations that first felt the driving force of the new industry led the others in this new move; but those other nations that made the transition to the mechanical technology at a later date also took to the same business-man's policy and came in for the same range of businesslike ideals in the conduct of their civil and political affairs at a correspondingly later date. The case of Germany or of Japan shows this concomitance in a particularly suggestive way.

Enhanced income from investments became the paramount incentive of civilised life; and the Captain of Industry—the substantial citizen who controlled much of the nation's workmanship and so came in for a largely enhanced income—became the paramount exponent of the community's aims and ideals as well as the standard container of all the civic virtues. Chief among these civic virtues was a steadfast cupidity,—as has already been noted in an earlier passage,—the steadfast spirit of business enterprise, of getting a safe margin of something for nothing at the cost of any whom it may concern. Nassau Senior about the middle of the nineteenth century explained that this is "The Natural State of Man," [2] as being that state of commercial felicity for which by a happy

[2] Senior, *Political Economy*, 5th ed. p. 85.

destiny mankind have been brought out upon the surface of this planet and placed under the governance of certain beneficent natural laws leading to this eventual consummation.

The coming of the new industry brought also certain secondary but very substantial consequences. As contrasted with what had gone before, the new industrial system dominated by the mechanistic technology, was highly productive; increasingly so as the mechanistic technology advanced and extended its range. Yet during all that period which can properly be called the era of free competition the industrial system never reached such a pitch of efficiency that it could properly be called inordinately productive; that is to say, production was not at that time continually in danger of outrunning the capacity of the market. In the ordinary lines of industry it was not at that time necessary constantly to restrict the output in order to maintain prices at a reasonably profitable level. Therefore that period—say, loosely, down to the middle of the nineteenth century—was, by and large, a period of free competitive production and increasing output, in England and in the English-speaking countries.

An immediate consequence of the increased rate of production was an increasing growth of the underlying population. At the same time the overseas trade was greatly stimulated; partly by the large output of marketable goods; partly by the direct effect which the new technology had on ship-building and navigation; and partly also by the fact that the new industrial arts made use of a constantly increasing amount and variety of new materials, many of which were brought from overseas. In the nature of things the new industrial system was bound to disregard national frontiers, both for the resources on which it drew and for the markets which it was fit to supply. So that free trade both in industrial materials and in marketable goods became an obvious foregone conclusion so soon as the new industry had got well under way. It is true, then as ever, national jealousies favored restrictions on trade, and business considerations—that is to say considerations of private gain for special interests—then and since then have decided against free trade, here and there from time to time. But it has been obviously and increasingly true that productive industry of the new order is always best served by an unrestricted exchange of goods and resources. Business considerations may call for obstruction of trade; technological considerations do not.

The growth of population and the growing extension of trade into foreign parts afforded an outlet for an ever increasing production of goods, at reasonably profitable prices, that is to say at increasingly profitable prices. So that business considerations during that time called for no vigilant restriction of output, on the whole; and the sagacity of the captains of industry was therefore habitually directed to a cheap and large output of goods rather than to a vigilant sabotage on production with a view to enhanced prices in a restricted market. The dominant note of ordinary industrial business was not then a carefully balanced sabotage on production, as has since then gradually come to be the case, but rather a rapaciously thrifty cost of production of an increased volume of output to be sold in a virtually unlimited market, at competitive prices, that were made profitable by low cost. It is true that, increasingly toward the close of that period, businesslike sabotage on production also comes to be habitual, so that industrial business enterprise takes on more of its later and maturer character of watchful waiting; but during the era of free competition it is, after all, the habitual drift of sound business practice to find a margin of gain in an increased output at a reduced cost, at the cost of the underlying population, by the help of improved processes and by work on a larger scale.

If the era of free competition be considered to have closed somewhere toward the middle of the nineteenth century, it may be said that during that period of some six or eight decades there was no very substantial addition to the range of materials commonly made use of in industry, and no very appreciable innovations were made in the nature of the processes commonly employed. The advance of the industrial arts in that time, although very substantial, consisted mainly in the further elaboration and refinement of the mechanical processes which were already in use, and the more extensive and diversified use of materials already in familiar use. Electricity, petroleum, and rubber had no share in industry then, and even that extensive use of structural iron and steel that has characterised the later age was still in its beginnings. Industrial chemistry was but a slight and inconspicuous matter, and the industrial uses of the rarer metals were still unknown. It is during the third quarter of the century that these things begin practically to edge their way into the everyday scheme of organised workmanship and become incorporated into the industrial system. The industrial system, the state of the industrial arts, as it stood before that date was complete without these things; since that time, since their invention has made them necessary, industry can not do without these things; and in that degree a new order has come into effect in industry.

But while little was added to the kind and variety of raw materials employed, the consumption of the staple

raw materials already in use increased greatly and continually. This fact, coupled with a continually increasing
consumption of goods, led to an enhanced market value of
all those natural resources which were commonly drawn
on in that time. So that many a fortune, great or small,
was amassed during that period by the simple expedient
of "sitting tight" while the market values of agricultural
and urban lands, timber lands, and lands underlaid with
mineral deposits, were gradually being bidden up by the
increasing volume of industrial uses and the increasingly
urgent needs of an ever larger underlying population.
The new values which so were added to the country's
riches were created by the advancing state of the industrial arts, but the new wealth which so came into being
was added to the possessions of those absentee owners
who were seized and possessed of these tangible properties.

The same process of creating tangible wealth by an
extension of industrial uses has, of course, gone on unremittingly since then, and indeed it has gone forward
all the while at an accelerated rate; and all the while the
increase has by settled law and custom continued to be
added to the possessions of absentee owners who have had
no part in that advance of the industrial arts by which
the new wealth has been created. The case of the mineral lands in America and the other Colonies will come to
mind; and the case of urban lands is well shown, e. g.,
by real-estate values on the island of Manhattan.[3]

England, and the other civilised nations in a lesser degree, came through this initial phase of the existing industrial situation with a greatly heightened industrial effi-

---

[3] The holdings of Trinity Church may serve as an instance of
unobstructed and unabashed absentee ownership at the cost
of the community.

ciency, a great and steadily growing number of gentlemen-investors, a steadily increasing population, and a large increase of material wealth. On the political side, this era of free competition laid the foundations of the British Empire. National wealth increased greatly, the kept classes made a notable growth in numbers and in the conspicuous consumption of superfluities, while the underlying population steadily fell into arrears, underfed and underbred in an ever more pronounced fashion as this era of free competition ran its course and brought the community nearer to Senior's "Natural State of Man."

Opinions will differ as regards the date at which the era of free competition closed, and there also are those who will say that it has not closed yet, that competitive production still dominates the market and still gives its character to the industrial system as it runs today. There is, in fact, much to be said for this latter view, and indeed much is said for it by those who wish to believe. Free competition still stands over as the popular ideal to which trade and production ought to conform; and in the nature of things it is distasteful to believe that the ideal state of things is already an irretrievably past phase of the state of things. And there is much to be said by those who believe that the competitive system still stands over in the main, and that it can be reinstated in full and intact by taking reasonable measures to that end.

But the question here is not what evidence and arguments might without violence to the facts in the case be written into a brief in advocacy of the competitive system, as being the only good and natural plan. The question here is wholly as to the run of the facts, for better or worse; and this reduces itself to a question as to the approximate date beyond which it seems reasonable to say that, on the whole, the rule of free competition ceased to govern productive industry and the market for the product of such industry. And this is in some degree a matter of opinion; although it seems reasonable, on the whole, to say that such a change in the industrial situation becomes effective sometime around the middle of the nineteenth century.

It is not that competition ceased abruptly at that date, whether in trade or in industry, or even that it ceased at all. It is only that in so far as touches the industrial situation as a whole the incidence of this competition has changed in such a way that the resulting situation can no longer be spoken of as a competitive system in anything like the sense in which that term has commonly been employed. But even so, there still are large and highly important divisions of productive industry within which competitive production still runs on according to the ancient plan. Such are, e. g., agriculture, as well as many of the minor lines of production which have not been made over on the pattern of the machine industry.

The competitive system has been dying at the top. Free competitive production has ceased to be the rule in what are sometimes called the "key industries"; those lines of production on whose output of goods or services the continued working of the industrial system as a whole depends from day to day. These are at the same time the lines of work in which the machine technology has been chiefly brought into effectual use, as well as the lines of production on which all the industrial arts chiefly draw for power, materials and equipment; as, e. g., coal, steel, oil, transportation, and structural work.

The competitive system has been dying at the top, and the decay has been spreading outwards and downwards as fast and as far as the other and lower branches of the industry have been sufficiently brought into line with the mechanical technology and so have become fit material for absentee ownership and control; that is to say, fit to be profitably managed on business principles. In great part this decay of the old-fashioned competitive system has consisted in a substitution of competitive selling in the place of that competitive production of goods that is always presumed to be the chief and most serviceable feature of the competitive system. That is to say, it has been a substitution of salesmanship in the place of workmanship; as would be due to happen so soon as business came to take precedence of industry, salesmanship being a matter of business, not of industry; and business being a matter of salesmanship, not of workmanship. That is to say in other words, competition as it runs under the rule of this decayed competitive system is chiefly competition between the business concerns that control production, on the one side, and the consuming public on the other side; the chief expedients in this businesslike competition being salesmanship and sabotage. Salesmanship in this connection means little else than prevarication, and sabotage means a businesslike curtailment of output.

Of course, neither salesmanlike prevarication nor businesslike curtailment of output are new inventions of the Victorian age. Both are as old as commercial enterprise. But during Victorian times things took such a turn as to throw these expedients of commercial business into the foremost place among the principles which have guided business men in their control of industry. What has been taking place is after all only a change in degree, but it is a change in degree of such magnitude as to create a change in kind.

As has already been indicated in earlier passages, this turn of things that so brought on a new order of competition and put the old-fashioned competitive system in abeyance, turns in the main on three peculiar features of the situation as it developed during the early half of the nineteenth century: (a) by a fuller development of the mechanistic technology industry was becoming excessively productive—beyond the current needs of business; (b) because of this fact and because the territorial expansion of the available market had then virtually reached its limits, the supply of industrial products had overtaken the demand; (c) there was a large and increasing use of credit, which in great part took the form of investment in corporation securities. Each of these causes worked toward the same outcome, and it would be difficult to say which of them is to be credited with the greater share in the outcome. They have all persisted in later times, and they still go to make up the situation in which the industrial system is placed. It might readily be made to appear that the use of credit has proved the more consequential of these causes that have converged to create the existing situation in industry, but it would likewise appear that this use of credit would presumably have had no such effect in the absence of an inordinately productive state of the industrial arts. Before this turn in human affairs thoughtful men were asking if business is good for industry, since then the engrossing question is whether industry is good for business.[4]

Seen in the historical perspective of today the era of free competition that so drew to a lingering close in early or middle Victorian times has the appearance of a period of transition, or in some respects even a period of

---

[4] The answer to both questions appears to be that business may be good for industry and industry may be good for business if not used to excess and not allowed to form a habit.

beginnings and pioneering, especially as regards the conduct of business and the businesslike control of industry; although, of course, it had no such appearance in the eyes of those who saw it all at the time.[5] As has already been remarked in an earlier passage, during the earlier decades that followed the Industrial Revolution the new mechanical industries were habitually conducted on a relatively small scale on a basis of self-ownership, with credit relations playing a subsidiary and essentially transient part, and by owners who exercised a personal supervision of the works from day to day and dealt with their hired workmen on something of a personal footing. In the typical case, the organisation and management had, on the whole, a good deal of an air of personal contact and personal understandings, both in its business transactions and in its direction of the work in hand. The business concern, which in the typical case was the same as the industrial manager, would commonly consist of a single man, with more or less workmanlike knowledge and experience, such as would make him a reasonably competent foreman of the works; or it was a private firm, in the nature of a partnership which included such a person. From this type-form there were many departures in practice, transiently or permanently. But through it all ran a visible presumption of self-help, personal initiative, and avoidance of debt. Aside from book accounts, the credit relations of this typical industrial concern would be slight and presumptively ephemeral.

In the course of the period in question, and as a major factor in bringing it to a close, business practice so far departed from this early footing of individual self-help

[5] So, e. g., to Nassau Senior that phase of commercialised industrial enterprise was the *terminus ad quem*, the "Natural State of Man"; and Senior is an eminently competent spokesman of his time.

that the prevalent form of industrial business concern presently came to be a more or less unwieldy partnership, commonly including silent or "sleeping" partners, rather than an individual employer-owner. And while the partnerships increased in size and number an increasing proportion of them also took on the corporate form of joint-stock companies or were replaced by chartered companies, impersonal corporations with limited liability.[6]

[6] This rapidly growing resort to incorporation presently led, in the English case, to the Companies Acts, in the fifties; and this may be taken as a convenient date to mark the transition from the earlier to a later phase of modern business organisation. By chance, perhaps, this coming of new things in business methods coincides somewhat closely in point of dates with the beginnings of certain new things in technology which have had far-reaching consequences for the later industrial system, very much as these new things in business which came on during the middle half of the nineteenth century have proved to be the beginnings of greater things in business.

CHAPTER V

The Rise of the Corporation [1]

THROUGH the latter half of the 19th century corporations multiplied and increasingly displaced other forms of business concerns, and took over more and more of the control of the industrial system. By this move the conduct and control of industrial production has more and more become a matter of corporation finance. Writers on Industrial History who deal with that period will commonly arrange their narrative and descriptions in the form of life-histories of the greater corporations and corporation financiers of the time, backed with supplementary matter on the movement of population and the state of the industrial arts.[2] Which makes it a history of business enterprise rather than of industry, and with which it is not usual to find fault on that account.

The corporation (or "company," in English usage) is a business concern, not an industrial unit. It is a business concern which has been created by a capitalisation of funds, and which accordingly rests on credit; in which it differs, at least in a marked degree, from the private firms and partnerships which it has superseded as the ordinary type-form of concern doing business in industry and commerce. It is an incorporation of absentee ownership, wholly and obviously. Hence it is necessarily impersonal in all its contacts and dealings, whether with

[1] Joint-stock Company, Societé anonyme, Aktiengesellschaft.
[2] Cf., e. g., Burton J. Hendrick, *The Age of Big Business*

other business concerns or with the workmen employed in the industry. It is a business concern only, and in the nature of the case its activities as a corporation are limited to business transactions of the nature of bargain and sale, and its aims are confined to results which can be brought into a balance-sheet in terms of net gain. The corporation's control and direction of industry is a financial control and direction; which always and necessarily takes effect in industry at the second remove only, by means of a business transaction which is of the nature of a bargain; in pursuit of a businesslike outcome which is statable in terms of outlay and income.

A corporation which does business in industry will employ technical experts to manage the work and oversee the processes into which its outlay goes and out of which its income is (indirectly) drawn; but such a corporation is not itself an organisation of technical personnel, nor can its corporate activities be stated in terms which have a technological meaning. Its end and aim is not productive work, but profitable business; and its corporate activities are not in the nature of workmanship, but of salesmanship. If it is an "industrial" corporation, so called, it will make use of technical ways and means, processes and products; but it makes use of them as ways and means of doing a profitable business. It has only an absentee beneficiary's interest in the work to be done. It is a pecuniary institution, not an industrial appliance. It is an incorporation of ownership to do business for private gain at the cost of any whom it may concern.

This is not said by way of finding fault or raising an issue. The rise of the corporation toward the middle of the century, and its subsequent growth, was not due to any access of iniquity; nor on the other hand does it appear to have resulted in increased hardship. It came on by force of circumstances, because the conditions and methods of business were maturing into such shape as to head up in this outcome.   The incentives which drove on to this outcome were the sound and laudable incentives of greater expedition and larger net gains to be got by a more exhaustive use of credit.   Corporation business is quite like any other form of business enterprise in being a quest of net profits at the cost of any whom it may concern.   It is only that at this juncture in the advance of technology and population, and consequently of trade and industry, business conditions were falling into such shape that larger net gains could be got by use of the corporate form of business organisation than by the methods and forms of procedure previously in use.

It has been usual, indeed it has long been an inveterate habit, among economists and public writers, to assume and say that the corporation came into use as a means of increasing the scale on which industry was carried on, by providing larger assemblages of material appliances and drawing them together into larger working units. Doubtless there is much truth in that opinion, or at least the facts will bear that construction.   It is, e. g., strongly borne out by the visible results in such an industry as railroading, and evidence to the same effect is not wanting in other lines of production and service.   But the use of a larger scale of production is a technological device, whereas the corporation is a business arrangement. The incentives which gave rise to the corporation and which have made it the dominant form of business organisation must accordingly be incentives of business; that is to say incentives of pecuniary gain, of increased net gain per cent. on the investment.

Safe and sane business men would go in for incorporation only on a good prospect of getting a little something more for nothing by following that lead, or on the promise of incurring a margin of net loss by failing to follow the lead. To employ a larger scale of production is a sound business proposition only so long as this larger scale will bring an increased net gain in the aggregate price of the output; which will be the outcome within limits and within certain lines of industry, and which doubtless held true and had its effect in some appreciable degree at the time when the corporation was coming into its dominant position in modern industrial business.[3]

But the corporation is always a business concern, not an industrial appliance. It is a means of making money, not of making goods. The production of goods or services, wherever that sort of thing is included among the corporation's affairs, is incidental to the making of money and is carried only so far as will yield the largest net gain in terms of money,—all according to the principle of "what the traffic will bear," or of "balanced return," which underlies all sound business, and more particularly all corporation business.

This principle has come to be formally recognised and accepted as good and final ever since the corporation came into general use as the standard form of business concern. Doubtless, and obviously, the spirit of it has always been present and decisive wherever men have done business, from time immemorial, but in concession to ancient prejudice it used to be decently covered over with professions of something else. It is only since the dominant interest of the civilised nations has shifted from production for a livelihood to investment for a profit, that this principle of net gain has come to stand out naked and

---

[3] Mr. Dewing discusses this point in a very competent fashion under "The Law of Balanced Return."—see A. S. Dewing, *The Financial Policy of Corporations*, vol. iv, ch. ii.

unashamed, as the sound and honest rule that should govern and limit the production of goods for human use. And the corporation incorporates this underlying principle of business enterprise more singly and adequately than any form of organisation that had gone before. Business enterprise may be said to have reached its majority when the corporation came to take first place and became the master institution of civilised life.

It is also a part of the folklore of Political Economy that the corporation—jointstock company—has exerted, and continues to exert, a creative force in productive industry, in that it draws out of retirement many small accumulated hoards of savings, and so combines them and puts them to work when they would otherwise remain idle. By this means the active capital is augmented by so much; which is believed to augment the materials and appliances of industry by so much, and thereby to increase the volume of work and output in a corresponding degree. This faith in the creative efficiency of capital funds and capitalised savings is one of the axioms of the business community. It is a safe presumption that no sound business man would question it. Savings will produce goods so soon as they are invested and capitalised. A more attentive scrutiny of this proposition should throw some light on the nature and uses of corporation finance.

The savings which are to be drawn out and mobilised, turned to use by corporation finance, are held and brought out in the shape of funds—money, coin, banknotes, savings-banks deposits, money borrowed on collateral, and the like. They are not material goods that can be employed in production. In practical fact, the savings in question have existed and continue to exist only in the

form of records of ownership, commonly evidences of
debt. What is transferred in the transactions by which
the savings are taken over into corporate capital is commonly some form of credit instrument; and the transactions result in an augmentation of the volume of outstanding credit instruments. Whether there are any
physically useful goods anywhere held in store back of
these funded savings—physical goods which are in any
special sense "represented" by these funds—is an open
question, with the presumption running strongly to the
contrary. Apart from warehouse receipts and the like,
which play a negligible part in these premises, the saved
up funds foot up to an absentee claimant's undifferen-
tiated claim on a share in the outstanding stock of merchantable goods at large. Any multiplication of such
claims, or any mobilisation of an added number of them,
adds nothing to the stock of goods on hand; it only reduces the share per unit of effectual claims, to answer to
the increased number of units. An immediate consequence of the mobilisation of savings by corporation
finance, therefore, will be an inflation of general prices, a
depreciation of the currency.

In any case it is not the underlying goods, if any, that
are mobilised in such a financial transaction, but the
funds. It is the funds that go to swell the capitalisation.
Capitalisation is a transaction in funds, not a physical
operation. The transaction is concluded in a transfer
of funds and the creation of a corresponding credit obligation, not in any corporeal transfer and delivery of
productive goods. It is a transaction in credit, in the
nature of a loan, by which the corporation financier comes
in for the use of additional funds and is enabled to increase the capitalisation and the purchasing-power of the
business concern for which he acts. These funds may be

invested in industry—materials, equipment, wages; in which case they constitute an addition to the purchasing-power which is thrown into the market for these things, without making any corresponding addition to the store of purchasable goods in hand which this increased power is to buy. If all goes well there follows a transfer of goods bought, but at a higher price than the same goods would have brought in the absence of the new purchasing-power which has been brought into the market by this transaction in corporation finance. And that is all that can be counted on for a certainty.

The total of useful goods in hand is the same as before, as counted by weight and tale; but the total wealth in hand has been increased by a rise of prices, by some multiple of the added purchasing power, as counted in money-values. Measured by physical units or physical usefulness the total effect is nil, at the best; but measured in money-values there has been an appreciable addition to the total wealth, represented immediately by the corporate capital in which the funds in question have been invested and indirectly by the enhanced level of prices. There has been a creation of funded wealth without an increase of material goods.

So far the result would appear to be quite unsubstantial. Money-values have been inflated by an inflation of credit, which has been capitalised. But men do not see it in that light; use and wont prevents them. In all these civilised countries where the price system has gone into effect men count their wealth in money-values. So much so that by settled habit, induced by long and close application to the pursuit of net gain in terms of price, men have come to the conviction that money-values are more real and substantial than any of the material facts in this transitory world. So much so that the final purpose of any businesslike undertaking is always a sale, by which the seller comes in for the price of his goods; and when a person has sold his goods, and so becomes in effect a creditor by that much, he is said to have "realised" his wealth, or to have "realised" on his holdings. In the business world the price of things is a more substantial fact than the things themselves. Therefore in all these civilised nations, where net gain in price is the master passion and where the corporation has come to be the master institution. the endless [4] use of credit has enabled the wealth in hand to multiply far and away out of proportion to the increased production of goods due to the advance of the industrial arts.

But corporation finance, even in that simple and obvious form in which it first went into action during the middle half of the nineteenth century, is not a small and easy matter, to be disposed of in a passing paragraph. It has, in fact, occupied many able writers through many well-considered volumes.[5] Yet there is a little something to be said here in the way of additional comment on the work of the corporation considered as the master institution of the business world during the period when the

[4] Endless in the sense that in the ordinary course of business no transaction of any consequence terminates in anything else than a new credit arrangement. And when one sells out and "realises" on his holdings the "reality" which he comes in for is invariably some form of fiduciary paper, some evidence of debt. Indeed, even if it were practicable to close out and "realise" in cash—say, in coin—it would not be sound business; it would be a losing game, except conceivably in the case of a banking concern which might have use for a store of specie on the basis of which to extend its credit transactions.

[5] Cf., e. g., E. S. Meade, *Corporation Finance;* H. W. Lyon, *Corporation Finance;* A. S. Dewing, *The Financial Policy of Corporations.*

business situation was maturing into the shape which it has taken on in more recent times.

If the nature and uses of the corporation be considered in terms of that earlier and simpler business practice out of which the corporate form of organisation arose, the case will stand somewhat as follows. The corporation arises out of a collective credit transaction whereby funds supplied by the stockholders (shareholders) are entrusted to the corporation as a going concern, to be administered for their benefit under certain specified limitations. The company so organised is, therefore, an impersonal incorporation of liabilities to the stockholders, and by employing these liabilities as collateral (formally or informally) it will then procure further capital by an issue of securities (debentures, typically bonds) bearing a stated rate of income and constituting a lien on the assets of the corporation. The securities outstanding make up the capitalisation, and the stated income rates borne by these securities are fixed charges on the corporate earnings. Such is the simplest case of corporation finance, neglecting certain minor facts that do not materially affect the typical working-out of the corporation's control of industry; which is the point of interest here.

Two main and consequential facts are obvious on the face of things: (a) an inflation of credit; and (b) a capitalisation of funds, essentially liabilities, with fixed charges. The inflation of credit has been spoken of above, as well as its immediate consequence in the inflation of prices. It may be worth while to note here in the same connection that the continued advance of the industrial arts during the same period has constantly been at work to offset or minimise that advance of prices which the credit operations of corporation finance have constantly been at work to produce. So that any statistical presentation of the actual course of prices during the period will not show in any adequate fashion how greatly the inflation of credit has acted to inflate prices. At the same time the inflation of credit has broken down from time to time in the way of crises and depressions, whereupon the process of inflation has had to begin over again. All of which confuses the case.

A further effect of the inflation should also be noted briefly. Inasmuch as in any community that is given to business enterprise men habitually rate their wealth and their gains in money-values, any inflation of money-values will bring on what is called "buoyancy" throughout the business community and lead to a heightened business activity and a spirit of confident adventure. Such a situation presents a promise of an uncommonly wide margin of something for nothing, and by the simple money-value logic of business it results in an increased volume of transactions and a consequent release of the industrial forces controlled by the business community. There results a period of prosperity, during which productive industry is speeded up to meet the larger demands of the market; so that for a time the industrial equipment and man-power may be allowed to run at something approaching full capacity. The eventual consequence of such a period of prosperity in that past era which is here in question was, as a matter of course, "overproduction," glut, depression, and commonly crisis with disastrous liquidation; but the prosperity would be no less actual for the time being, and it is to be set down to the credit of the credit-inflation out of which such a run of industrial activity has arisen. In later times the more perfect and comprehensive control of credit on a unified plan, and by collusion of the greater credit institutions, has virtually done away with these unadvised fluctuations of prosperity and depression; although even yet a general liquidation may be, and a general depression already has been, brought on by a credit-inflation of such unexampled sweep as to exceed the capacity of that apparatus of control that has been made and provided for the stabilisation of this business.

Throughout the period dominated by corporation finance the use of credit, therefore, has had much, if not all, to do with periodically speeding up business, and so speeding up production for the market; and the corporation, which has been the chief embodiment and vehicle of credit in the nineteenth century, has had its share in that work. It is true, there was always bound up with this periodical business prosperity a corresponding periodical liquidation and depression, which always brought curtailment and retardation in industry. And it is at least doubtful if the one could have been had without the other. The history of that period is a history of rythmically recurring fluctuations between prosperity and depression, recurring so constantly and typically as to argue that the two are inseparable phases of the same movement; which in turn would argue that any prosperity so brought on by credit inflation—also called "returning confidence"—can not have furthered the growth of industry or increased the volume of production in the long run, since each recurring wave of prosperity was always and unavoidably followed and offset by an equivalent wave of depression and retardation due to the same set of causes, leaving no net gain traceable to this cause. All of which leaves the point in doubt.[6]

But while the long-term use and value of credit inflation as a creator of prosperity is left in doubt, there is

[6] Cf. W. C. Mitchell, *Business Cycles.*

at least one other point, of a similar bearing, at which the long-term effect of corporation finance on industry is not similarly doubtful. The corporation is an incorporation of credit, capitalised on the basis of the funds invested and to the amount of its prospective earning-capacity. It carries fixed charges to an amount corresponding to its capitalisation—charges formally enforceable in the case of bonds and preferred stock (preference shares) and insisted on with tenacity in the case of the common stock. There is no provision for a shrinkage of assets, and but a slight and doubtful provision for a shrinkage of earnings. In other words, the corporation is organised for prosperity, not for adversity, and it is somewhat helpless in the face of adversity. It is not designed to carry on in a falling market. Fixed charges must be met, on pain of insolvency, and earnings can accordingly not be allowed to fall off materially. More particularly since it is the practice in sound corporation finance to capitalise any increase of earnings that looks at all promising, and cover them with an issue of securities bearing fixed charges. The principle involved in this practice has been called "Trading on the Equity."[7]

The reason for "trading on the equity" and so increasing the issue of securities with fixed charges as far as the corporation's earnings will bear, is the urgent need of more capital. The need of more capital in business is insatiable, or "indefinitely extensible," because funds are a means of competition and business is competitive. This abiding need of more capital has commonly beset the common run of corporations in brisk or ordinary times, and it may rise to the point of desperation in times of depression. All of which holds true in a particular degree for that earlier date which here is in question, be-

[7] Cf. Lyon, *Capitalisation,* ch. ii.

fore the present, twentieth-century, phase of corporation finance had come into action. There is always a disposition to trade on a thinner equity, to cover more nearly all assets with an issue of securities with fixed charges; which constitute a lien on the corporation's assets, and which will bring the concern to insolvency so soon as the earnings fall off materially, as they are likely to do in dull times. And the reason for this abiding need of more capital is the competitive use of funds in a rising market; the rise of the market being itself in the main caused by this competitive use of funds.

The competitive use of funds may, though it need not, involve a competitive increase of the production of goods. In brisk times there is likely to be something in the way of a competitive increase of the volume of output, but in ordinary times such an effect is not commonly to be observed. It remains true, of course, that the corporations are business concerns, and the competition between them is a business competition; that is to say, it is a competitive endeavour to realise the largest net gain in terms of price. So that the competitive endeavour always centers finally on salesmanship; and the stress of competition may accordingly fall on increased production in case and so far as an increased output can be counted on to bring an increased net return in terms of price, and not otherwise,—according to the well-known business principle of what the traffic will bear.

Witness the present situation (1923) as it has stood since the Armistice in 1918; the generality of business concerns are and have all this time been seeking additional funds, but evidently not to increase the output of goods, since neither the equipment controlled by these concerns nor the available man-power are or have been employed to much more than one-half their capacity.

Indeed, increased production of goods regardless of market conditions—i. e., regardless of what the traffic will bear—could have gone into action on very few hours notice and on an unexampled scale at any time during these years of unemployment and Watchful Waiting since the Armistice; but while such increased production has been quite feasible, technically, and quite urgently desirable as a matter of the consumptive need of goods, it would be suicidal as a matter of business. During all this time the traffic would not bear an increased production of goods. The result would, it is believed, be a calamitous liquidation, in which a greatly inflated credit situation would collapse, and would involve a cancellation of, perhaps, one-half of the money-values now carried on the books of the business community,—which is not to be contemplated, not to say with equanimity. It is true, the community, apart from the business concerns, would be that much better off in respect of useful goods and the other material amenities of life; but in any civilised nation the needs of business are paramount, and according to business principles (net gain in terms of price) it still is good and right that the popular need of work and goods should wait on the business need of net gain computed on outstanding credits.

This situation that has prevailed since the Armistice and has stood over as a product of that season of spectacular waste and profiteering covered by the War, is the same in kind as the situation which prevailed at any period after corporation finance first came into control of the leading industries in the nineteenth century. It is only an exaggerated case of that with which all civilised men are most familiar, in much the same measure in which they are civilised, and for the maintenance of which they have undergone unexampled sacrifices and are ready to undergo as much more. In short, it is business as usual, only more of it. It is business as usual under the régime of corporation finance. And such has been the nature of business-as-usual ever since and so far as corporation finance has taken over the control of industry; in the nineteenth century in such measure as the petty circumstances of the nineteenth century permitted, and in the twentieth century on that magnificent scale of unemployment, privation, and underfeeding that is now to be seen all over the place, rising here and there to the pitch of famine and pestilence. It is not possible, on sound business grounds, to let the industrial forces of the country go to work and produce what, in the physical sense, the country needs; because a free run of production would, it is believed, be ruinous for business; because it would lower prices and so reduce the net business gain below the danger point—the point below which the fixed charges on outstanding obligations would not be covered by the net returns. Hence what is conveniently called capitalistic sabotage or businesslike sabotage on industry.

Corporation finance has always proceeded on a capitalisation of credit, with fixed charges, carried as far as circumstances would permit. And circumstances have permitted this capitalisation of credit to go farther the more widely inclusive the scheme of corporation finance has become and the more capable the apparatus for stabilising credit has become. Which comes to saying that the need of a businesslike sabotage on industry, occasional or habitual, has grown measure for measure as the scope and volume of corporation finance has grown, and as the equilibrium of make-believe carried forward in the outstanding securities has grown more inclusive and more delicately balanced.

And all the while the industrial arts have grown more

efficient in detail, at the same time that the range of industries and products which have come under the rule of the mechanical industry has grown greater; new details and new ramifications have been added to the mechanical technology; new materials and new natural resources have continually been added to what was already in hand, and the whole has all the while been falling into a more close-knit system of interlocking industrial processes. All of which has gone, together, progressively to heighten the productive capacity per capita of an ever increasing and increasingly workmanlike population.

So the continued progress of the industrial arts has become a continued menace to the equilibrium of business, has forever threatened to lower the cost per unit and to increase the volume of output beyond the danger point,— the point written into the corporation securities in the shape of fixed charges on funds borrowed for operation under industrial conditions that have progressively grown obsolete. For the ceaseless advance of the mechanical technology has also the effect of lowering the production cost of the necessary equipment, as also the (physical) cost at which raw materials may be had. And the remedy by which this inordinate productivity of the industrial arts is to be defeated or minimised is always a businesslike sabotage, a prudent measure of unemployment and a curtailment of output, such as will keep prices running above that salutary minimum that is required to pay fixed charges on the funded make-believe and allow a "reasonable profit" on investments.

Something can always be done toward this end by a campaign of salesmanship, and quite as much has been done in that way as one would like to admit. But the greater work and the greater expenditure on salesmanship has come at a later date, later than that early phase of corporation finance with which the argument is immediately occupied here; so that any fuller discussion of salesmanship and its place in the economy of business will come more fittingly at a later passage. But the rise of salesmanship into the first rank among the matters with which business is concerned dates back to the same general period that saw the early rise of corporation finance. And salesmanship and sabotage have grown up together and have always been bound together in the strategy of business during all this time, so that the two may fairly be spoken of as the twin pillars of the edifice of business-as-usual in recent times. Salesmanship being the end and animating purpose of all business that is done for a price, that is to say business-as-usual, sabotage on production may even properly be counted as one of the expedients of salesmanship, although it is so greatly the first among these expedients as to put it in a class by itself among the duties of business enterprise. To increase sales and curtail the output is the appointed way of maintaining prices and increasing the net gain, which is the whole end and duty of business enterprise.

That period which has here been called the "era of free competition" was marked by a reasonably free competitive production of goods for the market, the profits of the business to be derived from competitive underselling. It is for such a "competitive system" that the economists have consistently spoken, through the nineteenth century and after, and the rehabilitation of it is still the abiding concern of many thoughtful persons. In practical effect it tapered off to an uncertain close in England about the middle of the century, in America something like a quarter-century later. So that it is a past phase. It meant a competition between producing-sellers, and so far as the plan was operative it inured to the benefit of the consumers.

Doubtless, such freely competitive production and selling prevailed only within reasonable bounds even in the time when it may be said to have been the rule in industrial business, and with the passage of time and the approaching saturation of the market the reasonable bounds gradually grew narrower and stricter. The manner of conducting the business passed by insensible degrees into a new order, and it became an increasingly patent matter-of-course for business enterprise in this field consistently to pursue the net gain by maintaining prices and curtailing the output.

It is not that competition ceased when this "competitive system" fell into decay, but only that the incidence of it has shifted. The competition which then used to run mutually between the producing-sellers has since then increasingly come to run between the business community on the one side and the consumers on the other. Salesmanship, with sabotage, has grown gradually greater and keener, at an increasing cost. And the end of this salesmanship is to get a margin of something for nothing at the cost of the consumer in a closed market. Whereas on the earlier plan the net gain was sought by underselling an increased output of serviceable goods in an open market. The old-fashioned plan, so far as it was effective, might be called a competition in workmanship; the later plan, so far as it has gone into effect, is a competition in publicity and scarcity.

In the workday actualities of the business the contrast between the ancient plan, that ruled the days before the coming of corporation finance, and the practice of later times is neither so broad nor so sheer as this characterisation would make it; but the difference is after all sufficiently visible, and it runs to the effect implied in this characterisation.

CHAPTER VI

THE CAPTAIN OF INDUSTRY

THE Captain of Industry is one of the major institutions of the nineteenth century. He has been an institution of civilised life—a self-sufficient element in the scheme of law and custom—in much the same sense as the Crown, or the Country Gentleman, or the Priesthood, have been institutions, or as they still are in those places where the habits of thought which they embody still have an institutional force.[1] For a hundred years or so he was, cumulatively, the dominant figure in civilised life, about whose deeds and interests law and custom have turned, the central and paramount personal agency in Occidental civilisation. Indeed, his great vogue and compelling eminence are not past yet, so far as regards his place in popular superstition and in the make-believe of political strategy, but it is essentially a glory standing over out of the past, essentially a superstition.[2] As regards the material actualities of life, the captain of industry is no longer the central and directive force in that business traffic that governs the material fortunes of mankind; not much more so than the Crown, the Country Gentleman, or the Priesthood.

[1] An institution is of the nature of a usage which has become axiomatic and indispensable by habituation and general acceptance. Its physiological counterpart would presumably be any one of those habitual addictions that are now attracting the attention of the experts in sobriety.

[2] He is also still a dominant figure in the folklore of Political Economy.

Considered as an institution, then, the captain of industry is the personal upshot of that mobilisation of business enterprise that arose out of the industrial use of the machine process. And the period of his ascendency is, accordingly, that era of (temperately) free competition that lies between the Industrial Revolution of the eighteenth century and the rise of corporation finance in the nineteenth, and so tapering off into the competitive twilight-zone of the later time when competition was shifting from industry to finance. But in the time of his ascendency the old-fashioned competitive system came up, flourished, and eventually fell into decay, all under the ministering hand of the Captain.

As is likely to be true of any institution that eventually counts for much in human life and culture, so also the captain of industry arose out of small beginnings which held no clear promise of a larger destiny. The prototype rather than the origin of the captain of industry is to be seen in the Merchant Adventurer of an earlier age, or as he would be called after he had grown to larger dimensions and become altogether sessile, the Merchant Prince. In the beginning the captain was an adventurer in industrial enterprise—hence the name given him; very much as the itinerant merchant of the days of the petty trade had once been an adventurer in commerce. He was a person of insight—perhaps chiefly industrial insight—and of initiative and energy, who was able to see something of the industrial reach and drive of that new mechanical technology that was finding its way into the industries, and who went about to contrive ways and means of turning these technological resources to new uses and a larger efficiency; always with a view to his own gain from turning out a more serviceable product with greater expedition. He was a captain of workmanship at the same time that he was a business man; but he was a good deal of a pioneer in both respects, inasmuch as he was on new ground in both respects. In many of the industrial ventures into which his initiative led him, both the mechanical working and the financial sanity of the new ways and means were yet to be tried out, so that in both respects he was working out an adventurous experiment rather than watchfully waiting for the turn of events. In the typical case, he was business manager of the venture as well as foreman of the works, and not infrequently he was the designer and master-builder of the equipment, of which he was also the responsible owner.[3] Typical of the work and spirit of these Captains of the early time are the careers of the great tool-builders of the late eighteenth and early nineteenth century.[4]

Such, it is believed, were many of those to whom the mechanical industries owed their rapid growth and sweeping success in the early time, both in production and in earning-capacity; and something of this sort is the typical Captain of Industry as he has lived, and still lives, in the affections of his countrymen. Such also is the type-form in terms of which those substantial citizens like to think of themselves, who aspire to the title. If this characterisation may appear large and fanciful to an unbelieving generation, at least the continued vogue of it both as a popular superstition and as a business man's day-dream will go to show that the instinct of workmanship is not dead yet even in those civilised countries where it has become eternally right and good that workmanship should wait on business. The disposition to think kindly of

[3] Cf. *The Engineers and the Price System*, ch. ii. "The Industrial System and the Captains of Industry."
[4] Cf. Roe, *British and American Tool-Builders*.

workmanlike service is still extant in these civilised nations, at least in their day-dreams; although business
principles have put it in abeyance so far as regards any
practical effect.

In fact, it seems to be true that many, perhaps most,
of those persons who amassed fortunes out of the proceeds of industry during this early period (say, 1760-
1860), and who thereby acquired merit, were not of this
workmanlike or pioneering type, but rather came in for
large gains by shrewd investment and conservative undertakings, such as would now be called safe and sane
business. Yet there will at the same time also have been
so much of this spirit of initiative and adventure abroad
in the conduct of industry, and it will have been so visible an element of industrial business-as-usual at that
time, as to have enabled this type-form of the captain of
industry to find lodgment in the popular belief; a man
of workmanlike force and creative insight into the community's needs, who stood out on a footing of self-help,
took large chances for large ideals, and came in for his
gains as a due reward for work well done in the service
of the common good, in designing and working out a
more effective organisation of industrial forces and in
creating and testing out new and better processes of
production. It is by no means easy at this distance to
make out how much of popular myth-making went to set
up this genial conception of the Captain in the popular
mind, or how much more of the same engaging conceit
was contributed toward the same preconception by the
many-sided self-esteem of many substantial business men
who had grown great by "buying in" and "sitting tight,"
and who would like to believe that they had done something to merit their gains. But however the balance may
lie, between workmanship and salesmanship, in the make-

up of the common run of those early leaders of industrial enterprise, it seems that there will have been enough of the master-workman in a sufficient number of them, and enough of adventure and initiative in a sufficient number of the undertakings, to enable the popular fancy to set up and hold fast this genial belief in the typical captain of industry as a creative factor in the advance of the industrial arts; at the same time that the economists were able presently to set him up, under the name of "Entrepreneur," as a fourth factor of production, along with Land, Labor, and Capital. Indeed, it is on some such ground that men have come to be called "Captains of Industry" rather than captains of business. Experience and observation at any later period could scarcely have engendered such a conception of those absentee owners who control the country's industrial plant and trade on a restricted output.

By insensible degrees, as the volume of industry grew larger, employing a larger equipment and larger numbers of workmen, the business concerns necessarily also increased in size and in the volume of transactions, personal supervision of the work by the owners was no longer practicable, and personal contact and personal arrangements between the employer-owner and his workmen tapered off into impersonal wage contracts governed by custom and adjusted to the minimum which the traffic would bear. The employer-owner, an ever increasingly impersonal business concern, shifted more and more to a footing of accountancy in its relations with the industrial plant and its personnel, and the oversight of the works passed by insensible degrees into the hands of technical experts who stood in a business relation to the concern, as its employees responsible to the concern for working the plant to such a fraction of its productive capacity as the condition of the market warranted for the time being.

So the function of the entrepreneur, the captain of industry, gradually fell apart in a two-fold division of labor, between the business manager and the office work on the one side and the technician and industrial work on the other side. Gradually more and more, by this shift and division, the captain of industry developed into a captain of business, and that part of his occupation which had given him title to his name and rank as captain of "industry" passed into alien hands. Expert practical men, practical in the way of tangible performance, men who had, or need have, no share in the prospective net gain and no responsibility for the concern's financial transactions, unbusinesslike technicians, began to be drawn into the management of the industry on the tangible side. It was a division of labor and responsibility, between the employer-owners who still were presumed to carry on the business of the concern and who were responsible to themselves for its financial fortunes, and on the other hand the expert industrial men who took over the tangible performance of production and were responsible to their own sense of workmanship.

Industry and business gradually split apart, in so far as concerned the personnel and the day's work. The employer-owners shifted farther over on their own ground as absentee owners, but continued to govern the volume of production and the conditions of life for the working personnel on the businesslike principle of the net gain in terms of price. While the tangible performance of so much work as the absentee owners considered to be wise, fell increasingly under the management of that line of technicians out of which there grew in time the engineering profession, with its many duties, grades, and divisions and its ever increasingly numerous and increasingly specialised personnel. It was a gradual shift and division, of course. So gradual, indeed, that while it had set in in a small way before the close of the eighteenth century, it had not yet been carried out completely and obviously by the close of the nineteenth, even in the greater mechanical industries. In fact, it has not yet been carried through to so rigorous a finish as to have warranted its recognition in the standard economic theories. In the manuals the captain of industry still figures as the enterprising investor-technician of the days of the beginning, and as such he still is a certified article of economic doctrine under the caption of the "Entrepreneur."

The industrial arts are a matter of tangible performance directed to work that is designed to be of material use to man, and all the while they are calling for an increasingly exhaustive knowledge of material fact and an increasingly close application to the work in hand. The realities of the technician's world are mechanistic realities, matters of material fact. And the responsibilities of the technician, as such, are responsibilities of workmanship only; in the last resort responsibility to his own sense of workmanlike performance, which might well be called the engineer's conscience. On the other hand the arts of business are arts of bargaining, effrontery, salesmanship, make-believe, and are directed to the gain of the business man at the cost of the community, at large and in detail. Neither tangible performance nor the common good is a business proposition. Any material use which his traffic may serve is quite beside the business man's purpose, except indirectly, in so far as it may serve to influence his clientele to his advantage.

But the arts of business, too, call all the while for

closer application to the work in hand. Throughout recent times salesmanship has come in for a steadily increasing volume and intensity of attention, and great
things have been achieved along that line. But the work
in hand in business traffic is not tangible performance.
The realities of the business world are money-values;
that is to say matters of make-believe which have the sanction of law and custom and are upheld by the police in
case of need. The business man's care is to create needs
to be satisfied at a price paid to himself. The engineer's
care is to provide for these needs, so far as the business
men in the background find their advantage in allowing
it. But law and custom have little to say to the engineer,
except to keep his hands off the work when the interests of business call for a temperate scarcity.

So, by force of circumstances the captain of industry
came in the course of time and growth to be occupied
wholly with the financial end of those industrial ventures
of which he still continued to be the captain. The spirit
of enterprise in him took a turn of sobriety. He became
patient and attentive to details, with an eye single to his
own greater net gain in terms of price. His conduct
came to be framed more and more on lines of an alert
patience, moderation, assurance, and conservatism; that
is to say, his conduct would have to fall into these lines
if he was to continue as a Captain under the changing
circumstances of the time. Changing circumstances
called for a new line of strategy in those who would survive as Captains and come into the commanding positions in the business community, and so into control of
the industrial system. It should perhaps rather be said
that the force of changing circumstances worked a change
in the character of the Captains by eliminating the Captains of the earlier type from the more responsible posi-

tion and favoring the substitution of persons endowed with other gifts and trained to other ideals and other standards of conduct; in short, men more nearly on the order of safe and sane business, such as have continued to be well at home in responsible affairs since then.

Under the changing circumstances the captains of industry of the earlier type fell to second rank, became lieutenants, who presently more and more lost standing, as being irresponsible, fanciful project-makers, footless adventurers, fit only to work out innovations that were of doubtful expediency in a business way, creators of technological disturbances that led to obsolescence of equipment and therefore to shrinkage of assets. Such men are persons whom it is not for the safe and sane Captains of the newer type to countenance; but who should be handled with circumspection and made the most of, as project-makers whose restless initiative and immature versatility is counted on to bring about all sorts of unsettling and irritating changes in the conditions of industry; but who may also, now and again, bring in something that will give some patiently alert business man a new advantage over his rivals in business, if he has the luck or the shrewdness to grasp it firmly and betimes. Under the changed circumstances the spirit of venturesome enterprise is more than likely to foot up as a hunting of trouble, and wisdom in business enterprise has more and more settled down to the wisdom of "Watchful waiting." [5]

[5] Doubtless this form of words, "watchful waiting," will have been employed in the first instance to describe the frame of mind of a toad who has reached years of discretion and has found his appointed place along some frequented run where many flies and spiders pass and repass on their way to complete that destiny to which it has pleased an all-seeing and merciful Providence to call them; but by an easy turn of speech it has

The changing circumstances by force of which the conduct of industrial business so gradually came under the
hands of a saner generation of Captains, actuated more
singly by a conservative estimate of the net gain for themselves,—these circumstances have already been recited in
an earlier passage, in sketching the rise and derivation of
the business corporation and the conditions which brought
corporation finance into action as the ordinary means of
controlling the output of industry and turning it to the
advantage of absentee owners. So far as these determining circumstances admit of being enumerated in an
itemised way they were such as follows: (a) the industrial arts, in the mechanical industries, grew gradually
into a complex and extensive technology which called for
a continually more exhaustive and more exact knowledge
of material facts, such as to give rise to engineers, technicians, industrial experts; (b) the scale on which industrial processes were carried out grew greater in the
leading industries, so as to require the men in charge to
give their undivided attention to the technical conduct,
the tangible performance of the work in hand; (c) the

also been found suitable to describe the safe and sane strategy of
that mature order of captains of industry who are governed by
sound business principles. There is a certain bland sufficiency
spread across the face of such a toad so circumstanced, while
his comely personal bulk gives assurance of a pyramidal stability of principles.

> "And the sons of Mary smile and are blessed—
>   they know the angels are on their side,
> They know in them is the Grace confessed,
>   and for them are the Mercies multiplied.
> They sit at the Feet, and they hear the Word—
>   they know how truly the Promise runs.
> They have cast their burden upon the Lord,
>   and—the Lord, He lays it on Martha's sons.
>   —RUDYARD KIPLING

business concerns in which was vested the ownership and control of the industrial equipment and its working also grew larger, carried a larger volume of transactions, took on more of an impersonally financial character, and eventually passed over into the wholly impersonal form of the corporation or joint-stock company, with limited liability; (d) the continued advance of the industrial arts, in range, scope, and efficiency, increased the ordinary productive capacity of the leading industries to such a degree that there was continually less and less question of their being able to supply the market and continually more and more danger that the output would exceed what the market could carry off at prices that would yield a reasonable profit—that is to say the largest obtainable profit; (e) loosely speaking, production had overtaken the market; (f) eventually corporation finance came into action and shifted the point of businesslike initiative and discretion from the works and their management, and even from the running volume of transactions carried by the business office of the concern, to the negotiation and maintenance of a running volume of credit; (g) the capitalisation of credit with fixed charges, as involved in the corporate organisation, precluded shrinkage, recession, or retrenchment of assets or earnings, and so ordinarily precluded a lowering of prices or an undue increase of output,—undue for purposes of the net gain. Business enterprise, therefore, ceased progressively to be compatible with free-swung industrial enterprise, and a new order of businesslike management went progressively into action, and shuffled a new type of persons into the positions of responsibility; men with an eye more single to the main chance at the cost of any whom it may concern.

Among these circumstances that so made for a new order in industrial business the one which is, presumably, the decisive one beyond the rest is the growing productive capacity of industry wherever and so far as the later advances in industrial process are allowed to go into effect. By about the middle of the nineteenth century it can be said without affectation that the leading industries were beginning to be inordinately productive, as rated in terms of what the traffic would bear; that is to say as counted in terms of net gain. Free-swung production, approaching the full productive capacity of the equipment and available man-power, was no longer to be tolerated in ordinary times. It became ever more imperative to observe a duly graduated moderation, and to govern the volume of output, not by the productive capacity of the plant or the working capacity of the workmen, nor by the consumptive needs of the consumers, but by what the traffic would bear; which was then habitually and increasingly coming to mean a modicum of unemployment both of the plant and the available man-power. It was coming to be true, increasingly, that the ordinary equipment of industry and the available complement of workmen were not wanted for daily use, but only for special occasions and during seasons of exceptionally brisk trade. Unemployment, in other words sabotage, to use a word of later date, was becoming an everyday care of the business management in the mechanical industries, and was already on the way to become, what it is today, the most engrossing care that habitually engages the vigilance of the business executive. And sabotage can best be taken care of in the large; so that the corporations, and particularly the larger corporations, would be in a particularly fortunate position to administer the routine of salutary sabotage. And when the Captain of Industry then made the passage from industrial adventurer to corporation financier it became the ordinary care of his office as Captain to keep a restraining hand on employment and output, and so administer a salutary running margin of sabotage on production, at the cost of the underlying population.[6]

But the account is not complete with a description of what the Captain of Industry has done toward the standardisation of business methods and the stabilisation of industrial enterprise, and of what the new order of business-as-usual has done toward the standardisation of the Captain and eventually towards his neutralisation and abeyance. As has already been remarked, he was one of the major institutions of the nineteenth century, and as such he has left his mark on the culture of that time and after, in other bearings as well as in the standards of business enterprise. As has also been remarked above, the Captain of Industry and his work and interests presently became the focus of attention and deference. The Landed Interest, the political buccaneers, and the priesthood, yielded him the first place in affairs and in the councils of the nation, civil and political. With the forward movement from that state of things in which business was conceived to be the servant of industry to that more mature order of things under which industry became the servant of business, and then presently industrial business of the simpler sort became the servant of the big business which lives and moves on the higher level of finance at large,— as this progression took effect and reshaped the Captain to its uses, the growth of popular sentiment kept pace with the march of facts, so that the popular ideal came to be the prehensile business man rather than the creative driver of industry; the sedentary man of means, the Cap-

---

[6] As someone with a taste for slang and aphorism has said it, "In the beginning the Captain of Industry set out to do something, and in the end he sat down to do somebody."

tain of Solvency. And all the while the illusions of nationalism allowed the underlying population to believe that the common good was bound up with the business advantage of these captains of solvency, into whose service the national establishment was gradually drawn, more and more unreservedly, until it has become an axiomatic rule that all the powers of government and diplomacy must work together for the benefit of the business interests of the larger sort. Not that the constituted authorities have no other cares, but these other cares are, after all, in all the civilised nations, in the nature of secondary considerations, matters to be taken care of when and so far as the paramount exigencies of business will allow.

In all this there is, of course, nothing radically new, in principle. In principle it all comes to much the same thing as the older plan which this era of business, big and little, has displaced. So long as nationalism has held sway, the care and affectionate pride of the underlying population has, in effect, ever centered on the due keep of the nation's kept classes. It is only that by force of circumstances the captain of industry, or in more accurate words the captain of solvency, has in recent times come to be the effectual spokesman and type-form of the kept classes as well as the keeper and dispenser of their keep; very much as the War Lord of the barbarian raids, or the Baron of the Middle Ages, or the Prince of the era of state-making, or the Priesthood early and late in Christendom, have all and several, each in their time, place and degree, stood out as the spokesman and exemplar of the kept classes, and served as the legitimate channel by which the community's surplus product has been drained off and consumed, to the greater spiritual comfort of all parties concerned.

It is only that the superstitions of absentee ownership and business principles have come into the first place among those "Superstitions of the Herd" which go to make up the spirit of national integrity. The moral excellence and public utility of the kept classes that now march under the banners of absentee ownership and business enterprise are no more to be doubted by the loyal citizens of the Christian nations today than the similar excellence and utility of the princely establishment and the priestly ministrations which have drained the resources of the underlying population in an earlier and ruder age. And the princes of solvency and free income no more doubt their own excellence and utility than the princes of the divine grace or the prelates of the divine visitations have done in their time. It is only a shifting of the primacy among the civilised institutions, with the effect that the princes and the priests of the Grace and the Mercy now habitually creep in under the now impervious cloak of the prince and priest of business; very much as the business adventurer of an earlier day crept in under the sheltering cloak of the prince and the priest of the Grace and the Mercy, on whom the superstitions that were dominant in that time then bestowed the usufruct of the underlying population. For in the nineteenth century the captain of business became, in the popular apprehension, a prince after the order of Melchizedech, holding the primacy in secular and spiritual concerns.

Men are moved by many impulses and driven by many instinctive dispositions. Among these abiding dispositions are a strong bent to admire and defer to persons of achievement and distinction, as well as a workmanlike disposition to find merit in any work that serves the common good. The distinction which is admired and deferred to may often be nothing more to the point than a conventional investiture of rank attained by the routine of descent, as, e. g., a king, or by the routine of seniority, as, e. g., a prelate.

There is commonly no personal quality which a bystander can distinguish in these personages. The case of the Mikado in the times of the Shogunate is perhaps extreme, but it can by no means be said to be untrue or unfair as an illustrative instance of how the predilection for deference will find merit even in a personage who, for all that is known of him, has no personal attributes, good, bad, or indifferent. The kings and prelates of Christendom are only less perfect instances of the same. It is in these cases a matter of distinction, of course, with no hint of achievement, except such achievement as a loyal deference is bound to impute.[7] It is usual, indeed it seems inevitable, in all such instances of the conventional exaltation of nothing-in-particular, that there is also imputed to the person who so becomes a personage something in the way of service to the common good. Men like to believe that the personages whom they so admire by force of conventional routine are also of some use, as well as of great distinction,—that they even somehow contribute, or at least conduce, to the material wellbeing at large. Which is presumably to be set down as one of the wonders wrought by the instinct of workmanship, which will not let men be content without some

[7] As a blameless instance of this human avidity for deference and exaltation of personages, a certain Square on Manhattan Island has lately been renamed in honor of a certain military personage who was once, in an emergency, appointed to high rank and responsibility because there was nothing better available under the routine of seniority, and of whose deeds and attainments the most laudatory encomium has found nothing substantially better to say than that it might have been worse. And it is by no means an isolated case.

colorable serviceability in the personages which they so create out of nothing-in-particular.

But where there is also achievement, great deeds according to that fashion of exploits that has the vogue for the time being, this will of itself create distinction and erect a personage. Such is the derivation of the captain of industry in the nineteenth century. Men had learned, at some cost, that their exalted personages created *ad hoc* by incantation were of something less than no use to the common good, that at the best and cheapest they were something in the nature of a blameless bill of expense. The civilised nations had turned democratic, so much of them as had a fairly colorable claim to be called civilised; and so they had been left without their indispensable complement of personages to whom to defer and to whom to impute merit. In so far as the ground had been cleared of institutional holdovers from pre-democratic times, there remained but one workable ground of distinction on which a practicable line of personages at large could be erected, such as would meet the ever-insistent need of some intoxicating make-believe of the kind. Democratically speaking, distinction at large could be achieved only in the matter of ownership, but when ownership was carried well out along the way of absentee ownership it was found to do very nicely as a base on which to erect a colorable personage, sufficient to carry a decently full charge of imputed merit.[8] It results that under the aegis

---

[8] Exception may be taken to all this, to the effect that the requisite personages can always be found in the shape of gentlemen at large—"country gentlemen" or "Southern Gentlemen," of what not—and "Best Families" who sit secure on a prescriptive gentility of birth and breeding. But in this bearing and seen in impersonal perspective, Gentlemen and Best Families are best to be defined as "absentee ownership in the consumptive phase," just as the captain of industry may likewise be spoken of

of democracy one's betters must be better in point of property qualifications, from which the civic virtues flow by ready force of imputation.

So the captain of industry came into the place of first consequence and took up the responsibilities of exemplar, philosopher and friend at large to civilised mankind; and no man shall say that he has not done as well as might be expected. Neither has he fallen short in respect of a becoming gravity through it all. The larger the proportion of the community's wealth and income which he has taken over, the larger the deference and imputation of merit imputed to him, and the larger and graver that affable condescension and stately benevolence that habitually adorn the character of the large captains of solvency. There is no branch or department of the humanities in which the substantial absentee owner is not competent to act as guide, philosopher and friend, whether in his own conceit or in the estimation of his underlying population,—in art and literature, in church and state, in science and education, in law and morals,—and the underlying population is well content. And nowhere does the pecuniary personage stand higher or more secure as the standard container of the civic virtues than in democratic America; as should be the case, of course, since America is the most democratic of them all. And nowhere else does the captain of big business rule the affairs of the nation, civil and political, and control the conditions of life so unreservedly as in democratic America; as should also be the case, inasmuch as the acquisition of absentee ownership is, after all, in the popular apprehension, the most meritorious and the most necessary work to be done in this country.

impersonally as absentee ownership in the acquisitive phase; which brings the case back to the point of departure.

CHAPTER VII

THE CASE OF AMERICA:
I. THE SELF-MADE MAN

In this matter of absentee ownership the case of America is peculiar in some respects, although the special features of the case are not such that it departs from the main line of the development in any material degree. Indeed, it might rather be said that America shows this development in the freest and fullest shape which it has anywhere attained hitherto. The special circumstances which have conditioned its growth in this country have brought the institution more swiftly to a more stable and mature state here than elsewhere. So that absentee ownership has become the master institution in American civilisation, speedily and summarily, with slighter reservations than in the older civilised nations. In this particular, at least, America may be said to stand at the apex of cultural growth among the peoples of Christendom. And America is followed closely by the other, newer peoples that have come up out of European colonisation; although it is doubtful if any of them will have the fortune to overtake America. There is some ground for thinking that these others may have made too late a start, so that an undue proportion of other ideals and principles, alien to the perfect dominance of absentee ownership, may be included in the effectual drift of popular sentiment in these other cases. But so far these others are coming along very nicely, and there is perhaps no ground for serious apprehension.

America is the oldest and maturest of the colonies founded by the English-speaking peoples, or by any of those Continental peoples which fall into the same class with the English in this connection, as, e. g., the Dutch or the Scandinavians. And the foundation and impetus dates back to that period of West-European culture when the principles of self-help, free contract, and net gain, achieved their ascendency, and before these principles had been pruned back by legal definition to fit a more conservative manner of thinking. It is, indeed, a point of distinction for the American case that here the pruning back of these popular principles of conduct was carried out to fit the working-out of these principles themselves, under such conditions of singleminded conviction that other institutional holdovers of the older order have not seriously troubled the outcome. It was the fortune of the American people to have taken their point of departure from the European situation during a period when the system of Natural Liberty was still "obvious and simple," fresh and crude, and consequently amenable to growth and adaptation on its own premises under the direct impact of the new material circumstances offered by the New World. Whereas later enterprises in colonisation have had their institutional point of departure blurred with a scattering of the holdovers that were brought in again by the return wave of reaction in Europe, as well as by those later-come stirrings of radical discontent that have questioned the eternal fitness of the system of Natural Liberty itself. The difference is not wide, and the American advantage is not a great one; nor need it make or mar the outcome in the end, since the colonists and the later-come inhabitants of these other new countries are, after all, the same thing over again in respect of their permanent traits of character. They are all made up of substantially the same hybrid mixture of races, so that by heredity they are all substantially the same people.[1]

In this matter those other, South-European or "Latin," peoples who have had a share in the colonisation of the new continents fall somewhat to one side. In this matter of absentee ownership after the pattern set by the system of Natural Rights, these others carry a serious handicap. It is their fortune, not their fault. At that period, when they were taking the lead in the winning of the New World, these South-Europeans were still living very busily in a more archaic and barbarian phase of the European culture, which belongs at a point in the sequence antedating the natural rights that make democracy. Their ideals and motives were, on the whole, of a visibly different order and have worked out in time to a different effect. Their enterprise in colonisation, as, e. g., the Spanish and in a degree the Portuguese, was an enterprise in pillage, inflamed and inflated by religious fanaticism and martial vanity; and it has worked out in the erection of a class of colonial nations which have hitherto scarcely proved fit to survive under this newer order of things that has been imposed by the mechanical industry and the business enterprise which makes use of the mechanical industry.

In effect, the English-speaking peoples, on the other hand, colonised with a view to the orderly exploitation of the natural resources; driven, on the whole, by motives and ideals of self-help, equal opportunity, and net gain. The difference may not be wide or substantial, nor is there by any means a sharp contrast between the English-speaking colonial pioneers and the South-Europeans

---

[1] Of course, in point of nationality they are, each and several, eternally distinct for the time being.

on these heads; not nearly so wide and sharp as this blunt phrasing of it will imply. But, in effect, a difference of this character is visible, and in its working-out this initial difference has told cumulatively in the outcome. And in the outcome the English-speaking colonial nations turn out to be addicted to democratic institutions, the mechanical industries, and business enterprise. It will not do to say that the English-speaking colonisation to which America owes its beginnings and its character was untouched by the spirit of plunder or unfamiliar with religious atrocities and warlike vanity; but while the difference may be one of degree rather than of kind, such measure of initial difference as there was appears to have made the outcome. And the difference in the outcome is too obvious to be overlooked by any but statesmen and lawyers.

America is the most mature of these English-speaking colonies. And in all of these colonial nations the mainspring of the enterprise and the enduring preoccupation of the people has been the exploitation of natural resources for private gain. In all of them the natural resources have progressively been taken over into private ownership on a reasoned plan of legalized seizure. It has been a sober and orderly-advancing seizure of these resources, conducted under rules designed to safeguard a democratically equal opportunity of seizure, and advancing as fast as the available resources have successively become, or have promised to become, valuable. The rules governing this progressive subreption have been drawn on lines that constantly call to mind the rules governing games of skill, where a formally even chance is prescribed for all players who "sit in." And these rules of equitable "grab" have also, on the whole, been lived up to with about the same degree of scruple that is commonly to be had in games of luck and skill. In either case, whether in the standard games of chance and dexterity or in the business of taking over natural resources and turning them to account, it is understood that any formally blameless evasion of the rules will rightly inure to the benefit of any competitor who so has been able to "beat the game." It is a principle of self-help. But in either case, too, there is a formal limit on profitable evasion, beyond which tact and salesmanship cease to be sportsmanlike finesse or businesslike ambiguity and become sharp practice or swindle.[2]

So there has been incorporated in American common sense and has grown into American practice the presumption that all the natural resources of the country must of right be held in private ownership, by those persons who have been lucky enough or shrewd enough to take them over according to the rules in such cases made and provided, or by those who have acquired title from these original impropriators.

With the (partial) exception of the agricultural lands, the ownership of these natural resources is always absentee ownership, and it has always been absentee ownership that has been aimed at in the efforts made to come into possession of them. And they are always acquired and held with a view to getting a larger benefit from them than their cost; that is to say, with a view to getting a margin of something for nothing at the cost of the rest of the community. These are commonplaces, of course,

---

[2] It is not easy in any given case—indeed it is at times impossible until the courts have spoken—to say whether it is an instance of praise-worthy salesmanship or a penitentiary offense. All that may turn on a point of legal verbiage, and it may also depend somewhat on the magnitude of the transaction and the business rating of the parties in interest; a large transaction is, on the whole, less likely to be found reprehensible.

which it should scarcely be necessary to call to mind.

The natural resources of America are, or have been, unexampled in abundance and availability, and they have always been the main factor on which the life and comfort of the inhabitants have depended. They are the indispensable means of life of the population at large, so that the livelihood of all the inhabitants from day to day is unavoidably bound up in their daily use. So long and so far as these resources can be turned to use without hindrance the American population will always be assured an abundant and easy livelihood. So much so that with free and full use of its unexampled natural resources and an unhindered employment of its workmanship this people may, or rather might, come in for an unexampled material abundance on unexampled easy terms. What stands in the way of this climax of material good fortune, immediately and directly, is the absentee ownership of these natural resources. And what stands in the way of discontinuing this absentee ownership of the country's resources is the moral sense of the American body of citizens; and in this they are in close accord with the working bias of their constituted authorities, whose chief care it is to safeguard and augment all rights of absentee ownership at all points.

Doubtless the discontinuance of absentee ownership in the country's resources would not of itself set the industrial system free to run at full capacity and so make the most of the country's workmanship; business considerations could not permit that, so long as business considerations continue to control the industrial system,—and there is other business to be taken care of than that which is occupied with the control of natural resources. But it remains true that absentee ownership of the country's resources stands first and obviously in the way of a continued full run of the country's productive industry. Should it occur to anyone to take exception to this broad statement, it should suffice to call attention to the fact that the raw materials drawn from these natural resources command a price beyond the cost of the workmanship that goes to bring out the supply. Should this, again, be questioned, there is the fact that the absentee owners of the country's coal, ore, oil, water-power, timber, quarries, water frontage, building sites, and the like, continue to hold these properties as a valued possession from which they derive a revenue. This is free income payable to the absentee owners of these things and constitutes an overhead charge on the country's productive industry; it goes into the cost of the goods produced, and is that much of a burden and restriction on the output. This should also be sufficiently obvious; but the moral sense of the body of citizens will tolerate no disallowance of this right of the absentee owners to get this legalised margin of something for nothing.

Natural resources are valuable to their owners not because the owners have produced these things nor because they have invested their "savings" in them, but because the community has use for them and is willing to pay something for their use,—because they are an indispensable means of living. Failing either the industrial usefulness which these things now have, or failing the continued willingness to allow the absentee owners a usufruct in these resources as a source of free income, they will no longer have value as assets, whatever they may have cost.[3] Natural resources are acquired, owned, and

---

[3] A classic illustration of the first point are the flint deposits of Denmark, which were of first-rate consequence as natural resources in the Stone Age; while the second point is covered by the case of the Negro man-power of the Southern States.

valued, as a source of free income; income for which no equivalent in useful work is given, whatever the cost at which these assets may have been acquired. At the same time they will be of no use, and so will have no value as assets, except as they are turned to use by the workmanship of the population. It is the state of the industrial arts that makes them natural resources, not the funds invested in their ownership. In the language of mathematics, the value of these things as a source of free income to their owners is a "function" of the workmanship of the population at large. And for the completeness of statement it should be added that the workmanship of the population is a "function" of the state of the industrial arts; which is a joint stock of technical knowledge and workmanlike habits ingrained in the population and carried on jointly by the country's man-power, which in this respect carries on as an indivisible going concern.

The absentee owner of natural resources is enabled to make them a source of free income, that is to say make them assets, by the power legally conferred on him to withhold them from use until his charge for their use is allowed him. What this charge will be is always a question of what the traffic will bear; which is the same as what will yield him the largest net return. But what the traffic will bear will vary indefinitely according to the circumstances of the case, and the value of given resources as assets will vary accordingly.[4] Aside from

which ceased to be assets as soon as the consent to its usufruct by absentee ownership was withdrawn.

[4] E. g., certain copper properties have varied greatly in their value as assets, with the continued discovery of further copper deposits, on the one hand, and with the increased requirements of electrical material, on the other hand. So also have nickel properties responded to changing circumstances of the same

changes in the industrial arts, the most considerable and most widely effective of these varying circumstances is the varying degree in which competition prevails among the owners of such assets.[5]

In the usual course, in the case of such staple resources as coal, oil, or the ores, the business of exploitation has at the outset commonly been competitive in a pronounced degree; that is, the owners have competed in the market by speeding up the output and underbidding on the price. The result has been low prices for the time being, and a rapid exhaustion, with waste, of the natural supply. Presently, as the holdings have been drawn together into the ownership of a smaller and more manageable number of absentee owners, these owners have more and more consistently acted in collusion, and in time have drawn together into combinations which have taken on a corporate character, at least in effect, and so have ceased to compete among themselves.[6]

order. And both, but particularly nickel, considered as a means of free income for absentee owners, have been greatly helped out from time to time by a protective tariff designed to safeguard and augment the free income of vested interests of this class. It is the whole wisdom of a protective tariff that when the charges so imposed by the absentee owners are so protected by a protective duty the traffic can be made to bear a heavier charge. In further illustration of the general statement above, it may be recalled that the discovery of the Minnesota iron ores and the gradual perfecting of the steel smelting processes, incontinently cut down the value as assets of those Cuban ore bodies whose American absentee owners were to have been safeguarded in their free income by the Spanish-American War. But there are no end of illustrative instances, since the whole use and value of these natural resources, as well as variations in their value as assets, turn on the state of technological knowledge, with which the owners of them have nothing to do.

[5] Compare, e. g., the case of the Texas oil fields with that of the anthracite coal field.

[6] The salt business, e. g., shows a very fair instance of this

The result is not that competition ceases or declines when the business of a given line of natural supply so outgrows what is called the competitive stage and passes under the control of a collusive or corporate combination of absentee owners, but only that it takes a new turn, commonly with an increased vigor and persistence. Instead of competing against one another, to their own mutual defeat, the absentee owners now turn their undivided competitive efforts against the consumers. It becomes a competition not within the business but between this business as a whole and the rest of the community. This stage of business maturity, which may be called the stage of vested interest, has progressively been reached in a very passable fashion by the generality of that absentee ownership that controls the necessary supply of raw materials used in the leading industries,— in what are sometimes called the "key industries."

There is, of course, the large exception of agricultural food products, and the partial exception of such a natural staple as crude oil, where the continued opening of new deposits and the continued growth of an under-supplied market continues still to trouble the business and its vested interests with a weedy crop of upstart competitors for the market. The agricultural soil, the natural resource from which the food-products are drawn, is not amenable to absentee ownership except in a partial measure, at least not yet; and agricultural food products have accordingly not yet been successfully handled on the non-competitive or collusive plan, so far as concerns their production; although there are typical cases of collusion and absentee control to be found among the concerns that own the business of milling, packing, and

gradual shifting from a competitive to a monopolistic footing.

marketing many of these food-products. And while crude oil is still troubled with irresponsible competitive production for an open market, of the kind sometimes called "wild-catting," the efforts toward a collusive stability of the business have, after all, been as successful as might reasonably be looked for. So that, on the whole, the owners and distributors are already engaged on a fairly secure and consistent collusive competition against the rest of the community.

The farmers who have to do with the great staples have, for some time past and repeatedly, endeavored to establish a collusive control of their market, with a view to narrowing and stabilising the margin between the prices they get and the prices which the consumers pay; but so far with no substantial results. It has quite uniformly worked out in nothing better than gestures of desperation. Their markets are controlled, but not by the farmers. Absentee ownership in farming has yet reached neither the extent nor the scale which would enable a collusive combination of farm-owners to determine what the traffic will bear and arrange the volume of output accordingly. All that matter is now taken care of by those massive vested interests that move obscurely in the background of the market and decide for themselves what the traffic will bear for their benefit at the cost of the farmers on the one side and the consumers of farm products on the other.

II. THE INDEPENDENT FARMER

The case of the American farmer is conspicuous; though it can scarcely be called singular, since in great part it is rather typical of the fortune which has overtaken the underlying populations throughout Christendom under the dominion of absentee ownership in its later developed phase. Much the same general run of conditions recurs elsewhere in those respects which engage the fearsome attention of these farmers. By and large, the farmer is so placed in the economic system that both as producer and as consumer he deals with business concerns which are in a position to make the terms of the traffic, which it is for him to take or leave. Therefore the margin of benefit that comes to him from his work is commonly at a minimum. He is commonly driven by circumstances over which he has no control, the circumstances being made by the system of absentee ownership and its business enterprise. Yet he is, on the whole, an obstinately loyal supporter of the system of law and custom which so makes the conditions of life for him.

His unwavering loyalty to the system is in part a holdover from that obsolete past when he was the Independent Farmer of the poets; but in part it is also due to the still surviving persuasion that he is on the way, by hard work and shrewd management, to acquire a "competence"; such as will enable him some day to take his due place among the absentee owners of the land and so come in for an easy livelihood at the cost of the rest of the community; and in part it is also due to the persistent though fantastic opinion that his own present interest is bound up with the system of absentee ownership, in that he is himself an absentee owner by so much as he owns land and equipment which he works with hired help,—always presuming that he is such an owner, in effect or in prospect.

It is true, the farmer-owners commonly are absentee

owners to this extent. Farming is team-work. As it is necessarily carried on by current methods in the great farming sections, farm work runs on such a scale that no individual owner can carry on by use of his own personal work alone, or by use of the man-power of his own household alone,—which makes him an absentee owner by so much. But it does not, in the common run, make him an absentee owner of such dimensions as are required in order to create an effectual collusive control of the market, or such as will enable him, singly or collectively, to determine what charges the traffic shall bear. It leaves him still effectually in a position to take or leave what is offered at the discretion of those massive absentee interests that move in the background of the market.[6a]

Always, of course, the farmer has with him the abiding comfort of his illusions, to the effect that he is in some occult sense the "Independent Farmer," and that he is somehow by way of achieving a competence of absentee ownership by hard work and sharp practice, some day; but in practical effect, as things habitually work out, he is rather to be called a quasi-absentee owner, or perhaps a pseudo-absentee owner, being too small a parcel of absentee ownership to count as such in the outcome. But it is presumably all for the best, or at least it is expedient for business-as-usual, that the farmer should continue to nurse his illusions and go about his work; that he should go on his way to complete that destiny to which it has pleased an all-seeing and merciful Providence to call him.

From colonial times and through the greater part of its history as a republic America has been in the main an

[6a] Cf. Wallace, *Farm Prices.*

agricultural country. Farming has been the staple occupation and has employed the greater part of the population. And the soil has always been the chief of those
natural resources which the American people have taken
over and made into property. Through the greater part
of its history the visible growth of the country has consisted in the extension of the cultivated area and the
increasing farm output, farm equipment, and farm population. This progressive taking-over and settlement of
the farming lands is the most impressive material achievement of the American people, as it is also the most serviceable work which they have accomplished hitherto. It
still is, as it ever has been, the people's livelihood; and
the rest of the industrial system has in the main, grown
up, hitherto, as a subsidiary or auxiliarly, adopted to and
limited by the needs and the achievements of the country's husbandry. The incentives and methods engaged
in this taking-over of the soil, as well as the industrial
and institutional consequences that have followed, are
accordingly matters of prime consideration in any endeavour to understand or explain the national character
and the temperamental bent which underlies it.

The farm population—that farm population which has
counted substantially toward this national achievement
—have been a ready, capable and resourceful body of
workmen. And they have been driven by the incentives
already spoken of in an earlier passage as being characteristic of the English-speaking colonial enterprise,—
individual self-help and cupidity. Except transiently and
provisionally, and with doubtful effect, this farm population has nowhere and at no time been actuated by a spirit
of community interest in dealing with any of their material concerns. Their community spirit, in material con-

cerns, has been quite notably scant and precarious, in spite of the fact that they have long been exposed to material circumstances of a wide-sweeping uniformity, such as should have engendered a spirit of community interest and made for collective enterprise, and such as could have made any effectual collective enterprise greatly remunerative to all concerned. But they still stand sturdily by the timeworn make-believe that they still are individually self-sufficient masterless men, and through good report and evil report they have remained Independent Farmers, as between themselves, which is all that is left of their independence,—Each for himself, etc.

Of its kind, this is an admirable spirit, of course; and it has achieved many admirable results, even though the results have not all been to the gain of the farmers. Their self-help and cupidity have left them at the mercy of any organisation that is capable of mass action and a steady purpose. So they have, in the economic respect—and incidentally in the civil and political respect—fallen under the dominion of those massive business interests that move obscurely in the background of the market and buy and sell and dispose of the farm products and the farmers' votes and opinions very much on their own terms and at their ease.

But all the while it remains true that they have brought an unexampled large and fertile body of soil to a very passable state of service, and their work continues to yield a comfortably large food supply to an increasing population, at the same time that it yields a comfortable run of free income to the country's kept classes. It is true, in the end the farm population find themselves at work for the benefit of business-as-usual, on a very modest livelihood. For farming is, perhaps necessarily, carried on in severalty and on a relatively small scale, even though the required scale exceeds what is possible on a footing of strict self-ownership of land and equipment by the cultivators; and there is always the pervading spirit of self-help and cupidity, which unavoidably defeats even that degree of collusive mass action that might otherwise be possible. Whereas the system of business interests in whose web the farmers are caught is drawn on a large scale, its units are massive, impersonal, imperturbable and, in effect, irresponsible, under the established order of law and custom, and they are interlocked in an unbreakable framework of common interests.

By and large, the case of America is as the case of the American farm population, and for the like reasons. For the incentives and ideals, the law and custom and the knowledge and belief, on which the farm population has gone about its work and has come to this pass, are the same as have ruled the growth and shaped the outcome for the community at large. Nor does the situation in America differ materially from the state of things elsewhere in the civilised countries, in so far as these others share in the same material civilisation of Christendom.

In the American tradition, and in point of historical fact out of which the tradition has arisen, the farmer has been something of a pioneer. Loosely it can be said that the pioneering era is now closing, at least provisionally and as regards farming. But while the pioneer-farmer is dropping out of the work of husbandry, his pioneer soul goes marching on. And it has been an essential trait of this American pioneering spirit to seize upon so much of the country's natural resources as the enterprising pioneer could lay hands on,—in the case of the pioneer-farmer, so much of the land as he could get and hold possession of. The land had, as it still has, a prospective use and therefore a prospective value, a "speculative" value as it is called; and the farmer-pioneer was concerned with seizing upon this prospective value and turning it into net gain by way of absentee ownership, as much as the pioneer-farmer was concerned with turning the fertile soil to present use in the creation of a livelihood for himself and his household from day to day.

Habitually and with singular uniformity the American farmers have aimed to acquire real estate at the same time that they have worked at their trade as husbandmen. And real estate is a matter of absentee ownership, an asset whose value is based on the community's need of this given parcel of land for use as a means of livelihood, and the value of which is measured by the capitalised free income which the owner may expect to come in for by holding it for as high a rental as the traffic in this need will bear. So that the pioneering aim, in American farming, has been for the pioneer-farmers, each and several, to come in for as much of a free income at the cost of the rest of the community as the law would allow; which has habitually worked out in their occupying, each and several, something more than they could well take care of. They have habitually "carried" valuable real estate at the same time that they have worked the soil of so much of their land as they could take care of, in as effectual a manner as they could under these circumstances. They have been cultivators of the main chance as well as of the fertile soil; with the result that, by consequence of this intense and unbroken habituation, the farm population is today imbued with that penny-wise spirit of self-help and cupidity that now leaves them and their work and holdings at the disposal of those massive vested interests that know the uses of collusive mass action, as already spoken of above.

But aside from this spiritual effect which this protracted habituation to a somewhat picayune calculation of the main chance has had on the farmers' frame of mind, and aside from their consequent unfitness to meet the businesslike manœuvres of the greater vested interests, this manner of pioneering enterprise which the farmers have habitually mixed into their farming has also had a more immediate bearing on the country's husbandry, and, indeed, on the industrial system as a whole. The common practice has been to "take up" more land than the farmer could cultivate, with his available means, and to hold it at some cost. Which has increased the equipment required for the cultivation of the acres cultivated, and has also increased the urgency of the farmer's need of credit by help of which to find the needed equipment and meet the expenses incident to his holding his idle and semi-idle acres intact. And farm credit has been notoriously usurious. All this has had the effect of raising the cost of production of farm products; partly by making the individual farm that much more unwieldy as an instrument of production, partly by further enforcing the insufficiency and the make-shift character for which American farm equipment is justly famed, and partly also by increasing the distances over which the farm supplies and the farm products have had to be moved.

This last point marks one of the more serious handicaps of American farming, at the same time that it has contributed materially to enforce that "extensive," "superficial," and exhausting character of American farming which has arrested the attention of all foreign observers. In American practice the "farm area" has always greatly exceeded the "acreage under cultivation," even after all due allowance is made for any unavoidable inclusion of waste and half-waste acreage within the farm boundaries. Even yet, at the provisional close of the career of the American pioneer-farmer, the actual proportion of unused and half-used land included within and among the farms will materially exceed what the records show, and it greatly exceeds what any inexperienced observer will be able to credit. The period is not long past—if it is past—when, taking one locality with another within the great farming sections of the country, the idle and half-idle lands included in and among the farms equalled the acreage that was fully employed, even in that "extensive" fashion in which American farming has habitually been carried on.

But there is no need of insisting on this high proportion of idle acreage, which none will credit who has not a wide and intimate knowledge of the facts in the case. For more or less—for as much as all intelligent observers will be ready to credit—this American practice has counted toward an excessively wide distribution of the cultivated areas, excessively long distances of transport, over roads which have by consequence been excessively bad—necessarily and notoriously so—and which have hindered communication to such a degree as in many instances to confine the cultivation to such crops as can be handled with a minimum of farm buildings and will bear the crudest kind of carriage over long distances and with incalculable delays. This applies not only to the farm-country's highways, but to its railway facilities as well. The American practice has doubled the difficulty of transportation and retarded the introduction of the more practicable and more remunerative methods of farming; until makeshift and haphazard have in many places become so in-

grained in the habits of the farm population that nothing but abounding distress and the slow passing of generations can correct it all.[1] At the same time, as an incident by the way, this same excessive dispersion of the
farming communities over long distances, helped out by
bad roads, has beeen perhaps the chief factor in giving
the retail business communities of the country towns their
strangle-hold on the underlying farm population.

And it should surprise no one if a population which has
been exposed to unremitting habituation of this kind has
presently come to feel at home in it all; so that the bootless chicanery of their self-help is rated as a masterly
fabric of axiomatic realities, and sharp practice has become a matter of conscience. In such a community it
should hold true that "An honest man will bear watching," that the common good is a by-word, that "Every-
body's business is nobody's business," that public office
is a private job, where the peak of aphoristic wisdom is
reached in that red-letter formula of democratic politics,
"Subtraction, division, and silence." So it has become
a democratic principle that public office should go by
rotation, under the rule of equal opportunity,—equal
opportunity to get something for nothing—but should go
only to those who value the opportunity highly enough to
make a desperate run for it. Here men "run" for office,
not "stand" for it. Subtraction is the aim of this pioneer
cupidity, not production; and salesmanship is its line of

---

[1] As a side issue to this arrangement of magnificent distances
in the fertile farm country, it may be called to mind that the
éducation of the farm children has on this account continually
suffered from enforced neglect, with untoward results. And
there are those who believe that the noticeably high rate of in-
sanity among farmers' wives in certain sections of the prairie
country is traceable in good part to the dreary isolation enforced
upon them by this American plan of "country life."

approach, not workmanship; and so, being in no way related quantitatively to a person's workmanlike powers or
to his tangible performance, it has no "saturation point." [2]

The spirit of the American farmers, typically, has been
that of the pioneer rather than the workman. They have
been efficient workmen, but that is not the trait which
marks them for its own and sets them off in contrast with
the common run. Their passion for acquisition has driven
them to work, hard and painfully, but they have never
been slavishly attached to their work; their slavery has
been not to an imperative bent of workmanship and human service, but to an indefinitely extensible cupidity
which drives to work when other expedients fail; at
least so they say. So they have been somewhat footloose
in their attachment to the soil as well as somewhat hasty
and shiftless in its cultivation. They have always, in the
typical case, wanted something more than their proportionate share of the soil; not because they were driven

---

[2] This civilised-man's cupidity is one of those "higher wants
of man" which the economists have found to be "indefinitely
extensible," and like other spiritual needs it is self-authenticat-
ing, its own voucher.

The Latin phrase is *auri sacra fames,* which goes to show
the point along the road to civilisation reached by that people.
They had reached a realisation of the essentially sacramental
virtue of this indefinitely extensible need of more; but the
aurum in terms of which they visualised the object of their
passion is after all a tangible object, with physical limitations of
weight and space, such as to impose a mechanical "saturation
point" on the appetite for its accumulation. But the civilised
peoples of Christendom at large, and more particularly America,
the most civilised and most Christian of them all, have in recent
times removed this limitation. The object of this "higher want
of man" is no longer specie, but some form of credit instrument
which conveys title to a run of free income; and it can accordingly have no "saturation point," even in fancy, inasmuch as
credit is also indefinitely extensible and stands in no quantitative
relation to tangible fact.

by a felt need of doing more than their fair share of work or because they aimed to give the community more service than would be a fair equivalent of their own livelihood, but with a view to cornering something more than their proportion of the community's indispensable means of life and so getting a little something for nothing in allowing their holdings to be turned to account, for a good and valuable consideration.

The American farmers have been footloose, on the whole, more particularly that peculiarly American element among them who derive their traditions from a colonial pedigree. There has always been an easy shifting from country to town, and this steady drift into the towns of the great farming sections has in the main been a drift from work into business. And it has been the business of these country towns—what may be called their business-as-usual—to make the most of the necessities and the ignorance of their underlying farm population. The farmers have on the whole been ready to make such a shift whenever there has been an "opening"; that is to say, they have habitually been ready to turn their talents to more remunerative use in some other pursuit whenever the chance has offered, and indeed they have habitually been ready to make the shift out of husbandry into the traffic of the towns even at some risk whenever the prospect of a wider margin of net gain has opened before their eager eyes.

In all this pursuit of the net gain the farm population and their country-town cousins have carried on with the utmost good nature. The business communities of the country towns have uniformly got the upper hand. But the farmers have shown themselves good losers; they have in the main gracefully accepted the turn of things and have continued to count on meeting with better luck or making a shrewder play next time. But the upshot of it so far has habitually been that the farm population find themselves working for a very modest livelihood and the country towns come in for an inordinately wide margin of net gains; that is to say, net gain over necessary outlay and over the value of the services which they render their underlying farm populations.

To many persons who have some superficial acquaintance with the run of the facts it may seem, on scant reflection, that what is said above of the inordinate gains that go to the country towns is a rash overstatement, perhaps even a malicious overstatement. It is not intended to say that the gains *per capita* of the persons currently engaged in business in the country towns, or the gains per cent. on the funds invested, are extraordinarily high; but only that as counted on the necessary rather than the actual cost of the useful work done, and as counted on the necessary rather than the actual number of persons engaged, the gains which go to the business traffic of the country towns are inordinately large.[3]

---

[3] It may be added, though it should scarcely be necessary, that a good part of the gains which are taken by the country-town business community passes through their hands into the hands of those massive vested interests that move obscurely in the background of the market, and to whom the country towns stand in a relation of feeders, analogous to that in which the farm population stands to the towns. In good part the business traffic of the country towns serves as ways and means of net gain to these business interests in the background. But when all due allowance is made on this and other accounts, and even if this element which may be called net gains in transit be deducted, the statement as made above remains standing without material abatement: the business gains which come to the country towns in their traffic with their underlying farm populations are inordinately large, as counted on the necessary cost and use-value of the service rendered, or on the necessary

III. THE COUNTRY TOWN

The country town of the great American farming region is the perfect flower of self-help and cupidity standardised on the American plan. Its name may be Spoon River or Gopher Prairie, or it may be Emporia or Centralia or Columbia. The pattern is substantially the same, and is repeated several thousand times with a faithful perfection which argues that there is no help for it, that it is worked out by uniform circumstances over which there is no control, and that it wholly falls in with the spirit of things and answers to the enduring aspirations of the community. The country town is one of the great American institutions; perhaps the greatest, in the sense that it has had and continues to have a greater part than any other in shaping public sentiment and giving character to American culture.

The location of any given town has commonly been determined by collusion between "interested parties" with a view to speculation in real estate, and it continues through its life-history (hitherto) to be managed as a real estate "proposition." Its municipal affairs, its civic pride, its community interest, converge upon its real-estate values, which are invariably of a speculative character, and which all its loyal citizens are intent on "booming" and "boosting,"—that is to say, lifting still farther off the

work done. But whether these net gains, in so far as they are "inordinate"—that is in so far as they go in under the caption of Something for Nothing—are retained by the business men of the town or are by them passed on to the larger business interests which dominate them, that is an idle difference for all that concerns the fortunes of the underlying farm population or the community at large. In either case it is idle waste, so far as concerns the material well-being of any part of the farm population.

level of actual ground-values as measured by the uses to which the ground is turned. Seldom do the current (speculative) values of the town's real estate exceed the use-value of it by less than 100 per cent.; and never do they exceed the actual values by less than 200 per cent., as shown by the estimates of the tax assessor; nor do the loyal citizens ever cease their endeavours to lift the speculative values to something still farther out of touch with the material facts. A country town which does not answer to these specifications is "a dead one," one that has failed to "make good," and need not be counted with, except as a warning to the unwary "boomer." [1] Real estate is the one community interest that binds the townsmen with a common bond; and it is highly significant—perhaps it is pathetic, perhaps admirable—that those inhabitants of the town who have no holdings of real estate and who never hope to have any will commonly also do their little best to inflate the speculative values by adding the clamour of their unpaid chorus to the paid clamour of the professional publicity-agents, at the cost of so adding a little something to their own cost of living in the enhanced rentals and prices out of which the expenses of publicity are to be met.

Real estate is an enterprise in "futures," designed to get something for nothing from the unwary, of whom it is believed by experienced persons that "there is one born every minute." So, farmers and townsmen together

[1] "The great American game," they say, is Poker. Just why Real Estate should not come in for honorable mention in that way is not to be explained off hand. And an extended exposition of the reasons why would be tedious and perhaps distasteful, besides calling for such expert discrimination as quite exceeds the powers of a layman in these premises. But even persons who are laymen on both heads will recognise the same family traits in both.

throughout the great farming region are pilgrims of hope looking forward to the time when the community's advancing needs will enable them to realise on the inflated values of their real estate, or looking more immediately to the chance that one or another of those who are "born every minute" may be so ill advised as to take them at their word and become their debtors in the amount which they say their real estate is worth. The purpose of country-town real estate, as of farm real estate in a less extreme degree, is to realise on it. This is the common bond of community interest which binds and animates the business community of the country town. In this enterprise there is concerted action and a spirit of solidarity, as well as a running business of mutual manœuvring to get the better of one another. For eternal vigilance is the price of country-town real estate, being an enterprise in salesmanship.

Aside from this common interest in the town's inflated real estate, the townsmen are engaged in a vigilant rivalry, being competitors in the traffic carried on with the farm population. The town is a retail trading-station, where farm produce is bought and farm supplies are sold, and there are always more traders than are necessary to take care of this retail trade. So that they are each and several looking to increase their own share in this trade at the expense of their neighbors in the same line. There is always more or less active competition, often underhand. But this does not hinder collusion between the competitors with a view to maintain and augment their collective hold on the trade with their farm population.

From an early point in the life-history of such a town collusion habitually becomes the rule, and there is commonly a well recognised ethical code of collusion governing the style and limits of competitive manœuvres which any reputable trader may allow himself. In effect, the competition among business concerns engaged in any given line of traffic is kept well in hand by a common understanding, and the traders as a body direct their collective efforts to getting what can be got out of the underlying farm population. It is on this farm trade also, and on the volume and increase of it, past and prospective, that the real-estate values of the town rest. As one consequence, the volume and profit of the farm trade is commonly over-stated, with a view to enhancing the town's real-estate values.

Quite as a matter of course the business of the town arranges itself under such regulations and usages that it foots up to a competition, not between the business concerns, but between town and country, between traders and customers. And quite as a matter of course, too, the number of concerns doing business in any one town greatly exceeds what is necessary to carry on the traffic; with the result that while the total profits of the business in any given town are inordinately large for the work done, the profits of any given concern are likely to be modest enough. The more successful ones among them commonly do very well and come in for large returns on their outlay, but the average returns per concern or per man are quite modest, and the less successful ones are habitually doing business within speaking-distance of bankruptcy. The number of failures is large, but they are habitually replaced by others who still have something to lose. The conscientiously habitual overstatements of the real-estate interests continually draw new trader's into the town, for the retail trade of the town also gets its quota of such persons as are born every minute, who then transiently become supernumerary retail traders. Many fortunes are made in the country towns, often fortunes of very respectable proportions, but many smaller fortunes are also lost.

Neither the causes nor the effects of this state of things have been expounded by the economists, nor has it found a place in the many formulations of theory that have to do with the retail trade; presumably because it is all, under the circumstances, so altogether "natural" and unavoidable. Exposition of the obvious is a tedious employment, and a recital of commonplaces does not hold the interest of readers or audience. Yet, for completeness of the argument, it seems necessary here to go a little farther into the details and add something on the reasons for this arrangement. However obvious and natural it may be it is after all serious enough to merit the attention of anyone who is interested in the economic situation as it stands, or in finding a way out of this situation; which is just now (1923) quite perplexing, as the futile endeavours of the statesmen will abundantly demonstrate.

However natural and legitimate it all undoubtedly may be, the arrangement as it runs today imposes on the country's farm industry an annual overhead charge which runs into ten or twelve figures, and all to the benefit of no one. This overhead charge of billions, due to duplication of work, personnel, equipment, and traffic, in the country towns is, after all, simple and obvious waste. Which is perhaps to be deprecated, although one may well hesitate to find fault with it all, inasmuch as it is all a simple and obvious outcome of those democratic principles of self-help and cupidity on which the commonwealth is founded. These principles are fundamentally and eternally right and good—so long as popular sentiment runs to that effect— and they are to be accepted gratefully, with the defects of their qualities. The whole arrangement is doubtless all right and worth its cost; indeed it is avowed to be the chief care and most righteous solicitude of the constituted authorities to maintain and cherish it all.

To an understanding of the country town and its place in the economy of American farming it should be noted that in the great farming regions any given town has a virtual monopoly of the trade within the territory tributary to it. This monopoly is neither complete nor indisputable; it does not cover all lines of traffic equally nor is outside competition completely excluded in any line. But the broad statement is quite sound, that within its domain any given country town in the farming country has a virtual monopoly of trade in those main lines of business in which the townsmen are chiefly engaged. And the townsmen are vigilant in taking due precautions that this virtual monopoly shall not be broken in upon. It may be remarked by the way that this characterisation applies to the country towns of the great farming country, and only in a less degree to the towns of the industrial and outlying sections.

Under such a (virtual) monopoly the charge collected on the traffic adjusts itself, quite as a matter of course, to what the traffic will bear. It has no other relation to the costs or the use-value of the service rendered. But what the traffic will bear is something to be determined by experience and is subject to continued readjustment and revision, with the effect of unremittingly keeping the charge close up to the practicable maximum. Indeed, there is reason to believe that the townsmen are habitually driven by a conscientious cupidity and a sense of equity to push the level of charges somewhat over the maximum; that is to say, over the rate which would yield them the largest net return. Since there are too many of them they are so placed as habitually to feel that they come in for something short of their just deserts, and their endeavour to remedy this state of things is likely to lead to overcharging rather than the reverse.

What the traffic will bear in this retail trade is what the farm population will put up with, without breaking away and finding their necessary supplies and disposing of their marketable products elsewhere, in some other town, through itinerant dealers, by recourse to brokers at a distance, through the mail-order concerns, and the like. The two dangerous outside channels of trade appear to be the rival country towns and the mail-order houses, and of these the mail-order houses are apparently the more real menace as well as the more dreaded. Indeed they are quite cordially detested by right-minded country-town dealers. The rival country towns are no really grave menace to the usurious charges of any community of country-town business men, since they are all and several in the same position, and none of them fails to charge all comers all that the traffic will bear.

There is also another limiting condition to be considered in determining what the traffic will bear in this retail trade, though it is less, or at least less visibly, operative; namely, the point beyond which the charges can not enduringly be advanced without discouraging the farm population unduly; that is to say, the point beyond which the livelihood of the farm population will be cut into so severely by the overcharging of the retail trade that they begin to decide that they have nothing more to lose, and so give up and move out. This critical point appears not commonly to be reached in the ordinary retail trade—as, e. g., groceries, clothing, hardware—possibly because there still remains, practicable in an extremity, the recourse to outside dealers of one sort or another. In the business of country-town banking, however, and similar money-lending by other persons than the banks, the critical point is not infrequently reached and passed. Here the local monopoly is fairly complete and rigorous, which brings on an insistent provocation to over-reach.

And then, too, the banker deals in money-values, and money-values are forever liable to fluctuate; at the same time that the fortunes of the banker's farm clients are subject to the vicissitudes of the seasons and of the markets; and competition drives both banker and client to base their habitual rates, not on a conservative anticipation of what is likely to happen, but on the lucky chance of what may come to pass barring accidents and the acts of God. And the banker is under the necessity—"inner necessity," as the Hegelians would say—of getting all he can and securing himself against all risk, at the cost of any whom it may concern, by such charges and stipulations as will insure his net gain in any event.

It is the business of the country-town business community, one with another, to charge what the traffic will bear; and the traffic will bear charges that are inordinately high as counted on the necessary cost or the use-value of the work to be done. It follows, under the common-sense logic of self-help, cupidity, and business-as-usual, that men eager to do business on a good margin will continue to drift in and cut into the traffic until the number of concerns among whom the gains are to be divided is so large that each one's share is no more than will cover costs and leave a "reasonable" margin of net gain. So that while the underlying farm population continues to yield inordinately high rates on the traffic, the business concerns engaged, one with another, come in for no more than what will induce them to go on; the reason being that in the retail trade as conducted on this plan of self-help and equal opportunity the stocks, equipment and man-power employed will unavoidably exceed what is required for the work, by some 200 to 1000 per cent.,—those lines of the trade being the more densely over-populated which enjoy the nearest approach to a local monoply, as e. g., groceries, or banking.[2]

It is perhaps not impertinent to call to mind that the retail trade throughout, always and everywhere, runs on very much the same plan of inordinately high charges and consequently extravagant multiplication of stocks, equipment, work, personnel, publicity, credits, and costs. It runs to the same effect in city, town and country. And in city, town or country town it is in all of these several respects the country's largest business enterprise in the aggregate; and always something like three-fourths to nine-tenths of it is idle waste, to be cancelled out of the community's working efficiency as lag, leak and friction. When the statesmen and the newspapers—and other publicity-agencies—speak for the security and the meritorious work of the country's business men, it is something of this sort

[2] The round numbers named above are safe and conservative, particularly so long as the question concerns the staple country towns of the great farming regions. As has already been remarked, they are only less securely applicable in the case of similar towns in the industrial and outlying parts of the country. To some they may seem large and loose. They are based on a fairly exhaustive study of statistical materials gathered by special inquiry in the spring of 1918 for the Statistical Division of the Food Administration, but not published hitherto.

There has been little detailed or concrete discussion of the topic. See, however, a very brief paper by Isador Lubin on "The Economic Costs of Retail Distribution," published in the *Twenty-second Report of the Michigan Academy of Science,* which runs in great part on the same material.

It is, or should be, unnecessary to add that the retail trade of the country towns is neither a unique nor an extravagant development of business-as-usual. It is in fact very much the sort of thing that is to be met with in the retail trade everywhere, in America and elsewhere.

they are talking about. The bulk of the country's business is the retail trade, and in an eminent sense the retail trade is business-as-usual.

The retail trade, and therefore in its degree the country town, have been the home ground of American culture and the actuating center of public affairs and public sentiment throughout the nineteenth century, ever more securely and unequivocally as the century advanced and drew toward its close. In American parlance "The Public," so far as it can be defined, has meant those persons who are engaged in and about the business of the retail trade, together with such of the kept classes as draw their keep from this traffic. The road to success has run into and through the country town, or its retail-trade equivalent in the cities, and the habits of thought engendered by the preoccupations of the retail trade have shaped popular sentiment and popular morals and have dominated public policy in what was to be done and what was to be left undone, locally and at large, in political, civil, social, ecclesiastical, and educational concerns. The country's public men and official spokesmen have come up through and out of the country-town community, on passing the test of fitness according to retail-trade standards, and have carried with them into official responsibility the habits of thought induced by these interests and these habits of life.

This is also what is meant by democracy in American parlance, and it was for this country-town pattern of democracy that the Defender of the American Faith once aspired to make the world safe. Meantime democracy, at least in America, has moved forward and upward to a higher business level, where larger vested interests dominate and bulkier margins of net gain are in the hazard. It has come to be recognised that the country-town situation of the nineteenth century is now by way of being left behind; and so it is now recognised, or at least acted on, that the salvation of twentieth-century democracy is best to be worked out by making the world safe for Big Business and than let Big Business take care of the interests of the retail trade and the country town, together with much else.   But it should not be overlooked that in and through all this it is the soul of the country town that goes marching on.

Toward the close of the century, and increasingly since the turn of the century, the trading community of the country towns has been losing its initiative as a maker of charges and has by degrees become tributary to the great vested interests that move in the background of the market.   In a way the country towns have in an appreciable degree fallen into the position of toll-gate keepers for the distribution of goods and collection of customs for the large absentee owners of the business.   Grocers, hardware dealers, meat-markets, druggists, shoe-shops, are more and more extensively falling into the position of local distributors for jobbing houses and manufacturers.   They increasingly handle "package goods" bearing the brand of some (ostensible) maker, whose chief connection with the goods is that of advertiser of the copyright brand which appears on the label.   Prices, and margins, are made for the retailers, which they can take or leave.   But leaving, in this connection, will commonly mean leaving the business—which is not included in the premises.   The bankers work by affiliation with and under surveillance of their correspondents in the sub-centers of credit, who are similarly tied in under the credit routine of the associated banking houses in the great centers.   And the clothiers duly sell garments under the brand of "Cost-Plus," or some such apochryphal token of merit.

All this reduction of the retailers to simpler terms has by no means lowered the overhead charges of the retail trade as they bear upon the underlying farm population; rather the reverse. Nor has it hitherto lessened the duplication of stocks, equipment, personnel and work, that goes into the retail trade; rather the reverse, indeed, whatever may yet happen in that connection. Nor has it abated the ancient spirit of self-help and cupidity that has always animated the retail trade and the country town; rather the reverse; inasmuch as their principals back in the jungle of Big Business cut into the initiative and the margins of the retailers with "package goods," brands, advertising, and agency contracts; which irritates the retailers and provokes them to retaliate and recoup where they see an opening, that is at the cost of the underlying farm population. It is true, the added overcharge which so can effectually be brought to rest on the farm population may be a negligible quantity; there never was much slack to be taken up on that side.

The best days of the retail trade and the country town are past. The retail trader is passing under the hand of Big Business and so is ceasing to be a masterless man ready to follow the line of his own initiative and help to rule his corner of the land in collusion with his fellow townsmen. Circumstances are prescribing for him. The decisive circumstances that hedge him about have been changing in such a way as to leave him no longer fit to do business on his own, even in collusion with his fellow townsmen. The retail trade and the country town are an enterprise in salesmanship, of course, and salesmanship is a matter of buying cheap and selling dear; all of which is simple and obvious to any retailer, and holds true all around the circle from grocer to banker and back again. During the period while the country town has flourished and grown into the texture of the economic situation, the salesmanship which made the outcome was a matter of personal qualities, knack and skill that gave the dealer an advantage in meeting his customers man to man, largely a matter of tact, patience and effrontery; those qualities, in short, which have qualified the rustic horse-trader and have cast a glamour of adventurous enterprise over American country life. In this connection it is worth recalling that the personnel engaged in the retail trade of the country towns has in the main been drawn by self-selection from the farm population, prevailingly from the older-settled sections where this traditional animus of the horse-trader is of older growth and more untroubled.

All this was well enough, at least, during the period of what may be called the masterless country town, before Big Business began to come into its own in these premises. But this situation has been changing, becoming obsolete, slowly, by insensible degrees. The factors of change have been such as: increased facilities of transport and communication; increasing use of advertising, largely made possible by facilities of transport and communication; increased size and combination of the business concerns engaged in the wholesale trade, as packers, jobbers, warehouse-concerns handling farm products; increased resort to package-goods, brands, and trade-marks, advertised on a liberal plan which runs over the heads of the retailers; increased employment of chain-store methods and agencies; increased dependence of local bankers on the greater credit establishments of the financial centers. It will be seen, of course, that this new growth finally runs back to and rests upon changes of a material sort, in the industrial arts, and more immediately on changes in the means of transport and communication.

In effect, salesmanship, too, has been shifting to the

wholesale scale and plane, and the country-town retailer is not in a position to make use of the resulting wholesale methods of publicity and control. The conditioning circumstances have outgrown him. Should he make the shift to the wholesale plan of salesmanship he will cease to be a country-town retailer and take on the character of a chain-store concern, a line-yard lumber syndicate, a mail-order house, a Chicago packer instead of a meat market, a Reserve Bank instead of a county-seat banker, and the like; all of which is not contained in the premises of the country-town retail trade.

The country town, of course, still has its uses, and its use so far as bears on the daily life of the underlying farm population is much the same as ever; but for the retail trade and for those accessory persons and classes who draw their keep from its net gains the country town is no longer what it once was. It has been falling into the position of a way-station in the distributive system, instead of a local habitation where a man of initiative and principle might reasonably hope to come in for a "competence"—that is a capitalised free livelihood—and bear his share in the control of affairs without being accountable to any master-concern "higher-up" in the hierarchy of business. The country town and the townsmen are by way of becoming ways and means in the hands of Big Business. Barring accidents, Bolshevism, and the acts of God or of the United States Congress, such would appear to be the drift of things in the calculable future; that is to say, in the absence of disturbing causes.

This does not mean that the country town is on the decline in point of population or the volume of its traffic; but only that the once masterless retailer is coming in for a master, that the retail trade is being standardised and reparcelled by and in behalf of those massive vested interests that move obscurely in the background, and that these vested interests in the background now have the first call on the "income stream" that flows from the farms through the country town. Nor does it imply that that spirit of self-help and collusive cupidity that made and animated the country town at its best has faded out of the mentality of this people. It has only moved upward and onward to higher duties and wider horizons. Even if it should appear that the self-acting collusive storekeeper and banker of the nineteenth-century country town "lies a-moldering in his grave," yet "his soul goes marching on." It is only that the same stock of men with the same traditions and ideals are doing Big Business on the same general plan on which the country town was built. And these men who know the country town "from the ground up" now find it ready to their hand, ready to be turned to account according to the methods and principles bred in their own bone. And the habit of mind induced by and conducive to business-as-usual is much the same whether the balance sheet runs in four figures or in eight.

It is an unhappy circumstance that all this plain speaking about the country town, its traffic, its animating spirit, and its standards of merit, unavoidably has an air of finding fault. But even slight reflection will show that this appearance is unavoidable even where there is no inclination to disparage. It lies in the nature of the case, unfortunately. No unprejudiced inquiry into the facts can content itself with anything short of plain speech, and in this connection plain speech has an air of disparagement because it has been the unbroken usage to avoid plain speech touching these things, these motives, aims, principles, ways and means and achievements, of these substantial citizens and their business and fortunes. But for all that, all these substantial citizens and their folks, fortunes, works, and opinions are no less substantial and meritorious, in fact. Indeed one can scarcely appreciate the full measure of their stature, substance and achievements, and more particularly the moral costs of their great work in developing the country and taking over its resources, without putting it all in plain terms, instead of the salesmanlike parables that have to be employed in the make-believe of trade and politics.

The country town and the business of its substantial citizens are and have ever been an enterprise in salesmanship; and the beginning of wisdom in salesmanship is equivocation. There is a decent measure of equivocation which runs its course on the hither side of prevarication or duplicity, and an honest salesman—such "an honest man as will bear watching"—will endeavor to confine his best efforts to this highly moral zone where stands the upright man who is not under oath to tell the whole truth. But "self-preservation knows no moral law"; and it is not to be overlooked that there habitually enter into the retail trade of the country towns many competitors who do not falter at prevarication and who even do not hesitate at outright duplicity; and it will not do for an honest man to let the rogues get away with the best—or any—of the trade, at the risk of too narrow a margin of profit on his own business—that is to say a narrower margin than might be had in the absence of scruple. And then there is always the base-line of what the law allows; and what the law allows can not be far wrong. Indeed, the sane presumption will be that whoever lives within the law has no need to quarrel with his conscience. And a sound principle will be to improve the hour today and, if worse comes to worst, let the courts determine tomorrow, under protest, just what the law allows, and therefore what the moral code exacts. And then, too, it is believed and credible that the courts will be wise enough to see that the law is not allowed to apply with such effect as to impede the volume or narrow the margins of business-as-usual.

"He either fears his fate too much, Or his deserts are small, Who dare not put it to the touch" and take a chance with the legalities and the moralities for once in a way, when there is easy money in sight and no one is looking, particularly in case his own solvency—that is his life as a business concern—should be in the balance. Solvency is always a meritorious work, however it may be achieved or maintained; and so long as one is quite sound on this main count one is sound on the whole, and can afford to forget peccadillos, within reason. The country-town code of morality at large as well as its code of business ethics, is quite sharp, meticulous; but solvency always has a sedative value in these premises, at large and in personal detail. And then, too, solvency not only puts a man in the way of acquiring merit, but it makes him over into a substantial citizen whose opinions and preferences have weight and who is therefore enabled to do much good for his fellow citizens—that is to say, shape them somewhat to his own pattern. To create mankind in one's own image is a work that partakes of the divine, and it is a high privilege which the substantial citizen commonly makes the most of. Evidently this salesmanlike pursuit of the net gain has a high cultural value at the same time that it is invaluable as a means to a competence.

The country-town pattern of moral agent and the code of morals and proprieties, manners and customs, which come up out of this life of salesmanship is such as this unremitting habituation is fit to produce. The scheme of conduct for the business man and for "his sisters and his cousins and his aunts" is a scheme of salesmanship, seven days in the week. And the rule of life of country-town salesmanship is summed up in what the older logicians have called *suppressio veri* and *suggestio falsi.* The dominant note of this life is circumspection.[3] One must avoid offense, cultivate good-will, at any reasonable cost, and continue unfailing in taking advantage of it; and, as a corollary to this axiom, one should be ready to recognise and recount the possible short-comings of one's neighbors, for neighbors are (or may be) rivals in the trade, and in trade one man's loss is another's gain, and a rival's disabilities count in among one's assets and should not be allowed to go to waste.

One must be circumspect, acquire merit, and avoid offense. So one must eschew opinions, or information, which are not acceptable to the common run of those whose good-will has or may conceivably come to have any commercial value. The country-town system of knowledge and belief can admit nothing that would annoy the prejudices of any appreciable number of the respectable townsfolk. So it becomes a system of intellectual, institutional, and religious holdovers. The country town is conservative; aggressively and truculently so, since any assertion or denial that runs counter to any appreciable set of respectable prejudices would come in for some degree of disfavor, and any degree of disfavor is intolerable to men whose business would presumably suffer from it. Whereas there is no (business) harm done in assenting to, and so in time coming to believe in, any or all of the commonplaces of the day before yesterday. In this sense

[3] It might also be called salesmanlike pusillanimity.

the country town is conservative, in that it is by force of business expediency intolerant of anything but holdovers. Intellectually, institutionally, and religiously, the country towns of the great farming country are "standing pat" on the ground taken somewhere about the period of the Civil War; or according to the wider chronology, somewhere about Mid-Victorian times. And the men of affairs and responsibility in public life, who have passed the test of country-town fitness, as they must, are men who have come through and made good according to the canons of faith and conduct imposed by this system of holdovers.

Again it seems necessary to enter the caution that in so speaking of this system of country-town holdovers and circumspection there need be no hint of disparagement. The colloquial speech of our time, outside of the country-town hives of expedient respectability, carries a note of disallowance and disclaimer in all that it has to say of holdovers; which is an unfortunate but inherent defect of the language, and which it is necessary to discount and make one's peace with. It is only that outside of the country towns, where human intelligence has not yet gone into abeyance and where human speech accordingly is in continued process of remaking, sentiment and opinion run to the unhappy effect which this implicit disparagement of these holdovers discloses.

Indeed, there is much, or at least something, to be said to the credit of this country-town system of holdovers, with its canons of salesmanship and circumspection. It has to its credit many deeds of Christian charity and Christian faith. It may be—as how should it not?—that many of these deeds of faith and charity are done in the business-like hope that they will have some salutary effect on the doer's balance sheet; but the opaque fact remains that these business men do these things, and it is to be presumed that they would rather not discuss the ulterior motives.

It is a notorious commonplace among those who get their living by promoting enterprises of charity and good deeds in general that no large enterprise of this description can be carried through to a successful and lucrative issue without due appeal to the country towns and due support by the businesslike townsmen and their associates and accessory folks. And it is likewise notorious that the country-town community of business men and substantial households will endorse and contribute to virtually any enterprise of the sort, and ask few questions. The effectual interest which prompts to endorsement of and visible contribution to these enterprises is a salesmanlike interest in the "prestige value" that comes to those persons who endorse and visibly contribute; and perhaps even more insistently there is the loss of "prestige value" that would come to anyone who should dare to omit due endorsement and contribution to any ostensibly public-spirited enterprise of this kind that has caught the vogue and does not violate the system of prescriptive holdovers.

Other interest there may well be, as, e. g., human charity or Christian charity—that is to say solicitude for the salvation of one's soul—but without due appeal to salesmanlike respectability the clamour of any certified solicitor of these good deeds will be but as sounding brass and a tinkling cymbal. One need only try to picture what would be the fate, e. g., of the campaigns and campaigners for Red Cross, famine relief, Liberty Bonds, foreign missions, Inter-Church fund, and the like, in the absence of such appeal and of the due response. It may well be, of course, that the salesmanlike townsman endorses with the majority and pays his contribution as a mulct, under compunction of expediency, as a choice between evils, for fear of losing good-will. But the main fact remains. It may perhaps all foot up to this with the common run, that no man who values his salesmanlike well-being will dare follow his own untoward propensity in dealing with these certified enterprises in good deeds, and speak his profane mind to the certified campaigners. But it all comes to the same in the upshot. The substantial townsman is shrewd perhaps, or at least he aims to be, and it may well be that with a shrewd man's logic he argues that two birds in the bush are worth more than one in the hand; and so pays his due peace-offering to the certified solicitor of good deeds somewhat in the spirit of those addicts of the faith who once upon a time bought Papal indulgences. But when all is said, it works; and that it does so, and that these many adventures and adventurers in certified mercy and humanity are so enabled to subsist in any degree of prosperity and comfort is to be credited, for the major part, to the salesmanlike tact of the substantial citizens of the country towns.

One hesitates to imagine what would be the fate of the foreign missions, e. g., in the absence of this salesmanlike solicitude for the main chance in the country towns. And there is perhaps less comfort in reflecting on what would be the terms of liquidation for those many churches and churchmen that now adorn the land, if they were driven to rest their fortunes on unconstrained gifts from *de facto* worshippers moved by the first-hand fear of God, in the absence of that more bounteous subvention that so comes in from the quasi-consecrated respectable townsmen who are so constrained by their salesmanlike fear of a possible decline in their prestige.

Any person who is seriously addicted to devout observances and who takes his ecclesiastical verities at their face might be moved to deprecate this dependence of the good cause on these mixed motives. But there is no need of entertaining doubts here as to the ulterior goodness of these businesslike incentives. Seen in perspective from the outside—as any economist must view these matters—it should seem to be the part of wisdom, for the faithful and for their businesslike benefactors alike, to look steadfastly to the good end and leave ulterior questions of motive on one side. There is also some reason to believe that such a view of the whole matter is not infrequently acted upon. And when all is said and allowed for, the main fact remains, that in the absence of this spirit of what may without offense be called salesmanlike pusillanimity in the country towns, both the glory of God and the good of man would be less bountifully served, on all these issues that engage the certified solicitors of good deeds.

This system of innocuous holdovers, then, makes up what may be called the country-town profession of faith, spiritual and secular. And so it comes to pass that the same general system of holdovers imposes its bias on the reputable organs of expression throughout the community—pulpit, public press, courts, schools—and dominates the conduct of public affairs; inasmuch as the constituency of the country town, in the main and in the everyday run, shapes the course of reputable sentiment and conviction for the American community at large. Not because of any widely prevalent aggressive preference for that sort of thing, perhaps, but rather because it would scarcely be a "sound business proposition" to run counter to the known interests of the ruling class; that is to say, the substantial citizens and their folks. But the effect is much the same and will scarcely be denied.

It will be seen that in substantial effect this country-town system of holdovers is of what would be called a "salutary" character; that is to say, it is somewhat intolerantly conservative. It is a system of professions and avowals, which may perhaps run to no deeper ground than a salesmanlike pusillanimity, but the effect is much the same. In the country-town community and its outlying ramifications, as in any community of men, the professions made and insisted on will unavoidably shape the effectual scheme of knowledge and belief. Such is the known force of inveterate habit. To the young generation the prescriptive holdovers are handed down as self-evident and immutable principles of reality, and the (reputable) schools can allow themselves no latitude and no question. And what is more to the point, men and women come to believe in the truths which they profess, on whatever ground, provided only that they continue stubbornly to profess them. Their professions may have come out of expedient make-believe, but, all the same, they serve as premises in all the projects, reflections, and reveries of these folks who profess them. And it will be only on provocation of harsh and protracted exposure to material facts running unbroken to the contrary that the current of their sentiments and convictions can be brought to range outside of the lines drawn for them by these professed articles of truth.

The case is illustrated, e. g., by the various and widely-varying systems of religious verities current among the outlying peoples, the peoples of the lower cultures, each and several of which are indubitable and immutably truthful to their respective believers, throughout all the bizarre web of their incredible conceits and grotesqueries, none of which will bear the light of alien scrutiny.[4] Having

---

[4] There is, of course, no call in this Christian land to throw up a doubt or question touching any of the highly remarkable

come in for these professions of archaic make-believe, and continuing stubbornly to profess implicit faith in these things as a hopeful sedative of the wrath to come, these things come to hedge about the scheme of knowledge and belief as well as the scheme of what is to be done or left undone. In much the same way the country-town system of prescriptive holdovers has gone into action as the safe and sane body of American common sense; until it is now self-evident to American public sentiment that any derangement of these holdovers would bring the affairs of the human race to a disastrous collapse. And all the while the material conditions are progressively drawing together into such shape that this plain country-town common sense will no longer work.

IV. THE NEW GOLD

America has been a land of unexampled natural resources. Some day China and the Russian dominions will presumably outbid America in that way, both as to the abundance and the availability of their natural re-

verities of the Christian confession at large. While it will be freely admitted on all hands that many of the observances and beliefs current among the "non-Christian tribes" are grotesque and palpable errors of mortal mind; it must at the same time, and indeed by the same token, be equally plain to any person of cultivated tastes in religious superstition, and with a sound bias, that the corresponding convolutions of unreason in the Christian faith are in the nature of a divine coagulum of the true, the beautiful, and the good, as it was in the beginning, is now, and ever shall be: World without end. But all the while it is evident that all these "beastly devices of the heathen," just referred to, are true, beautiful and good to their benighted apprehension only because their apprehension has been benighted by their stubborn profession of these articles of misguided make-believe, through the generations; which is the point of the argument.

sources, and Brazil and Argentine come into the same class in this respect, as also other less well known regions in the low latitudes. But the material resources of these countries are to be counted with in the future rather than in the past; and, for the present at least, a good part of them are to be counted in as a source of supplementary and subsidiary materials required for use in the industries of the countries lying in the temperate latitudes, not as countries that are abundantly endowed with a balanced allowance of those raw materials that go to make the basis of that system of industry which runs on the existing state of the industrial arts. Something to the same general effect may be said for all the greater fertile lands in the low latitudes. As the case stands just now these regions are outlying tributaries to the industrial system that centers in the north-temperate latitudes, and they come into the industrial scheme as a necessary compliment to the ways and means of this industrial system rather than a basis for self-balanced industrial commonwealths at home. All of that may be due to change presently. The state of the industrial arts is unstable, now as always, and it would be idle to speculate on what is due to come of it all in the remoter course of time and change. But for the present and the calculable future the seats of the mighty in this industrial system lie in the north-temperate latitudes, and for the immediate present and that recent past that goes to make the current situation, America comes easily first in this matter of abundant and available natural resources.

That such is the case may be called an historical accident. The state of the industrial arts as it has taken shape in this recent past has brought productive industry to depend, in the main and perforce, on that range of natural resources with which America is peculiarly well

endowed. It is no serious stretch of language to say
that this current state of the industrial arts has made
America a land of abundant resources, inasmuch as these
industrial arts have made these material facts of the
American continent serviceable for industrial use. In the
absence of that mechanical industry that arose in Europe
in the eighteenth century and that system of mixed farming which runs along with the mechanical industry, the
natural resources of America would count for little. So
that the current state of the industrial arts might even
quite warrantably be said to have created this natural
wealth of the country,—converted otherwise meaningless
elements of physiography and mineralogy into industrial
wealth. It all was of little use or value, counted for little
as wealth or as means of production, until the coming
of this state of the industrial arts. And it is of course
also conceivable that in the further course of time and
change men may learn to do well enough without the use
of this range of materials; whereupon these resources
would cease to be resources, by that much. But all that
lies beyond the calculable future.

In the same connection it may, at the risk of tedious
iteration, be worth while to recall that this state of the industrial arts that now makes the outcome is, like any
other, of the nature of a joint stock of technical knowledge and proficiency, held, worked, augmented, and carried forward in common by the population at large; indeed, by the population of the civilised world at large,
not by any one class or country unaided or in isolation.
It is a joint stock of technical knowledge and workmanlike
habits, without the use of which the existing material
wealth of the civilised nations would not be wealth. Also,
in the same connection it should also be recalled that the
American plan is and has been, consistently from the be-

ginning, to convert all these unexampled natural resources to absentee ownership, with all haste and expedition, so soon as they have become valuable enough to be worth owning,—all the while that it is the community's workmanship that gives them whatever value they have.

This American plan began at the beginning, and has continued. It is not peculiarly American, except in the sense that it has been worked out more consistently and more extensively here than elsewhere, and that it has been worked into the texture of American life and culture more faithfully. In the last analysis, the difference in this respect between the Americans and the other civilised nations will probably resolve itself into a difference of opportunity, and there is no wide difference at that. This American plan or policy is very simply a settled practice of converting all public wealth to private gain on a plan of legalised seizure.

First among these natural resources to fall under the American plan were the fur-bearing animals. The fur trade, of course, was not a matter of the first magnitude, and it is now a scarce-remembered episode of pioneering enterprise; nor does it now count in any appreciable degree among the useful means of livelihood, in great part because business enterprise has run through that range of natural resources with exemplary thoroughness and expedition and has left the place of it bare. It is worth while to speak of it here only because it shows a finished instance of business-as-usual converting community goods to private gain without afterthought. It is a neat, compact, and concluded chapter of American business enterprise.

Bound up with the enterprise there is also an unwritten chapter on the debauchery and manslaughter entailed on the Indian population of the country by the same businesslike fur trade; one of the least engaging chapters of colonial history, lapping over far into the nineteenth century, and leaving more than one distasteful sequel to run into the future. Indirectly and unintentionally, but speedily and conclusively, the traffic of the furtraders converted a reasonably peaceable and temperate native population to a state of fanatical hostility among themselves and an unmanageable complication of outlaws in their contact with the white population. The traffic has, of course, also had its effect on the latter, chiefly by way of what may be called sclerosis of the American soul.

But the Americans have forgiven themselves for the fur trade and its hideous accessories and have nearly forgotten it all; nor is the fur trade in any case to be counted in as a factor in the economic situation as its runs in recent times. The Great Adventure of the Americans has, after all, been the seizure of the fertile soil and its conversion to private gain. Their dealing with the soil has been the largest of these enterprises in absentee ownership, both in respect of its extent in time and space and in its social and civil consequences; and this has already been spoken of, in its main bearings and at some length. Yet there is at least one further, and very consequential, feature of the case that should come in for mention, if not for extended discussion, as a grave and instructive incident in the working-out of this American plan.

In the North this enterprise in land-values has run off in the manner and with accessory consequences somewhat as described in the last two preceding sections But the case of the South, and the institutional value of the soil in that section, has been different. In the South the private usufruct of the soil injected into American life the "peculiar institution" of Negro slavery. The soil, crops, topography and climate of the North were, on the whole, not suited to agricultural exploitation on a large scale by use of forced labor; whereas the soil and crops of the South lent themselves very passably to that manner of absentee ownership in agriculture. So the more fertile tracts in the South fell into the shape of "plantations" rather than farms; and the large scale, with forced labor and absentee coercion, became the type-form of Southern husbandry. The consequence has been that while Negro slavery tapered off and faded out in the North before it had time to give its character to the industrial system and to mold the scheme of social values and usages into its own image, in the South Negro slavery became the "peculiar institution" about which "the scheme of things entire" circled and gravitated, and which gave its color and bias to all the local conventions and principles of honor and honesty; until, in the end, Negro slavery has left its mark on the culture of that section so deeply etched into the moral tissues of its people that the bias of it will presumably not be outgrown within the calculable future. In the South that bias is still right and good which the exacting discipline enforced by this "peculiar institution" once made right and good to them and so ingrained it in their common sense; very much as the equally peculiar institution of the Country Town has made the moral bias and the spiritual outcome in the North.

This is not saying that the Country Town has counted for nothing in the South,—the county-seat politics and social amenities of that section are not to be overlooked; nor did Negro slavery leave the North untouched. Negro slavery presumes a Negro slave-trade. And the slave-trade was a Northern enterprise in the main, centering chiefly in New England, it is said; and it has doubtless had its effect in giving a certain implacable effrontery to the commercial spirit of that section, while it also had something substantial to do with the early accumulation of commercial fortunes in New England.[1]

Aside from agriculture and real estate, the progressive seizure of natural resources and their conversion to private gain falls under several main heads, somewhat as follows:—gold and other precious metals, timber, coal, iron and other useful metals, petroleum, natural gas, water-power, irrigation, transportation (as water-front, right-of-way, and terminal facilities).

For the time being the great ones among these are: coal, iron, transportation, and perhaps oil. As the case stands just now, coal, iron, and transportation together can make and remake the industrial balance, and the control of either one of the three can mar it, as is shown by current events. These are public interests of course, public utilities, if that term is to be applied at all in a community where the custom is to turn every public need to account as a means of private gain, and to capitalise it as

[1] The slave-trade never was a "nice" occupation or an altogether unexceptionable investment—"balanced on the edge of the permissible." But even though it may have been distasteful to one and another of its New-England men of affairs, and though there always was a suspicion of moral obliquity attached to the slave-trade, yet it had the fortune to be drawn into the service of the greater good. In conjunction with its running-mate, the rum-trade, it laid the foundations of some very reputable fortunes at that focus of commercial enterprise that presently became the center of American culture, and so gave rise to some of the country's Best People. At least so they say.

Perhaps also it was, in some part, in this early pursuit of gain in this moral penumbra that American business enterprise learned how not to let its right hand know what its left hand is doing; and there is always something to be done that is best done with the left hand.

such. One must quite naturally hesitate about speaking of a "public interest" or a "public utility" which is carried on the books of a private corporation as a capitalised source of income. It seems incongruous.

While gold and the chase after it is not to be reckoned among the country's greater enterprises in point of permanent importance for industry, yet it ranks in the popular esteem as the greatest and most glorious of them all, the most picturesque and the most affectionately familiar in men's mind. It stands out as the type-form of that manly enterprise which aims to get something for nothing at all costs. So that, one thing with another, for its bald honesty and its picturesque qualities as well as by the concrete and tangible nature of the reward which it offers for spent manhood, the quest of gold has always a place in the rosy foreground of all pioneering.

It is not that the bountiful earth gives up its gold, or its other precious minerals, without cost to the finder, but it always remains his aim and his actuating hope that he may come in for much of it at next to no proportionate cost; in which, it is true, he is commonly disappointed. But "Hope springs eternal in the human breast." The actuating hope of the prospector is something for nothing, although his work will more commonly bring nothing for something. But there is also another sense in which it can be said even more truly that the gold which is found and brought out is a clear case of something for nothing. The gold is added to the outstanding purchasing power, while nothing is thereby added to the purchasable goods in hand. So that its finder or producer, at whatever cost, comes in for a share of the useful goods already on hand, without anything having been added to the community's material wealth.

Wherever gold has been found or procured in recent

times the tale of it runs always to the same effect, whether in California, Australia, South Africa, or Alaska. And it runs to this effect:—Many ablebodied men, at a very appreciable cost for equipment and subsistence, engage in this adventure for a considerable length of time, hard at work under conditions of some hardship, and subject to a death-rate which invariably exceeds that of equally robust men in the common run of employments. The greater number of these men come through the adventure alive, most of them without seriously impaired health,—unless the period covered by the enterprise should run longer than has commonly been the case. Some of them, relatively few, come in for large fortunes. Many of them, an appreciable fraction of those who come through alive, come out of it with modest gains, or at least without pecuniary loss. The greater number, perhaps ninety per cent. or so, of those who come out alive, come through with nothing to show for the time, work, and equipment which they have staked on the lucky chance, nothing but a harsh experience and an increased age. Meantime, as the period of free adventure draws to a close, the gold-bearing properties will have been taken over by absentee corporations, after having served their turn as stakes in what is reputed to be the most doubtful game of hazard known to men.[2]

[2] Although it is not greatly to the point, yet it may be noted by way of parenthesis, that many funds are also invested in worthless, "wild-cat," and spurious mining stocks in the course of that speculative investment that gathers about any one of the greater gold discoveries, and that the funds so invested in profitless make-believe will doubtless in all cases greatly exceed the total value of the gold produced up to the date at which the gold-bearing properties have finally passed into the possession of absentee corporations and are being worked on the basis of corporate business-as-usual. Of course, all this traffic in speculative mining shares has no great or material

The total value of the gold produced, one year with another, is also doubtless appreciably less than the total of the work and equipment expended on its discovery and production during the same period. And the same relation between cost and output holds true for any given gold field also, through its earlier years, while individual initiative is still running free; but in the adventurous years of the beginning the difference between total costs and the total value produced will be still wider than it is after the work has been standardised and stabilised under corporate control. There is always a net loss in the production of gold, but the net loss is larger during the earlier years of novelty and adventure. Even if the time, expenses, and wear and tear of the unsuccessful seekers are left out of the account—as being perhaps no more than a fair equivalent of the "pleasures of the chase"—it still will hold true that the total cost of producing the supply of gold habitually exceeds the total value of the product by several hundred per cent.[3] And the

significance for anyone else than the buyers and sellers. The speculative losses of over-sanguine investors and the speculative gains of the over-facile salesmen who create and dispose of mining stocks have only a speculative interest to anyone but themselves. Like other games of chance and skill it is a closed circuit of profit and loss. It foots up to a transfer of purchasing power from the buyers, who get nothing, for a price, to the sellers, who dispose of the same commodity, for the same price. It is of interest as being a typical case of salesmanship; an exploit of salesmanship *in puris naturalibus,* as one might say; that is to say, it runs off wholly on the plane of make-believe, without ulterior consequences or sequelae. It has something of that detachment from material fact which distinguishes the publicity enterprise of Holy Church.

[3] Cf. W. S. Jevons, *Investigations in Currency and Finance* (London, 1884) pp. 70–73. "But in itself gold-digging has ever seemed to me almost a dead loss of labour as regards the world in general—a wrong against the human race, just such as is that of a Government against its people, in over-issuing and depreciating its own currency."

same will hold true in a less degree for the other precious and semi-precious metals and minerals.

And all the while it holds true that, loosely speaking, the production of gold is of no industrial use and no material service to the community at large. What may have to be admitted in qualification of this broad statement is so slight and doubtful that it may be neglected without serious oversight. The gold supply is a supply of specie, on which money and money-values are based. The productive use of the metal in industry is altogether of secondary consequence, particularly such use as can claim to serve any material need. What goes into the industrial arts goes in chiefly as a means of conspicuously wasteful consumption; a need which is doubtless real enough, but which could also doubtless be met as adequately in the absence of a gold supply, or by use of any smaller gold supply, without apparent lower limit.[4]

Men who are intimately acquainted with the gold deposits of Alaska and their working, and who have had the benefit of a full acquaintance with the work of the U. S. Geological Survey in that region, have been at pains to estimate and compute on the basis of the statistical information which so can be drawn on, and have come to the result that the total expenditures which have gone into the production of gold in the Alaskan field, up to the year 1919, have exceeded the total value of the output of gold by some 500 per cent., rather over than under. So that the gold output of Alaska has cost something like six dollars per dollar. Which may be taken as a fair index of the value of the Alaskan gold fields to the American people at large; except that when the matter is appraised from the point of view of the community at large the time and work of the unsuccessful seekers, as well as the lost lives, would have to be counted in among the total costs. Which would raise the cost of the gold appreciably over 1000 per cent. of its purchasing value. Cf. also "The World's Gold Supply," by William A. Berridge, in *The Review of Economic Statistics* (Harvard University Press), *Preliminary Volume II.* pp. 181–199.

[4] What has happened to platinum during the past quarter-century may be taken as a passably conclusive object-lesson

The gold supply is useful as specie. This has to do with business, not with industry, except as industry is controlled by business. And here, again, one meets with the paradox that, while gold is extremely valuable and does good service as specie, a smaller supply of bullion would doubtless serve the same purpose quite as well. Indeed, a greatly increased supply would be inconvenient, and if carried very far an increasing supply would seriously impair or conceivably destroy the usefulness of gold as specie. The immediate and substantial effect of an increased supply of specie is to decrease the purchasing-value of the money unit; that is to say, a depreciation of the dollar and a consequent advance of the general price level.

Otherwise it leaves things very much as before, except for certain indirect consequences which may be more or less serious. So, e. g., other things equal, an increased

on this head. In the early nineties platinum still had virtually no use as a decorative precious metal. Then its price began to rise, strongly and steadily, chiefly because of its increasing employment in the electrical industry, and in some degree by a slighter but increased use in photography and dyeing. Then progressively, as the price advanced and so made the decorative use of platinum increasingly and conspicuously wasteful, the decorative use as well as the conventional beauty of platinum steadily gained ground and assurance; until the metal is today imperatively required as an indispensable ingredient in all the more exacting and honorable confections of the jeweler's art,—at a price ranging some ten or twenty fold higher than the point of departure. No slight is to be put upon platinum, as touches either its beauty or its serviceability, in taking note of the fact that at a sufficiently lower price it would be no more sought after as a personal adornment than some of the several alloys which rival it in visual effect. Indeed, except for the declining value of gold, brought on by the increased supply, and the rising value of platinum, due to scarcity, it is extremely doubtful if the latter metal could have found any special favor as an object of beauty, or could in any degree have displaced gold as an article of personal ornament.

supply of specie will depress the purchasing-value of annuities, insurance payments, fixed salaries and fees, and similar incomes, and it will also lighten the effectual burden of fixed charges payable on long-term loans and the like, and so will depress the purchasing-value of outstanding securities which carry a stated rate of income. Its direct and proximate effect is, therefore, to undo the stability of the money-unit, depreciate it, and so derange prices, in the direction of an advance; to alter the effectual terms of loans outstanding, to the advantage of the debtor; to bring on an effectual redistribution of property as counted in goods, to the disadvantage of creditors, annuitants, and holders of securities drawn in terms of money; and, perhaps the most consequential outcome, effectually to lighten the burden of outstanding corporation securities, and thereby enable the corporations to increase the volume of their obligations and their capitalisation. So also, by further indirect effect there will commonly follow an increased activity in business —and therefore in industry—due to the inflation of prices. The whole matter is summed up in saying that an increased supply of specie brings depreciation of the money unit. And it should be added that business men commonly welcome such depreciation, so long as it is not known by that name. Such depreciation (or inflation), within reasonable limits, is "good for trade."

In point of material usefulness, then, it seems fair to say that the production of gold is pure waste—more especially the production of more than is currently taken up in the arts—and that this waste commonly exceeds the total value of the product. But in point of expediency for business it appears to be very much the other way. The effect on business appears to be altogether "salutary," as it would be called. That is to say, continued production of gold in excess of what is consumed in the arts will bring business prosperity—the only prosperity known to civilised men—by raising prices. The surplus of gold depreciates the money unit; which inflates prices; which provokes to increased activity in business by holding out a prospect of larger gains in money; which involves larger sales; which calls for a larger industrial output; which speeds up industry and increases the percentage of employment both of the plant and of the industrial man-power. So also, this inflation of prices and increased activity of business will increase the rate and volume of the business turnover and of the business earnings—as counted in terms of the depreciated money unit —and will thereby inflate capital values, and so make credit easier by inflating the values of the collateral. Doubtless, no other single circumstance will affect the business situation in so invariably acceptable a manner as a surplus output of specie, such, e. g., as was had during the closing years of the nineteenth century and the opening years of the twentieth.[5]

[5] The statement is put in this form because it applies without reservation only under the conditions which prevailed in the late nineteenth century and for a few years after its close, gradually changing into a new order of things as the twentieth century has advanced. Since then it will apply only with lessened force. Indeed, until the War brought on the present international complication of insolvent credits, the American system of money and credit seemed in a fair way to become independent of any surplus productions of gold or of any store of specie, if need be.

In short, the statement applies to the older situation; when the banks and other credit establishments were still doing business in severalty, at least in the main; and it will apply with gradually lessening force since and in so far as these concerns that do business in credit have effectually been drawing together for concerted action on a collusive plan; and more particularly will it not hold true in the earlier fashion since the establishment of the Federal Reserve has enabled this collusive plan of

The surplus output of gold takes effect on the conduct of business along two main lines. Directly and immediately it acts to inflate prices—in so far as it is not offset by the Federal Reserve's remedial control of credit and currency—and so it inflates the business men's expectations of gain, and thereby speeds up business and industry; for among the securely known facts of psychology, as touches the conduct of business, is the ingrained persuasion that the money unit is stable;[6] the value of the money unit being the base-line of business transactions. Therefore an inflation of prices is rated as an accession of wealth. Therefore such an inflation will impart confidence and buoyancy and raise great expectations, by a tropismatic stimulation of the business men's sensibilities if not by logical inference; and logic is after all a feeble defense in the face of a tropismatic stimulation, as is abundantly shown by the history of business cycles.[7]   And when so

team-work in credit to be enforced with a reasonable measure of centralised control. The stability (at least *de jure*) of the money unit and of the country's credit arrangements is no longer conditioned on the supply of specie in any such intractable fashion. Yet a surplus production of the money metal, at any cost, continues always to be a fortunate circumstance for the conduct of business.

[6] This persuasion or presumption prevails wherever the price-system has fully gone into effect. It may fairly be called the spiritual precipitate of the price-system. It affects not only the business men, properly speaking, but the underlying population as well. It is known not to accord with fact, but still it remains a principle of conduct. It has something like an instinctive force; or perhaps rather, it is something like a tropismatic reaction, in that the presumption is acted on even when it is known to be misleading. And it is a necessary assumption in business, since business is necessarily done in terms of price; so that money values unavoidably constitute the base-line to which transactions are finally referred, and by measurements upon which they are ultimately checked, controlled, adjusted, and accounted for.

[7] Cf. W. C. Mitchell, *Business Cycles,* perhaps especially chapter xiii.

borne up on the resulting "wave of confidence" the business men are in a frame of mind for new commitments; which turns the wave of confidence into a wave of prosperity.

Money-values are the underlying realities of the business man's world, the substance of things hoped for, the evidence of things not seen. Therefore an inflation of prices is a business gain, and a decline of prices is a business loss. And one must not do business at a loss. Therefore the staple remedy for declining prices is to do no business until "things look up again." Therefore such business as ·is concerned with productive industry will aim to correct low or declining prices by slowing down, curtailing output, holding back,—in short, sabotage. So long as the case is not desperate—that is to say so long as the failure of the price situation can be covered over with plausible make-believe—so long the business-like remedy will be a steadfast application of sabotage, while waiting watchfully for things to take a turn. But so soon as the case grows desperate—that is to say when the unreality of the money-values involved can no longer be overlooked, even with the best endeavours of make-believe —then there is no remedy within the range of assumptions on which business is conducted. Therefore, in this last extremity there comes a break-down, a slaughter of the innocents, called a period of liquidation; which violates the premises of business-as-usual.[8]

[8] In the present spectacular conjuncture which had followed upon the War and the Armistice, e. g., it is a matter of common notoriety that the scale of prices went out of touch with the material realities of production and consumption some years ago and has so continued since then; that the present scale of money-values, in tangible property and in securities, is quite unsound; that the outstanding volume of credit obligations has turned into a fantastic tissue of footless make-believe; and that the only way out of a desperate situation is to go to work.

In ordinary times as well as in hard times, such as the present, it is of necessity the constant care of the business men who control industry to guard against an over-supply of their industrial output,—a running balance of sabotage on production with a view to maintain prices. It is the immediate effect of a surplus output of gold to inflate prices by depreciating the money unit. Therefore it relieves the need of this businesslike sabotage on the output of industry by that much. Therefore it brings a run of

It is equally notorious that there is a desperate need of goods for consumption; and that the needed raw materials, industrial plant, and manpower are ready to hand—urgently ready to be turned to productive use.

All this is well known to all concerned and has been quite evident all through these years while this situation has run on and grown steadily worse. The established rights of ownership (absentee ownership) vest all discretion in this matter in the country's business men—and in the Business Administration which has been installed to serve their needs; so that it is for them, and their Business Administration, to say what is to be done about it. And it is also plain enough what need be done. They are all agreed that the thing to do is to go to work; to make use of the country's raw materials, equipment and manpower for the production of useful goods. But to take these known facts by their only handle, to acknowledge the known facts and act upon them, would not be "a sound business proposition." Indeed, it can not be done without violating the premises on which sound business is conducted,—the premises of unshrinkable values and net gain. Therefore the best that the collective wisdom of the business community and the Business Administration knows how to propose after some three or four years of deliberation is "Nothing doing."

There is wide-spread and steadily increasing privation among the underlying population, increasing unemployment of plant and man-power, increasing discontent, increasing indebtedness, steady shrinkage of use-values, due to consumption, wear and tear, and neglect. And all the while the business men, who alone have the power to act, are bound by their unshrinkable money-values; and so they hold back and wait watchfully for the eventual breakdown, under a smoke-screen of optimistic talk; watchfully and with a manly attempt at self-delusion.

prosperity in business, a reduction of unemployment in industry, and a run of increased production. Its great merit is that it offsets, in its degree, this habitual need of curtailing the output of industry. It is a psychological factor, and it owes its efficacy to this inveterate habit of rating wealth in terms of money-values instead of use-values; and this habit rules the case wherever and in so far as the price-system has taken effect.

But in recent times the mastery of the price-system has taken a peculiar turn, in that corporation finance has, in effect, supplanted private initiative, and so has taken over the direction of business enterprise and the control of the material fortunes of the community. And the surplus output of gold stands in a somewhat special relation to corporation finance. A corporation is an incorporation of credit, an organisation of funds, a capitalisation of obligations. Loosely its capital value is measured by its outstanding obligations, and the whole is rated and administered on the basis of the current money-values of these obligations. This is the measure of its rating and the basis of its commitments. Its everyday business transactions, too, large and small, are in the nature of transactions in credit. At the same time —if it is an industrial concern in any sense—the corporation is possessed of tangible assets (natural resources, raw materials, industrial plant, right of way, etc.) as well as intangibles (of the nature of credit instruments, monopolies and custom). All these are valuable, and all will serve as collateral at the same time that they are means of earning. Any increase in the money-value of these assets, tangible or intangible, is an increase of the corporation's assets and therefore an accession of wealth, in the only sense in which wealth can be taken account of in corporation finance.

Any inflation of money-values due to an increased supply of specie will enhance the corporation's assets, while it leaves the outstanding obligations at the old figure. Inflation, therefore, signifies net gain to the corporation in all its book-values; and its assets will serve as collateral to float that much more debt, with a fixed charge.

In the last analysis, of course, all this gain that comes to the corporation from this inflation of prices comes at the cost of its senior creditors, the holders of its outstanding securities with a fixed rate, the purchasing power (or use-value) of whose claims shrinks by as much as the money unit has depreciated. But except in an extreme case, and very tardily then, the creditors will not see it that way. Nor have they any remedy if they should come to see it that way. On the contrary, they are elated with the improved solvency of the corporation whose securities they are holding. For these creditors, too, like other men who live by and under the price-system, go on the assumption that money-values are the final reality of things, and that they can lose nothing so long as the face value of their paper is undiminished and the solvency of their debtor remains unimpaired. It is true, these creditors may know better, as a matter of deliberate information, but they do not know it with such effect as to shake their faith in the realities of the price-system or to influence their conduct in any degree.

Among other things, then, this depreciation of the currency affects the corporation's assets and enhances their carrying-capacity as collateral; which enables the corporation to contract new credit-obligations, add something to its capitalisation, and so to take on an additional overhead of fixed charges. The income-rate on the new capitalisation is fixed formally by the terms of the instrument which covers it (e. g. in the case of bonds and similar debentures) or informally and more flexibly by usage, presumption, and financial expediency (e. g. in the case of stocks). When the inflated assets have so been capitalised and hypothecated they are, in effect, standardised at a stated value and become unshrinkable, except by way of enforced liquidation. So they come to stand at these inflated values as staple assets, on which it is then imperative to "earn" a net gain answering to the fixed or customary income-charge ordinarily borne by securities of the class which covers them.[9] So the traffic must be made to bear such charges in perpetuity as will yield that rate of net gains which is called for by this expanded recapitalisation. And the staple procedure dictated by sound business principles in such a case is to increase the schedule of charges and curtail the output. It is perhaps unfortunate that there is no other way out

[9] The guaranteed earnings of the American railways, as now provided by law, is instructive on this head; both as regards capitalised inflation and as regards the unshrinkable values of assets that have once been covered with securities of the approved forms. The railroad properties have, in great part, ceased to yield earnings. Logically this state of things should call for their recapitalisation at such a lower figure as would answer to their shrunken earning-capacity. But business principles, vested interests, and corporation finance do not admit deflation of assets in the ordinary course of business.

It may be mentioned as something outside the ken of American statesmen and financiers and abhorrent to American principles of sound business that certain European industrial corporate concerns lately (1921–1922) have, under severe pressure, been writing off a very appreciable proportion of capital on which no earnings can be had. But then, there were no American statesmen at hand to succor these Europeans in distress. The parallel case of the American railways and their (actually) valueless assets will point the difference. The American plan is to let the taxpayers make up the shrinkage. America is, after all, the land of unshrinkable absentee ownership.

according to the canons of business-as-usual, since there is after all a limit to this method of making the traffic bring a reasonable net gain on inflated capitalisation.[10]

It apears, then, that so far as concerns the output of gold—and other precious metals—there is much to be said for this American plan of exhausting the country's natural resources by seizure and conversion to absentee ownership, regardless of cost and as expeditiously as may be. This particular range of natural resources has, in effect, no use-value; so that their loss or exhaustion entails no material loss on the community directly,—apart from the excessively high cost of their exhaustion by this method. Indirectly but immediately, it is true, by operation of the added purchasing-power which the new specie gratuitously brings into the market, the community at large loses so much in useful goods as this added purchasing power will account for; which will, by use of fiduciary currency, bank checks, and other forms of credit-extension, foot up to some multiple of the initial value of the new specie that is brought to market,—say some ten times the value of the new specie, or some such figure. But this loss the community bears gladly, and in fact counts it as so much gain measured by the purchasing-value of the new specie. The country is so much richer per capita, counted in terms of the depreciated money unit. So great is the magic of the price system and its frame of mind. Beyond this there is to

[10] The case of the American railways, again, illustrates the point; in that the schedule of charges in this case has been advanced to such a point that the total net earnings have apparently been falling off. In the absence of a guarantee it should not seem likely that the railways would charge more than the traffic will bear; but with standard earnings guaranteed there may even be a certain economy in making the charges high enough to discourage traffic in a moderate degree.

be set down to the credit of the new specie the creation of a wave of prosperity by inflation, and the creation also of enlarged opportunities for corporation finance.

V. The Timber Lands and The Oil Fields

The American Plan of seizure and conversion as it has worked out in the case of the land and the precious metals has been greatly complicated with ulterior consequences and secondary effects, not aimed at and not contemplated in the original design. The like is not true in the same degree in respect of those other natural resources which are more usually spoken of as such; as timber, coal, iron, oil, gas, waterpower, irrigation waters. Harbor facilities and transportation lines should also be included among these. The history of the large and many enterprises that have had to do with taking over these articles of national wealth can, of course, not be recited here, nor need it be. The records are full and accessible, for all such facts relating to these public utilities as the public has a right to inquire into under this American plan.

Publicity touching these matters is no part of the American plan. Yet, to recall what the ordinary course of events has been like, and what has been the commonplace outcome of absentee ownership and business enterprise in this field, it is necessary to show some of the characteristic practices and incidents that have marked this pioneering enterprise. And this can be shown as well, and perhaps more simply and concisely, in lumber than in any other one line of natural resources.

There have been many picturesque incidents and not a few spectacular episodes in the course of this pioneering enterprise; but all such it will be necessary to avoid, since that which is of interest here as bearing on the present argument is not the colorful atmosphere of this thing but only its workday nature, causes, and outcome—the industrial significance of its ordinary working-out. The case as a whole, of course, as an object-lesson showing the merits and qualities of the American Plan, runs not on picturesque episodes but on standard practice and workday outcome.

What has been done with the country's timber supply is a well defined and characteristic case, showing how absentee ownership functions in taking over the country's natural resources and using them up. As a characteristic feature of the case it may be called to mind at the outset that much of what has happened to the stand of hardwood timber has happened as an episode by the way, a side-issue of pioneer farming. The greater proportion of the original stand of hardwood, together with an appreciable fraction of the pine and hemlock, was got rid of in all haste in clearing the land to get at the soil. It would be hard to say how much of this hurried work of destroying the stand of timber is to be set down to the account of absentee ownership. There can be no question as to the broad fact that the practice of competitively taking over land more rapidly and in larger parcels than the requirements of cultivation called for will have increased the rate and volume of this waste. For more or less, so much is to be set down to the account of absentee ownership. It would perhaps be an overstatement to say that this practice has doubled the waste of timber incident to bringing the soil under cultivation, though it is not an extravagant overstatement. The enterprise in "land-grabbing," as it has been called, has involved a great deal of hasty work by men who have commonly been short of equipment and "working capital" and who have been driven to many shifts by present need and so have gone on a plan of hurried exploitation instead of economical use.[1]

The pine and other evergreens have been taken care of by enterprising lumbermen driven by a businesslike pursuit of immediate net gain without afterthought. The like is also true for much of the hardwood timber; for such of it as has not been included in the "farm areas." The greater and better part of the stand of pine timber east of the plains—and much of the hemlock, spruce, and cedar—was run through and virtually exhausted during the latter half of the nineteenth century.

In pursuance of this American plan of lumbering as shown in the pine-timber country the usual procedure of the business men who conducted the enterprise was to acquire title to tracts of timber-land by one means and another. There was a shady side to some—quite a large

[1] So, e. g., in much of the country where the ground was covered with hardwood timber it was in its time not unusual for the impecunious settlers to raise some slight funds for urgent use by hastily felling the stand of timber, burning it, and selling the ash, which was used for making potash. So also, in the same sections as well as in many places where the land was timbered with pine and hemlock, it has not been unusual to construct fences by felling the timber along the fence-line in such a way as to make a barrier of it to serve the purpose of a fence by cumbering the ground. These Independent Farmers were commonly very nearly penniless, and so were driven to many ingenious devices to find ready money, at the same time that their competitive enterprise in land-grabbing scattered them and their work out over wide spaces of half-wild country with long distances and atrocious roads, leaving them far out of reach of reasonable transportation. They were (commonly) unable to buy or to bring in anything like the equipment and materials required in their work. So they took this way out of present difficulties at the cost of the future; and the future, which has now become the present, is paying the cost in a scarcity of timber.

proportion, they say—of the transactions involved in so acquiring title to these timber-lands or to the stand of timber on them; but this somewhat prevalent shady complexion of the enterprise at this point is not of particular interest here. Title was acquired under the broad principle that all is fair in competitive business; particularly so long as any dubious practices are carried through at the cost of the community at large.

According to the standard routine of the time, as seen, e. g., in the pineries of Michigan, Wisconsin, and Minnesota, these tracts of timber-land would then be "lumbered" as expeditiously as might be;[2] that is to say, as the practice ran through the larger and busier part of that half-century, the high-grade and accessible pine timber was taken out, turned into lumber, and marketed. The inferior grades of pine timber—the smaller sticks (say, under eighteen inches in the butt), the crooked and short sticks (say, under sixteen feet length), and other kinds than White pine (as, e. g., "Norway," "pitch," "jack," or "bull" pine)—were left standing or fallen, together with the greater part, sometimes all, of the hemlock, spruce, fir, cedar, tamarack, and any scattered bodies of hardwood. So also the slashings (approximately one-half of the total mass of material in each tree) were left on the ground. So soon as these loppings were suffici-

---

[2] The time allowed for stripping any such given tract and "getting out" its first-class timber would commonly be limited to the number of years which the laws of the state allowed delinquent taxes to run before title to the land reverted to the state. Hence the need of despatch. This period was commonly long enough for the purpose if no time were wasted; and as a matter of economy it was accordingly not usual to pay taxes on the timber-lands during this interval while the desirable timber was removed. So that much of the timber-lands reverted to the state for delinquent taxes after the stand of timber had been cut or burned.

ently dry—say, in two or three years—they would presently be fired, by accident or design, and the tract would then be burned over, destroying whatever timber had not been taken out.

When account is taken of the frequent spread of these fires into uncut tracts of standing timber, it is probably within the mark to say that something more than one-half of the original stand of timber was lost in these unavoidable fires. This standard routine of American lumbering, including the destruction by fire, did not vary greatly from place to place, and it has held true with little abatement throughout the period. It is doubtless within the mark to say that this enterprise of the lumbermen during the period since the middle of the nineteenth century has destroyed very appreciably more timber than it has utilised,[3] although some practice of economy has come into the business toward the close of the period, and more particularly since the beginning of the present century.[4]

[3] Cf. e. g., U. S. Department of Agriculture, Forest Service-circular 171. "The Forests of the U. S. and their Uses," pp. 9–11.

[4] There has been an increasing endeavour to turn by-products and waste products to account, and more economical methods and appliances have come into use. The latter point is illustrated, e. g., by the gradual introduction of the gang-saw, and presently the band-saw, in place of the circular saw in the sawmills which turn the saw-logs into lumber. The circular saw is an American invention, at least in respect of its larger use and as a standard appliance for reducing saw-logs to lumber. In this larger use, in the use of these circular saws of large diameter, the unavoidable waste of material is larger than the corresponding waste involved in the use of the gang-saw, larger by something more than 100 per cent. But the circular saw is expeditious, and it does not require so extensive or so massive an equipment, at the same time that it and its equipment are more readily portable. And so long as waste of material has little or no commercial value the circular saw is preferred. But it makes sawdust of something like one-fourth to one-third of the lumber-

None of this passionate endeavour of the lumbermen to get rich quick has been wilfully destructive. It is only that as it has been conducted, and as it could not but be conducted according to sound business principles, a destructive waste of the timber supply has been involved in it and a greater waste and destruction has unfailingly followed it up. It is always sound business practice to take any obtainable net gain, at any cost and at any risk to the rest of the community. The Captains of Industry who have been engaged in this enterprise of disemboweling the country's timber resources and who have profited by it have been quite within their rights and within the ethics of business. Not only so; commonly if not invariably their conduct is heartily approved and admired by their fellow citizens, and they have come through the adventure with a greatly augmented self-respect and a very notable conviction of well-doing.

They, the successful ones, have become substantial citizens, bearing all the stigmata of civic substance and merit. And after the pattern of substantial American citizens they have, not unusually, gone on and acquired further merit by devoting some part of their takings to conspicuously humane works. There are towns, not a few, that have been named in reverent memory of these enterprising men, and there are many parks, hospitals, museums, libraries, fountains, school and town edifices, and other municipal works, in many towns and cities in these states, which bear their name and carry forward the memory of their munificence. Indeed, so highly do their fellow citizens esteem their meritorious work in so having disembowelled the country's timber resources, that

content of a saw-log, whereas the gang-saw's or the band-saw's allowance for sawdust will be perhaps one-tenth to one-fourth of the lumber-content.

they have not uncommonly been called by popular vote to take over the business of governing the country whose resources they have disembowelled, in legislative and administrative office, in the states and in the Federal Government. There is, broadly speaking, no fault to be found with them or their works, or at least no fault is found, by themselves or by their fellow citizens. Their rating, in the popular esteem and in their own, is reflected by the fact that a very appreciable and honorable number of these men have proved to be substantial and public-spirited enough to find their way into the federal senate, sometimes even at a cash outlay which it might be inconvenient to specify; and here they have honorably "stood pat," embattled in defense of the principles of business-as-usual, and have honorably kept faith with all the vested interests. In short, they run meritoriously true to the American ideal of the self-made man who knows that his work is well done.

In the end, that is to say since the end of the timber resources has very crudely come in sight, a more economical plan of seizure and conversion has gone into effect, more economical and also more conclusive in the matter of seizure and conversion. It became evident some time ago that the timber-lands were by way of becoming valuable holdings for eventual profit. Therefore title to the major part of what was left was presently acquired by interested individuals and corporations, to be held for an eventual rise in the prices of lumber. And the rise in lumber was looked for as due to come so soon as the increasing scarcity of timber and the collusive strategy of these large absentee owners could be effectually brought to bear on the market. And, indeed, the anticipated advance came on with reasonable promptitude, so soon as the major part of the remaining stand of timber had passed securely under the control of these larger absentee owners. And the outcome has been such a schedule of prices as the traffic could be made to bear on this basis of organised collusion. In the end this remnant of the original stand of timber promises to cost the community as much at the hands of these collusive absentee owners as the original stand of timber would have been worth in case it had been managed on a plan of deliberate economy and conservation from the outset. And its value to its absentee owners is measured by its cost to the community, which in turn is measured by what the traffic can be made to bear in the case of a tariff-protected necessity under competent monopoly management.[5]

The Lumber Interest shows the American plan as it has worked out in a moderately large and well defined field. In principle, what has been done with other, larger natural resources does not differ essentially from the case of the timber lands. The details are different, of

[5] There is, of course, no monopoly control of the timber supply, *de jure;* no more than there is such a control *de jure* in anthracite or bituminous coal. The law does not tolerate such control, *de jure.* But the present argument is concerned only with the state of the case *de facto.* And *de facto* it will not be questioned that in the case of the timber supply, as is uniformly to be expected under this American plan of expeditious seizure and conversion to private ownership, the spectacularly wasteful competition among enterprising pioneers has now run its course and has worked out in a system of collusive management in behalf of these larger absentee owners who have acquired title to (virtually) all that is left. Whereby it has come about, as happens uniformly where an effectual monopoly control has taken over the output of one of the necessaries of life, that the competition which once used to run between the lumbermen producing for an open market now runs between this group of absentee owners and the underlying population. So the group of absentee owners of the remaining stand of timber make the terms under due cover of law, which the underlying population will have to take, *de facto,* but which they can leave, *de jure.*

course, inasmuch as these others come into the industrial system each in ways of its own. So far as the peculiar circumstances of each case will permit, these others, too, show the characteristic traits of the American plan,— initial waste and eventual absentee ownership on a large scale and on a quasi-monopolistic footing. And wherever and so far as the course of enterprise has had a chance to work out, the outcome is monotonously the same,—collusive management under absentee control at the cost of the underlying population.

But these larger items of the country's natural resources—as coal, iron, water-power, or transportation lines—are the material of the country's "key industries." They are, therefore, the substance of the country's industrial system, and it would be a bootless undertaking to go into a discussion of them except as organic factors in that balanced system of industrial processes in which they are the major forces engaged. They can only be taken conjointly, and their joint life-history is the life-history of American industry as it has run on since the mechanical technology began to dominate American industry during the latter half of the nineteenth century.

Coal and iron have already reached a passably settled state of collusive management under corporation control on a basis of unqualified absentee ownership. Water-power is still in process of being taken over and converted to absentee gain, helped along covertly and overtly by official and legislative furtherance; no doubt conscientiously so, in the main, since the legislators as well as the administrative and judiciary officials are commonly men with a sound business-man's bias; men whose best knowledge and belief runs to the effect that such gainful absentee enterprise at any cost to the underlying population is "good for business"; that the common good turns on the unremitting acceleration of absentee business traffic; which is conditioned on increasing net gains for the interested parties. And the costless transfer of these necessaries of life to these absentee owners is an obvious means of increasing their net gains; thereby provoking them to do business with the underlying population; which is the good end to which in the nature of things a businesslike administration should bend its energies.

So the country's water-power is unobtrusively passing into the hands of duly constituted vested interests, to be turned to account for the benefit of duly accredited absentee owners, all in due accord with the American Plan. So also the transportation system is still in process, but in an advanced stage of the process, of approach to that settled state of vested interest which confers an inalienable right to a flow of free income computed on an immutably inflated capitalisation. The railways, e. g., should not have much farther to go along that road. What chiefly remains to be done would seem to be that which the authorities already have in hand,—to make the taxpayers chargeable for suitable earnings on the railway corporations' capitalisation, as a fixed overhead charge on the cost of living, without apology or afterthought. So that matter will have been arranged.[6]

[6] Such a course falls in with the temper of a Business Administration, at the same time that it is wholly consonant with that popular sentiment that is animated with business principles. Any sound business concern is capitalised on that rate of net gain which it has been found that the traffic will bear; and in effect it is held, in law and custom, that any reputably large business concern duly capitalised on this basis, and of some years' standing, is duly entitled, has a vested right, to a net income in perpetuity answering to this capitalisation so arrived at. Therefore, when earnings fall off—due, perhaps, to businesslike incapacity—it should be the part of economy and clean management to cut out meaningless intermediate steps in the process of getting these legitimate gains out of the underlying popula-

In coal, iron, and transportation the conversion of public necessities into private assets has already reached a passably settled and conclusive state, so that these means of production are now securely held in absentee ownership and managed on the sound business principle of charging what the traffic will bear. Their use is regulated on the steady presumption of rendering no greater service than that minimum which will yield a satisfactory net gain to their absentee owners. That is to say, as regards these natural resources their employment has been brought to a basis of "sound business," so that the abiding care of the businesslike management is to avoid an excessive output. An excessive output in this connection means such a full and sustained employment of plant and man-power as would overstock the market and lower profits. Hence a watchful curtailment of output, unemployment, and sabotage.[7]

ion, by making the suitable rate of net gains for this business a fixed overhead charge upon the underlying population in the shape of a tax. There is no use of having taxpayers if they are not to be made use of in such an emergency.

[7] This is by no means intended to say that this running sabotage on production and output constitutes the whole duty of the corporate management which takes care of the interests of the absentee owners of these natural resources. There are also always the many and various cares of corporation finance, and there is the running administrative routine of "hiring and firing" the working personnel with a view to lower costs, and this duty is forever complicated with "labor troubles" that arise out of refractory human nature. But sabotage, in that inoffensive sense in which the word is used here, remains after all the first and unremitting duty incumbent on these executives, in so far as their business is conducted on the sound principles of net gain in terms of price, as is commonly the case. And this sabotage, graduated un-employment, and parsimonious hiring and firing, entails "labor troubles," in the nature of things. On this head the situation in coal since the Armistice is typical rather than exceptional. So also in steel. So persistent, or rather chronic, have been the labor troubles in these industries

On the other hand Oil, that is to say the business in crude oil, is still in an immature phase of its development, resembling the earlier lumbering enterprise, and marked by a headlong competitive rush to disembowel the available resources expeditiously and at any cost. In the course of nature the older oil-fields have passed this stage *of development and have duly come to rest secure and orderly under the absentee ownership and absentee management of economically regular corporations, of the large and stable type which is known colloquially as Big Business. So also is very much of the business of refining, transporting and marketing the output. These things have already come in under the head of business-as-usual and are managed discretely by collusion and coercion on the principle of what the traffic will bear; that is to say, these lines of business run on a settled plan of competition between the absentee owners and the underlying population, according to which the absentee management makes the terms for the underlying population on the principle of what the traffic will bear. As business concerns these corporate interests have already become enterprises in salesmanship simply, and conduct their affairs quite in conformity with the later approved canons of salesmanship, as touches both their outstanding securities and their marketable products and services.[8]

There still is much pioneering enterprise in the

during these years while the necessary sabotage on production has run high, that the management have found it necessary to call in the help of many "under-cover-men" and armed guards as well as the armed forces at the disposal of the local and state authorities. The authorities so called in have even found it necessary transiently to resort to "martial law." The salutary modicum of sabotage on production is no light care.—Cf., e. g., *Public Opinion and the Steel Strike,* ch. i; also *Report on the Steel Strike of 1919,* especially ch. vii.

[8] Cf. Joseph E. Pogue, *Economics of Petroleum,* ch. i.

production of the crude oil, designed to get rich quick on a moderate outlay. Many "independent" concerns are engaged in this enterprise, a number of which—perhaps the greater number—are unrecognised subsidiaries of the large absentee corporations which handle the refined. The affiliations of these "independent" oil concerns are surrounded with much painstaking obscurity. For such of them as are in any degree independent in fact, the manœuvres of the greater corporations are conditioning circumstances to be guessed at and taken account of. The great corporations stand as massive impersonal vested interests which move obscurely in the background of the market and make the terms on which business may be transacted; and it is for the "independents" to make their peace with them on such terms as may be had. Having come to terms with the master corporations, the enterprising knights of trover and conversion who are "developing" the newer fields go about their business of disemboweling the country's oil resources in all haste and without afterthought.[9]

The greater number of these "independent" concerns are scantily equipped for the work; although the total expenditure on equipment and work in the field greatly exceeds what would be required to produce the crude oil on any reasonably economical plan. They are also commonly under-manned, in the sense that the working personnel in the field includes too small a proportion of suitably skilled and experienced workmen and too scant a staff of technical experts; too scant, that is, for economical working. Also they are commonly ill prepared for contingencies, whether of a financial or a mechanical

[9] Cf. Pogue, *Economics of Petroleum,* chapters i, ii, iv and xv.

nature; partly because they commonly do not have the benefit of competent technical advice and experience; partly because much of this enterprise still carries the mark of "wild-cat" and still does business in a hurry on a chance and a "shoe-string"; and partly also because unfavorable contingencies are not infrequently arranged for them as a matter of business strategy in behalf of the vested interests that move in the background. And quite as a matter of routine there is a notorious initial waste of the output (both oil and gas) when a well is brought in. This waste commonly goes on for some time at a high percentage, and the waste of gas will often run on nearly unchecked through the life of the well, for want of storage capacity, pipe-line connections, etc.

Much of this enterprise is of the nature of a competitive duplication of work and equipment. The independent producers, many of whom are corporations of some standing, are competitive leaseholders of plots of ground bounded by survey lines, lines of ownership, not by the natural boundaries of the "pools" which they are engaged in exhausting. These leased plots of ground touch one another along the geometrical lines of the survey. So, under the spur of businesslike initiative the leaseholders each and several bend their efforts to get the better of one another by cutting in on one another's oil-contents underground along these dividing lines. All and several sink many wells rapidly on these competing plots of ground, taking care to crowd many new wells up against the dividing lines and into the corners of their leaseholds, to draw off underground what it would be larceny to take over after it reaches the surface; until the resulting number of wells (and "dry holes") sunk in any given neighbourhood is several times as many, at several

times the cost that would be needed to get out the underlying oil on any reasonable plan.[10]

This clamorous waste and manhandling of the oil
resources runs on quite as a matter of business routine,
and the recital of any part of the story here may well
seem a piece of aimless tedium. It runs on in this fashion
from the outset, but it is plain that the enterprise is in
all cases due to head up eventually in a collective control
of the output by large absentee owners. The older fields
show what is to be expected in that respect and how it is
likely to be done. The waste which this pioneering enterprise in oil involves, and the excessive cost of it, will not
run to so high a percentage of the output as in the case of
the gold production (some 500 per cent. for the Alaskan
gold), but counted in absolute figures the total of wasteful
costs and wasted output entailed by private initiative in
the production of oil is doubtless larger than the corresponding total for gold.

The whole of this routine of waste and inefficiency is
a matter of course under the American plan of seizure
and conversion; and it is at least a blameless exercise of
private initiative, commonly regarded as a meritorious

[10] Any detail map of such an oil-field will show this duplication of wells as one of its striking features. Wherever four
leaseholds meet, e. g., one expects to find four (or more) competing wells, sunk in all haste, crowded into the four corners
as near as the dimensions of the machinery or of the law will
permit, in a race to encroach on one another's oil-contents and
draw off the oil which one well would handle with less waste.
Such duplication of wells is also enforceable at law, as certain
recent court-decisions have established. A leaseholder who fails
to crowd in quickly into a competing corner of his leasehold is
liable to damages at the suit of the lessor.

Cf., e. g., C. G. Gilbert and J. E. Pogue, *Petroleum—A Re-
source Interpretation* (Bulletin 102, part 6, U. S. National
Museum, 1918,) ; see also J. E. Pogue, *Economics of Petroleum*
(New York, 1921), pp. 31–46, and map on p. 33.

work. It is, in effect, no more than an exemplary working-out of the American citizen's dearest constitutional rights, and there is no fault to be found with it all on any score of irregularity. In its time and under the given conditions of law and custom it is sound business enterprise; just as the Big Business and monopoly control in which it invariably heads up is also sound business. It is all in the day's work. It has seemed necessary here to recall these workday incidents of business-as-usual in oil, just because they show a concrete and exemplary working-out of absentee ownership as it affects the country's natural resources.

PART II

CHAPTER VIII

THE NEW ORDER OF BUSINESS

WHAT has just been described, or sketched, hastily in these brief chapters on the progress of industrial America in the nineteenth century has evidently been a process of continued growth, a cumulative sequence of complex changes. And the new order of things which now faces the Americans is an outgrowth of a period of unexampled changes. So there has arisen a situation which foots up to a new order of things; although the new order carries over much of the old order out of which it has arisen. The changes that have been going forward have taken effect primarily and most profoundly in the material circumstances which condition the life and work of this people. The material conditions, the ways and means of living and of procuring a livelihood, have been altered in a very substantial degree. At the same time these material and technical changes have also put a strain on the received canons of knowledge and belief and on the established order of law and custom; although the strain to which they have been subjected has not yet brought on any substantial measure of change in these principles of use and merit that govern belief and conduct.

The changes that have been going forward have not affected all parts of the scheme of life in anything like the same measure. The drive of change has not been the same, and the rate of change has therefore not been the same throughout. The driving forces of change have taken direct effect in the industrial arts, and have touched matters of law and custom only at the second remove. Habits of thought have therefore not been displaced and shifted forward to a new footing in law and morals in anything like the same measure in which men have learned to use new ways and means in industry. The principles (habits of thought) which govern knowledge and belief, law and morals, have accordingly lagged behind, as contrasted with the forward drive in industry and in the resulting workday conditions of living.

As is always the case, in the nature of things, so in this case, too, the changes that have taken effect in the material circumstances are the creative factors which have gone into action, as a driving force and a controlling agency, and have set afoot a new line of habituation. And as is always the case, in the nature of things, the new pattern of knowledge and the new elements of belief and conviction which these new habits of workday living are pushing forward are finding acceptance and endorsement only tardily and by way of reluctant concession to the *force majeure* of continued and rigorous habituation. In point of time, these adaptations of knowledge and belief come after the fact. And any departure from ancient precedent in law and morals will come into effect still more tardily, still farther in arrears. So much so that opinionated persons are quite able to believe that no substantial change need take place or can take place in that range of habitual "action patterns" in which law and morals are grounded, at least not in America. Indeed, it is something of a boast among Americans of the stricter observance that American law and custom have suffered no change, in principle, since the date of the Federal Constitution. In principle, that is to say in respect of its underlying habits of thought, the working system of American law and custom is held to be the finished product of a process of growth which came to a ripe conclusion some 150 years ago. This rigorously retrospective position is formally binding on the judiciary and the legal profession. It overlooks the service rendered by legal fiction and constructive precedents, of course; but there is after all a modicum of truth in the contention,—so much as will enable the judiciary and the legal profession to rest their arguments on it, *pro forma*.

It results that in so far as the new order of things departs from the old it has not the countenance of law and custom, except by way of legal fiction. Or to turn the proposition about, in so far as the new order of things departs from the old, the American system of law and order as embodied in the Federal constitution is out-of-date, except by way of legal fiction. The Federal constitution was framed by the elder statesmen of the eighteenth century; whereas the new industrial order of things is created by the technicians of the twentieth century. There is accordingly a discrepancy between the run of material facts in the present and the canons of law and order as stabilised in the eighteenth century. In the same fashion, though in a less formal conflict, the traditional system of knowledge and belief also is holding out against the pressure brought by the revolution in industry. Such is necessarily the case with any stable system of usages and beliefs and with any established order of law and custom; and it holds true with particular cogency in this American case, where the rate and volume of change in the material conditions of life during this interval have been large and swift beyond example.

The established system of knowledge and belief, law and order, came out of the remoter past that lies back of the period of its own stabilisation, and it embodies the habits of thought and the frame of mind that were engendered in still earlier generations by habituation and precedent in the course of that past experience. In this sense, then, it is necessarily out-of-date by so much as the material circumstances which condition the present have departed from those past conditions to which it owes its rise and fixation; and, indeed, by so much more as the working scheme of knowledge and belief, law and order, in that past time carried forward and perpetuated habits of thought, preconceptions, principles, that are of still older date.

The new order of things has arisen out of the past by a change in degree carried so far as to result in an effectual change in kind. In the American case this change in the material conditions of life has gone so far as to amount to a break with the past; while the system of legal and customary rights, powers, immunities, and privileges stands over on the base given it by the elder statesmen of the past, except for legal fiction.

The changes which have made this break with the past and have set up this discrepancy between the current conditions of life and the received rules which govern the conduct of life,—these changes have been, primarily and immediately, changes in the material circumstances of the case, due to a progressive change in the state of the industrial arts and to a continued growth of population. And in both of these respects the rate and volume of change have been large, beyond example. And this altered state of their material circumstances has not yet had time to affect the spiritual animus, the frame of mind, of the American community, at all seriously or substantially; nor has it all at all seriously affected their outlook on things even in those matters of knowledge and belief that have to do directly with the industrial arts and the material welfare of the community.[1]

It is true, business enterprise and business methods have undergone some measure of reorganization, designed to get the benefit of the new opportunities offered by the new scale of work that has been brought into action by the continued advance of the industrial arts. So that business has been conducted on a larger scale and at a swifter pace, and with a wider sweep of credit relations— all due in great part to improved mechanical facilities; but the spirit in which American business is conducted, as well as the law and custom which formally govern its powers and procedure, are still the same spirit and the same principles of law and morals that have long been familiar to the horse-trading farmer and the collusive retailers of the country towns.[2]

The material circumstances which underlie and enable the new order, which supply its working forces and limit its powers, are the state of the industrial arts and the man-power of the underlying population; and these forces have come up into their present state by an irrepressible

[1] The country town has apparently been the chief agency by which this stable and peevish quietism of American knowledge and belief has been kept in repair, as indicated in an earlier passage.

[2] Of course, what so is said of a new order of things will apply only *de facto,* not *de jure.* Indeed, that is the point in argument. *De jure,* of course, the current state of things in the American industrial world differs in no degree from the situation of a hundred years ago. And the difficulties and perplexities, and animosities, that have lately been coming to a head under this new industrial order have arisen out of the growing divergence between the state of things *de jure* and the state of things *de facto.* It is, perhaps, necessary to add that *"de facto"* is here used not in the sense of a convenient prevarication, as in latterday diplomatic usage, but rather as designating the material circumstances of the case.

growth, and they are still engaged in a sweeping advance which is pushing them farther and farther from their point of departure. But the control of these industrial powers, and the decision as to what, when, and how much work shall be done by them, is vested in the absentee owners of the country's resources. And these owners and their business agents go into this work of directing and restraining the work in hand with such powers and preconceptions as have been conferred on them according to a scheme of law and custom that was worked out and stabilised in an alien past for purposes that are alien to this latterday state of the industrial arts and out of touch with the latterday state of population. The New Order, therefore, is by way of being a misfit. It is an organisation of new ways and means in the way of industrial processes and man-power, subject to irresponsible control at the hands of a superannuated general staff of business men moving along lines of an old-fashioned strategy toward obsolete ends.[3]

This new order of things in American business and industry may be said to have arisen so soon as a working majority of the country's industrial resources, including the transportation system, had been brought securely under absentee ownership on a sufficiently large scale, in

[3] It is not intended to cast aspersions on this general staff of business men who so administer the country's industrial affairs for the benefit of its absentee owners. They are superannuated, not in point of physical senility but only in point of their aims and methods, bias and preconceptions. By interest, training, and perhaps by native gift, they are holdovers out of a past order of conceptions, which cannot be defined in terms of the later industrial processes or in terms of the man-power engaged. They are responsible men, of course, but their responsibility runs in such terms and to such effect that it has no meaning within the system of the latter-day technology.

sufficiently large holdings, to make these national resources and the industries which make use of them amenable to concerted surveillance and control by the vested interests that represent these larger absentee owners. Of course, there is no sharply drawn date-line to mark the beginning of this new dispensation; *de jure* it does not exist. But the *de facto* rise of the new order may be conveniently dated from about the turn of the century. Loosely speaking, that large-scale control of the industrial forces which has made the outcome, dates back to the ten or twelve years overlapping the end of the century. The "era of trust-making," sometimes so called, that ran for some years from, say, 1897 onward, was concerned in this transition to a new footing in American business.

This appears to make the New Order a new order of business. And so it is, in the sense that the New Order is an order of things in which business considerations are paramount. Its distinctive characteristic on this head being that it is an order of things in which Big Business is paramount. But Big Business still is business of the old familiar kind, with the old familiar aims to be worked out in the old familiar spirit.

Big Business is paramount in the New Order. But all the while the conditioning circumstances which underlie this new order of business enterprise are circumstances of a material, tangible, mechanical, technical nature, ways and means of doing tangible work, not merely new and improved ways and means of doing business. Business has to do with the intangibles of ownership, and only indirectly with the tangible facts of workmanship. Under the new dispensation as under any other, the whole duty of business enterprise is to come in for as large and secure a net gain as may be, to acquire title, to "make money," and therefore to turn all tangible means and performances to account for this intangible but paramount purpose of acquiring title. The new expedients that have been brought into action in the conduct of business are contrivances and expedients designed to serve this intangible end; new ways and means of responding to the call of those new opportunities for gain that arise out of tangible changes in the industrial system,—for it is out of the tangible performance of this industrial system that the gains of ownership are drawn and it is to these tangibles of industrial work and products that title is to be acquired. And the tangible changes affecting the industrial system have been going forward as an unremitting proliferation, a continuous advance in the scale and articulation of the industrial process at large.

No new order of business and industry has sprung up suddenly and complete at any given date, even though a visible change has taken effect within a reasonably short time. It is only that somewhere about the turn of the century a critical point was reached and passed, without much visible change of circumstances at the time. The new system, in business and in industry, has in fact been maturing into its present working shape through some twenty years past. And it is still feasible for legally-minded persons to believe that no substantial change has taken effect for a longer period than that. Nor will it do to say that this new growth has now run its course to a finality; although it should perhaps not come as a surprise if the present phase of it turns out to mark something like a station in the course of events, possibly even something of a new point of departure. Certain indications that the present situation may constitute such a critical phase, and may mark a new departure, will be brought into the argument in a later passage and in another connection.

The critical pass, the point at which the New Order may be said to have set in, was reached and passed so soon as a working majority of the country's industrial resources had been brought under absentee ownership on a sufficiently large scale for collusive management. But this is not intended to say that at that period anything like a statistical majority of the natural resources had been taken over into large holdings; but only that, loosely about that period, an effectual working majority of those natural resources and industrial plants which are immediately engaged in the so-called "key industries" had already passed into absentee ownership on so large a scale as to enable an effectual collusive control of these things by the vested interests concerned, such a degree of control as to make a reasonably concerted check on production in these key industries a manageable undertaking.[4]

In effect, whether by intention or not, the country's industrial system as a working whole, as an industrial going concern, was thereby brought under control and became subject to a varying degree of sabotage at the hands of the vested interests in these key industries.

[4] Effectual concert of action in this bearing does not involve anything like a formal collusive arrangement, such as would constitute a "conspiracy in restraint of trade" in the opinion of the courts. E. g., even now slightly more than one-half of the steel production of the country is in the hands of "independent" concerns which have no corporate connection with the Steel Corporation; at least no such relation is visible to the courts or avowed by the corporation executives. Yet it is a fact accepted as a matter of course and of common notoriety that the policy pursued by the Steel Corporation, e. g., in its "labor management" and its campaign for the "open shop," will in the nature of things govern the conduct of the Independents in the same connection.—Cf. *Report on the Steel Strike of 1919*, by the Commission of the Interchurch World Movement (New York, 1920), where this state of the case is very much in evidence throughout the findings of the Commission.

That is what is meant by calling them "key industries." The business concerns that have to do with other branches of production and trade necessarily wait on the movement of things in these key industries. That is also a matter of course and of common notoriety. Not that the businesslike management of one and another of these key industries will aim to administer sabotage to any or all of the underlying and outlying members of the industrial system. That is not the intention; it is only the effect. Indeed, in so curtailing employment and output in the underlying and outlying industries by curtailing the output in the key industries the business management of these latter unintentionally curtail the fund of wealth from which the owners of the key industries are to draw their run of free income. So that it is, in effect, at a sacrifice of the long run of gain that the management of the key industries "grabs off" an enhanced rate of earnings for the time being, by curtailing its output and advancing its price schedule. But then, business enterprise, particularly American business enterprise, habitually looks to the short run. And there are reasons why Big Business in particular should conduct its operations with a view to the short-time returns.[5]

The working schedule throughout the rest of the industrial system is conditioned from day to day on the rate, volume, and balance of work and output in these key industries; inasmuch as the secondary, underlying and outlying branches of the system are, in effect, engaged on what may be called continuation work, which draws unremittingly on the output of the key industries for power, raw materials, transportation, and mechanical equipment,

[5] Cf., "On the Nature of Capital," second paper, reprinted in *The Place of Science*, pp. 352–386, especially pp. 373–386.

and which presently will unavoidably halt when the flow of these indispensable ways and means of production is clogged by obstructive manœuvres and curtailment in the key industries. So also, the habitual and deliberate failure of the key industries, for business reasons, to run at their full productive capacity acts, in effect, to set the pace, to adjust the rate and volume of employment and output throughout the rest of the industrial system at a lower average than would otherwise be the rule. Any degree of concerted control over these natural resources, as it takes effect in the curtailment or speeding-up of these main industries that so lie at the tactical center of the system, will effectually govern the movements of the country's industrial system at large, as a comprehensive going concern.

And this control, and the running balance of sabotage which is its chief method of control and its chief material consequence, all takes effect in an impersonal and dispassionate way, as a matter of business routine. Absentee ownership and absentee management on this grand scale is immune from neighborly personalities and from sentimental considerations and scruples.[6]

It takes effect through the colorless and impersonal channels of corporation management, at the hands of businesslike officials whose discretion and responsibility extend no farther than the procuring of a reasonably large— that is to say the largest obtainable—net gain in terms of price. The absentee owners are removed out of all touch with the working personnel or with the industrial work

[6] Cf., e. g., Testimony of E. H. Gary before the Senate Commission to investigate the Steel Strike of 1919–1920, vol. I; and *Report on the Steel Strike of 1919* by The Interchurch World Movement (New York, 1920), throughout, and especially sections II ("Ignorance") and V ("Grievances and Control").

in hand, except such remote, neutral and dispassionate contact by proxy as may be implied in the continued receipt of a free income; and very much the same is true for the business agents of the absentee owners, the investment-bankers and the staff of responsible corporation officials. Their relation to what is going on, and to the man-power by use of which it is going on, is a fiscal relation. As industry, as a process of workmanship and a production of the means of life, the work in hand has no meaning for the absentee owners sitting in the fiscal background of these vested interests. Personalities and tangible consequences are eliminated and the business of governing the rate and volume of the output goes forward in terms of funds, prices, and percentages.

But all the while the work in hand goes forward in terms of mechanical power, fuel, raw materials, mechanical equipment, chemical processes, man-power, and technical design and surveillance,—matters hidden, perhaps mercifully, from the absentee owners who come in for that free income on which the strategy of these vested interests converges. Thereby the absentee owners as well as their absentee business managers are spared many distasteful experiences, saved from reflecting on many dreary trivialities of life and death,—trivialities on the balance sheet of assets and liabilities, although their material counterfoil in terms of life and death among the underlying population may be grave enough to those on whom their impact falls. But the absentee owners and their business agents are also by the same screen of absentee immunity barred out from knowing what to do, or from doing anything at all to the purpose in case of need, in case these trivialities of life and death head up in a tangle of discord and mutiny such as to jeopardise the orderly run of their free income, after the fashion which is now becoming familiar to all men.[7]

The strategy of business—the strategy of getting a larger net gain in dollars—dictates what is to be done or left undone; and having so dictated, it moves on to the next thing in the same line. There is no place in Big Business for considerations of a more material sort or of a more sentimental sort than net gain within the law. It moves on that particular plane of make-believe on which the net gain in money-values is a more convincing reality than productive work or human livelihood. Neither the tenuous things of the human spirit nor the gross material needs of human life can come in contact with this business enterprise in such a way as to deflect its course from the line of least resistance, which is the line of greatest present gain within the law.

This line of least resistance and greatest present gain runs in the main by way of a vigilant sabotage on production. So true is this and so impassively binding is this duty of businesslike sabotage, that even in a crisis of unexampled privation, such as these years since the War, the captains of Big Business have been unable to break away and let the forces of production take their course; and this in spite of their being notably humane persons, imbued with the most benevolent sentiments. With an eye single to the net gain, business strategy still continues

---

[7] "The conditions described have caused me deep concern. The first intimation months ago that such a situation existed . . . led me to institute prompt inquiry, with the hope that any just grounds for criticism might be removed forthwith. That these efforts, long since under way and still in progress, have not been more quickly effective has been and is a disappointment."—Cf. also *The Epistles of Saint John of the Standard to the Holy Brotherhood of the Long Bow. Passim.*

impartially to dictate a conscientious withdrawal of efficiency.[8]

The state of things brought on by the War and perpetuated by the businesslike Peace which has followed after, is complicated enough in detail; but the outline of things so far as regards the main circumstances which govern business and industry is not especially obscure. When relieved of those personalities and moralities that commonly cloud the argument, the case will stand somewhat as follows. There is a very large inflation of credits, both in the set form of loan credits and in fiduciary currency, in all the civilised nations. The inflation in America, taking one thing with another, may perhaps be rated at something like 100 per cent., rather over than under.[9] Hence money-values have advanced, resulting

---

[8] Here as in other passages of this argument "Sabotage" is taken to mean "A Conscientious Withdrawal of Efficiency," with whatever tactics of artifice and effrontery may be required to give it effect. The phrase is said to have originated among the I. W. W.; but it is no less convenient for use in the present connection. Like aims call for like procedure.

It will be said, of course, as it has been said, that this comfortless and perplexing situation of the immediate present has been precipitated by the War, and that the difficulties and distress involved in this present state of things are the difficulties of recovery from the devastation and disorganization incident to the War. But it is by no means certain that very much the same state of things would not have come on anyway, before long, as the rightful outgrowth of that run of forces that have been at work in business and industry during these past two decades, while the New Order has been coming into its own, and that the fatalities of the War have only brought it all to a head more sharply and perhaps more speedily than might otherwise have happened. The situation is a complicated one, and further analysis may reach a different result.

[9] This is at present (1923) over the official figure, so far as official figures have been given out. Indeed, inflation has been denied for America, apparently in good faith. The dollar is still claimed to be at par and redeemable. It is needless to ques-

in an effectual recapitalisation of American business concerns, their assets and their presumptive earnings.[10]   At the same time the aggregate wealth of the country, as counted by weight and tale and use-value, has fallen off greatly, as has also the man-power available for productive work.   Hence there has arisen a discrepancy between the country's material wealth and the business community's capitalised wealth, which may in a manner of speak-

tion the fact here.   The dollar may be redeemable in some sense *de jure; de facto* the depreciation is effective.   Official statistics of prices make it something like 60 or 70 per cent. over the level of 1914; the effectual inflation still seems to run appreciably over the official figures.

Under the exacting surveillance of the Federal Reserve, the banking community have hitherto exercised a very salutary collusive control of credits, which has upheld the effectual inflation and so prevented any precipitate liquidation.   They have indeed effected a slow and temperate retrenchment of credits, which may conceivably have gone far enough to offset the continued shrinkage of assets that has run along at the same time, due to idleness, consumption and wear and tear.   Nor, conceivably, need America experience a period of acute liquidation so long as the effectual bankruptcy of virtually all civilised Europe does not pass from *de facto* to *de jure;* provided always that the Federal Reserve continues to administer the American credit situation with a firm hand, and provided also that the nation's Business Administration does not live up to its election promises in the way of businesslike legislation.   It may yet be within the power of the American banking community and the Federal Reserve to postpone the formal bankruptcy of Europe indefinitely, if European statecraft can be brought to substitute common sense for politics in any sensible degree.   All this appears to be known to those who control the American credit situation and to be acted on by them.

[10] The capital value of a business concern at any given time, its purchase value as a going concern, is measured by the capitalised value of its presumptive earnings; which is a question of its presumptive net earning-capacity and of the rate or coefficient of capitalisation currently accepted at the time; and the second of these two factors is intimately related to the rate of discount ruling at the time.

ing be called a divergence between the country's wealth *de facto* and its wealth *de jure;* between the country's wealth in hand considered as a business proposition (which has increased) and its material wealth considered as a proposition in livelihood (which has decreased). The country is richer in money-values and poorer in use-values.

But capitalisation and earnings are a business proposition; livelihood is not. And in any civilised country, like America, business controls industry; which means that production must wait on earnings. Under these circumstances it is, as a matter of common honesty, incumbent on the business men in charge to keep this—in a sense fictitious—capitalisation intact, and to make it good by bringing current earnings up to the mark. And they have been endeavoring to do this by curtailing employment and output to such a point that the resulting smaller volume of output at the resulting increased price per unit will yield the requisite increased total price-return. Among the expedients by which it is sought to save the capitalisation intact is a concerted effort to reduce wages.[11]

---

[11] It will be noted that all this businesslike strategy falls properly under the head of sabotage. It is, in effect, a traffic in privation, of course. It is also business-as-usual. No fault need be found with it, since there is no help for it. It is not a matter of personal preference or moral obliquity. It is not that these captains of Big Business whose duty it is to administer this salutary modicum of sabotage on production are naughty. It is not that they aim to shorten human life or augment human discomfort by contriving an increase of privation among their fellow men. Indeed, it is to be presumed that they are as humane as they profess. But only by shortening the supply of things needed and so increasing privation to a critical point can they sufficiently increase their (nominal) earnings, and so come off with a clear conscience and justify the trust which their absentee owners have reposed in them. They are caught in the net of

It is evident that in its main lines this precarious situation that has been precipitated by the War, and the Peace, does not differ notably, unless in degree, from the orderly run of business and industry during the times of peace immediately preceding the War. The drift of things in that time set visibly in the direction of such an outcome as the War has brought to a head. Then as since then over-capitalisation was the rule;[12] as a standard practice

business-as-usual, under circumstances which dictate a conscientious withdrawal of efficiency. The question is not whether this traffic in privation is humane, but whether it is sound business management; which reduces itself to a question of whether the underlying population will put up with a sufficient degree of privation for a sufficiently long time. And the underlying population of this country is notoriously tolerant as regards all those things that are done in the name of business.

[12] "Over-capitalisation" is here used for brevity only, and in a particular technical sense, applicable in this connection and not necessarily serviceable for general use. It is intended to cover the well-known fact that in current practice business capital, the capital value of any successful business concern, has habitually and increasingly exceeded the value of the material wealth which underlies it. The fact is perhaps most obvious in the case of corporate capitalisation, but it is scarcely less true for going concerns which are not incorporated. In other words, the total capitalised assets of the country's business concerns have habitually, and increasingly, exceeded their total tangible assets.

Of course there is nothing reprehensible in this business practice. It is a matter of sound business routine. Such "over-capitalisation" is one of the ordinary consequences, as it is also an evidence, of good management; being in great part a capitalisation of "good-will," so called. But it involves two consequences that are worth noting in this connection:—it results that (a) the total wealth of the country counted as assets, funded capital values, is very appreciably larger than the same total when counted as itemised material wealth in hand; and (b) these assets on which the earnings of business are to be computed are notably larger than the holdings of materially productive goods employed. Which brings up the paradox that the ordinary net earnings of business must exceed the ordinary net product of industry from which alone these net earnings are to

there has been more or less of a running sabotage on production, that is to say more or less unemployment of equipment and man-power; there has been intermittent and, on the whole, increasing discord and distrust between the workmen in the larger industries and their corporate employers, rising with increasing frequency into hostilities in the way of strikes and lockouts, while there has also been a rapidly increasing use of strike-breakers, labor spies ("under-cover men"), armed guards, hired "deputies," state police and other armed forces, to keep the peace, uphold the rights of property and make good the absentee owners' claim to a reasonable net gain. By and large, the system of civilised business and industry appears to have been moving forward as a whole and in an orderly fashion toward some such state of balanced inaction and suspended hostilities as that which has been precipitated by the War.

At first sight this view seems to be sound, but a closer scrutiny may leave it in doubt. On the face of things, it looks as if the business community which controls the country's industrial forces had for some time past been engaged in a concerted movement of cumulative over-capitalisation and sabotage; while the industrial man-power has been increasingly and systematically falling

be drawn. Which gives added precision to the statement that business management is businesslike and capable only in so far as it gets something for nothing.

The case of the American farm population, too, comes in for sharper definition in the light of this paradox. The assets of the going concerns in business yield earnings in excess, as a reward of sound business management. On the other hand, as is known to statisticians, the assets of the farmers yield, on an average, next to no earnings, perhaps none. The ordinary income of the average farm where the equipment is owned by the cultivator will foot up to scant wages for the labor expended by the farmer and his household.

into an attitude of cross-purposes and ill-will. There is scarcely a question about the intractable attitude of the industrial man-power, and the steadily rising pitch and sweep of it. Nor is there a tenable doubt as regards the increasing resort to over-capitalisation and sabotage on the part of the business community. But there is at least a reasonable doubt as to how far the business managers have been moving in concert in this matter. Their dutiful denials have, of course, no significance except as a ground of suspicion. But the circumstantial evidence in the case is not convincing.

The War, and the businesslike Peace, have brought the economic system as a whole to a state of balanced inaction by a general and uniform check, which gives the resulting situation of sabotage on employment and output the appearance of concerted action on a deliberate and comprehensive plan. But there is no good evidence of widely concerted inaction in that businesslike sabotage that prevailed in the pre-war period. And there is at least a reasonable doubt whether the present apparently concerted inaction, after the War, is the outcome of deliberate choice arrived at in concert by the business community at large acting in collusion. Superficially it has the appearance of conspiracy, of course; and the evidence is perhaps reasonably conclusive that the large employers have been working together the past two years on a common understanding to break down the labor unions, in the well-known campaign for what is called the "open shop." But there is no good evidence of any similarly wide concert of action on their part in earlier years. They have showed no capacity for concerted action on such a scale in the past. Except for the banking community, who are held under passable control of a coercive kind by the great credit establishments at the financial center, acting under the coercive surveillance of the Federal Reserve, the American business community have showed no great aptitude for such intelligent and sustained concert of action as this would imply.

There has in the past, from time to time, been an effectual concert of action within certain groups, among the business concerns which take care of certain industries; as, e. g., in steel, coal, lumber, oil, copper, electrical and building supplies, and in a degree in transportation. But the resulting inaction and curtailment, so far as it has affected the industrial system at large, has been somewhat haphazard. It has had the appearance of being governed by uncoördinated yielding to the pressure of circumstances, tracing back to curtailment of supplies from one or another of the key industries or to measures taken in the centralised credit business. The industrial business concerns at large have commonly appeared to act in severalty, yielding to a common pressure, rather than moving by a common impulse and looking to a shrewdly balanced sabotage on employment and output as a whole. Of course, in ordinary times there is a routine of sabotage, a restriction of output to meet the market, which goes into the day's work of all sizable concerns that do business in productive industry; but all that has been a matter of routine business within each concern; which is something quite different from such a nation-wide campaign of inaction and hostilities as has held up the country's industry since the War.

The question may be put in this way:—Is this post-bellum state of resolute inaction in business and of unemployment and hostilities in industry the rightful outgrowth of the ordinary agencies that have been at work during the past two decades? or is it all a transient derangement of things, due to transient causes extraneous to that system of absentee ownership and finance that makes the New Order of things? And if the latter appears to be the case, if this post-bellum complication of hardships and inaction does not belong in the orderly course of things under the New Order, what should then reasonably be looked for in the calculable future as an outcome of continued growth along the line of the past two decades? What is reasonably to be looked for as the outcome of absentee ownership and control on this large scale as it is working out on the ground of an increasingly large and close-knit industrial-system, and an increasingly large and compact underlying population?

It is a question of human behavior under pressure of changing circumstances with a minimum of change in the formal rules which govern this behavior. Apparently it should involve a question of the degree and direction of change to be looked for in the law and the administrative procedure that touches the conduct of industry and business. Which becomes, in effect, a question of what the courts, the legislatures, and the administrative officials are likely to decide in these premises. There should apparently be small ground for doubt on that head, in the light of what has been taking place. So that the answer to this part of the question may be taken for granted, with a fair degree of confidence.

As has been customary in recent times, so also during the past two decades the courts and legislatures have, on the whole, acted to safeguard and fortify the rights, powers and immunities of absentee ownership whenever there has been occasion, and the administrative officials have acted in the same sense with celerity and effect, to the best of their knowledge and belief; in all of which the constituted authorities have doubtless acted in good faith and have followed out the logic of law and custom that has been bred in them by precept, example and tradition. There need be no apprehension of interference with the course of things from that side, so far as the course of things is dictated by the needs of absentee ownership. It may accordingly be assumed that the case of America as it runs into the calculable future will continue to be ordered on the lines of absentee ownership without much afterthought, governed by business enterprise carried on with an eye single to the largest net gain in terms of price. The law allows it and the court awards it. The changes to be looked for are such changes as are initiated from outside the jurisdiction of law and custom.

There are three somewhat divergent main lines, at least, along which the resulting new growth may move; according as one or another of the country's main business interests comes to dominate the situation, alone or in a combination. (a) The funded power, the control of credit, in the hands of the associated banking-houses and the Federal Reserve, may be able to govern the course of business to such effect as to safeguard the interests of absentee ownership at large, maintain a steadily rising overcapitalisation of absentee assets, and assure an indefinitely continued increase of net gains on investments and credit commitments. The drift just now appears to set in that direction. These agencies may be able to maintain such a balanced and stable progressive expansion of assets and earnings. In any case, the dominant position of this community of "investment-bankers," moving in concert under the steady surveillance of the Federal Reserve, will exercise an influence of this kind and will greatly affect the outcome. (b) At the same time it is conceivable that the vested interests which own and control the main natural resources and the key industries may take the lead, with the support of the banking community. Ownership of these tangible assets that underlie the country's industrial system, the underlying material resources and equipment, will enable these corporate interests to draw together on a concerted plan of common action and set the pace for the country's industry as a whole by limiting output and service to such a rate and volume as will best serve their own collective net gain. In so doing they will be in a position progressively to draw the industrial system as a whole in under their own absentee ownership, without material reservation, at least to the extent of coming in for the effectual usufruct of the whole,— somewhat after the fashion in which the packers, millers, and railways, now enjoy the usufruct of the farming community in the Middle West, but with a stricter authority. In this connection it is to be recalled that there is already a far-reaching identity both of personnel and of corporate interests between the group of corporations who control the key industries on the one side and the banking community on the other, and this coalescence or consolidation of the masters of tangible assets with the masters of credit and solvency is visibly on the increase. So that what should be looked for is quite as likely to be an effectual coalescence and concert of these two powers, the bankers and the key industries, rather than the dominance of either one as against the other. (c) There is also the possibility that the business concerns which control the natural resources and the great industries will continue to act by groups as in the recent past, each group taking measures for itself in what may be called group severalty, and each group of Interests [13] seeking its own immediate advantage by charging what the traffic will bear, at the cost of any other vested interests and of the under-

[13] As, e. g., railways, steel, oil, anthracite coal, bituminous coal, packers, millers.

lying population. In so doing these collusive groups of industrial concerns will necessarily be working more or less at cross purposes, and will thereby carry on a haphazard and fluctuating sabotage on employment and output, after the pattern that had become familiar during the years before the War. Such is the tradition of business enterprise in industry and of that "competitive system" that still lives in American tradition, and there is always the chance that the conservative spirit of the American business may preclude any effectual departure from this familiar plan of mutual distrust and sharp practice. In the background of any such pattern of semidetached group action there is, of course, always the collusive banking community to be counted with; and there remains therefore the question of how far the banking community will tolerate cross purposes between groups of industrial business concerns.

There is also the more obscure question of what the industrial man-power and the underlying population will say to it all, if anything. In strict consistency, of course, under the dispassionate logic of established law and custom, neither the industrial man-power nor the underlying population come into the case except as counters in the computation of what the traffic will bear. Anything like reasoned conduct or articulate behavior on their part will scarcely be looked for in this connection. Yet there remains an uneasy doubt as touches the *de facto* limits of tolerance.

CHAPTER IX

The Industrial System of the New Order

THAT new order of things which has been coming to a head since the close of the century is especially plain to be seen in the conduct of business. Business runs on something of a new footing. But it is a new order of material conditions that has enabled this new dispensation in business to come on and go into action. It runs on an altered state of the industrial arts, coupled with a continual growth of population. And the new dispensation in business has arisen out of the endeavours of the business men to profit by the enlarged opportunities which these altered material conditions have offered them. It has been their work to turn the new industrial situation to account for their own gain while working under rules of the game of business that have come down from the old order.

This has involved a progressive change. It has taken time and experiment as well as the help of legal counsel to discover and work out suitable expedients of business procedure and to get into the habit of them. At the same time the underlying industrial situation has been subject to a continued, cumulative, alteration; an advance in mass and extension, in the scale and range of operations, as well as in the complexity, balance, and precision of details. Therefore the new order of business procedure has gone into action in a progressive and tentative fashion. And for the same reason it has never reached the end of its development; nor, indeed, is there any promise of its reaching anything like a final state of stability and finished growth in the calculable future; for the reason that the state of the industrial arts which underlies it is forever unstable. And just now the industrial arts are in a state of unexampled instability. And the business men who aim to benefit by the use and control of these industrial arts will have to take them as they come, and it is the habitual procedure of these business men that determines what the methods and organization of business will be.

There is little that can be said in the way of confident forecast as touches the future of the industrial arts or as regards any final outcome of this continued advance in technology and in the consequent sweep and scale and articulation of the industrial system; and the business community will have to face these new exigencies as they arise. Yet in one respect, at least, the course of things in the recent past may be taken to indicate the nature of the situation which the business management will have to deal with as time goes on. As it stands now the industrial system is inordinarily productive. Its productive capacity per unit of the factors engaged—the coefficient of productive capacity—has in recent times continually been increasing at a continually accelerated rate, and the situation holds a clear promise of a still more inordinate productive capacity in the course of further time and change. The technicians are forever occupied with contriving new ways and means designed to compass that end.[1]

---

[1] As has been remarked in an earlier passage, "inordinate" is here employed in something of a technical sense, as meaning excessively and unguardedly productive, beyond the ordinary

In so speaking of a "New Order of Things" there is no intention to imply that the new is divided from the old by a catastrophic break of continuity. To use a geologic figure of speech, there has been no faulting of the strata. No sudden thrust has upset the orderly advance of technological knowledge and practice. There has been an orderly cumulative advance which has gone forward without serious interruption and at a constantly increasing rate of advance. It is an instance of cumulative growth, which has now passed a critical point of such a nature as to give rise to a new situation which differs effectually from what went before.

In the case of America this cumulative growth of the industrial arts and of the industrial system has been particularly notable since about the middle of the nineteenth century. Coupled with this advancing industrial situation and conditioned upon it, there has at the same time gone forward a sweeping progressive reorganisation of the business community, which has placed the country's business affairs on a footing of credit and corporate ownership. With the result that toward the close of the century the financial community, who command the country's solvency and dispense the country's credit, found themselves in a position to take over the control and the usufruct of the country's industrial system by taking over the ownership of those strategically dominant members of the indus-

needs of business in ordinary times. That is to say, if the available resources in the way of materials, equipment and man-power were to be employed under competent technical management with a view to maximum production, the output of industry would be greatly in excess of what the traffic will bear, considered as a business proposition. Not that the output would exceed the consumptive capacity of the underlying population, but only that it would be too large to yield the maximum net gain in terms of price to the business concerns of the country. "Inordinate" refers to the needs of business, not to livelihood.

trial system that are known as the "Key Industries." Since then the key industries have been progressively taken over into the absentee ownership of the country's credit institutions, and this absentee ownership has progressively been consolidated and arranged in manageable shape. The arrangement has now been brought to a passable degree of balance and stability, although the work has not been brought to a neatly finished conclusion; nor need it be. Nor is there any present likelihood that this working arrangement will be rounded out into a statistically all-inclusive block of absentee ownership in the hands of a formally consolidated going concern of investment-bankers.

Irrepressible new technological advances are forever running out new ramifications of industry, which are forever requiring further attention at the hands of these captains of ownership. So that the work of taking things over is an endless task, at the same time that something less than universal ownership will serve the purpose quite handsomely. All that is needed for the purpose of an effectual usufruct of the country's work and output is a strategically effectual control of the country's industrial system as a going concern, and that much is now an accomplished fact. The several branches and strata of the industrial system overlap and interlock in such a way as to vest a strategically effectual control of the whole in the hands of those who command the standard natural resources and control the key industries. All that remains needful to be done is to bring the several absentee concerns who control the key industries to a settled and facile footing of collusion, and much has been accomplished along that line these last few years.

In America, as an outcome of the nineteenth century,

the industrial work of the community has fallen into the shape of a three-fold division or stratification of industries which work together in a balanced whole, a moving equilibrium of interlocking processes of production: (a) the primary, initial, or key industries, so called, which command the greater natural resources of the country and turn out the prime staple necessaries of the mechanical industry in the way of power, transportation, fuel, and structural material; (b) the secondary or continuation industries, manufactures, which turn these crude supplies and services into consumable goods and distribute them; (c) agriculture.

This may seem a gratuitous and illogical classification, particularly as regards agriculture. It is quite evident, of course, that agriculture has to do with the greatest and most essential of the country's natural resources, at the same time that it is the indispensable source of supply for a wide and varied range of staple industries. So it is as usual as it is unquestionably proper to class agriculture with the "extractive industries," and not unusual to give it the first place in that class; and there is no fault to be found with that arrangement. The conventional scheme would be: (a) extractive industries; (b) manufactures; (c) distribution. Which would be a sound logical plan and classification of productive industry, in the absence of business considerations.

On the other hand the three-fold division which is spoken for above is drawn in view of those business considerations that are decisive for the conduct of industry here and now. It is not intended to violate or set aside the grouping of industries that has been usual in the theoretical speculation of the economists, but is made only for present convenience. What is aimed at is a convenient definition of the facts for the present argument, which has to do with the relations between business and industry in America in the twentieth century; and the three-fold division spoken for above answers this purpose. Each of these three industrial groups or strata occupies a peculiar place in the industrial system, in respect of ownership and business connections.. There are at the same time no sharp lines of division between the three groups. They overlap, interlock and blend; and each group will show doubtful and marginal cases; but in the large, as component factors in the framework of the industrial system, each group stands out by itself, typically distinct from the rest, particularly in respect of the business considerations by which each is bound or actuated.

At the same time it is also not to be overlooked that these three strata of productive industry are marked by characteristic differences on the technological side, as well as in respect of the business considerations that govern them. They each stand on a somewhat special and distinctive footing in the industrial arts; all the while that they all move within the framework of the modern industrial system and are, each in its degree, dominated by that mechanical industry that gives its distinctive character to the system as a whole and as contrasted with what has gone before. But the three groups or departments of industry do not share alike or in the same degree in that characteristic shift to a mechanical footing that has resulted from the industrial revolution of the past one hundred and fifty years.

As it runs now, the industrial system centers in quantity production of goods and services by use of inanimate energies engaged in mechanical work, or engaged in chemical processes that are of a mechanical nature and effect. Typically, the standard processes of this modern industry engage inanimate forces and materials; or materials and forces which can effectually be applied on a mechanical plan. In this respect the current state of the industrial arts differs notably from its own past as well as from the industrial systems that still prevail among outlying and backward peoples,—backward, that is, in respect of the mechanical technology. In the main and typically, this state of the industrial arts is a technology of physics and chemistry; having to do with inanimate ways and means, and carrying on its most characteristic work by use of inorganic processes and materials.

But all the while it remains true, of course, that this mechanistic state of the industrial arts has come out of a past phase in which workmanship ran on another plan; a past in which the industrial arts were dominated by a different range of conceptions. Through some ninety-nine per cent., at least, of this past period of experience and growth the industrial arts have been, in the main and typically, a technology of animate (human) energies, workmanlike manipulation, and organic processes of fecundity, growth and nurture; and there are many holdovers out of the organic technology of the past that still make up a very substantial part of the industrial system.

Agriculture, e. g., still rests on a body of such old-fashioned holdovers, much of it of unknown antiquity and out of touch with the logic of the mechanical industry. Yet in the main and as contrasted with what has gone before, and allowing for extensive holdovers, the industrial system that engages the civilised nations runs on a technology of physics and chemistry, and its work converges on quantity production of mechanically standardised goods and services. Therefore manufactures are the focus of the industrial system. It is a technology of manufacture, of mechanical standardisation and quantity production; and the same technical principles and procedures are all the while reaching out into the outlying fields of agriculture and back into the other extractive industries that have to do with the primary supply of power, fuel, and raw and structural materials.

As the case now stands the manufacturing industries are able and ready to meet all current needs of the market by the use of the existing equipment and man-power, and the technicians and workmen are ready at any time to extend, amplify and intensify the available equipment and industrial processes to take care of any new growth in the demand for goods. The manufacturing industries, where mechanical power and quantity production rule the case, are inordinately productive, in the sense that they are ready at any time to cover a demand for goods greatly in excess of their ordinary output.

It is one of the features of the current situation that there is always an available slack which can be taken up in case of need, a margin of unemployed equipment and man-power ready to go to work, and a fringe of technical knowledge which has not yet been turned to account but which is fit to speed up the quantity production of staple goods at any point where an additional output may be called for. In effect, the work and output of the manufacturing industries are not now limited by the productive capacity of their equipment, workmen, or technical processes. But they are subject to limitation on the one side by the available supply of power and materials, and on the other side by the market for their output; and the available supply of power and essential materials is limited, in the main and decisively, by the current output of the key industries which command the country's staple resources; which output in turn is limited by consideration of what the traffic will bear, at the hands of the absentee owners of the staple resources and their business agents. On both sides, therefore, the output of staple goods in the manufacturing industries is limited, not by productive capacity or by capacity for consumption, but by business considerations. And the business considerations which chiefly decide what the volume of output of manufactured goods shall be are the considerations which govern the key industries and their output of power, fuel, and raw and structural materials.

It follows that the manufacturing industries as a class are dependent immediately on the key industries and on the terms which the management of the key industries may choose to offer them, somewhat arbitrarily. From which it follows also that the manufacturers as a class necessarily conduct their enterprise on a short-term plan; governed by the visible supply and the orders outstanding; since the management of the sovereign key industries, like other business men, keep their own counsel as to what they will do about their own business,—when and how and how far they may see fit to alter the terms on which they are willing to supply the necessary materials of industry. So the manufacturers must hold themselves ready to slack off or to speed up, to widen or narrow the margin of unemployment, with a vigilant eye to the main chance and waiting watchfully for any adroit manœuvres in the key industries.

So also it follows that the manufacturing industries as a class are on a competitive footing; competing for the available supply of power and primary materials, but more particularly competitors for custom in the market. This competition has been taking on a special character during the past two or three decades, not contemplated in the manuals of economic theory, and as it is in some degree a novel development due to a complication of cir-

cumstances and calling for detailed analysis, a fuller consideration of it will best be deferred to a later chapter.

The place and nature of the key industries in the industrial system scarcely require elaborate discussion here.
They are such as the name, "key industries," implies.
And they are key industries because they command the
main run of the country's staple resources. Technologically the key industries come into the same class with manufactures, and some of the best work of applied chemistry
and physics is to be found here; as, e. g., in metallurgy
and the refining of petroleum. But as business concerns
the key industries stand in a special relation to the industrial system. They hold the initiative by virtue of
their hold on the staple natural resources; and by active
collusion or by routine which has been settled on lines
of collusion they have during the last few decades come
to exercise a decisive control over the industrial system
at large, so that the country's industry will now speed up,
slack off, or shut down, very much as the massive concerns
in the background among these key industries may decide;
and their decision in these matters is, of course, guided
not by consideration of serviceability to industry at large
or to the livelihood of the underlying population but by
pursuit of the largest obtainable net gain for themselves.

Of course, there is in this respect no difference in principle between the business management of the key industries and business-as-usual anywhere else. It is only
that the business of the key industries is in a peculiarly
fortunate position, such a position of virtual monopoly
and free initiative as all business men in all lines of enterprise aim to achieve if they can. It should be added that
this strangle-hold of the key industries upon the country's
industry at large has been gaining in breadth, rigor, and

security, and that the present outlook is for further gains of the same nature.[2]

In practice there is no sharp line to be drawn between the key industries and the common run of manufactures. They all belong together within the lines of the machine industry, and the business interests which control them make no account of any technical distinction between the two groups of industrial enterprises. In coal, oil, steel, and transportation, e. g., the business concerns interested have been reaching out among the manufacturing industries which draw on them for service and materials, and have been acquiring an interest also in the business of distribution. And many manufacturing concerns have on occasion, for security and despatch, reached back among the key industries and secured a hold on some needed line of staple resources. As an illustrative instance, corporate interests whose business centres in the extraction, refining, and transportation of petroleum and its products have gone largely into merchandising business as distributors of their own output, wholesale and retail, and at the same time they are also to be found intimately interested in a business way in linseed oil and the manufacture of paints and pigments, as, e. g., white-lead, as well as in soaps, candles, unguents, medicines, and cosmetics. So also there are industrial business concerns that have to do with manufacturing and that would have to be classed as manufactures in the technological respect, at the same

[2] The past three or four years (1920-1923) have shown how these matters stand. The country's industry has hung in a state of suspended animation while the business concerns that take care of coal, iron and transportation have been engaged—no doubt righteously and legally—in bringing the man-power employed in those industries to profitable terms by a campaign of protracted unemployment and privation.

time that they occupy a strategical position of much the same character as the key industries. Such are, e. g., the meat-packers and the flour-millers; and there are other concerns interested in sugar, gas, electricity, telephones, trolley lines, and the like, that fall more or less patently in the same doubtful or ambiguous class.

Among all these, that group of business concerns of which the packers and millers are the type-form occupies a special position, peculiarly difficult to classify. On the formal face of things they are manufacturers, but in effect they command those natural resources from which their raw materials are drawn. In effect their command of the tributary agricultural resources is so unqualified that it will scarcely be an over-statement to say that they hold these natural resources of the farming region in usufruct, with power of use and abuse. It is also quite safe to say that this usufruct of the farm resources has been capitalised and included among the assets of these corporations so as to count in a substantial way in the current market value of their outstanding corporate securities. Of course it does not follow, nor need one entertain a suspicion, that the corporate interests in question have ever abused the power which their virtual monopoly of the country's resources in meat and grain so vests in them. The point of interest here is rather that the cleavage between the key industries and the common run of manufactures is by no means neatly observed in business practice, although the technical distinction between the two is fairly obvious. The trail of the net gain will cross technological frontiers as readily as national frontiers.[3]

[3] The underlying principle of it all was formulated in another connection by Jacob Fugger back in the 16th century: . . . "er wäre kleinmutig . . . wollte verdienen dieweil er konnte."— Quoted by Sombart, *Moderne Kapitalismus,* first edition, vol. I. p. 396.

The third of these contrasted industrial groups, or strata, in the three-fold division spoken for above, the farm community, is more sharply set off from the rest of the industrial system, both technologically and in respect of the business relations by which it is governed. In both respects farming is on a footing different from the rest; and the reason for its different business footing is its different technological character.

Outside of farming, the main body of the industrial system has undergone a revolutionary experience during the past one-hundred-fifty years. The industrial system at large, outside of farming, has been reshaped by the machine industry and that standardised quantity-production which the machine industry has brought into action. The industrial system at large is dominated by the technology of physics and chemistry; it is essentially a system of mechanical power, inanimate materials, and inorganic processes. On the other hand agriculture still rests on a body of industrial arts that are older than the Industrial Revolution,—older even than that handicraft system which the technology of physics and chemistry has been displacing. In farming, these mechanical appliances and applications of mechanical power are still "labor-saving devices," and they still come into the case only as accessory ways and means which "facilitate and abridge" the manual operations of the husbandman. All these things have hitherto touched agriculture only in a superficial way. They do not make the output; they only help along in the manipulation and distribution of it.

The agriculture from which the civilised peoples draw their livelihood and on which civilised life depends is a system of "mixed farming" which does not differ, in its elements, from the mixed farming of neolithic Europe some ten or twelve thousand years ago. It is mixed farming. That is to say it makes use of a certain equipment of domestic animals and crop-plants; and the equipment as well as the methods and purposes of it all are still, in their elements, the same as ruled the case in the husbandry of neolithic Europe. The industry still continues to turn out essentially the same output of grain, milk, butter, cheese, eggs, meat, wool, and hides; and it turns out these necessaries of civilised life by recourse to the same technology of breeding and nurture, fortified by a variety of mechanical helps.

But these mechanical helps and expedients do not make the output and "are not of the essence of this contract." Farm produce is still an output of those processes of growth and nurture that date back for their technological character to the domestication of plants and animals in prehistoric times. And the mixed farming of the civilised nations still rests on the technological foundations that were laid for it when the crop-plants and domestic animals found their way into neolithic Europe. Improvements in methods and appliances have been many and various, but those improvements and advances that have cut at all deeply into the substance of husbandry have been advances in breeding and tillage; that is to say, they have continued the work of domestication which the neolithic husbandmen already had taken in hand some ten or twelve thousand years ago. The methods of breeding and nurture as well as the equipment of livestock and crop plants have been improved and extended, and the farmers' work has been "facilitated and abridged" here and there by the use of many mechanical contrivances, as well as by the introduction of more productive contrivances in the way of crop-plants unknown to neolithic Europe, as, e. g., corn (maize) and potatoes and cotton;

but all the while it remains true that those technological improvements and advances which have counted substantially toward an enhanced output of farm produce have continued to be something in the nature of elaboration and refinement on the same old procedure of breeding and nurture that supplied the necessaries of life in neolithic times.

There is no call to undervalue the service which the machine industry and industrial chemistry have rendered, but when all has been said and allowed for it remains true that these agencies of the Industrial Revolution have not made farming over in their own image, and that husbandry is after all a matter of the skilled breeding and nurture of animals and crop-plants; and the conditioning circumstances which govern these elemental processes of breeding and nurture are still the ancient circumstances of space, air, rainfall, sunshine, soil, and seasons. These conditioning circumstances still govern the farm industry and the life of the farm population. The American husbandry, mixed farming, is necessarily spread abroad over the face of the land. Livestock and crops live and multiply only in that way, and the farm population under whose skilled care they live and multiply will have to live with them. That is the neolithic way.

Quantity-production and the large-scale process come into this mixed farming mainly by way of a figure of speech. It is true, the farm unit has been growing larger gradually during the past half or three quarters century, both on an average and in the typical case; and that such has been the drift of things during this interval is due to mechanical improvements, to the use of mechanical power and the like applications of the technology of physics and chemistry; but it also remains true that husbandry is not built upon these inanimate factors, and that, in the large, the scale and pace of things in farming still wait on the processes of breeding and nurture, not on the massing of inanimate forces and the concatenation of inanimate chemical reactions.

The farm population is still given over to a workday surveillance of these processes of breeding and nurture. Farm life is still a neighborhood life of homely detail and seasonal fortuities; and the inveterate habituation to which the farm population is subject still makes for the good old spirit of parochialism and personalities, of neighborhood gossip and petty intrigue. The organisation of the work necessarily runs to small-scale parcelment and isola‹ tion; relatively small working units which are necessarily masterless and self-directing in their processes of work, however greatly they may be tied-up, hampered and retarded by pecuniary obligations to absentee owners outside.

Because of this necessary parcelment, and because of the intimately personal character of the farmer's technical knowledge and proficiency, he is still the "independent farmer" in respect of the day's work. Only in a slight, external, and essentially inconsequential way, are the farm population subject to that wide-sweeping, impersonal, mechanistic discipline of standardisation and mass movement that gives its character to the industrial system at large. The abiding and pervasive factors of habituation for the husbandman and his folks are still the homely movements of human nature working in collusion with the animate forces of plant and animal life, settled habits of thought that have to do with breeding and nurture. With the result, among other things, that the rural community is still shot through with prehistoric animism in a degree that passes the comprehension of any person whose habits of thought have been shaped by the technology of physics and chemistry. So it has come about that the rural community is still the repository of timeworn superstitions, magical, religious, and political, such as would do credit to the best credulity of neolithic man.[4]

Technologically speaking, and seen in the light of the latterday industrial arts, agriculture is grounded in a system of holdovers that have come down from remote antiquity and embody habits of thought that are suited to the institutional structure of those good old days; days which antedate not only the machine industry and Big Business, but the era of handicraft as well. By technical necessity the farming industry is still conducted on a plan of dispersion, discontinuous parcelment, and individual responsibility, so far as regards the day's work. But in point of business relations the farmer is caught in the net of the system at large; which is a system of absentee ownership and works out in a network of credit, markets, organised salesmanship, corporate capitalisation, and Big Business managed on the principle of what the traffic will bear. To the farmer and his folks all these things are external circumstances over which he has no control, but to which he and his folks are required to conform on pain of "getting left." He is within the system but not of it. He and the work of his hands are in it as a bone of contention; something for adroit salesmen to buy cheap and sell dear, and something to which absentee title is to be acquired by a tactical use of credit.

[4] To this pervasive animistic credulity of the rural community the salesmanlike folks of the country town have to "play up," in their unremitting pursuit of profitable customers. So that by force of salesmanlike pusillanimity the country towns are driven to underbid the lowest survivals of neolithic animism in a competitive endeavour to conform to all holdovers of superstition that may conceivably have a commercial value; as has been explained in an earlier passage.

Reluctantly but as a matter of course the farmer and all his work and ways are involved in the all-pervading system of credit, for more or less. It is a business system, and business runs on credit, and the Big Business which dominates the system begins and ends its work within the convolutions of credit. In the rural community, on the other hand, the rule still runs that indebtedness is an "incumbrance" to be got away from as fast and far as may be. That is to say, the farmer is a victim of the credit system, not a manipulator of it. His property is not assets to be employed as collateral by use of which to swell his capitalisation, but "production goods," visible means of support to be jealously kept clear of the money-lender, if such a thing were possible.[5]

The farmer and his folks and work are bound by the run of the market, but he does not create or control the run of the market by any exercise of deliberation or discretion on his part. It is not his market, except in the sense that he is dependent on it. Perhaps he "ought" to control his market, and make the terms on which he will buy and sell; but in practical fact his choice in the matter goes no farther than to take or leave the terms that are offered him. The run of the market is made for him and he can take it or leave it, but mostly take it lest a worse thing befall him. The run of the market is made up on the principle of what the traffic will bear for Big Business,

[5] Right lately, the farmers and their delegates among the nation's official personnel have been much occupied with contrivances for facilitating and amplifying "farm credits," designed to bring agriculture and the farm population within the pale of the credit-system and enable them to turn their assets to account as collateral on which to expand their effective capitalisation. Of course, as seen from another angle, the whole project may also look like a contrivance to induce the farm population to increase their liabilities and overhead charges beyond what their earning-capacity will bear.

by those massive business interests that move obscurely in the background,—railway interests, ware-house interests, jobbing interests, packing interests, milling interests, farm-implement interests, coal interests, oil interests, steel interests, cordage interests, and the like.

And every once in a while the farmers make a broad gesture of collusive strategy and concerted action. Every once in a while there springs up a hope, born of desperation, that the massive interests which move in the background of the market are to be set at naught by the farmers' taking thought together in a business way; or they are to be confounded by some intelligent alignment of rural political forces. And always this collusive strategy of the rural communities disintegrates into a parcelment of self-seeking detail and mutual sharp practice, and always the political mass-action of the independent farmers runs out in a dust-heap of parochial chicanery. And the rural community remains an inalienable domain of that business enterprise that buys cheap and sells dear.

In respect of industrial articulation, as regards technical interdependence and mutual support among the members or strata of the existing system, the case stands somewhat as follows. The industrial arts, the employment of this technology of physics and chemistry, come to a head in the manufacturing industries, dominated by standard mechanical processes and quantity production. This industrial system owes its unexampled productivity to the mechanistic technology of the manufacturing industries, and the apex of technological growth is in that field. These industries draw on farming and the key industries for mechanical power, man-power and materials, at the same time that they supply ways and means that are indispensable to the work in farming and the key industries.

The whole constitutes a balanced system of work, a moving equilibrium of interlocking processes, in which the efficiency of any given part is conditioned on the due working of all the rest. No part of the system can do its share of the work in isolation or in severalty, and any degree of failure or curtailment at any point, in rate, volume or quality of output, entails a degree of curtailment and inefficiency throughout the system. The dominant factor in this moving equilibrium of work, technologically speaking, is the manufacturing industry, and it is on the output of this industry that the efficiency of the industrial system converges.

Such is the technical character of the system as an industrial organisation, and such would be its working balance and articulation in the absence of other incentives and considerations than the production of useful goods. But under the existing system of ownership that consideration is not decisive. The incentive of business is not to produce goods but to make money, and business considerations are decisive in the control and management of the industrial system. And the articulation and balance of the industrial system as it is organised for business purposes is accordingly a different one. Technologically the apex of the system is the manufacturing industry, but in the business organisation of it the key industries are at the apex; and they hold this dominant position by owning the right to retard or curtail the supply of necessary power and materials that goes to the manufacturing industries. Industrially the country's farming is the primary source of its livelihood, and therefore of its available man-power, but in the business organisation the farm community serves as ways and means of that commercial enterprise that handles the country's manufactured products, which in turn is subject to such businesslike curtailment and retardation as the pursuit of profits in the key industries may entail.

What has just been said about the industrial system describes the situation in America. And what is true of America will hold true with an inconsequential change of words for the industrial system more at large, to include the civilised nations, in about the same measure in which they are civilised; or a more guarded statement would be, in the same measure in which they are included in the framework of the modern European civilisation. In many of the characteristic features of the case America may be taken as an exemplar of the civilised world, particularly as regards the civilised world's present status in industry and business.

The civilised nations, in the degree in which they are civilised, are all unavoidably bound together in a single working system of industry, and they are now similarly bound up in a comprehensive system of business enterprise; although the articulations of business run on lines somewhat different from those technological lines of specialisation and mutual support that bind the civilised peoples in an inclusive organisation of industry. In the industrial respect, as determined by the state of the industrial arts, the civilised peoples are held in a net-work of interlocking processes of work, so close-knit and so far-reaching as to make them a single going concern working together toward a maximum quantity production of staple goods by use of the world's known resources of mechanical power, raw materials and man-power. All this is quite obvious, and it is coming to be quite familiar, at large and in detail, to the technical men within whose horizon these matters lie.

But in respect of their business interests, or rather in

respect of the strategy of their business men, the civilised nations are not similarly bound together in a coöperative commonwealth. Business enterprise, being competitive, runs at cross purposes. And it is these cross purposes of business enterprise that chiefly obstruct the due articulation of industrial undertakings and so act to derange and curtail the work in hand, both in the industrial system at large and in the detail conduct of industrial undertakings within any given national frontiers. As the matter stands now the division between nations is a division of business interests, and national policies are chiefly occupied with the competitive cross purposes of vested interests which do business under one flag and another. This, too, is quite obvious, and it is a familiar matter of course, at large and in detail, to the absentee owners and statesmen who have to take care of these matters.

CHAPTER X

THE TECHNOLOGY OF PHYSICS AND CHEMISTRY

As is well known and has often been described, the machine industry of recent times took its rise by a gradual emergence out of handicraft in England in the eighteenth century. Since then the same industrial arts have progressively been getting the upper hand in all the civilised nations, in much the same degree in which these nations have come to be counted as civilised. There has been a progressive mechanisation of the ways and means of living as well as of the ways and means of productive industry, and this mechanisation has in recent times been going forward at a constantly accelerated rate, and it is still in progress, with no present promise of abatement or conclusion.

Not until the middle of the nineteenth century can it be said that this mechanical industry, and the consequent mechanical organisation of work and life, had got the upper hand in any country outside of Great Britain; although the machine and its procedure had begun to make serious inroads in all those countries that came within the sweep of European commerce. Since then, by progressive diffusion of the machine industry and progressive advance in technology, the state of the industrial arts at large has so far been remodeled that this mechanical industry now stands dominant at the apex of a complex and comprehensive industrial system which includes the civilised world in a net-work of ways and means drawn on a mechanical plan.[1]

[1] The limits and ramifications of this industrial system run in a peculiar fashion, on peculiar lines of coincidence. Loosely and for the time being, but with such a degree of consistency as to make it worth noting, this state of industry has made itself at home only among those peoples that get their livelihood from the mixed farming of the temperate latitudes,—from that manner of husbandry which traces back to neolithic Europe and which still makes use of substantially the same equipment of crop-plants and domestic animals that came into use at that time. It may all be a matter of fortuitous coincidence. It is not easy to find an organic connection or correlation between the mechanical technology and this special type of mixed farming; and yet it is also not easy to avoid the tacit assumption that the two are in some way intimately bound up together; and certain opaque facts of recent experience argue that way.

E. g., the Great War was carried on as a contest of mechanical appliances, a competitive enterprise in the technology of mechanics and chemistry, backed by man-power whose livelihood was drawn from this type of mixed farming. This great adventure involved and made use of substantially all those peoples whose industry is regulated by the mechanical technology and whose subsistence is drawn from this type of husbandry, and virtually no others; and in the end the decision was reached on these two counts; technological mastery, and the food-supply of the temperate latitudes. Throughout the conflict, underlying all the pursuit of funds and munitions and conditioning it, ran the desperate need of a standard subsistence—grain, meat, milk, animal fats, wool, leather—all standardised on the basis of that mixed farming that has come down from neolithic times. And as if to complete the experiment and bring the relative value of these two factors in the fight to a conclusive test, there has been the continued run of hostilities that have engaged European (and American) statecraft since the return of peace.

The most notable of these is the case of Russia. The obstinate and hitherto inconclusive endeavour of the Associated Powers to break Soviet Russia has been, in the main, a contest between finance, commerce and mechanical industry on the one side and mixed farming on the other side. It has been a conflict of desperation between the most advanced among the industrial and commercial nations on the one side and the most nearly neolithic population of peasant farmers on the other, in which the Allied and Associated Powers have endeavored to bring the peasant

The mechanical industry, with its technology of physics and chemistry, stands dominant at the apex of the industrial system. So far as the technology of physics and chemistry has taken effect, the industrial system at large has fallen into line as an orderly ramification of productive processes that work together as a rounded and balanced whole, an industrial going concern, a composite of interlocking ways and means organised on an impersonal plan of give and take. It centers about the use of mechanical power and inanimate materials, to be turned to productive account by use of specialised and standardised processes of mechanics and chemistry in charge of technicians and technically skilled workmen. The standardised processes of production according to this mechanistic plan interlock in a moving equilibrium of wórk, in a sensitively balanced interdependence of supply and output. From which it results that any curtailment, disproportion, or retardation at any point will entail retardation and derangement of the work throughout the system; and a degree of failure at any point will entail a more than proportionate degree of derangement through all the ramifications of work that are touched by this give and take. Any degree of obstruction or shortage at any critical point will set up a more than proportionate volume of retardation and de-

farmers to terms by shutting them off from the use of the industrial and commercial system of Christendom and turning the resources of that system against them. Hitherto the peasant farmers have, on the whole, held their ground against the forces brought to bear by the financiers and the captains of industry, and the likelihood of their being brought to reason seems, on the whole, increasingly remote. At the same time the peasant farmers of Russia appear all the while to be shaping the course of things more and more to their own notion at home. European civilisation appears not yet to have passed the stage at which mixed farming is the prime conditioning factor in its material fortunes.

rangement in the rest of the working mechanism. The due working of the whole or of any part is accordingly conditioned on the due allocation of power-resources and materials, as well as on the unhampered employment of all the available technical insight and man-power. A withdrawal of efficiency at any critical point, in respect of power, materials, man-power, or technical guidance, entails derangement and lowered efficiency of the working whole. Of capital importance among these critical points in the industrial system are the "key industries," so called because they stand in this critical and commanding relation to the whole.

The later advances in the industrial arts have taken such a turn as to throw the technicians more and more into a position of immediate and unremitting responsibility, in all this mechanical organisation of work. So that the industrial system, drawn on this mechanical plan, will do its work in a competent fashion only on condition that competent technical men are placed in charge of it, at large and in detail, unhampered by other than technical considerations. The industrial system has progressively been taking on this character of mechanical articulation and mechanical intolerance. At the same time, and indeed by the same move, the technicians, in whose habits of thought this state of the industrial arts lives and has its being, have become more and more broadly addicted to the mechanistic logic of the inorganic sciences and more intolerant of all those conventional truths and amenities that lie beyond the borders of tangible fact. Workday preoccupation with these exacting and nicely balanced matters of fact gives them a character of intolerantly impersonal skepticism touching all things that are of the nature of imponderables. It is a constructive skepticism, since the engineer's work is constructive work, but it is skepticism none the less. They are engaged on contriving and directing ways and means of doing things, but it is ways and means of doing things in space of three dimensions, and the technician's preoccupations do not lap over into the realm of the imponderables.[2]

Neither the industrial system nor the brotherhood of technicians, in whose habits of thought this industrial system is contained, have yet reached that unmitigated state of mechanisation and brute logic which this description of it would imply. But it is headed that way and is moving at a constantly accelerated rate. There still are large remnants of old-fashioned human nature in the make-up of the twentieth-century engineer, such as once grew and flourished in the mellower days of handicraft and illiteracy. But then, the engineer is something new under the sun, and that impersonal outlook on things, which his training is likely to entail has not yet had time to be conventionalised into a settled matter of common sense; just as those material sciences of physics and chemistry on which he feeds are also something new, in some degree still alien to the common-sense scheme of things.

In effect, the technician has come up and grown great as a factor in productive industry, has grown to be one of the major institutions in modern life, in very much

[2] "To these from birth is belief forbidden; from these till death is relief afar,
They are concerned with matters hidden; under the earth-line their altars are.

They do not teach that their God will rouse them a little before the nuts work loose;
They do not preach that His Pity allows them to leave their work whenever they choose."
RUDYARD KIPLING, "The Sons of Martha."

the same degree and in the same time as the financier, the captain of solvency, has displaced the captain of industry and become the paramount factor in business. So that while the technician is now, and increasingly, the paramount factor in technology, he is by no means master of the industrial system or of the economic situation; inasmuch as the economic situation is a composite of industry and business, and the conduct of business is not entrusted to the technicians. The technicians and the business men are the outstanding factors in the case, the conjugate foci of the economic system; and the orbit of the economic world now swings about these two foci, which are beginning to draw apart.

An earlier chapter has endeavored to describe the rise, dominance, and eventual decline or disintegration of the Captain of Industry, considered as one of the major institutions of civilised life. As the name implies, he set out with being a pioneer in industrial enterprise, a designer, builder and manager of industrial equipment and a foreman of the work in hand.[3] At the same time he was a business man and took care of the financial end of the enterprise, buying and selling, "hiring and firing," investment and promotion. Presently, as the mechanical industries of which he was a captain grew greater and advanced to a larger scale, with an increasingly detailed and exacting specialisation and standardisation of processes and products, and with an increasing resort to credit, the Captain of Industry under the pressure of circumstances gradually divested himself of his technical or industrial functions and tapered off into a business man of the commercial type. His attention and energies were taken

[3] Cf. J. W. Roe, *English and American Tool Builders*, (Yale University Press, 1916.)

up more and more exclusively with the run of the market, with margins of cost and profit, and especially with the ever increased exactions and opportunities of credit and investment. By the middle of the nineteenth century the captain of industry, considered as a staple article of institutional furniture, had in effect run out or gone in the discard in the British industrial community; and by the same date he had risen into dominance and was beginning to disintegrate in the American world of affairs.[4] As a "business proposition," that is to say as a staple requisite among the ways and means of profitable business, the captain of industry was already beginning to shift over into, or to be displaced by, the company promoter, the financial magnate, and the corporation financier. It should scarcely be necessary to trace the course of his disguises and mutations from that point on, through the succeeding half-century of projects, promotions, and corporation finance that has eventually given rise to the captain of solvency, investment-banker, and corporation excutive of the twentieth century.

The discontinuance and disintegration of the captain of industry was due to the continued advance of the industrial arts. This advance took such a turn, in the way of specialisation and complexity, that no industrial enterprise of standard size and grade could continue to be competently managed under the divided attention of any one man; divided between the mechanical requirements of the industry and the financial requirements of the busi-

---

[4] Beginning with the civil-war period the center of the American stage is occupied by a swiftly increasing company of financial magnates and manipulators, e. g., "Commodore" Vanderbilt, Jay Cooke, "Jim" Fiske, Oakes Ames, Jay Gould, and presently John D. Rockefeller, Andrew Carnegie, J. J. Hill.—Cf. Burton J. Hendrick, *The Age of Big Business;* Isaac Lippincott, *Economic Development of the United States.*

ness. It was an advance in the scale and complication of equipment and work, in specialisation and standardisation, in applied mechanics and chemistry, which entailed the substitution of technical precision in the place of rule-of-thumb; and along with this progressive change in the technical complexion of the case there was a similarly exacting growth in the business to be done, an increasing volume and an increasing nicety and multiplicity of details. Out of this increasing recourse to detailed, exact, objective knowledge there arose the industrial experts, engineers, technicians, who progressively took over the industrial functions of the captain of industry and left him free to devote his attention to business alone.

In the third quarter of the century chemical science also began to take effect as a material factor in technology, and about the same time electrical science rose into consequence as an industrial force. Chemical processes had of course had their part in the industrial arts before that date, but it had on the whole been a matter of chemical rule-of-thumb rather than of chemical science, of general information and common notoriety rather than exact and calculable processes worked out by detailed experiment and computation in the chemical laboratories. Neither the industrial chemist nor the industrial laboratory had been counted in among the ways and means of production.

Metallurgy, e. g., as well as much of the work in dyeing, tanning, baking, brewing, and the like, have always been of the nature of chemical industry; but it was not until the middle of the nineteenth century and after that these things began to bulk large in the industrial arts and then fell into the hands of the chemical technicians and took their place in the technological scheme as recondite matters of applied science. All these things had been matters of accumulated experience and had held their place in the common sense of the day's work, along with the familiar use of the mechanical principles and appliances,—familiar in their elements to all men by common notoriety. They were matters which any intelligent layman could understand and turn to account on a footing of workday information helped out by some slight touch of special experience, of the nature of an informal apprenticeship. But by insensible process of growth all these matters of technological use and wont took on a more exacting character, such as gradually to take them out of the untrained reach of businesslike laymen, however ingenious and intelligent, and thereby gave rise to a new factor of production, the technicians, engineers, experts, men grounded in the material sciences and instructed in the specialised application of them.

So the interval since the middle of the nineteenth century stands in contrast to what went before, as a more or less sharply defined period of special growth in the industrial arts, during which the mechanical industry has progressively shifted to a footing of applied science, and during which also the immediate designing and conduct of the work has progressively been taken over by the technicians. At the same time and by force of the same drift of circumstance the captain of industry, the owner-employer, business manager, has progressively been shifted to one side,—to the business side, the "financial end." Being a layman in matters of industry—that is to say in matters of technically applied science—the business man has perforce become an absentee, an outsider so far as concerns any creative work. Though he is an outsider with a deciding vote on what goes on inside. The "division of labor" has taken this turn. It has progressively eliminated and removed the businesslike layman from the effectual personnel of industry and has progressively vested the effectual management of production in these technical men.

Not that this progressive elimination of the laymen has yet been completed, even as regards responsible work of a technical nature. Indeed, it is still an article of popular belief, grounded in traditional common sense, that the control of productive industry must in the nature of things be entrusted to absentee laymen, even in those lines of production where the work can not effectually be carried on without the constant attention of technically trained men. Even within the mechanical industries the displacement of businesslike laymen by competent technicians has not yet gone so far as to vest full discretion in the technical experts, even in the conduct of mechanical details. At the best or farthest it can be said that the technicians decide in detail what is to be done, if anything, and how it is to be done; while the absentee laymen decide summarily what and how much is not to be done. Such is the state of the case in detail in those lines of production where the mechanical industry has already taken effect in a passably complete degree. But in the large, in what may be called industrial affairs, in the planning and execution of projects that call for a comprehensive technical balancing and articulation of large industrial processes,—in these larger conjunctures, where any lack of technical insight and sobriety will have particularly grave and far-reaching consequences,—there the discretion and control continues to be exercised by absentee laymen who take measures on other than technical grounds.

It will be seen that neither the induction of technicians into the responsible conduct of industry nor the elimination of laymen from work that is of a technical nature is yet nearly complete. Nor, it should be added, is such an outcome desired. It is contrary to common sense and would not be allowed by law and custom. Indeed, it is a safe presumption that any outspoken proposal or project to hasten or precipitate this progressive retirement of businesslike laymen from the superior management of these technical affairs would turn out to be seditious, so soon as the jurisdiction of the courts could be brought to bear on the question. It would involve the abrogation or disallowance, in whole or in part, of the rights of absentee ownership; and absentee ownership is safeguarded by a special clause of the American constitution. There need be no apprehension that the present unreserved control of the industrial arts by businesslike laymen will be discontinued, just yet. While it is quite evident that the conduct of productive industry, especially in its larger and more difficult undertakings, calls progressively for a more profound and wider technical insight and a more single-minded technical discretion and control, yet the general staff of the industrial system continues to be made up of businesslike laymen.

The state of the industrial arts, as it runs on the lines of the mechanical industry, is a technology of physics and chemistry. That is to say, it is governed by the same logic as the scientific laboratories. The procedure, the principles, habits of thought, preconceptions, units of measurement and of valuation, are the same in both cases, so far as regards any furtherance of the work in hand. Other considerations may come into the case, other preconceptions, principles, units of valuation; but these others can come into bearing only as factors of disturbance from outside the orderly procedure of the work in hand, and can only deflect, retard, and curtail the work in hand.

The mechanistic technology makes use of the same range of facts as the laboratories, handled in the same impersonal way and directed to the same manner of objective results. In both cases alike it is of the first importance to eliminate the "personal equation," to let the work go forward and let the forces at work take effect quite objectively, without hindrance or deflection for any personal end, interest, or gain. It is the technician's place in industry, as it is the scientist's place in the laboratory, to serve as an intellectual embodiment of the forces at work, isolate the forces engaged from all extraneous disturbances, and let them take full effect along the lines of designed work. The technician is an active or creative factor in the case only in the sense that he is the keeper of the logic which governs the forces at work. And he can be said to make these forces work and to have created the results that emerge under his hands, only in the sense that he has taken due care to see that these impersonal forces work out according to the logic which his experiments and calculations have formulated out of the ascertained behavior of the brute facts.

These brute forces that so are brought to bear in creative industry are of an objective, impersonal, unconventional nature, of course. They are of the nature of opaque fact. Pecuniary gain is not one of these impersonal facts. Any consideration of pecuniary gain that may be injected into the technician's working plans will come into the case as an intrusive and alien factor, whose sole effect is to deflect, retard, derange and curtail the work in hand. At the same time considerations of pecuniary gain are the only agency brought into the case by the business men, and the only ground on which they exercise a control of production. Their office is to take care of the pecuniary interests of the absentee owners. In the nature of things, by force of the rights of ownership, they can, at will, selectively obstruct, forbid, curtail, deflect, derange, retard; but they can not bear a creative hand in what is going forward, inasmuch as their knowledge, interest, insight, and reasoning concerning the work that is going forward are not drawn in terms of the forces which enter creatively into the case. Yet, for good and conclusive reasons the final control of all these matters vests in the businesslike laymen. They are reasons of absentee ownership, and they are good and conclusive because they are a matter of settled habit. The claims of absentee ownership are as irrelevant to the conduct of industry as a fourth dimension of space is to the calculations of the mechanical engineers; but the claims of absentee ownership after all are paramount, and they are sound and conclusive according to established law and custom.

The technology of physics and chemistry is not derived from established law and custom, and it goes on its way with as nearly complete a disregard of the spiritual truths of law and custom as the circumstances will permit. The realities with which the technicians are occupied are of another order of actuality, lying altogether within the three dimensions that contain the material universe, and running altogether on the logic of material fact. In effect it is the logic of inanimate facts. The realities of technology are such things as wind and weather, topography and water courses, soil, climatic regions, coastlines and harbors, contour lines and geological formations, fuel, ores and fluxes, temperatures and chemical values, energy, mass, tensile strength, velocities, inertia and impact.

Progressively imbued with these habits of thought and driven by these preconceptions, the technicians had from the outset been working along these lines of tangible, impersonal reality; and by the middle, or the third quarter, of the nineteenth century they were coming within sight of their technological frontiers as drawn by the available knowledge of useful things in that time. Their achievement up to that time was in substance a technology of mechanics, fairly well rounded out. Not that the resources of mechanics had been worked out, nor even that the domain of mechanical power and mechanical appliances had been fully explored. The technological potentialities of mechanics were not nearing exhaustion, but the technicians of that time—inventors, designers, engineers— were after all in a position to say that, in the large and in its elements, they knew then what manner of things they had to do with and what manner of things they could reasonably promise to do with them. They had at their command those elements of mechanical power, mechanical contrivance, and structural material that would work out in a rounded system of mechanical operations, complete in itself, a balanced and self-contained going concern of productive industry. The further work in sight, within the frontiers of their technological province, was a work of further extension, articulation, and perfection of mechanical contrivances and processes; substantially a work of continuation and elaboration.

Seen in the perspective of a later time this technological situation of the middle nineteenth century is notable for what it got along without. It has a provincial air. But seen in the light of its own time it was passably complete, except for further practicable extensions and refinements of mechanical detail. There had been worked out a practicable and effectually inclusive system of transportation by land and water, by use of mechanical structures and mechanical power, competent and capable of extension and enlarged capacity at will. So there was also a competent mechanical system of lighting, capable of further elaboration but complete in its elements, even to the nineteenth-century inventions of the friction match and the lamp-chimney,—so far complete, in effect, that the next move in that connection has been in the nature of "obsolescence by supersession." The tool-builders of the early nineteenth century had pushed their work through to the construction of a finished series of machine-tools which still continue, with improvements and extensions in detail, to meet the needs of the mills and machinists. And, in great part as an effect of these machine-tools, standardisation of mechanical units, units of gauge, work, and materials, was beginning to dominate the life of industry and was giving rise to those principles of interchangeable parts and automatic process that lie at the root of quantity production. The industrial system as a working whole was falling into shape as a mechanical articulation of standard processes.

But taken as a whole and seen in the perspective of the twentieth century the mechanical industry of that time looks like a technological province. Industrial electricity and industrial chemistry had virtually no place in that scheme of things. There was no petroleum, virtually no industrial use of rubber, and virtually no use of cement. These things were not precisely unknown, but they were things which it was not then quite necessary to know anything about. The working scheme of things got along well enough without them. Refrigeration was still unknown, industrially; the hermetically sealed tin had not become a part of daily life; and the internal-combustion engine had not been invented, not even the rudimentary Otto gas-engine. As an after-effect of Faraday's experiments and speculations on "The viscosity of the magnetic field" in the second quarter of the century, the

dynamo and the electrical industry came into the tech-
nologist's world in the course of the latter half of the
nineteenth century. Over the same interval of time, taking its departure from the experiments and speculations of
Berthelot on the synthesis of organic compounds in the
third quarter of the century, industrial chemistry has arisen
and by insensible degrees has run its creative tentacles
through the technological system from the ground up.[4a]

It is true, chemical processes had been in daily use from
the earliest times, in metallurgy, tanning, fermentation, and
the like; but it is a significant fact that the phrase, "industrial chemistry," was not known and not needed until the
other day. So also electricity was not unknown, and
there is no call to overlook or minimise the industrial use
of such appliances as the Morse telegraph; but a "live
wire" is a conception that arose in the last quarter of the
nineteenth century, and "volts," "amperes," and "kilo-
watts" are units of measurement that were not needed
until the other day. In the third quarter of the century
the technical vocabulary was still complete without these
neologisms, and the logic of industrial procedure was
complete without the conceptions for which they speak.
Since that time chemical and electrical engineers and appliances have been multiplying on the face of the land like
the frogs of Exodus, until the only remaining certainty
is that if there is any root or branch of industry that is
free from them today they will invade it tomorrow.

It is of the essence of this mechanical plan of industry
that the work to be done is done on a mechanical plan.
The logic of it is the logic of inanimate forces and
masses deliberately liberated according to design. Where-
ever chemical and electrical science come into the scheme
of work they fall into line as ways and means in the carry-

[4a] Cf., e. g., Slosson, *Creative Chemistry.*

ing out of a complex mechanical process. The activities and materials which the mechanical industry makes use of and the ways and means by which it makes use of them are of a brute nature, mechanical, inanimate, such that the time, place, rate and volume of their operation can be arranged at will.

Even where animate factors are employed, as they are increasingly employed in the processes of fermentation and the like, these animate materials, too, are handled on a mechanical plan. They are liberated and controlled in the mass, impersonally, according to calculated design, in terms of volume, "cultures," media, concentrations, temperatures, time allowance, with the same freedom and the same nicety of computed effect as the reagents of inorganic chemistry. The whole callous procedure belongs to the mechanical order of things. It has none of the solicitous personal concern that goes, e. g., to make up the day's work of a shepherd. The seasonal work of husbandry and the farmer's dealings with his crops and livestock continues to have a quality of personality—the farmer lives with these things, even where mechanical appliances and standardised feeding, fertilisers and irrigation, have gone farthest in the way of bringing mixed farming into line with the impersonal drive of the machine process.

This mechanical system of work has the peculiar quality that it can be managed at will, that it is not subject to seasonal and fortuitous circumstances over which men have no control; "acts of God" do not intervene except by human neglect or ignorance. The system is complex, intricate and extensive; daily growing more complex, intricate and extensive; but it is a creature of human information and initiative, and all its complex and interwoven motions have been formulated out of experience and run wholly within the lines of known objective fact. It is a creation out of known mechanical fact and the knowledge that has gone to its making and that continues to go to its maintenance and working is of the nature of data. There are no mysteries in the mechanical technique and no occult or magical agencies in the way of a trend, bent, reservation, or inscrutable eventuality. Such obscure factors as may come into the case are taken over and allowed for as known variables of hitherto unascertained magnitude; and the system moves on in terms of the calculated brute factors, the data, with such margin of allowance for error as experience has shown to be called for; for in this technology even the margin of ignorance that has to be allowed for and circumvented is carried as a datum to which a working value is assigned on grounds of expert approximation. The technology of physics and chemistry is altogether matter-of-fact, and its facts are of the nature of data, brute, refractory, impersonal and irresponsible. It is open and aboveboard, but it is also exacting and implacable.

The mechanical system of industry is manageable at will, in detail and at large, but only on the proviso (a) that all technical knowledge that is in use must be accessible, without restraint or reservation, to all the technicians concerned, and (b) that there must be no interference on other than technical grounds. Restraint or reservation, holding out information in the way of trade secrets, injects an incalculable element of error into all related lines of work. The industrial system is an edifice of interlocking processes of work, each of which is a reasoned method of procedure, and the reasoning on which each proceeds is based on the information available as to what is going on and what is intended in all the rest; information as to the methods of work, current and prospective, and the nature, rate and volume of output as well as the kind, quality and quantity of materials employed. For none of these interlocking processes of work is carried on, or can be carried on, independently of the rest. Any degree of isolation involves a degree of error in the specifications of the work, and any withholding of information consequently brings perplexity and derangement to all the rest.

This will hold true in a special degree for the great staple industries, but it is true also in a degree for all subsidiary lines of production. They are bound in a network of give and take of such a nature that the lines of interdependence are endless. The correlation and running adjustment in the work to be done is taken care of by calculation based on the available data as to what is being done in one line and another and what is in prospect, on information or inference as to the kind and quantity of what each and several of these lines of production are ready to give and what and how much they will take. In so far as these calculations governing the kind, rate and volume of work to be done are based on guess-work they are bound to run over or under the true figures and so to result in waste and scarcity and therefore in a more or less pronounced derangement all down the line.

Secrecy and mystification may be "good for trade," but they are altogether bad for industry; sabotage may be indispensable in business although it is invariably disastrous to production. A trade secret is a "business proposition" and may be profitable to its keeper, and the like is true for all secrecy of accounts; at least such is believed to be the case. Unemployment of materials, equipment, and man-power, curtailment of output, may be a sound business proposition and may bring gain to the business; at least the belief is commonly acted on. But all these things are invariably wasteful in their industrial bearing, and invariably bring derangement and retardation in the related lines of industry, which will on occasion amount to disaster; and the net loss to industry always exceeds the net gain to the business.

The mechanical industry in that simpler form in which it stood before the coming of industrial chemistry and electricity, was, even then, taking on this character of articulation and interplay of productive processes, so that even at that date the industrial system made up a loosely balanced going concern of production. And as fast and far as the mechanisation of industry gained, in scope, range, volume and territorial extension, the articulation of working processes grew continually closer and the balance of give and take within the system grew more exacting and more critical. Yet these matters had not then gone so far as to bring home to the thoughtful men of that time the critical importance of a due balance, proportion, and articulation among the interlocking processes of the industrial system.[5]

[5] In 1832 Charles Babbage spoke as of a matter of course in restating Adam Smith's observation, that "Perhaps the most important principle on which the economy of a manufacture depends, is the *division of labor* amongst the persons who perform the work." (*On the Economy of Machinery and Manufactures,* chapter xviii. "On the Division of Labor.") Babbage's observations on the British industrial system were made at a time when British manufactures were still managed, in the main, by captains of industry of the traditional type, on a plan of unguarded competitive production for an open market; the scale of work and equipment was still relatively slight, and specialisation had not gone far; standardisation of processes, appliances, and output was still in its beginnings. (See Babbage, ch. x, "Of the Identity of Work when it is of the Same Kind," etc.) The machine process and quantity production had not at that time taken effect as pace-maker and prime mover in in-

When the growth of industrial chemistry and electricity set in there also set in, by insensible degrees, a new era in the articulation of industrial processes. The contrast between what went before and what followed after is by no means sharp, but it is fairly wide; more particularly, it has grown wide as time has gone by. The difference between before and after is due in part to the continued growth of those technological factors that had made the situation of the earlier time, in part to the intrusion of new agencies which made for increased complexity of operations and a larger scale. It would scarcely be an overbold figure of speech to say that under the old dispensation of the middle nineteenth century the technological plan of things was drawn in two dimensions, whereas under the new technological dispensation, so far as chemical and electrical science have taken effect, the industrial system and its growth may be said to move in space of three dimensions.

The number and interplay of technological factors engaged in any major operation in industry today are related to the corresponding facts of the middle nineteenth century somewhat as the mathematical cube is related to the square; and the increase and multiplication of these technological factors is going forward incontinently, at a constantly accelerated rate.

dustry in so obvious a fashion as to force this new state of things on his attention.

It is even more significant that at a still later date, in the fifties and sixties, from observation of the same industrial system, Karl Marx set up a doctrine which makes "Labor Power" the sole creative factor as well as the common measure in all productive work. Neither of these men is unduly bound by the traditions of economic science, and yet neither one of them was provoked by the run of the facts as he saw them to conceive the industrial system at large as a going concern. They were still content to speak of industry as an affair of detachable factors and independent segments of work going on in severalty.

By the middle of the century the work of designing and supervising the processes of production was already beginning to pass into the hands of specially trained experts, engineers, technicians. It was beginning to exceed the best powers of intelligent laymen working on a footing of general information. The course of things since then, and the rate and scope of the change that has been going forward, is shown by the exuberant growth of the engineering professions, in numbers, competency, and diversity, as well as by their ubiquitous place in the workday conduct of industrial undertakings. In the twentieth century the technicians have become one of the standard factors in production; as much so as the country's natural resources of timber, coal, oil, and ores. Indeed, these things are natural resources, instead of being features of the landscape, because the technicians know how to turn them to account. And the extent and variety of the country's natural resources are constantly increasing, because and by so much as the technicians are continually learning to make use of a larger number and variety of these things. The question of natural resources is, after all, a question of technical insight.

In the beginning the technicians came into the case by progressive infiltration, as designers, consultants, overseers of special details that were too recondite to be taken care of by intelligent laymen on a footing of general information. And these technical details that required expert attention grew continually more urgent and more numerous; they coalesced into ever larger composite working units and fell into progressively closer, more numerous and more exacting articulations among themselves and with the sources of mechanical power and useful materials; with the result that every successive move in this technological growth and complication made two technicians grow where one grew before; and all the while the meshwork of technology has grown and tightened, and always a technician stands at every apex of growth. Until today, throughout the system of the mechanical industries, it has become a matter of course that the conduct as well as the designing of any industrial plant or process that is to make use of the advanced industrial arts cannot safely be entrusted to others than technically trained men. The safe and sane plan of common sense now dictates that industrial operations must be conducted by competent technicians. And this holds true in a special degree for the larger operations and the more formidable organisations of work and equipment, where many technological factors and a wide range of materials and processes are drawn together for teamwork in quantity production on an extensive scale. So it should also hold true in a superlative degree as regards the oversight and control of the industrial system at large as a going concern; the balance, articulation, and mutual support among the several lines of production and distribution that go to make up the system.

However, the rule of the technicians does not go all the way. It began with taking over minor details and fractional outlines of design and operation, and it has hitherto progressed only so far as to cover now what may be called the major details of the industrial system. The planning and surveillance of productive industry at large, in those bearings that are of capital systematic importance, have not yet been taken over by technically trained men. All that is still in the hands of laymen working at cross purposes. Plainly, this capital work of correlation, apportionment, balance and continuity, control of the mutual give and take among the several lines and branches of production, should call for the most intelligent and most scrupulously dispassionate exercise of technical insight and deliberation. Technologically speaking, this is the apex of the industrial system. The work should logically devolve on a technical General Staff. But hitherto all this work of sovereign technical jurisdiction remains in the hands of laymen working at cross purposes, and it continues to be conducted on certain broad principles of ignorance, neglect and sabotage; all in deference to the paramount rights of absentee ownership.

The sovereign jurisdiction in all this highly technical scheme of industry vests in the non-technical business men. Their dealings with the industrial system and all its works are governed not by the calculus of productive work but by the calculus of net gain in terms of price. In the nature of things, the aims, considerations and rulings injected into the run of work by these laymen on these grounds are irrelevant, incompetent, and impertinent, and not germane to the case of creative industry; being grounded in that alien fourth dimension of the economic situation that is called Business Expediency.

To put these generalities and abstractions in more concrete terms, so far as scant space will permit. The industrial system is a composite organisation of work which falls into three interlocking divisions or strata of industrial undertakings, as has already been shown in an earlier passage:—the Key Industries, Manufactures, and Farming. These three groups or classes of industrial undertakings differ from one another not so much in their technological character and relations as in the business considerations which govern them. Technically the two first named belong together as a high-wrought and wide-sweeping application of the mechanical industry, while the same scheme of mechanical processes and appliances laps over into the work of farming also.

As working parts in the system, the several industrial undertakings which make up its three divisions are all inextricably bound together in an endless web of give and take. They are, each and several, mutually continuations of one another. Co-ordination and mutual aid between these three divisions of the industrial system, at large and in detail, is the first requisite of production on this plan. At the same time it is something which can be duly taken care of only by eternal vigilance and unhampered teamwork on the part of a suitable corps of technically trained and experienced men. Whereas, in practice, by force of the rights of ownership, all these matters are habitually taken care of by afterthought and guesswork.

Technically speaking, there is, e. g., no break of continuity in the working-up of lumber, from the time when the lumberman takes it off the stump to the time when it comes out from under the hands of the house-carpenter in the shape of finished floors, doors and casings in place, or the time when the cabinet-maker has turned it out as furniture, or when the builder of sign-boards has worked it into the scenery along the highway and inscribed it with the legend, "Eventually, why not now?" Industrially, in all its ramifications, this wood-working is an unbroken sequence of special processes of work; each successive process of elaboration is standardised with a view to the shape in which its material comes in, to the power and appliances by which the work is to be done, and by the standard shapes in which the same material is to be passed on into the next succeeding process in the industrial chain. And at every point in the sequence it

is of the essence of the case that the work should go forward in unbroken continuity, supplied at a known rate
and volume of materials of standard kinds, gauges and
grades. Uncertainty, interruption, or evasion at any
point counts unavoidably as derangement and unemployment throughout the sequence of work. In practice,
for reasons of business expediency, there is deliberate
evasion, delay, and uncertainty at as many points in this
sequence of work as there are subdivisions of ownership
along the way; for alongside the chain of working processes there runs an equal chain of businesslike owners
working at cross purposes with one another.

The like holds true, only in a more formidable way, for
the steel industry. Technically it is of the essence of the
case that the right ores and the suitable coke and fluxes
should go, without hindrance, to all those steel-works that
are fit for the work in hand and necessary to turn out
such a rate and volume of output as will meet the working needs of the industries concerned, and that they should
go to no others; due regard being had to the means of
transportation and the points of delivery. Technologically speaking, the working-up of the steel supply into
finished products begins with the selection of the ores
and other raw materials and with the location and planning of the steel works, including due provision for the
housing and livelihood of the man-power engaged. From
that point on the work goes forward—or should go forward—in a calculated sequence of standardised processes
and products, designed to run in unbroken continuity
and to supply the ways and means of work through the
further stages of elaboration, in standard units of kind,
gauge, grade, and delivery, as assigned by competent technicians working in concert. So, e. g., the production of
any given article of farm implements or machinery tech-

nically begins with the selection of ores, fluxes and processes suitable to make a steel of the special character required, it runs through a chain of processes by which the parts are fashioned and assembled, and it ends only when the transportation agencies have delivered the implement on the ground where it is to be used; and even then the case continues in the way of sundries, repairs and replacements, until the life-history of the implement is concluded. All of which is contained in the technological premises and is capable of detailed and unambiguous specification in mechanical units of the kind familiar to the engineers, and none of which can go forward except in some sort of articulate correlation with all the rest. Ambiguity comes in only when business considerations enter, and ambiguity unavoidably comes in wherever business considerations enter.

In practice, the production of steel is a "business proposition." It is controlled by an absentee management with an eye single to the net gain of absentee owners. Steel production is a "key industry"; that is to say, the business men who control it are able to withhold resources and limit the output of one of the prime requisites of other industries at will. It is the invariable practice of "safe and sane" management to limit the output to "what the traffic will bear,"—that is to say, to what will yield the largest net gain to the absentee owners. The business management of such a "key industry" have no responsibility and incur no blame for any derangement, waste or unemployment which this "safe and sane" business practice entails on the rest of the industrial system.[6] It is

[6] The present (1919–1923) situation shows what these entailed consequences are like.—Cf., e. g., *Waste in Industry*, by the Committee of the Federated American Engineering Societies, (New York, 1921, chapters i, ii, xi, xii; also *Report on the*

only that the calculus of business runs in terms that are not commensurable with the calculus of the industrial process. The calculus of business is a calculus of money-value, which is not a mechanical or material fact; whereas the calculus of industry is a calculus of mechanical, tangible, material values. From which it follows that any intrusion of business strategy into the conduct of industry will be sabotage.

The case is of the same complexion when turned the other way about. Farming, e. g., draws on the machine industries, and therefore eventually on the key industries in steel, coal, oil, transportation, etc., for its necessary equipment and workday supplies. But at the same time the output of grain, meat, and dairy products makes up the livelihood of the man-power that is consumed in these key industries and in subsidiary and accessory ramifications of the industrial system. These elements of the community's livelihood run through a technically continuous process of working-up and distribution, by use of mills, packing houses, railways, retailers, and the like; and technically it is of the essence of the case that this process of production, working-up, and distribution should go forward in unbroken continuity on a concerted schedule of work and output, with no avoidable shortage, waste, delay, or evasion along the way. In practice the transportation, milling, packing, distribution, and retailing, is controlled by absentee owners with an eye single to their own net gain in terms of price, by a strategy of evasion, secrecy, shortage, waste, and delay.

This sketch of the technological system and its work-

Steel Strike of 1919, by the Commission of the Interchurch World Movement; and *Public Opinion and the Steel Strike,* by The Same. (New York, 1921.)

ing is evidently overdrawn as well as incomplete. It describes the possibilities of the case rather than the actual run of things. There are good and sufficient reasons why the industries which embody this technology of physics and chemistry do not in practical fact reach this pitch of productive work, as well as why the balance and articulation of industrial processes are not nearly so complete, comprehensive and exacting as this description would imply. The largest and most generally applicable of these reasons for under-efficiency is the all-pervading sabotage that is brought into the work by the present businesslike control of production and distribution; and the nature and consequences of this businesslike management will merit a more detailed analysis and exposition. But there are also other infirmities in the situation, partly intrinsic to the technology and its personnel, partly due to use and wont, law and custom, knowledge and belief prevalent in the community.

The infirmities of the technology, as such, are in the main the infirmities of growth and consequent obsolescence. The technological scheme is engaged in an unremitting growth, which proceeds by cumulative change in detail, and the apices of growth are numerous and more or less isolated, even if account be taken only of the more significant and substantial changes that are going forward. What may be called the cross-references or inosculations of the technological growth come into bearing only by further contrivance which proceeds on further familiarity with the new elements of knowledge, such as comes only on the ground of something like common notoriety.[7] It will commonly take some time for any new

[7] So, e. g., the use of reënforced concrete came out of a technological symphysis involving several elementary facts of workday knowledge and practice, each of which had been a matter of

method or process to find its way into the various uses which it will eventually serve, and to be tested out in these uses; and there is commonly some practical doubt and hesitation, to be tested out in detail, as to the rate and extent in which an improved or alternative process will eventually supersede earlier methods of doing the work.[8] These things take time and carry a margin of uncertainty, hesitation, experiment, and obsolescence, such as to leave the system as a whole in a chronically unfinished and incompletely balanced state, due to continued growth. In a sense, the technological system is never fully abreast of itself.

The technological system is an organisation of intelligence, a structure of intangibles and imponderables, in the nature of habits of thought. It resides in the habits of thought of the community and comes to a head in the habits of thought of the technicians. This technology of physics and chemistry that goes to make the mechanical system of industry is an organisation of habits of thought which run on the ground of mechanistic logic, the logic of impersonal activities which run wholly within the confines of the three dimensions of space. It makes no use of conventional, sentimental, religious, or magical truths. But the habits of thought of the community run, in the main, on conventional, sentimental, religious, and magical lines, and are governed by the logic native to that order of realities.

The received system of institutions which governs hu-

common notoriety since a date older than the birth of the men at whose hands the new move was made.

[8] E. g., the partial and gradual supersession of the Bessemer Converter by the Open Hearth and the recourse to the "basic" process in steel making, with the consequent shifting to a different range of iron ores and a partial relocation of the industrial plants.

man thought and conduct among the civilised peoples is a fabric of conventional, sentimental, religious, and magical habits of thought. These institutions are of a spiritual nature; that is to say, the logic by which they are actuated runs wholly outside the confines of the three dimensions of space. As seen from the standpoint of physics and chemistry, they are of a supernatural or praeternatural complexion. The mechanistic logic of physics and chemistry comes into this institutional order of things as an interloper, a non-conformist with an alien strain. The technology of physics and chemistry, therefore, works under something of a handicap, in an institutional environment imbued with a logical bias that is alien to its bent and inhospitable to its free growth.

Like other men, the technicians are citizens of the world in which they live and creatures of the institutional environment out of which they spring. Such is the declaration of the material sciences, and such is the deliverance of the mechanistic logic on that head. Like other men, the technicians and the technically trained workmen come through their years of growth and use and wont with more or less of the same logical bias that pervades the community at large,—a bias of the animistic order that runs on conventional proprieties, moralities, religious and magical symbols and superstitions. Under these circumstances, the measure in which these men who carry on the mechanical technology achieve a mastery of its mechanistic logic is always a matter of more or less. Their mentality is more or less of an addiction to matter-of-fact habits of thought governed, with more or less mitigation, by the mechanistic logic, and always carrying more or less extensive adhesions of that tissue of superstitions that goes to build up the Christian gentleman and the patriotic citizen. It is only that in the technicians and technically trained workmen the miraculous convictions of religion and the magical "forced movements" of nationalism have suffered a degree of sterilisation. It is a question of more or less, and it is the constant care of the pillars of society to see that the degree of sterilisation suffered by these antiquities of the human spirit shall in no instance exceed a salutary modicum.

In the civilised scheme of education and training for the young, solicitude converges on those elements of knowledge and belief that run outside the confines of the three dimensions of space. The foundations of knowledge and belief are laid in the miracles of the faith and the magic of national allegiance. It is a matter of course to all right-minded citizens of all the Christian nations that a child must first learn to say his prayers and salute the flag.[9] In the institutional scheme of the civilised nations the beginning of wisdom is the fear of God; whereas in the technology of physics and chemistry the beginning of wisdom is to forget Him. And some forget Him more, others less, but none altogether. Latterly, as an aftermath of the atrocities of war, an increased stress has been laid on bending the young idea to religious devotion and patriotic fervor, and thereby, in effect, bending the incoming generation away from the bias of the mechanistic logic; which will count for what it may be worth in defeat of the technological spirit.[10]

[9] In point of institutional value these things are of the first consequence, but when brought within the three dimensions of space and submitted to the logic of physics and chemistry the potent sacraments of Holy Church are no different from the futile incantations of the Black Art, and the Star-spangled Banner (Long may it wave!) foots up as a wasteful exposure of a woollen fabric to the elements.

[10] All the while it is not to be overlooked that the case of America is bound up with the case of Europe, in respect of its technological science and man-power. Technologically, America

At the same time the commercial bent of the community at large and of its educational system works to the same general effect. The old generation of engineers have been pretty well commercialised by lifelong attendance on business expediency in the service of business concerns whose sole standard of efficiency is net gain in terms of price. By inveterate habit these elders go to their day's work in a spirit of salesmanship; and their outlook on the engineer's work is an outlook on what it will bring, quite as much as on what it will do. In all this the elder engineers are quite at one with the common sense of the community at large as well as with the settled convictions of the substantial citizens who pursue the net gain and stand as pillars of society. Under the aegis of these pillars of society and borne up by the commercialised common sense of the underlying population, those who have the care of schooling the country's young men are diverting more and more of the country's educational resources to the service of salesmanship, training for a business career. By so much as this endeavor to divert the schools to the service of salesmanship has the designed effect it acts to draw off talent and training from the service of workmanship and to curtail the reserve of human material on which the technological advance will be able to draw. At the same time its acts in its degree pervasively to lessen the single-mindedness of that contingent of young men who go into the work of technology.

is after all a province or outlier of the European general body; so that America faces a virtually assured decline in this respect, —presumably a fatal decline. The technical man-power lost in the War is not being replaced; the conditions imposed by the businesslike Peace do not permit it; particularly not in those countries of continental Europe on which the continued growth and maintenance of technical science have come to depend.

CHAPTER XI

Manufactures and Salesmanship

Loosely, the organisation-table of industry falls into three main branches or divisions: The Key Industries; Manufactures; and Farming; as has already been shown in an earlier passage. These lines of division are not sharp and clear; the running contact and interdependence between these divisions being close and critical, as has also appeared already. But such a three-fold division is, after all, effectual, and it is readily to be seen in the large. So also, the network of business organization and management runs into three similar divisions, although in the organisation of business the lines of cleavage are even less clear and less fixed.

Of these three divisions, the Key Industries stand at the apex of the industrial system and control the issues of industrial life for the rest. The control which is exercised in this way at the apex is exercised not for the benefit of industry at large but for the profit of the owners (and management) of the key industries, as has also appeared already. The manufactures—continuation industries—and their management stand in a relation to the rest of the community which is analogous to that in which the key industries stand to the rest of the industrial system; but with the difference that the management of these continuation industries have only a vicarious or delegated power, in that their initiative and discretion are

284

bounded by the measures which may be taken independently by the management of the key industries.

Whenever and in so far as the use of mechanical ways and means is the ruling factor in the work to be done, the processes of industry are inordinately productive, as has already been explained. Therefore it is necessary for the businesslike management of these industries to observe a degree of moderation, if the market is not to be overstocked to an unprofitable extent. It is necessary to regulate the rate and volume of output with a view to profitable prices, and this will involve more or less unemployment of the available equipment and man-power, a variable margin of unemployment, a strategic withholding of productive efficiency for business ends. This Conscientious Withdrawal of Efficiency is what is had in mind here in speaking of Sabotage. The urgency of such a salutary margin of sabotage on output, as well as the ordinary width of the margin, has increased unremittingly during the past half-century, and this increasing urgency of it has been more particularly notable during the past two or three decades.

It is by this reasonable restriction of output that the management of the key industries controls the issues of life for the rest of the industrial system. So it is also by measures of the same character that the management of the manufacturing industries governs the conditions of life for the rest of the community, in a businesslike endeavor to meet the needs of the market in a profitable way. For one reason and another the Farmers, on the other hand, are not in a position to apply such a salutary modicum of sabotage to their work and output or to regulate prices to their own liking in the same way. They are too many, too scattered, too widely varied in their work and their interests, besides being inveterately rooted in self-help and sharp practice. So that the Farmers are by way of being the residuary losers, at whose cost much of this business is carried on.

Ever since this country began to make the turn from an agricultural to an "industrial" footing, the American manufacturing industry has been producing for a closed market. The American tariff policy also took on an aggravated form about that time, and this has contributed greatly to restrict the available market to the purchasing power of the home population, at the same time that it has enabled American special interests to maintain a high level of prices for their output. The volume of this closed market has continually grown greater, with the growth of population and the use of larger resources; but the productive capacity of the manufacturing industries has also continually increased at a more rapid rate, due to the same circumstances and to the additional factor of a continually increasing efficiency in the industrial arts. Industry has continued to be "inordinately" productive, increasingly so. Therefore the urgency of a strategic limitation of the output has also continually increased. The various concerns that have been doing business in manufactures have been competitive sellers in a limited market whose purchasing capacity has habitually fallen short of the productive capacity of the industries which supply the marketable output. On pain of bankruptcy, therefore, it has been incumbent on these business concerns to use moderation and limit their saleable output to the needs of the market,[1] and at the same time to compete among themselves for profitable sales. Any business concern's need of sales is indefinitely extensible, while

---

[1] "The needs of the market," of course, means "what the market will carry off at profitable prices."

the total volume of sales at any given time is fixed within a narrow margin. Salesmanship is the art of taking over a disproportionate share of this run of sales, at a profitable price.

These business concerns are competitive sellers, but they are so circumstanced by their closed market that they can, on the whole, not underbid one another at all effectually in the price of their wares. Underbidding involves an enlarged aggregate output, which implies an enlarged market. In effect, their competitive strategy is confined to two main lines of endeavour:—to reduce the production-cost of a restricted output; and to increase their sales without lowering prices.

On the cost side of this account, again, their constant recourse has been, habitually and increasingly, to endeavour to keep production-costs down by keeping down wages.[2] On the side of sales and salesmanship the out-

[2] Other items that enter into production-costs, as, e. g., the staple raw and structural materials and the power employed, are scarcely amenable to manipulation from the side of the manufacturing business. It is, on the whole, a question of take it or leave it. The business concerns who dispose of the key industries and the staple natural resources are massive bodies and occupy a secure position at the apex of the system, and those who deal with them find it unprofitable to kick against the pricks. Except for the somewhat special case of those manufacturing concerns which do business in farm products, there is small chance of practicing parsimony in production at the cost of any others than the hired man-power. And as a business proposition parsimony becomes a question of shifting production-cost to someone else.

On the other hand the provocation to parsimony in wages is insidious and speciously promising. The industrial man-power is voluminous, but it is scarcely compact enough to be called massive. Hitherto and for the time being it seems quite unlikely that these workmen can be drawn together in such massive formation as would enable them to make head against the business concerns which, between them, control the key industries and the manufactures and transportation system. By force of circumstances

come has been a continued increase of selling-costs and a continually more diligent application to salesmanship. Under both of these heads the passing years of the new century have shown a rising curve, and under both heads the rise has been steeper since the War.

There is no call here to go into the merits of trade-unionism and collective bargaining for wages, or to review the run of "labor troubles" in recent times. These topics are controversial and irritating, and also they are of the nature of subsidiary detail, so far as concerns the present argument. But the broad fact that hired labor is of the essence of the situation under absentee ownership can not similarly be left on one side. Hired labor is an essential factor in the case, and the fact that the man-power employed in industry necessarily goes to its work for wages—on the principle of "hiring and firing" —has grave consequences for the conduct of industry and its efficiency.

As has been explained in an earlier passage, and as is sufficiently evident, the industrial system is a running balance of interlocking processes which stand in such relations of give and take that no one section or process or

these concerns that make up the great body of the business community work together, in effect, to a common end in their negotiations with the hired workmen; the common end being the defeat of the workmen and the consequent shifting upon them of so much of the production-costs as the traffic will bear. In this contest the employer-owners present a massive formation, at the same time that they habitually find themselves legally and morally in the right, resting their case on ancient principles of law and custom; so that any intervention from the side of the constituted authorities will habitually work out to their profit. The bias of the established order and of its appointed keepers runs in favor of business; so that the keepers of law and order will, in effect, be the guardians of the business interests against all comers. And the same bias of principles still runs also throughout the body of hired workmen.

sequence of processes engaged in the work is independent of the rest. Wherever and so far as the mechanical industry has gone into effect the measure of team-work between the constituent processes engaged is the measure of its productive efficiency. When and so far as this running balance of give and take falls away, the system will not work. It is a system of mechanical powers and skilled workmanship running on the mechanically standardised team-work of its constituents; and the factor which finally shapes and carries out this creative team-work in the concrete details of production is the disciplined man-power engaged. It is as an embodiment of disciplined workmanship that this man-power enters creatively into the work of production; and as such it is indispensable. It is true, of course, that the man-power without the due equipment, material resources, and technical direction, will come to naught as a creative force. So will also these other factors in the case without the due man-power, duly trained. By itself any one of them is of no account, but each is indispensable in the combination. It is only in team-work, duly balanced, that these things become creative industrial forces. The only dispensable factor in the case is the owner.

It is by force of his workmanship that the workman counts at all for production. But wherever and so far as absentee ownership has taken effect, it is by force of his salesmanship that he takes his place in the shop. The whole duty of salesmanship is to sell dear and deliver a minimum. With their turn for succinct speech, the Romans covered it all with the maxim: *Caveat emptor.* It is as an articulation in a working team that the workman does work, if any; but it is as a detached salesman of man-power that he comes in for his job.

Since and so far as the mechanical state of the indus-

trial arts has gone into action, industry has been placed on
a footing of absentee ownership and labor has become a
commodity, to be sold dear and delivered at a minimum.
At the same time the régime of absentee ownership perforce excludes personal relations and personal considerations between workmen and employers,—the type-form of
employer under this régime being an impersonal incorporation. So far as human infirmities of a sentimental sort
will permit, therefore, the wage relation under this régime
should fall into wholly impersonal, or depersonalised,
lines; with no recourse to the blandishments of the huckstering salesman and with an unashamed appeal to the
objective facts of demand and supply.

The "employment market," or "labor market," has
visibly been approaching this finished shape, progressively
ever since the country began to make the turn from agriculture and neighborhood workmanship to an industrial
footing on the mechanical plan; but it should also be evident to any moderately dispassionate observer that this
progressive approach to objective nakedness in the negotiations of the employment market has not yet reached
the last conceivable degree of perfection. This failure
to reach perfection, during the past two or three quarter-
centuries of habituation to the new régime, appears to be
due to the very tenacious hold of ancient habits and
transmitted preconceptions; and perhaps also to a workmanlike bent which appears to be innate in the race, and
which will not tolerate an unreserved shift from workmanship to salesmanship.[3] The traditional preconcep-

[3] If a native bent of this kind is to be ascribed, it should apparently be with the reservation that severe and protracted ad-
verse habituation will very greatly, if not altogether, neutralise it
in any given case, and that there also are an appreciable number of individuals in whom this bent is of so slight a force, by
comparison with their other propensities, as to leave them vir-

tion which came down from the old order of industry, under the régime of husbandry, handicraft and neighborhood workmanship, ran imperatively to the effect that human work should be of some objective human use, and it has been a slow-dying prejudice. The bias of salesmanship on the other hand is, as it has always been, to get a margin of something for nothing, and the wider the margin the more perfect the salesman's work. The population which underlies the régime of absentee ownership and hired labor, and which makes up the industrial manpower, have come out of that earlier dispensation of unguarded workmanship, and they still carry over a residue of its habits of thought. Should they finally lose this residue of workmanlike sentiment that now cumbers their negotiations with the absentee corporations, the system of mechanical industry conducted on a basis of investment would evidently no longer work. That is to say, it would no longer yield a net output of goods and services. Even something less than a total loss of the workmanlike animus would bring this industrial system to a stalemate. The state of the case may be described by saying that there is a critical pitch or level of effectual workmanlike animus which must be maintained if the industrial system is to work along as a self-sustained going concern of production. Any decline below this critical level would bring the great industrial adventure to a close, presumably after a more or less protracted period of disorder and decay.[4]

tually exempt from its bias.—Cf. *The Instinct of Workmanship,* ch. ii and iv; also John Dewey, *Human Nature and Conduct,* perhaps especially Part II, sections ii, iii and iv.

[4] In effect, the question has been entertained by some, whether American industry, as well as the industry of civilised Europe, has fallen below this critical level of effectual workmanship since the War. Other causes have contributed,—as, e. g., the

The industrial man-power entered upon this era of mechanical industry and absentee ownership well imbued with the animus of workmanship and of salesmanship, both. The two habits of thought are, both of them, a legacy come down from the era of handicraft, household industry, and neighborly bargaining. And together they lie at the root of the established order of rights, obligations and immunities in industry and business. In America particularly the actuating incentives of life have been these two, to the passable exclusion or abeyance of other spiritual prime-movers, more particularly through that formative period during which the working principles of Americanism were matured, assimilated, and stabilised. The frame of mind in which the familiar use of "hiring and firing" is grounded dates back to the old order; when the individual workman still was technically complete and self-sufficient in his work, and entered on any undertaking as a self-sufficient salesman of his own rounded personal skill, dexterity and judgment, in a bargain with a personal employer.

By degrees, as absentee ownership has progressively taken over the ways and means of industrial life, the relation of the workman to the work in hand has lost the personal note and has come to be the relation of a hired

destruction of equipment, man-power, and morale, caused by the War, and the reinforcement of business principles brought on by the Peace,—and it is also by no means clear that the visible decline of the workmanlike animus is not a transient recession under stress. Yet the question is by no means an idle one, whether these several causes driving to a common objective have not, between them, put the situation in the way of assured eventual wreck. At the best it is a point in doubt. Of these causes of decay the two formidable ones are the loss of workmanlike morale and the over-growth of salesmanlike enterprise. Either or both should be sufficient, "in the absence of disturbing causes."

man to his job. By degrees also, as the workmen have progressively learned that they are transients and by-standers in whatever concerns the organization and aims of any given industrial enterprise, they have also learned to draw together on a more or less lucidly collusive plan to make the most of their position in the impersonal employment market. The resulting organisations of workmen have been "trade unions"—that is to say they have been drawn on lines of workmanship—but they have been formed for a businesslike purpose. The avowed spirit of the thing has been the spirit of salesmanship. The unions have been orgr nized with a view to drive a bargain, and from the outset it has been their constant aim to sell dear, and from near the outset they have also aimed to deliver a minimum. Through it all there has run the ancient bent of workmanship, to the effect that a workman has work to do as well as a job to hold. But with time and continued experience in businesslike negotiations it has by degrees been borne in upon them that as a business proposition it is the first duty of a workman to hold a job; that he has work to do is a secondary consideration.

In all bargaining, in all transactions of merchandising and price-making, the limitation of the merchantable supply is of the essence of the case. And the more single-minded and salesmanlike the parties to the transactions may be, the more diligently will they consider ways and means of limiting the supply to such a point as will most profitably enforce a scarcity value of their vendible output. In the course of time and continued attention to salesmanship, therefore, the unions and their members have been learning that, as regards the work to be done in holding their jobs, it is to be their constant concern to devise plausible ways of withholding it. In the nature of

things,—that is to say in the nature of salesmanship,—
the unions are organizations for the restraint of trade.
It is a delicate question, hitherto not finally decided, how
far they are to be accounted "conspiracies" in restraint
of trade. Necessarily they are of that general complexion, being business organizations; and they have been
continually taking on more of that businesslike complexion, since there can be no effectual salesmanship without
some limitation on the supply of the vendible goods.
The American Federation of Labor may be taken as a
type. The outcome is that both parties to the negotiations in the employment market have now reached a passably unequivocal recognition of this state of things. Employers and workmen, both, have come to realise that the
sole decisive argument on either side is a refusal to go
on. The rest of the voluminous disputation which habitually surrounds their negotiations is known to both parties
to be so much verbiage designed to cloud the issue.

Hitherto this outcome has not been worked out to a
finished clarity. There still remains, especially on the side
of the workmen, a lingering sense of unworthiness in so
putting salesmanship in the place of workmanship. The
habitual position taken by the employer-owners in these
disputes is fairly clear and unembarrassed, but hitherto
the workmen have been unable to go all the way along
these lines of salesmanlike strategy, such as to draw them
together into an inclusive and massive formation driving
to a common onset against a common adversary; such,
e. g., as has sometimes been sketched out under the dread
catchword of "One Big Union." They are still tangled
in personalities, not realising that their common adversary
is a state of affairs rather than a conspiracy of sinners.
And there is also still extant among them a tenacious
residue of that ancient way of thinking according to which

a workman should work for a living and should, in some moral sense, be able to claim a livelihood for which he is ready to work. In one way and another they are unable to see their own case in the untroubled perspective of salesmanship, in which it is to be seen that the chief end of man is to get a margin of something for nothing, at the cost of any whom it may concern. Their spiritual complexion is not yet fully commercialised, even though the great body of them may already have begun to realise that sabotage is the beginning of wisdom in industrial business. They may already believe it with their head, but they do not yet know it with their heart.

Something is also to be said in abatement on the other side, on the side of the business men who manage the industries and who hire and fire. They too are not quite clear, have not yet come into a fully objective appreciation of the facts in the case; although the remnant of handicraft tradition that sticks in their habitual thinking is not precisely to the same effect, and can scarcely be rated as a handicap. Stripped of its adventitious verbiage the position habitually taken by these substantial citizens comes to this, that in common honesty the workmen should work for a living and the owner-employers should invest for a profit; leaving the substantial citizens to decide what may be a suitable livelihood for the workmen. In substance the constituted authorities of the nation also fall into line with the substantial citizens on this head: as how should they not? Again it is a position taken on grounds of inveterate prepossession rather than objective reasoning. Neither side has yet contemplated the converse of this proposition, that the owner-employers should invest for a living and the workmen should work for a profit; leaving the workmen to fix on a suitable livelihood for the employer-owners.

Traditional prepossessions apart, the one of these prop-
ositions is about as good as the other, of course; and
neither of them falls in with the objective run of facts
under the new order of business, as conducted on the impersonal footing of absentee ownership. Under the dispassionate logic of business, neither party is bound in
common honesty to anything more than selling dear and
delivering a minimum. So also, the common good does
not lie within the range of incentives that govern these
negotiations; nor, indeed, within the range of considerations which set the limits of tolerance; except so far as
"the common good" is taken to mean "business-as-usual."
And with each recurring wrangle the preamble of vituper-
ation and sanctimony becomes more abridged and the argument shifts more quickly and more overtly to its final
terms,—the "big stick" of coercive inaction, passive resistance, unemployment, sabotage. The parties to the bargaining have come to be avowed adversaries who are
learning to line up as enemies, habitually preoccupied
with projects of mutual defeat. It should accordingly
not be a question of whether, but only of how soon the
strategy of mutual defeat will result in an inclusive defeat
of the combined forces of industry and business; and
that should apparently resolve itself into a question of how
soon the industrial man-power will, in effect, learn the complete lesson of salesmanlike sabotage,—the employer-
owners have already learned it well enough to serve the
turn.

And all the while the constituted authorities of the nation constitute a Business Administration whose duties
are prescribed for them by that provision of the Constitution which provides that citizens must not be deprived of
their property except by due process of law; which being
interpreted means, in effect, that the powers and immu-

nities of absentee ownership are to be enforced and safeguarded by any suitable use of force and at any cost to
the taxpayers. Circumstances have turned in such a way
as to make this the large and ordinary application of this
proviso. And by the same turn of circumstances the constituted authorities have, in effect and in the main, become
attorneys for one party to the industrial quarrel, thereby
stimulating irritation and quickening the convergence of
events to a blind corner. The industrial system requires
that the management and the industrial man-power should
be engaged on an increasingly close team-work in production; in effect and increasingly, on grounds of sound business they are giving much of their attention to teamwork
in sabotage.

But in all these manœuvres of businesslike management the industrial man-power is, after all, the party of
the second part. The business enterprise that is of the
first as well as of initial consequence is the enterprise of
the business men who have the responsible management
of industry. It is on them that the responsibility rests and
the interest centers. And the argument therefore returns to the policies and tactics habitually employed among
concerns which do business in the manufacturing industries
and supply goods for the market, and to the circumstances
which surround and determine their activities. This ru-
bric covers also the merchandising business, wholesale
and retail, as well as the manufacturing business in the
narrower sense, which delivers the merchantable goods
for distribution in the market. There is no longer a consistent cleavage between these two lines of enterprise,
and a practicable line of distinction between them can no
longer be drawn,—so far as concerns the present argument. Together they make up that field of enterprise

that has to do with the output and distribution of merchantable goods, as contrasted with the key industries on the one hand and the farm population on the other hand.

As has already been remarked in an earlier passage, the great objective circumstance which dominates the business of supply and distribution is the fact of a closed market. This circumstance determines the volume of the output, within a fairly narrow margin of fluctuation. It is an objective actuality, so far as bears on the traffic of the manufacturers and merchants, stubborn as objective facts habitually are. But it is after all an actuality created by the convergence of several circumstances, each of which may be resolved into matters of use and wont. These determining circumstances which set the bounds of the market are such as: (a) the running balance of sabotage on the output of raw and structural materials, administered for their own ends by the management of the key industries and by those interests that stand in a similar relation of arbitrary control to the output of farm products; the ground on which this initial sabotage is carried out being the absentee ownership (or usufruct) of natural resources, and its end being an enhanced free income for the management and their absentee owners; (b) the price system, which decides that the end of endeavor shall be to make money rather than to make goods, and so decides that the making of goods shall be used with wise moderation as a means of making money; the end sought being therefore a maximum aggregate price, as contrasted with a maximum output of goods; (c) by force of the same price system, the purchasing-power of those who buy the merchantable goods is limited by their available funds for expenditure, as contrasted with their productive power; (d) within this framework of prescriptive convention, essentially in the nature of inveterate ceremonial observances, there is drawn by authority the factitious bar of a tariff in restraint of trade, by which the bounds of the market are drawn closer and the available purchasing power is restricted to a higher price level.

The outcome of it all is simple enough. These various business concerns are competitors for a closed volume of traffic. Or more specifically, they are competitive sellers each of which necessarily endeavors to increase his net share in the available purchasing fund; the total volume of purchasing funds available at any given time being fixed within a relatively narrow margin of fluctuation. So that each of these competitive sellers can gain only at a corresponding loss to the rest. At the same time there is, by and large, no outlook for competition in this market by the method of increased output at substantially reduced prices. That expedient was tried and found wanting. The large and progressively larger net returns do not come on that footing, on the whole.[5] That type of competition presumes an open market and a declining price level, all of which is obsolete.

The manufacturers and merchants, therefore, are engaged on a business of competitive selling in a closed market in which prices may fluctuate but can not substantially decline; a market in which one seller's gain is an-

---

[5] It is not to be overlooked, of course, that there are such phenomena as the Ford cars and the chain-stores and mail-order houses, which cut into the profitable traffic on a footing of quantity production and underbidding. But all men know these concerns to be disturbers of the peace and enemies of society, whom the business community at large would be glad to outlaw. They are the filibusters who drive a trade on the too trustful integrity of the business community at large and the too lenient justice of the nation's Business Administration.

other's loss.[6] The business reduces itself to a traffic in salesmanship, running wholly on the comparative merit of the rival commodities, or rather of the rival salesmen. One result has been a very substantial and progressive increase of sales-cost; very appreciably larger than an inspection of the books would show. The producers have been giving continually more attention to the saleability of their product, so that much of what appears on the books as production-cost should properly be charged to the production of saleable appearances. The distinction between workmanship and salesmanship has progressively been blurred in this way, until it will doubtless hold true now that the shop-cost of many articles produced for the market is mainly chargeable to the production of saleable appearances, ordinarily meretricious. So, e. g., whatever its other (and undeniable) merits may be, the vogue of "package goods" is to be credited wholly to salesmanship, and its cost is chargeable in the main to that account.

The designing and promulgation of saleable containers, —that is to say such containers as will sell the contents on the merits of the visual effect of their container,—has become a large and, it is said, a lucrative branch of the business of publicity. It employs a formidable number of artists and "copy writers" as well as of itinerant spokesmen, demonstrators, interpreters; and more than one psychologist of eminence has been retained by the publicity agencies for consultation and critical advice on the competitive saleability of rival containers and of the labels and doctrinal memoranda which embellish them. The cost of all this is very appreciable, but it is a necessary cost. Taking them one with another, it is presumably

---

[6] As this matter was recently summed up at a staff conference of a certain noted advertising concern: "Blank has got the market; it is our problem to dislodge him."

safe to say that the containers account for one-half the shop-cost of what are properly called "package goods," and for something approaching one-half of the price paid by the consumer. In certain lines, doubtless, as, e. g., in cosmetics and household remedies, this proportion is exceeded by a very substantial margin; in these lines, indeed, the choice of suitable—that is to say saleable—containers surrounded with suitable—that is to say saleable —doctrinal sentences, is the matter of grave moment; the specific nature of the contents being, on the whole, of subsidiary consequence, if any.[7] It is also the confident testimony of persons who are in a position to know, that except for line and color, shape and surface, of the containers, and apart from verbal differences in the doctrinal matter which surrounds them, any distinctive character in these various articles of intimate personal use is something very difficult to get at.[8]

[7] This is not said by way of aspersion. In these intimate matters of health and fabricated beauty the beneficent workings of faith are manifest; if it should not rather be said that the manifest benefit derived from these many remedies, medicaments, lotions, unguents, pastes and pigments, is in the main a work of faith which acts tropismatically on the consumer's bodily frame, with little reference to the pharmaceutical composition of the contents of the purchased container, provided that they are not unduly deleterious. The case may, not without profit, be assimilated to certain of the more amiable prodigies wrought in the name of Holy Church, where it is well known that the curative efficacy of any given sainted object is something quite apart from its chemical constitution. Indeed, here as at many other points salesmanship touches the frontiers of the magical art; and no man will question that, as a business proposition, a magical efficacy is a good thing to sell.

[8] All the while, it appears on inquiry that the number of distinct articles—distinct in point of name and container—carried in stock under the head of "Toilet Goods" on the first floor of a well-known New-York department store exceeds 10,000. So it also appears on the same inquiry that floor space so devoted to the distribution of these 10,000 yields larger net

Saleable containers are only the beginning of wisdom in latterday manufacture and merchandising. But they merit attention as being typical and illustrative of the latterday growth of salesmanship and of the latterday spirit of business at its homeliest and best. They are typical of the ways and means of salesmanship also in the respect that they serve a useful purpose for the consumer in the way of convenience and cleanliness at the same time that they enable the contents to be sold at an enhanced price. There is always something of such a variable fringe of substantial service attaching to the ordinary ways and means of salesmanlike publicity, whether in the way of containers or in that standard run of doctrinal pronouncements that will come to mind as the type-form of such publicity; [9] and it is the ordinary duty of the salesman to make it appear that this outlying fringe of usefulness is the whole end and purpose of it all. One will be a competent salesman in much the same measure as one effectually "puts over" this line of make-believe.

The concerns which do business in this field are compet-

earnings per square foot than any other similar area of floor space employed by this prosperous business concern. Of course the 10,000 items are not all, or nearly all, containers of fabricated beauty, but even a cursory view of the premises will find such containers very much in evidence, and will also show that this particular case presents nothing exceptional.

[9] This is, of course, not intended to say that the net effect of these things, apart from their beneficial effect on sales, is ordinarily of a serviceable character; but only that there are mitigating circumstances. Materially speaking, these things are in the nature of nuisances, but there is something to be said in abatement. There is commonly a variable, often negligible, fringe of serviceable information, and the like, attaching to their salesmanlike use. In their net effect, sign-boards, placards, car-cards, posters, electrical blinkers, and the like devices, are a public nuisance, of course—*de facto,* not *de jure*—but to a variable, though fractional, extent their subsidiary and unintended effects may often be serviceable.

itors in a closed market. That is to say, they are competitors for a share in the available purchasing-power that comes into the market, so that the one concern gains at the others' cost. From which it follows that any device or expedient which approves itself as a practicable means of cutting into the market, on the part of any one of the competitive concerns, presently becomes a necessity to all the rest, on pain of extinction. The means of "getting ahead" is also the means of "keeping up." Any concern which neglects its opportunities and falls behind is in a way to fall out of the game.[10] The net aggregate result is a competitive multiplication of the ways and means of salesmanship at a competitively increasing net aggregate cost. The selling-cost per unit of the goods sold rises accordingly, and the price to the consumer rises to meet the enhanced selling-cost. The rising cost of salesmanship becomes a rising overhead charge on the business, regulated by the pressure of competitive selling, but hitherto trending upwards, apparently with a gradually accelerated rise.

[10] There are exceptional cases, perhaps more apparent than convincing, where old established merchant-houses have continued to do business in a modest but profitable way on a footing of clientèle and goodwill coming down from the custom of past years. Indeed, such a house will have a substantial advantage so long as its clientèle holds out, in that it incurs but a minimum of expense for publicity at the same time that it comes in for its volume of sales at the enhanced prices which the rising costs of publicity at large entail. Increased sales-costs entail rising prices and widening margins for the general body of competing concerns, while the old established firm, which rests its business on its ancient clientèle, shares in the rising prices and widening margins without a porportionate share in the rising costs of publicity. So that a concern so placed will be in a position to maintain its volume of net earnings even while the volume of its custom is shrinking. The circumstance is perhaps best to be rated as a case of past salesmanship capitalized and carried over as intangible assets.

As is the case with other business charges and expenditures, the effectual limit on sales-costs, including whatever is to be counted in as ways and means of selling, is what the traffic will bear. But sales-costs present some slight peculiarities in this respect, being subject to certain peculiar circumstances. By use of the proper expedients—which may be taken to mean the same as saying, by judicious expenditure of sufficiently large sums—the sales of any given line of merchantable goods, or of any given concern dealing in such goods, may be increased indefinitely. This is a well-assured proposition in folk-psychology. Beyond a certain point (to be determined by experience) an increase of sales will be had only at an increasing sales-cost per unit of goods sold; and beyond a certain further point (similarly to be determined by experience) any further increase of sales will cost more than it will bring,—that is to say the selling-cost per unit will then exceed the seller's net price-margin over production-cost, which is more than the traffic will bear. A judicious expenditure on sales-cost should evidently approach this point, without passing it.

But the other sellers in the same market, whether they sell the same line of goods or other lines, are competitors for the same custom and will push their sales-enterprise on the same plan. Which puts the sellers, all and several, on the defensive against one another's salesmanship; which comes to a competitively defensive expenditure on sales-costs, of such a character that none of the competing sellers can afford to fall short in his expenditures on salesmanship,—on penalty of failure. That is to say, as a business proposition, the traffic in manufacturing and merchandising will no longer bear a scant overhead charge in the way of sales-costs; or such a charge as would once have been called a reasonable overhead on that score. The conditions imposed by a closed competitive market have taken such a turn that parsimony in the matter of sales-costs will be fatal, in the ordinary case. He who hesitates is lost. Taking one such sales-enterprise with another, what the traffic will bear appears, in effect, to run between the two points indicated above, but to rise consistently toward the higher. Judicious expenditure on salesmanship, therefore, will play between these limits, touching the higher limit more frequently than the lower; with certain consequences to be noted presently.

The experience of the last few years, since salesmanship has come unequivocally to take the first place in the business of manufacturing and merchandising, has also brought out a further peculiar circumstance which attaches to this enterprise of selling goods and services in a closed market. A large, and increasing, number of the competing lines lend themselves effectually to large-scale production in the matter of salesmanship. Judicious and continued expenditure on publicity and the like expedients of salesmanship will result in what may fairly be called a quantity-production of customers for the purchase of the goods or services in question.[11] Experience has shown what might be expected, that the cost of pro-

[11] There is, of course, no actual fabrication of persons endowed with purchasing-power *ad hoc,* although much of the language employed by the publicity-agencies appears to promise something of that kind; nor is there even any importation of an unused supply of such customers from abroad,—the law does not allow it. Viewed in the large, what actually is effected is only a diversion of customers from one to another of the competing sellers, of course. But as seen from the isolated standpoint of any given selling-concern it foots up to a production of new customers or the upkeep of customers already in use by the given concern. So that this acquisition and repair of customers may fairly be reckoned at a stated production-cost per unit; and this operation lends itself to quantity production.

duction per unit of customers by the use of the later perfected methods and appliances of sales-publicity is subject
to the well-known economic law of increasing returns,
very much as it applies to quantity production generally,
wherever machine processes are employed on an appreciably large scale.

It may be called to mind, though the fact should be
familiar enough, that with the continued growth and
standardisation of the business and its procedure in recent
years, very much of sales-publicity has with good effect
been reduced to mechanical units of space, speed, number, frequency, and the like. Much the same is true for
very much of the other apparatus of salesmanship, including a reasonable proportion of the personnel. It has
accordingly become practicable now to check and tally this
work and its major effects in units of tangible performance. So that the fabrication of customers can now be
carried on as a routine operation, quite in the spirit of
the mechanical industries and with much the same degree
of assurance as regards the quality, rate and volume of
the output; the mechanical equipment as well as its complement of man-power employed in such production of
customers being held to its work under the surveillance of
technically trained persons who might fairly be called publicity engineers. Such technicians are now diligently bred
and trained for this use by all the reputable seminaries of
learning.[12]

[12] The schools, on private foundation or at the public charge,
are turning a greatly intensified and amplified attention to the
needs of salesmanship and the propagation of salesmen, and they
are turning out a rapidly swelling volume of graduates in this
art of "putting it over." Indeed, this scholastic propagation of
salesmen may fairly be cited as an example of quantity. production; standardised both in its processes and in its output.

The production of customers by sales-publicity is evidently

It is familiarly known to economists that up to a certain, fluctuating but effectual, limit an increasing volume of output may be turned out by methods of quantity production at a decreasing cost per unit. This law of increasing returns, or decreasing cost, will apply in the production of customers by large-scale publicity very much as in the large-scale mechanical industry generally. In the business of sales-publicity this upper limit of increasing returns is relatively high. So that up to a fairly high limit the aggregate sales-costs on a larger volume of sales will be progressively more reasonable, relatively to the net aggregate returns from the sales. The rule does not apply throughout or uniformly, but it applies rather widely and in an increasing number of lines, particularly among the staple lines of merchandise. It follows that within the application of the rule the larger selling-concerns, with larger funds and expenditures, will have something of an advantage over concerns of a smaller and middling size.

It should and appears to follow that so far as this rule of quantity-production applies, the larger advertisers among these competing concerns will tend to displace those of a smaller and middling size. The latter will drop

the same thing as a production of systematised illusions organised into serviceable "action patterns"—serviceable, that is, for the use of the seller on whose account and for whose profit the customer is being produced. It follows therefore that the technicians in charge of this work, as also the skilled personnel of the working-force, are by way of being experts and experimenters in applied psychology, with a workmanlike bent in the direction of what may be called creative psychiatry. Their day's work will necessarily run on the creative guidance of habit and bias, by recourse to shock effects, tropismatic reactions, animal orientation, forced movements, fixation of ideas, verbal intoxication. It is a trading on that range of human infirmities which blossom in devout observances and bear fruit in the psychopathic wards.

out of the running, inconspicuously. This traffic in publicity and customers runs within a closed market, as has already been remarked, and it feeds on a loosely fixed aggregate volume of purchasing-power; so that at any given time, whatever increase of custom is gained by any given selling-concern will be lost by others, and whatever custom is shifted by publicity to any given commodity (e. g., yeast-cakes) is thereby shifted away from another or others (e. g., soap-powders).[13] Hitherto the rule appears to hold good, on the whole, that the large selling-concerns and the large adventures in publicity are gaining at the expense of the smaller ones and are displacing the latter, particularly those of a middling size. The rule is by no means hard and fast, no more so here than in the industrial use of quantity-production. And it is also noticeable that the growth of these larger absentee selling-concerns is not greatly reducing the number of those small-scale concerns that continue to do business on a footing of intimate personal attention to their customers, and that carry their point by word and gesture. What may be called "hand tooling" still holds its place in the field of salesmanship. Very much as is the case in productive industry, where many minor and intimate trades and crafts still find a living in the crevices of the industrial system, so here also.

In this market virtually all sellers (manufacturers and merchants) are competitors of virtually all other sellers, irrespective, on the whole, of the diversity of goods offered for sale. The total offering of goods for sale

[13] In strict accuracy and to avoid the appearance of oversight, it should be added that such a closed market, that is to say the volume of purchasing-power available, will be narrowed by approximately so much as these expenditures on salesmanship may amount to in the aggregate.

takes up the total volume of available purchasing-power.[14] But not all kinds and classes of merchantable goods lend themselves equally to propaganda by methods of the large-scale absentee salesmanship. The quantity-production of customers is visibly more applicable in some lines than in others. The experience of the past few years teaches, on the whole, that articles of intimate personal use and articles of conspicuous personal use lend themselves in some peculiar degree to this manner of propaganda. The volume of publicity devoted to the sale of such articles, as well as the resulting increased volume of sales, argues quite unequivocally to that effect. These articles and their consumption bear, or are plausibly alleged to bear, in a felicitous way on the personal well-being or the personal prestige of the consumer; and customers appear to be peculiarly open to argument and persuasion on these heads.[15]

As has already been remarked, the quantity-production

[14] There is the qualification, to be noted for what it may be worth, that the current, very urgent, sales-publicity may be presumed to divert a little something from savings to consumptive expenditures, and so may add that much of a margin of funds to the volume of purchasing-power currently available for expenditure on advertised goods. For what it may be worth, this unremitting impulsion to spend rather than save is to be counted in as a factor in the case.

[15] It has long been a commonplace among those who are interested in these matters that proprietary remedies, "patent medicines" and the like—what are sometimes called "nostrums"—can always be marketed with a good profit by use of a suitable kind and amount of publicity, somewhat irrespective of any inherent merit in the goods,—provided always that the seller-proprietor and his publicity-agent go about the business with the requisite lack of scruple. Something to the same effect holds true of sales-enterprise in many productions of commercialised art, which are plausibly alleged to be conducive to the prestige of the consumer; as e. g., grave-stones, lap-dogs, parlor-furniture, cosmetic pigments, fashionable dress and equipage generally.

of customers by appliances of publicity is a craft which runs on applied psychology. The raw material in which the work is to be done is human credulity, and the output aimed at is profitable fixed ideas. Current experience in publicity appears to show that among the human sensibilities upon which a sagacious salesmanship will spend its endeavors the most fruitful are Fear and Shame. Human credulity appears to be peculiarly tractable under the pressure of a well conceived appeal to fear and shame, and to set into obstinate and extraordinary shapes (action patterns) on relatively slight habituation along these lines. The fear and shame on which the sales-publicity[16] proceeds in its work of turning credulous persons into profitable customers are the fear of mortal disease and the fear of losing prestige. It is not easy, nor perhaps is it worth while, to attempt any hard and fast distinction between the sense of shame and the fear of losing prestige; at least in this connection and for the present argument. These are ubiquitous traits of the race. The former rises, apparently, to a gradually advancing pitch of sensibility (and credulity) with advancing age; while the latter, the solicitude for instant personal prestige, counts for more in the period of adolescence and early maturity.[17] So the

[16] Of the secular order, as contrasted with the propaganda of the Faith; for it is to be remarked—and it carries a comfortable note of authentication for salesmanship at large—that the stupendous spiritual edifice of Holy Church also rests quite secure on this profitable gift of credulous and lasting fear stabilised with tireless publicity.

[17] The fear of losing prestige has often been confused with personal vanity; a mistake due to incomplete analysis of the facts in the case. Closer attention to certain everyday facts, e. g., will satisfy any passably judicious bystander that the spirit which chiefly moves the young generation in these premises is not a boundless aspiration to out-bid and out-run all competitors and reach a preëminent notoriety for a splendid and colorful personal presence. Cosmetic pigments and preposterous

publicity agents of the sovereign remedies "throw a scare into" the old generation, while the salesmen of the proprietary beautifiers work on the aspirations of the young. The beautifiers are in the nature of "pacifiers." Between them they account for a very large and lucrative volume of absentee salesmanship, as well as a large aggregate of sales-costs, and a large diversion of custom from other lines of expenditures. The intrinsic merits of this traffic in fear and credulity will call for no reflections.

Salesmanship which has to do with merchandising follows two main lines: publicity (advertising), and personal bargaining.[18] Of the two, quantity-production of pub-

garments are applied to the person with a view to avoid falling short of the blamelessly best, to avoid unfavorable notice rather than to achieve notoriety, to "keep up with the times," rather than to set the pace. And it is to this fear of derogatory notoriety that the expert advertisers of these ways and means of fabricated beauty address themselves and adapt the flow of their intoxicating verbiage. Even a cursory view of advertising matter bearing on this point will show that its dominant note is minatory; it runs, by constant suggestion, on the evil case of those foolish virgins who "get left" in the matter of personal prestige.

On any common-sense reflection it should seem highly improbable that anything but unreasoning fear would drive any person to the habitual use of these singular means of adornment. It is also known to ethnologists that practices of a similar nature and of somewhat the same æsthetic value among the peoples of the lower cultures—as, e. g., tattooing and scarification, tooth-filing, nose-boring, lip-buttons—rest directly and unequivocally on the fear of losing prestige. And at this point, as indeed at many others, it is profitable to call to mind that the hereditary human nature of these Europeans and their colonies is still the same as that of their savage forebears was in the Neolithic Age, some ten or twelve thousand years ago.

[18] Salesmanship which is not immediately concerned with merchandising is less closely bound up with these two standard ways and means; as, e. g., in the manœuvres of salesmanship by which business is conducted in the key industries and in the money market. The more habitual recourse here is sabotage, an expert

licity has been gaining over the personal bargain ever since the business of selling began its advance to the large scale. Publicity is absentee salesmanship, and fits into the run of things along with absentee ownership. It is as an expedient of merchandising *in absentia* that publicity has fully come into its own.[19] But while sales-publicity has been gaining ground, it is doubtful if personal bargaining has lost ground, even relatively to the increased volume of sales. What is not doubtful is that between them the two account for a larger employment of manpower and a larger consumption of materials than ever before, whether counted in absolute figures or relatively to the aggregate volume of goods sold. In other words, more time, effort, and equipment—per unit of merchandise—goes into salesmanship, now than in the past; the sales-cost per unit is larger now, whether the unit be counted in terms of price or by weight and tale.

The cause of this advancing sales-cost is quite simple: —production-cost by modern industrial methods being less, the margin which can be taken up in sales-cost is more. In the nature of things sales-cost will rise to the

restriction of supply, though by no means to the entire neglect of publicity and bargaining. These lines of business will be considered in a later chapter.

[19] In its elements, of course, sales-publicity is nothing new; but in its eventual working-out under absentee ownership it has disclosed a character and significance beyond anticipation and beyond ancient example. Yet much of the doctrinal matter that goes into print in behalf of yeast-cakes, "style-plus" clothing, lipsticks, face-creams, and the like, still reads not unlike that ancient achievement in publicity, the royal preamble to the Code of Hammurabi, said to date from the twenty-first century B. C. There is in both the same diligent attention to over-statement and the same unfailing avoidance of all that is to be said in abatement.

And as has already been indicated, the normal guide of sales-publicity is the old Latin formula:—*Suppressio veri, suggestio falsi.*

maximum which the traffic will bear. If the net returns to any or all of the sellers who are already in the market should rise to any figure that can be called inordinate, one or another of two alternatives will follow. The sellers already in the market will competitively push their sales-cost, their expenditures on publicity and bargainers, to such a figure as to leave no inordinate returns; or new sellers will see their chance to come in for a profit and so will cut into the volume of sales and the margin of returns.

Both methods are in constant operation. Just now their action is masked and in some degree held in abeyance, in that the situation is undergoing a somewhat sweeping change. The large-scale publicity has made good as a profitable enterprise, and the large-scale competitors have not yet begun that closer-shorn and truceless competition among themselves for dominant control of the market, which is presumably coming to a head in due time. It is all contained in the workday premises of absentee ownership and absentee salesmanship. For the time being, the pioneers in this large sales-publicity are enjoying the fruits of their businesslike initiative, in the way of generous net returns; particularly the very large ones among them, who are having things very much their own way; which means low shop-costs, ample sales-costs, high selling-prices, and lucrative margins, with large aggregate net returns. But very much as is true in the mechanical industry, so also in this large-scale mechanical publicity, what one concern with ample funds can do another concern with funds of the same amplitude in the same or another line of merchandising can do as well, just so soon as the pioneers have sufficiently proved the case. The pioneers—the current sellers of soap-powders, yeast-cakes, rubber heels, motor cars, "cost-plus" clothing for young men, and the like—are due presently to be over-taken, and their easy market cut into by others who are ready to do just as well, with the result that sales-costs by this method will rise to the maximum which the traffic will bear, leaving no more than ordinary returns on the investment. The net result in the end should be a further increase of the prices paid by consumers and a further growth of advertising agencies and their business.

The number of concerns and the aggregate capital and personnel engaged in the business of sales-publicity is already very considerable, and the growth in all these respects, as well as in the volume of the business hitherto, goes on unchecked, with a very promising outlook for continued growth at an accelerated rate in the near future.[20] The growth of this business, and the growing necessity of it as a means of competitive selling, has been particularly notable during the past dozen years; and at the same time it has undergone an extensive standardisation and specialisation, by which the work has come to be effectually subdivided and apportioned among the per-

---

[20] The oldest existing advertising agency, according to figures supplied by the New York Council of the American Association of Advertising Agencies (known to the trade as the A. A. A. A.) was founded in 1864. It is still one of the largest, most reliable and most successful. It has now a business turnover of something approaching $15,000,000, and has established branch offices in several of the larger American and European cities. The life-history of this corporation may fairly be taken as typical of the business. It has been successful from the outset and has done an increasing volume of business since its foundation, but its largest growth and most gratifying success lies within the past decade. Its business turnover for the current year runs in excess of that of any previous year; not even excepting 1920, when the Treasury decision to the effect that expenditures on advertising are exempt from the Income Tax led to an extraordinary increase in such expenditures.

sonnel within each concern at the same time that the field
of publicity has been divided among the several concerns,
according to locality and according to the nature of the
work, particularly according to the ways and means employed, as, e. g., between news-print and "outdoor advertising." [21]

[21] Something may conveniently be said of the comparative
merits, costs, volume, and present standing of these two chief
divisions of sales-publicity. During the past year, e. g., at a
conference of the well-informed men of the country, interested in
these matters, the estimate was offered that "national" advertising
(as distinguished from "local") in the newspapers of the country amounts at present to some $600,000,000, rather over than
under. Well-informed persons within the body of conferees have
held that $700,000,000 or $750,000,000 would be nearer the facts.
The total expenditures for advertising in 1922, in newspapers and
magazines, has been some $800,000,000; while estimates for 1923
run over $1,000,000,000.

Of outdoor advertising, Mr. E. O. Perrin, of the Media Department in the J. Walter Thompson Co., says that, "until
1919 it amounted to about $5,000,000. Since then, the increase has
been tremendous, and last year (1921) the total volume of outdoor advertising in the United States exceeded $30,000,000.—
Prices vary greatly—according to size and location—some of the
spectacular displays rent at extremely high figures. The big
Wrigley (chewing-gum) electric sign at Times Square, New
York, costs the advertiser $108,000 a year."—E. O. Perrin, "The
Development of Outdoor Advertising," in *The J. Walter Thompson News*, February, 1922. At a conference of outdoor advertisers the previous year in Baltimore it was stated, on a deliberate
estimate, that that year's expenditures on sign-boards alone—
what are known in the trade jargon as "Bulletins" and "Posters"
—were running over $60,000,000.

"In the city of Chicago . . . it is possible to secure forty-eight
painted walls and bulletins at a cost of $1,250 per month. The
cost of a full page for one insertion in Chicago's largest newspaper is $1,708. In Kansas City, a display of one hundred
standard twenty-four sheet posters costs $755.60 per month, as
against $1,064 for one full page in the leading newspaper. A
representative poster campaign covering the entire country and
consisting of 17,196 posters would cost the advertiser about
$140,000 per month." (The Same.)

News-print publicity, as the use of printed matter in circulation may conveniently be called, is doubtless the largest "medium" employed for the making of sales; as it is also the most familiar and habitual, as well as the most costly in the aggregate, whether cost be counted in terms of the work and materials consumed, in the price paid for it by the advertisers, or in what it adds to the prices paid for goods by the consumers. It will include primarily advertising matter in newspapers and periodicals, but it includes also circulars, circular letters, and leaflets distributed by mail or by hand, and there is also to be counted in virtually all of the very considerable and constantly increasing number of trade periodicals devoted to special lines of the manufacturing and merchandising business, as well as the pages of trade-news and business information carried by the common run of papers, dailies, weeklies and others. On a deliberate estimate based on such data as are readily available it appears that advertising matter of the standard forms

"In this connection it is interesting to note that although the outdoor medium was first used on a large scale by the makers of patent medicines, it is now employed by nearly every type of advertiser. . . . The use of outdoor advertising during the Liberty Loan drives, as well as in recent political campaigns, is too well known to need comment.

"Outdoor advertising is now conducted by a large number of companies scattered all over the country, many of whom are in competition with each other in various territories. . . . The Thomas Cusack Company. Considerably more than half of the total volume of outdoor advertising in the United States last year was placed by that organization. The Thomas Cusack Company owns and operates both paint and poster plants in several hundred cities and towns throughout the country, and also places advertising in nearly all the small independent plants. In fact this company is the only organisation through which complete national campaigns can be secured. There are now between seven and eight thousand men on the Thomas Cusack payroll." (The Same.)

will account for something like one-half of the space occupied by printed matter in newspapers, including weeklies, rather under than over, and something appreciably less than one-half of the printed space in magazines, taking them one with another. If to this total of what would be listed as advertising space proper be added the trade-news, fashion, and financial columns, of the newspapers and the papers and magazines that are wholly or chiefly occupied with the interests of salesmanship, the total will rise appreciably over one-half the printed matter that goes into circulation in the way of newspapers and magazines. In point of expense the aggregate which is so devoted to sales-publicity doubtless runs very appreciably over one-half of the total of printed matter; advertising matter, financial news, and business comment and review being on the whole the most costly reading matter that goes to the make-up of a newspaper, both in the production of its "copy" and in the typographical composition and press work.[22]

[22] It is. accordingly, scarcely an over-statement to say that something like one half of the wood-pulp that goes through the paper mills, together with one-half the man-power and mechanical equipment engaged in the paper industry and the printing trades, is consumed in the making of competitive sales, the net effect of which is to raise the prices paid for goods by the consumers. The yearly consumption of newsprint paper in the United States and Canada is about 2,600,000 tons, according to figures submitted at a meeting of the Canadian Pulp and Paper Association.

As giving some indication of what the figures for expenditure on sales-publicity are like, in the periodical press outside of newspapers, it is reported on reliable authority that the total advertising revenues of 72 publications of this class for 1920 came to $132,414,799. This was the year immediately affected by the decision which exempts advertising expenditures from the income tax. The corresponding figures for 1919 were $97,208,791, those for 1918, $61,312,888. The corresponding total for "Color Copy" (1920) was $39,644,545. As a maximum value of adver-

The two major divisions of sales-advertising are "News-Print," and "Outdoor" Advertising.[23] But there are also many and various minor devices employed in the service of absentee salesmanship, which between them make up a sufficiently formidable total. They comprise, e. g., such things as show-windows,[24] indoor display of wares, decorative interiors, posters and personnel, trade marks, "slogans," demonstrators, decorative and doctrinal containers.

None of these ways and means are new, in principle, though some of them, as, e. g., the "spectacular" outdoor signs, are as new in detail as the mechanical devices which they turn to account. Nor is their use confined to what would be precisely called sales-publicity. Yet in all the use of these things there is this much in common, that they are

tising space in periodicals of this class, a single (preferred) page of a single issue of the presumed leader among them sold, in the winter of 1921, at the standard rate of $11,000; coupled with an engagement to buy the same space at the same rate in 13 issues during the year. This price does not cover the preparation of the illustrations or the reading matter, which are supplied at the expense of the advertiser.—Cf. *Advertising in National Publications* 1914–1920, Curtis Publishing Company, 1921. (For private circulation.) Expenditures for advertising in newspapers are said to run about seven times as high as what goes to the magazines.

[23] Outdoor displays have been classed under three standard forms: Bulletins ("Any outdoor sign which is handpainted in colors"); Poster ("A lithographed paper sign which is pasted on a metal panel"); and Spectacular displays ("An electric display built on a skeleton steel frame with flashing devices").

[24] "Big corporations with many branches have separate window display departments with a staff of men expert in various branches of the art, designing, color, and some even have a psychologist on the staff to decide whether the finished effect will prove alluring to the public.

"The great amount of material used in these windows has already made itself felt in several industries, the Copper and Brass Association figuring that 2,000,000 pounds of copper will be consumed during 1922."

employed competitively in an endeavour to draw on the sympathies and the substance of the underlying population; they are useful as a means by which those who make use of them come in for a competitive share in the usufruct of the underlying population, its services, workmanship, and material output. They have all been turned to account, early and late, in such enterprises as public loans, recruiting campaigns for army and navy, electioneering campaigns, campaigns for contributions to charities, relief, and such demi-military enterprises as the Red Cross; and most notably of all for the Propaganda of the Faith.

NOTE TO CHAPTER XI

Writers who discuss these matters have not directed attention to the Propaganda of the Faith as an object-lesson in sales-publicity, its theory and practice, its ways and means, its benefits and its possibilities of gain. Yet it is altogether the most notable enterprise of the kind. The Propaganda of the Faith is quite the largest, oldest, most magnificent, most unabashed, and most lucrative enterprise in sales-publicity in all Christendom. Much is to be learned from it as regards media and suitable methods of approach, as well as due perseverence, tact, and effrontery. By contrast, the many secular adventures in salesmanship are no better than upstarts, raw recruits, late and slender capitalisations out of the ample fund of human credulity. It is only quite recently, and even yet only with a dawning realisation of what may be achieved by consummate effrontery in the long run, that these others are beginning to take on anything like the same air of stately benevolence and menacing solemnity. No pronouncement on rubber-heels, soap-powders, lip-sticks, or yeast-cakes, not even Sapphira Buncombe's Vegetative Compound, are yet able to ignore material facts with the same magisterial detachment, and none has yet commanded the same unreasoning assent or acclamation. None other have achieved that pitch of unabated assurance which has enabled the publicity-agents of the Faith to debar human reason from scrutinising their pronouncements. These others are doing well enough, no doubt; perhaps as well as might reasonably be expected under the circumstances, but they are a feeble thing in comparison. Saul has slain his thousands, perhaps, but David has slain his tens of thousands.

There is, of course, no occasion for levity in so calling to mind these highly significant works of human infatuation, past and current. Nor should it cast any shadow of profanation on any of the sacred verities when it is so called to mind that, when all is said, they, too, rest after all on the same ubiquitously human ground of unreasoning fear, aspiration, and credulity, as do the familiar soap-powders, yeast-cakes, lip-sticks, rubber tires, chewing-gum, and restoratives of lost manhood, whose profitable efficacy is likewise created and kept in repair by a well-advised salespublicity. Indeed, it should rather seem the other way about. That the same principles of sales-publicity are found good and profitable for the traffic in spiritual amenities and in these material comforts should serve to show how deep and pervasively the scheme of deliverance and rehabilitation is rooted in the merciful gift of credulous infatuation. It should redound to the credit of the secular arm of sales-publicity rather than cast an aspersion on those who traffic in man's spiritual needs; and should go to show how truly business-as-usual articulates with the business of the Kingdom of Heaven. As it is with the traffic in these divinely beneficial intangibles, so it is with the like salesmanship on the material plane; the marvels of commercial make-believe, too, seek and find a lodgment in the popular knowledge and belief by way of a tireless publicity, such as blessed experience has long and profitably proved and found good in the Propaganda of the Faith. Ways and means which so have proved gainful to His publicity-agents and conducive to the Glory of God—indeed indispensable to the continued upkeep of that Glory—are being drawn into the service of the secular Good of Man; so attesting the excellence of that devoutly familiar form of words which describes the *summum bonum* as a balanced ration of divine glory and human use. It is worth noting in this connection that those Godfearing business men who administer the nation's affairs appear to realise this congruity between sacred and secular salesmanship; so much so that they have on due consideration found that investment in commercial advertising is rightfully exempt from the income tax, very much as the assets and revenues of the churches are tax-exempt. The one line of publicity, it appears is intrinsic to the good of man, as the other is essential to the continued Glory of God.

There is more than one reason for speaking of these matters here, and for speaking of them in a detached and objective way as mere workday factors of human conduct,—leaving all due sanctimony on one side for the time being, without thereby questioning the need and merit of such sanctimony as an ordinary means of grace, or the expediency of it as a standard vehicle of sales-publicity in putting over the transcendent verities of the Faith. It all implies no call and no inclination to lay profane hands on these verities. Taken objectively as a human achievement, the high example of the Propaganda of the Faith should serve as a moral stimulus and a pacemaker. The whole duty of sales-publicity is to "put it over," as the colloquial phrasing has it; and in the matter of putting it over, it is plain that the laurel, the palms, and the pæan are due to go to the publicity-agents of the Faith, without protest. The large and enduring success of the Propaganda through the ages is an object-lesson to show how great is the efficacy of *ipse dixit* when it is put over with due perseverence and audacity. It also carries a broad suggestion as to what may be the practical limits eventually to be attained by commercial advertising in the way of capitalisable earning-capacity.

Commercial sales-publicity of the secular sort evidently falls short, hitherto, in respect of the pitch and volume of make-believe which can be put over effectually and profitably. But it also falls short conspicuously at another critical point. It is of the nature of sales-publicity, to promise much and deliver a minimum. *Suppressio veri, suggestio falsi.* Worked out to its ideal finish, as in the promises and performance of the publicity-agents of the Faith, it should be the high good fortune of the perfect salesman in the secular field also to promise everything and deliver nothing.

Hitherto this climax of salesmanlike felicity has not been attained in the secular merchandising enterprise, except in a sporadic and dubious fashion. On the other hand, hitherto the publicity-agents of the Faith have habitually promised much and have delivered substantially none of the material advertised, and have "come through" with none of the tangible performances promised by their advertising matter. All that has been delivered hitherto has—perhaps all for the better—been in the nature of further publicity, often with a use of more pointedly menacing language; but it has always been more language, with a moratorium on the liquidation of the promises to pay, and a penalty on any expressed doubt of the solvency of the concern. There have of course, from time to time, been staged certain sketchy prodigies, in the nature of what the secular outdoor advertisers would call "spectacular displays," apparently designed to demonstrate the nature and merits of the goods kept in stock. These have not infrequently been highly ingenious, and also quite convincing to such persons as are fit to be convinced by them. They have carried conviction to those persons whose habitual beliefs are of a suitable kind. But as viewed objectively and as seen in any other than their own dim religious light, these admirable feats of manifestation have been after all essentially ephemeral and nugatory hitherto; very much of a class with those lunch-counter sample-packages that are designed to demonstrate the expansive powers of some noted baking-powder, in miniature and with precautions. They are after all in the nature of publicity-gestures, eloquent, no doubt, and graceful, but they are not the goods listed in the doctrinal pronouncements; no more than the wriggly gestures with which certain spear-headed manikins stab the nightly firmament over Times Square are an effectual delivery of chewing-gum. *Bona-fide* delivery of the listed goods would have to be a tangible performance of quite another complexion, inasmuch as the specifications call for Hell-fire and the Kingdom of Heaven; to which the most heavily capitalised of these publicity concerns of the supernatural adds a broad margin of Purgatory.

There is, of course, no call and no inclination to take the

publicity-agents of the Faith to task for failure to deliver the goods listed in their advertising matter. Quite otherwise, indeed. Since the sales-publicity from which these publicity-concerns derive their revenue plays on unreasoning fear and unreasoning aspiration, the output of goods listed in their advertising matter, falls under the two general heads of Hell-fire and the Kingdom of Heaven; so that, on the whole, their failure to deliver the goods is perhaps fortunate rather than otherwise. Hell-fire is after all a commodity the punctual delivery of which is not desired by the ultimate consumers; and according to such descriptive matter as is available the Kingdom of Heaven, on the other hand, should not greatly appeal to persons of sensitive taste, being presumably something of a dubiously gaudy affair, something in the nature of three rings and a steam-calliope, perhaps. It might have been worse.

This failure to deliver the goods is brought up here only as an object-lesson which goes to show what and how great are the powers of sales-publicity at its best; as exemplified in a publicity enterprise which has over a long period of time very profitably employed a very large personnel and a very extensive and costly material equipment, coupled with no visible ability or intention to deliver any material part of the commodities advertised, or indeed to deliver anything else than a further continued volume of the same magisterial publicity that has procured a livelihood for its numerous personnel and floated its magnificent overhead charges in the past. In this lucrative enterprise the Propaganda of the Faith employs a larger and more expensive personnel and a larger equipment of material appliances, with larger running expenses and larger revenues,—not only larger than any given one line among the secular enterprises in sales-publicity, but larger than the total of all that goes into secular sales-publicity in all the nations of Christendom.

Of such sacred sales-publicity concerns operating as certified agents for this marketing of supernatural intangibles, the Census of 1916 enumerates 202 chain-store organizations, comprising a total of 203,432 retail establishments occupied exclusively with the sale of such publicity to the ultimate consumers; of whom there is one born every minute, and who are said to be carried on the books of these retailers to the number of 41,926,854. It has been confidently estimated, on the ground of these data, that the effectual number of paying customers will be approximately 90,000,000; regard being had to the very appreciable floating clientèle and the great number of effectual consumers attached to and associated with the customers of record. The stated value of "church property" is $1,676,600,582. These tangible assets are exempt from taxation.

The figures of this enumeration are suggestive, but it takes account of only such establishments as are formally chartered to do business exclusively in the retail distribution of sacred sales-publicity. It covers no more than the certified apparatus for retail merchandising of the output. If regard be had to the equipment and personnel engaged in the fabrication, sorting, storage, ripening and mobilisation of the output, these figures will be found impossibly scant. If regard be had to the very considerable number of schools for the training of certified publicity-agents in Divinity and for generating a suitable bias of credulity in the incoming generation, as well as to the mighty multitude of convents, clubs, camps, infirmaries, retreats, missions, charities, cemeteries, and periodicals, in whole or in part given over to this work and its personnel, at home and abroad, it will be evident that any of the figures commonly assigned, whether for the material equipment, the receipts and disbursements, or for the operative personnel engaged on the propaganda, should freely be doubled, at least.[1]

The man-power employed in this work of the Propaganda is also more considerable than that engaged in any other calling, except Arms, and possibly Husbandry. Prelates and parsons abound all over the place, in the high, the middle, and the low degree; too many and too diversified, in person, station, nomenclature, and vestments, to be rightly enumerated or described,—bishops, deans, canons, abbots and abbesses, rectors, vicars, curates, monks and nuns, elders, deacons and deaconesses, secretaries, clerks and employees of Y. M. C. A., Epworth Leagues, Christian Endeavors, etc.,

[1] Cf. Part I of Report on *Religious Bodies,* 1916 by the Bureau of the Census.

beadles, janitors, sextons, sunday-school teachers, missionaries, writers, editors, printers and vendors of sacred literature, in books, periodicals and ephemera. All told—if it were possible—it will be evident that the aggregate of human talent currently consumed in this fabrication of vendible imponderables in the nth dimension, will foot up to a truly massive total, even after making a reasonable allowance, of, say, some thirty-three and one-third per cent., for average mental deficiency in the personnel which devotes itself to this manner of livelihood.[2]

[2] Extra Services at St. Patrick's
Special Holy Week services are scheduled for each day at St. Patrick's Cathedral.

To-morrow night there will be a sermon by the Rev. W. B. Martin and benediction of the Blessed Sacrament, while the tenebræ will be sung at 4 P.M. in commemoration of the sufferings and death of Christ.

On Holy Thursday communion will be given every half hour between 6 and 9 A.M. and at 10 A.M. There will be pontifical mass, blessing of the holy oils, and procession to the repository. The tenebræ will be sung at 4 P.M. and the holy hour will begin at 8 P.M.

On Good Friday adoration at the repository will take place from 8 to 10 A.M., followed by singing of the sacred psalms, sermon, unveiling of the holy cross, procession to the repository, mass of the presanctified, and reverencing of the holy cross.

The Passion sermon on Friday will be preached by Mgr. Lavelle, rector. The tenebræ will be sung at 4 P.M.

The blessing of the new fire will take place at 8 o'clock on Saturday. The paschal candle and the baptismal font also will be blessed.

Mass on Easter Sunday will be pontificated by the archbishop, who also will give the papal blessing. Pontifical vespers will take place at 4 P.M.—*The Globe and Commercial Advertiser,* New York, Tuesday, March 27, 1923.

CHAPTER XII

THE LARGER USE OF CREDIT

THE pivotal factor in the business enterprise of this new era is the larger use of credit which has come into action during the last few decades; larger in absolute scale and volume as well as in the ratio which it bears to those underlying tangible assets on which it is conceived to rest. This volume of credit is more widely detached from all material objects and operations, and increasingly so.

The business men of the nineteenth century, too, habitually conducted their affairs on a basis of credit, with slight, infrequent and inconsequential recourse to transactions in cash or in kind; increasingly so as the century advanced and as the credit system progressively matured into something like that stability and self-sufficiency which it now has attained. Prices ran on a credit basis, as a workday matter of course and of convenience, and virtually no payments of any consequence were made or expected to be made in any other medium than credit-instruments; so that the price-system had already in the nineteenth century become, in effect, a system of credit-prices. The banknote currency employed was a volume of credit-instruments, to which the underlying specie-reserve stood in the relation of a contingent emergency fund and a base-line of inflation. The "deposit currency" which served as the chief medium of exchange and method of payment was somewhat more widely out of touch with any cash basis, being related to the underlying specie-reserve at the second remove only. At no time would the price-level decline to or near its cash base-line, except in a convulsive way in times of commercial crisis. At such times the familiar credit-instruments by use of which business was carried on would fall somewhat under suspicion, transiently, and the margin of price-inflation would then be greatly narrowed.[1]

So soon as business picked up again and brisk times returned after these periods of partial deflation, the habitual credit-inflation would regain any lost ground and would then ordinarily run to a slightly higher level than before. Through all this fluctuating price-inflation that so made hard times or prosperity there runs a certain air of irresponsibility or fortuity, particularly through the earlier half or three quarters of the century. The business community was still unable to control its necessary credit relations at all effectually. The country's credit relations were not ready to be organised on a reasonably compact and inclusive plan, such as would combine stability with a sufficiently flexible administration of details. They were therefore subject to ungoverned seasonal and local contingencies, which upset the balance between credits and debits from time to time and so spread derangement and consternation abroad through the business community.

The precise point of the difficulty appears to have been

[1] The ordinary width of this margin of inflation is a matter for conjecture rather than computation. It varied appreciably even in ordinary times, and it grew gradually wider on the whole as the century advanced. Toward the close of the century a reasonable estimate would perhaps make it something between 500 per cent. and 1000 per cent. of what the price level might conceivably have been in the absence of bank credit. But since substantially no business was conducted on any other than a credit basis there are no data on which to base a secure opinion.

that there was no effectual concert or collusion governing the use of credit at large in that earlier time. The
debits and credits on which business was kept afloat were
not subject to effectual joint control; there was no effectual pooling of assets and liabilities. So that debtors
and creditors, even those of the larger sort, were still
somewhat at cross purposes; with no effectual teamwork
between those massive creditors and debtors, who, between them, make up the substantial core of the business
community. The large debtors were not identified with
their creditors in point of management and control, at
least not in a degree sufficient to maintain a reasonably
stable balance of things on a basis of community interest.
In more concrete terms, the general run of the key industries had not been tied up with the larger banks.

This difficulty has since been obviated, at least in a
great degree if not altogether. The larger lines of ownership, both in the industries of the country and in its credit
institutions, have been drawn together on somewhat common ground, with such effect that those massive debits
and credits which are of decisive consequence for the
stability of the credit system, in the large, are now owned,
or can be managed, in a collective fashion and to a common end. Therefore the level of credit-prices is now
quite reasonably under control, at the hands of the parties
most largely interested in its maintenance. So much so
that there should no longer be any serious apprehension
that the credit system may break down at an inopportune
moment or that the price-level will suffer any material
decline. A break might, of course, come on advisedly,
by concert among those massive credit concerns which
have, in effect, taken over the administration of the general body of credit. But such an eventuality need scarcely
be contemplated; or if so, it may be contemplated with

equanimity, inasmuch as it could be brought on only by deliberate action of the chief parties in interest, and therefore presumably only for their common good.[2]

Such has been the outcome in the large and in substantial effect. It has brought a new and more stable order of things in business, as well as a new and more precarious order of things in industry. The outcome takes effect in a large and sweeping fashion; but it has come into action by way of a multiplicity of shifting details, as is necessarily the case where a new order of things arises by a process of habituation to new circumstances. It is the upshot of many minor changes which have converged—or are converging—to this effect, by drift of circumstance rather than by reasoned design, perhaps even without any degree of effectual prevision on the part of those who have been the chief actors in the case. It is

[2] The run of things in these respects since the War should be sufficiently reassuring to anyone who might be apprehensive. An inflated capitalisation has been kept intact as a whole and has steadily been increased, and inflated market prices have been maintained without substantial abatement during these years, at the cost of persistent inaction in industry; in the face of extreme provocation to go to work and a very appreciable run of popular hardship and discontent due to continued unemployment and restriction of output. Whereas, if those concerns which control the financial end of things had kept their hands off and let the inflated credit situation come to a head, a drastic liquidation of the country's business affairs would doubtless have gone into effect in due course and brought on an effectual retrenchment in capitalisation and prices; whereupon the country's industries would shortly have got under way and would speedily have made good the wastes of the War, and supplied all ordinary needs. Indeed, there is no reason to doubt that the resulting industrial production, if it had been allowed to run free, would by this time (1923) have added as much to the tangible wealth of the country as would equal all the book-values of those inflated assets which their financial guardians have been safeguarding with unemployment and commercial paper through these years of privation and unrest.

also worth noting that the resulting state of things, in the respect which is in question here, has not been formally acknowledged or recognised by the parties concerned,— unless the need of occasionally denying its existence be accepted as amounting to an admission of it; and more particularly it has no legal existence. Indeed, the actual state of things in this respect is doubtless quite impossible *de jure;* which will of course mean only that it is something new, newer than the traditions of the law.

Its roots run through the economic tissues of the nineteenth century, and the historical date of its beginnings would have to be assigned on grounds of taste and preconception by any historian who might deal with this matter, and it would accordingly differ greatly according to his point of view and his point of attention. But since the argument here is concerned with the business situation as it has been taking shape during the past two decades, it should answer the present purpose to strike into the run of things in the nineties for a point of departure, and give attention chiefly to the changes which have come on since that period; letting that which has already been said in earlier chapters serve by way of orientation; particularly what has been said on the rise of corporation finance and on the increasing resort to credit during the century.[3]

A convenient point of departure for the rise of the

[3] Many excellent manuals and monographs have dealt with the conduct of business in the late nineteenth century; so many and so well as to make any selective citation difficult as well as invidious. But because the argument leans on these two in a peculiar degree, special reference is made to the analysis of the business situation at the close of the century as contained in W. C. Mitchell's *Business Cycles,* and in the chapters on Credit and Capitalisation in *The Theory of Business Enterprises.*

new era in business enterprise may be found in the late nineties; and the new departure may be said to have been set afoot in the financiering of mergers and holding-companies during those years by the late J. Pierpont Morgan and those others who presently followed his lead.

In that time the holding-company came to stand as the advanced and perfected type-form of corporate ownership and control as employed in the conduct of industrial business. It was a well-considered advance over the earlier methods of absentee ownership and absentee management. In point of form, the holding-company is of a more perfect order of absenteeism, in that by this device the lawful owner draws back farther by one remove from any personal relation with the property which he owns and from which he derives an income; whether the property in question be tangible assets or a vested usufruct. At the same time the owner's claim on and control over his property shifts to a more impersonal or statistical footing, if possible; to a footing of standardised quantitative allotment in terms of percentual units. His relation to the property and its use thereby comes to carry a slighter effectual responsibility for any action taken, or for any tangible outcome of such action taken by the corporate management to which he has in effect delegated his rights and powers. In the holding-company, even more obviously than in the ordinary corporation, the owner delegates the powers of ownership, and retains only its rights and immunities. So also it leaves him a correspondingly slighter chance of personally influencing any action taken by the management.

The holding-company has commonly been of a large size; and that fact has likewise had the effect of submerging the individual owner and his personal bias and initiative. The result is a pronounced degree of impersonality and standardised routine. So also, in the practical conduct of its affairs by the holding-company, the effectual control and management of any corporate business has passed into the hands of a relatively smaller minority of the ultimate owners, and at the same time the effectual control exercised by this relatively small minority of the owners has taken on a more unequivocally statistical character. So much so, indeed, that their effectual oversight and control will ordinarily touch nothing more tangible or more personal than certain figures supplied by the corporation's accountants; commonly numbers running to some half-a-dozen digits, having to do with certain price-totals.

The holding-company is no longer viewed with apprehension, as it once was; nor does it hold that dominant place in the business of credit and capitalisation which it held about the turn of the century. Not that it has gone out of use or out of mind. It has been proven and found good and has become a part of the standard apparatus of business, a commonplace formality of the routine. But at the outset, when the holding-company was coming into use, it was the effectual means of reorganising the business of the key industries on an enlarged, more elaborate and more manageable plan. It served to bring these industrial business concerns together into larger agglomerations than had been practicable up to that time, and it served also to detach the ownership of these concerns from their management more widely and effectually than before. By this move the whole apparatus and management of industrial business was placed on a foundation of credit in a more unqualified fashion than before, and thereby the management of the business was enabled to "trade on a thinner equity" [4] than had been practicable

[4] The expression, "trading on the equity," as employed in this

in the past. Corporation finance was enabled to take on still more of the character of standardised routine. So that the holding-company has been an instrument and an exemplar of that drift of things in the conduct of business which has brought on the current state of things, and which has made the difference between the situation of the nineties and that of the present.

Much of the use which the holding-company has served has been that of standardising the routine of "big business" and familiarising the business community with that larger scale and wider detachment that is characteristic of the ordinary use of credit and the ordinary duties of ownership in this later time. In a very passable fashion men have learned all that now, so that it is no longer beset with the distrust of the unknown,—which is said to be a nearly universal infirmity of sound business men. What the use of the holding-company once served to drive them to has now become a familiar matter of course.

Something to much the same effect is to be said for the use of "interlocking directorates," which also once loomed up in popular apprehension as a formidable, if not a menacing, innovation in the conduct of business. The interlocking directorate has also not passed out of use. It, too, is still a convenient arrangement for purposes of mutual understanding and support. But these purposes for which these devices were once resorted to as a means of constraint, have now become habitual matters of routine; and the devices therefore have ceased to claim that degree of attention which they were once presumed to merit. They are no longer of the essence of the case.

connection, is borrowed from W. H. Lyon, *Capitalisation,* where a very competent discussion of this principle is to be found in chapter ii.

The late J. Pierpont Morgan saw an opportunity and turned it to account. It is not likely, and it does not appear, that he rated himself as a path-finder or in any sense as the pioneer of a new era in business enterprise, or that he harbored any ambition or design to change the face of the business community. For all his large initiative and his large powers and responsibilities, he was a notably unassuming person; being apparently driven by nothing more spectacular than the habitual incentives of safe and sane business of the larger sort;[5] although his larger initiative led him beyond his contemporaries and associates, and at times, indeed, led him close to the frontiers of sound business practice.

The undertakings which are associated with his memory at this point, and which played a typical part in leading over to the new era, may be described in general terms somewhat as follows. At that time (late nineties) there were a large number and variety of established business concerns doing business primarily in certain of the key industries, notably steel, ore, coal, and railways. Many of these concerns were in a moderately bad way financially, for one reason and another. They were, not uncommonly, unable to command such a volume of credit as was needed in the conduct of their business. They were commonly over-capitalised—in excess of their market value as going concerns and notably in excess of the value of their tangible assets. So they were carrying overhead charges somewhat in excess of what their current earnings would warrant; and their earnings were declining rather than otherwise.

This state of their affairs was due in some measure to a more or less pronounced obsolescence. It was in part

[5] As is related of Jakob Fugger, "Er wollte verdienen dieweil er könte."

an obsolescence of their industrial plant, but with more critical effect these concerns also suffered from a rapidly growing obsolescence of locality, particularly as related to the means of transportation on which they depended for their supply of raw materials and for the delivery of their marketable output. In some instances their business facilities were also going out of date; their markets were in process of obsolescence, through a shifting of the population, through changes of custom and usage, through being cut under by other concerns doing business in the same market. There had been ceaseless change in the technique of these industries during the life-time of these business concerns; and more particularly during the lifetime of the "underlying companies" and industrial plants on which these industrial business concerns were based; for the greater number of those concerns that are in question here were composite organisations, built up out of previously existing corporations and firms, by merger, purchase, and consolidation. And throughout this period of industrial growth, changes in the processes of industry and in the localisation of the various industries had been going forward; due in great part to the growth and redistribution of the population and to continued extensions and enlargement of the transportation systems. New natural resources also continued to be drawn into the industrial system and to be engrossed by certain of the larger owners. All of which conspired to put these business concerns out of date and out of joint with the conditions of the market. Perhaps the gravest of the factors which contributed to this obsolescence and perplexity of these industrial business concerns was the competitive character of their market, both for raw materials and labor and for disposal of the output; and this competitive market was all the more precarious because the productive capacity of the existing plants was already greater than the market would carry off at a profitable price, even within the shelter of a high protective tariff. The most embarrassing appears to have been the inconsiderate competitive position taken by those Carnegie properties which presently came to play so magisterial a rôle in precipitating the formation of the U. S. Steel Corporation.[6]

Not infrequently the management of these previously established industrial business concerns was in the hands of elderly and opinionated owners, who had an old-fashioned sentimental interest each in his own corporation, as being his own creation, and whose occupation would be gone in case their own concern were to be merged with others or sunk in an inclusive holding-company. These survivers of an earlier business régime were by way of being "captains of industry" of the obsolete sort, in that they commonly combined some degree of technical training, experience, and aspiration, with a customary knowledge of the markets and of corporation finance. And they were commonly out of date in both respects, by force of what may be called obsolescence by displacement in technical practice and in financial usage. They were patriarchal holdovers, with much of the intolerance that will commonly invest the self-made patriarch. Things had been moving forward in matters of knowledge and practice during the lifetime of

[6] For descriptions and argument on this movement in the nineties and after, Cf. the testimony of various witnesses before the U. S. Industrial Commission, in the Commission's *Report,* vols. I, IX and XIII. So also W. Z. Ripley, *Trusts, Pools and Corporations;* E. S. Meade, *Trust Finance,* and *Corporation Finance;* W. S. Stevens, *Industrial Combinations and Trusts;* C. W. Gerstenberg, *Materials of Corporation Finance;* A. S. Dewing, *Corporate Promotions and Reorganization.*

these elderly captains and their establishments, and among the forward changes were such as made imperatively for a larger scale and a more far-reaching team-work in the processes of production, a larger use of credit, and for a more carefully guarded competition in the markets. And none of this fell in readily with the settled habits of these elderly captains or with the standing business relations among their several concerns.

These industrial business concerns, and their under-lying companies and plants, had in their time been projected with a view to the traffic of a fairly open competitive market, and they had expanded by successive extensions and accretions, and so had grown to maturity under conditions which that traffic had created. With the progressive filling-out and closing-in of this market they found themselves, progressively, in the position of competitive producers for a closed market of variable volume. They were consequently somewhat overstocked with industrial plants of a fair productive capacity, which not unusually duplicated one another, and which had been placed somewhat hastily by rule of thumb in somewhat haphazard locations, and had grown from relatively small beginnings by a process of patchwork and extension. And all the while their combined productive capacity rather exceeded the capacity of their market—at any such price as would afford them a "reasonable profit" on their output. In this sense the market was closing in. It was becoming too narrow for a free run of output at the price-level at which these enterprises had been projected. The period of competitive business in the key industries was closing. So that continued open competition among them became "cutthroat competition"; such as to entail present and prospective decline of their earning-capacity. As one consequence of this situation, they were greatly in need of additional credits for use in their business, at a time when their credit capacity was falling off and their liabilities were already becoming distressingly burdensome.

When the affairs of the corporations in the key industries had reached this pass, the dean of the banking community saw his own occasion in the present needs and the dubious prospects of these industrial business concerns. Of course there were others, too, and not a few, who were ready to see the same opportunity and to profit by it so soon as it had been placed before them in an object-lesson. The conjuncture was essentially that of a sweeping transition and realignment, incident to the passing of the common run of the key industries from a footing of competitive business in an ample market to a footing of collusive traffic in a closed market too narrow for unguarded competitive production.[7]

As the event has taught, the executive use of the country's credit resources in a large way and on a reasoned plan was the appointed means by which the due reconstruction of the business was to be worked out, and also the means by which the needful running collusion in the further conduct of the business was to be enforced and regulated. The holding-company and the merger, together with the interlocking directorates, and presently the voting trust, were the ways and means by which the banking community took over the strategic regulation of the key industries, and by way of that avenue also the control of the industrial system at large. By this move the effectual discretion in all that concerns the business management of the key industries was taken out of the

---

[7] There is, of course, no sharp date-line to be drawn in such a case, but 1897 will serve to mark this turn of affairs as well as any.

hands of corporation managers working in severalty and at cross purposes, and has been lodged in the hands of that group of investment bankers who constitute in effect a General Staff of financial strategy and who between them command the general body of the country's credit resources. This general staff, or inner group, command the credit resources of the country at large; although it would presumably not do to say, at least not just yet, that they—the large business financiers and their banking-houses—own or comprise or constitute the credit resources of the country.

Out of this drift of things the "Investment Banker" has emerged, to serve as a powerful instrumental factor in working out the new alignment of ownership and industrial business, and presently to take his place as one of the essential workday institutions of the business community. It should perhaps be remarked that he is not yet in existence *de jure,* but only *de facto.* Just yet he is still in process of standardisation as regards his precise nature and uses; so that no sharply defined description of him and his work can be drawn, just yet, although there is some thing to be said of him and his functions.[8] He is the source or the channel, as the case may be, of capitalisation and of corporation credit at large,—a source if he amounts to a banking-house of the first magnitude, a channel if his place in the economy of Nature is that of a subordinate. At the same time and in his appropriate degree he is the standard container of such credit and the standard repository, original or vicarious, of the larger intelligence and discretion in these fiscal matters. He initiates movement or pressure in the conduct of business,

[8] Cf. A. S. Dewing. *The Financial Policy of Corporations,* vol. II, ch. ii and vii. In the same connection see also The Same, vol. III, ch. ix, on the *Voting Trust.* Also Hastings Lyon, *Corporation. Finance,* Part II, ch. ii and iii.

or he transmits initiative and pressure. In point of pedigree, considered as an institution, his formal line of descent out of the past traces back to the business of underwriting, as it ran in the time before the banking community had taken over the general initiative and foresight in the conduct of industrial business. But he is also rooted in the business of commercial banking and banks of issue, as well as in the trust-companies that have come up and grown great in his own time; and then there is about him, too, a broad hint of the bill-broker of earlier times. In point of form, he is affiliated with his client-corporations as creditor, underwriter, sponsor, banker, broker. In effect, he is the comptroller of their fiscal affairs and, within reason, the master of their solvency; being custodian of their absentee owners' interests at large.

Hitherto, and in so far as it has touched the larger contingencies of business, this work of initiative, discretion, foresight, and control, which has become incumbent on the country's investment bankers, has habitually taken effect by way of collusion or concerted action. This concert of action is of the essence of the case. It is by virtue of such concert among the larger and more responsible ones that they constitute in effect the General Staff of the business community—what may be called the One Big Union of the Interests. Under the surveillance of this general staff, it has become incumbent on the investment bankers as an organized body to deal with the run of business as an organic moving equilibrium. This highly responsible task enjoins a collusive sobriety, a collective and concerted moderation, such as is intended in the colloquial phrase, "sitting tight." The investment bankers collectively are the community custodians of absentee ownership at large, the general staff in charge of the pursuit of business. And since the conduct of industry is incidental to the pursuit of business, the state of industry and the rate, volume and balance of production also are dependent on their sagacity and goodwill. So that it is here, if anywhere, that responsibility for the country's material welfare may be said to rest.

In his time, the great pioneering creator of mergers and holding-companies came to stand as the chief of investment bankers and the dean of the congregation of corporation finance. And from that time on, the investment bankers have progressively taken over the control of industrial business in the large. Investment-banking as it is conducted now, owes its rise and character to the circumstances of that time, and it has continued to work out along much the same lines to which it was then brought by the experience of Morgan and his associates. This financial enterprise may therefore be said to have arisen out of the mobilisation of those banking resources which were already employed in underwriting corporate capitalisations, and to have arisen as an enterprise in mergers, recapitalisations, and bonuses; but it presently fell into settled lines as a standardised routine of investing funds and allocating credits. This standardised routine of investment and allocation is what engrosses the energies of the community of investment bankers. It is also the ways and means by which they, working together as a general staff of financial strategy, govern the country's business at large and so regulate the ordinary rate and volume of productive industry. In all this, the continued merging of old concerns and creation of new ones goes forward as a routine matter of administration incident to the allocation of credits. And the credits are —also as a routine matter-of-course—allocated with an eye single to the greater gain of the investment bankers who see to the allocation of them.

In its beginnings, in the nineties, this enterprise in mergers and recapitalisation was primarily concerned with bringing certain elderly units of the industrial business community to terms, by a persuasive use of financial pressure; to prevail upon them to surrender their several corporate powers and enter into some arrangement in the way of a merger, commonly under the form of a holding-company. By this means these concerns ceased to govern their own affairs individually, were drawn in under a centralised management, and so ceased to be effectual competitors in the market. In the main this reorganisation had to do with business concerns which were in the position of holdovers in the key industries, and more particularly such of them as were in financial straits, as a good proportion of them were.

In this connection it has also been believed, on circumstantial evidence, that the great financier, and after him also the lesser ones, would now and again take pains to manœuvre such an embarrassed concern into financial extremities; such as would incline its management to surrender the controlling interest and to allow a suitable "bonus" to the captains of finance who managed the reorganisation.

During the early years of the period it was this bonus that was the immediate object sought by the reorganising financier, and the chief incentive to the reorganisation. The bonus commonly took the form of a block of securities issued in the name of the new incorporation. And it was commonly quite a substantial bonus, so as to take up a very appreciable percentage of the new capitalisation. This bonus which the underwriter of the new corporation securities came in for appears to have been the valuable consideration sought by these financiers in undertaking these early mergers and recapitalisations. It does not appear that these financiers commonly set out with the purpose of taking over the management of the incorporations which they created. But the transactions which they entered into in their pursuit of the bonus entailed commitments and obligations which stood over after the initial transactions had been concluded. The recapitalisation and its endorsement at the hands of the financier, or investment banker, together with the practice of taking over his bonus in the form of a block of securities issued by the new incorporation, entailed a continued community of interest between the investment banker and the new incorporations which he had created. A community interest of a special sort, in that it committed the investment banker—the financier and his banking-house—to a continued responsibility for the success of the new incorporation; which in turn vested the banker with power to act, and lodged in his hands a virtually plenary discretion in the oversight and management of the new incorporation. The outcome has been that the banking-houses which have engaged in this enterprise have come in for an effectual controlling interest in the corporations whose financial affairs they administer. And it is this outcome that has proved to be the enduring and decisive factor in the new business situation created by this recourse to mergers and recapitalisations under the auspices of the investment bankers.

At least in some very consequential instances, the further course of events and the further manœuvres and commitments in the way of recapitalisation and credit extensions, were also governed by the pressure of necessity bearing on the investment bankers in the case. The financiering bankers were involved in the affairs of their client corporations in such a critical fashion as to require a further move of coalition and recapitalisation, as a measure of safety. That consolidation of interests which resulted in the U. S. Steel Corporation, e. g., was precipitated by pressure of this kind. At the same time it is worth noting that the financier who, under pressure, carried out this consolidation of the steel interests came in for a bonus in the form of a block of the new corporation's securities bearing a face value of $50,000,000; in which sum the new corporation formally became indebted to its sponsor, as payment for his services.[9] This bonus was in the nature of an addition to the corporation's capitalisation. And it may be added that in the end, after some further financial manoeuvres, the securities which made up this bonus came to be worth fully their face value.

The bonus which so lay at the root of these early reorganisations of industrial business habitually took the shape of a block of corporation securities representing new capital values added to the total capitalisation in the operation of recapitalising the underlying properties; the capitalised value—face value, book value—of these properties being thereby augmented by that much. Such has been the standard usage. It is in effect a matter of routine. The bonus which so entered into the total capitalisation represented no acquisition of new capital; in the sense that it added no new funds and no new tangible assets to the total; but only new liabilities, added to the total of the corporation securities that resulted from recapitalisation. That is to say, according to the standard routine in the matter, the total outstanding securities, representing the

[9] There was also a block of 6 per cent. gold bonds, secured by a lien on the tangible assets of the Carnegie properties, payable to Andrew Carnegie for having brought the required pressure to bear on the great financiers, and for allowing the Carnegie steel properties to go into the coalition at an inflated valuation.

previous capitalisation of the underlying companies, were increased by that much without any corresponding increase of the underlying assets. It was a transaction in credit pure and simple, a creation of new credit values; or it was a redistribution of the old values under cover of a make-believe creation of new assets.

Also habitually, apart from any underwriter's bonus, in any such reorganisation the total capitalisation of the resulting collective holding-company is made somewhat larger than the sum of the outstanding capital securities of the underlying companies, and very appreciably larger than the aggregate market value of the underlying tangible assets. Habitually, as a matter of standard usage, the recapitalisation of industrial properties in this way has resulted in an increased volume of outstanding corporation securities, with or without, but commonly without, any increase in the underlying material assets. This addition to the volume of outstanding capital securities arising out of any such reincorporation may run to fifty per cent., of the total previous capitalisation of the underlying companies, or to some such figure, more or less.

The outcome of successive reorganisations has accordingly been a series of successive recapitalisations at a successively higher figure, resulting in a progressively increased volume of outstanding credit instruments and involving a corresponding progressive revaluation of the underlying assets at a progressively enhanced figure. As a rule rather than as an exception, in the key industries, the operation has been repeated in several successive recapitalisations of the same properties into successively larger coalitions. In effect it has been a creation of new values by an extension of credit. And in the main this progressively increased valuation of these corporate assets has been justified by the event. Indeed, the assets of the larger coalitions which have been created in this way have habitually increased in value even apart from and in excess of any such credit operations designed to add something to the face value of the outstanding securities.[10]

Such transactions in corporation finance were the outstanding feature of the business situation during the ten or a dozen years which overlapped the turn of the century, and the like transactions have continued to be an active factor in the conduct of industrial business since then; most notably and with the gravest consequences in the key industries. There has been a continued run of consolidations with recapitalisation at a higher figure, and new incorporations with flotations of new securities. The visible purpose of them, as seen from the side of the investment bankers, and the presumptive aim of the transactions, as transactions in corporation finance, has been the creation of new capitalised wealth by new extensions of credit. The benefit of the newly created capitalisations has, in the main, inured to the investment-banking houses which have carried on this work. In great part, the gains which accrue from investment banking still are derived from transactions of this class.[11]

[10] So, e. g., the market value of the securities of the U. S. Steel Corporation, or of the various Standard Oil subsidiaries, has persistently gone over par, even when large issues of stock-dividends have been set afloat.

[11] It has not been customary to describe transactions of this class in precisely these terms. It is even doubtful if writers on corporation finance and investment banking would accept what has been said above as a faithful description of the relevant facts. Habitually, the point of view of such writers, and more particularly their point of attention, has been somewhat different from the perspective which governs the present argument. It has been customary to discuss transactions in corporation finance from the side of the tangible assets and their use, rather than from the side of investment and valuation. The argument here is concerned with the workday uses of credit in transactions of capitalisation.

Recapitalisation at an increased figure has been the standard practice in reorganising and merging industrial business concerns during this period. New incorporations on any reasonably large scale have followed the same general principle, in that the capitalisation has commonly exceeded the value of the underlying assets. And with a very fair degree of generality this inflation of the capital-values of corporations and their assets has proved to

When new incorporations or reorganisations, involving new and larger flotations of securities, are here spoken of as transactions looking to the creation of capitalised wealth by new extensions of credit, it is not intended to say that such new extensions of credit will enlarge the existing volume of "productive goods." It is not intended to say that such addition to the outstanding credit obligations will create material assets, or will in any way directly add to or augment the country's tangible possessions, or enhance the tangible performance of the country's productive industry. As a matter of tradition, it has been customary to believe that some such effect will commonly follow indirectly from such new and increased capitalisation, but that is a question with which the argument is not concerned at this point. Immediately and traceably, the creative effect which these transactions have is altogether in the nature of a creation of intangible assets. Indirectly and presumptively, by what may be called a repercussion of optimism, there may also result something in the way of increased industrial activity and an enlargement of industrial plant; but all that lies outside the immediate operations of investment banking or corporation finance. Such tangible facts are not of the same order of things as an issue of fiduciary paper.

Intangible assets may be created by a suitable extension of credit embodied in corporation securities, as has been abundantly shown by the run of things during the past quarter-century. To their owners these intangible assets will be an effectual item of capitalised wealth, as is likewise shown by the experience of the same years. It is true, such intangible assets constitute no part of the country's material possessions and have no creative part in the tangible performance of the country's industrial forces. They are wholly in the nature of an absentee claim to a share in the country's income; in the last analysis, of course, a claim on the product of industry, to which all the while they have contributed nothing By and large, intangible assets consti-

be sound; in the sense that the inflated corporations have presently, if not from the outset, approached or reached such an earning-capacity as to justify their inflated capitalisation. The assets so created by a transaction in credit have proved to be sound assets, good property.

The increased earning-capacity of such inflated recapitalisations has been conditioned on an advance of the price-level for the sales from which the earnings are

tute a valid claim to get something for nothing; and such a claim may be created by an extension of credit; and to its owner it is wealth to the amount of what it is worth. It is also a marketable commodity, and it may be employed as collateral by means of which to procure a further extension of credit, which may be turned to account in the same way and with the like ulterior effect.

These intangible assets, capitalisations of usufruct, which so are created and added to the existing book-values of the country's wealth, constitute a new claim on the existing volume of income; therefore they constitute a substraction from the body of income which would otherwise go to other, earlier claimants. The owners of these newly created intangibles, therefore, come in for the effectual value of their newly acquired assets at the cost of a corresponding loss to the general body of owners. By force of these transactions, in credit and capitalisation, the existing property owners and workmen lose as much as the owners of the new assets gain, plus the cost of the operations. The loss which so falls on the general body of owners (and workmen) is a loss only in the material respect, by weight and tale of the things which their incomes will purchase, not a loss in respect of the book-values of their assets. The credit extension which goes to the creation of these new assets will mask the confiscatory character of the transaction by adding the face value of the new assets—and ordinarily something more—to the outstanding volume of market values. The new credits go into the market as an addition to the current volume of purchasing-power; thereby correspondingly lowering the purchasing-power of the money unit. It foots up to an inflation of the total volume of wealth in hand as rated in terms of price, with no corresponding increase of tangible possessions; whereby the investment bankers and their clients come in for an increased share of the wealth in hand, at the cost of the general body of owners and workmen. —Cf. also *Theory of Business Enterprise,* ch. iii, pp. 99–132, ch. iv, pp. 148–168, 174–176.

drawn, or on keeping up the established price-level in the face of declining production-costs. To maintain or advance the level of prices in this way requires an effectual freedom from unguarded competition in the market, among the business concerns engaged in the traffic; and the most advantageous arrangement for the purpose will be a virtual absence of competition; such as has been the rule, e. g., in the steel business, and such as has come near being the rule in coal. This can be accomplished by a reasonable degree of collusion and concerted action. By this means the margin of earnings is enlarged, at the same time that the hazards of the business are greatly reduced or virtually eliminated.[12]

The required degree of concerted action, or the needful reasonably collusive regulation of things, has not called for a close-knit organisation of the banking community in set form, or, indeed, for anything like a formally defined compact of joint action among the ruling captains of solvency and their underlying banking-houses. These latterday transactions in credit and capitalisation are of so transparently gainful a nature as to enjoin on all the parties in interest what amounts in effect to a collusive regulation of things, even in the absence of any provision for a formally concerted plan of action. The transactions which make the outcome are large, particularly such of them as are patently worth-while and worth bearing a hand in, and the business procedure in the case has already fallen into something of a standard routine,

---

[12] By "sound business management," proceeding on such a reasonable understanding among themselves, the investment bankers who command the credit resources of the country are enabled to trade on a progressively thinner equity; so that they are able safely to enlarge the volume of outstanding credit, indefinitely, by means of a progressive creation of intangible assets on which to base a further extension of credit, etc.

in pursuance of which this manner of large and lucrative transactions recur in a somewhat orderly succession; and the operations are of such a character as to make it plain to the meanest understanding that they will be carried through to a safe and lucrative conclusion only by such team-work among the several investment-concerns as will obviate all cross purposes, and will at the same time provide a broad collective reserve of credit resources and eliminate all hazard of unforeseen contingencies. And bankers are imbued with a reasonably conservative spirit, such as will conduce to safe and sane business of this kind.

Any member of the banking community who might so far exceed the limits of conventionally blameless cupidity as to be led into cross purposes and fall short of reasonable team-work at a critical juncture, would expect to be counted out of the game at the next turn. He would lose that most essential item among his own intangible assets, the goodwill of his fellow bankers, deprived of which he would no longer come in for that steady run of workday business that makes the broad foundation of his earnings. At the same time he would, in effect, cease to be an investment banker. Such is the turn which things have taken. In effect, whether it runs to commercial banking or in the field of investment, banking is essentially not now a competitive business, except collectively as against the underlying population. And investment banking in an eminent degree is a line of enterprise in which it is incumbent on all the parties in interest to take hands and help, in which one good turn deserves another, and in which there can be no tolerance for men who wantonly disregard the rules of the game. Any flotation of securities, but more particularly any major operation of such a character as to promise large and easy gains, is in practical effect an occasion for mutual support among the makers of credit, and for faithful teamwork throughout an extensive network of banking-concerns, who are bound in an orderly system of correspondence and through whose hands the credit instruments that are to be marketed will have to pass on their way to those investors who may be called the ultimate consumers of this product. For any bank or banker it is the part of wisdom faithfully to "stand in" and in all sobriety to take an equitable share in the margin of profit that is to be derived from these sales of credit.

This bond of union and concert that so holds the investment bankers to a profitable routine of team-work in disposing of this running output of credit instruments is greatly strengthened by the fact that the country's commercial banking is already established on the same lines of team-work and joint interest; it is taken care of by the same community of bankers, governed by a like routine of equitable give and take, in pursuance of which also all excesses and delinquencies are penalised with automatic punctuality. In the business of commercial banking, too, the superior discretion and initiative are perforce vested in the massive financial concerns that inhabit the country's financial metropolis, and whose massive resources enable them to create credit somewhat at will, and to regulate its expansion and allocation. By force of circumstances these banking concerns of the first magnitude make up the living nucleus of the banking community, and by force of circumstances it is the part of wisdom as well as of professional ethics for the lesser and outlying members of the craft to wait faithfully on the motions of these masters of solvency, who by force of circumstances constitute the General Staff of the banking community.[13]

The investment banker, severally and collectively, is custodian of the credit-interests of his own banking-house and of his clients. He is a custodian with plenary discretion, *de facto;* the exigencies of absentee ownership make him so. In the nature of the case these interests are the interests of absentee ownership, like other credit

[13] In due time this force of circumstances, which so has drawn the banking community together in a centralised ramification of equitable give and take under the collusive surveillance of the great credit houses of the metropolis, has been given a local habitation and a name, by act of a businesslike Congress, in the installation of the Federal Reserve Board. The working-out of this measure appears to have been wholly salutary and to have fallen quite neatly in with the drift of circumstances that has shaped the men and structure of Big Business. It is true, the surveillance and disciplinary powers formally vested in the Board neither derive from nor devolve upon the massive banking-houses of the metropolis; nor, on the other hand, do they extend by specification to anything beyond commercial banking and the issuance of fiduciary currency. But it is the same concatenation of banking concerns, bound in the same inclusive system of financial correspondence, by which the commercial paper and the paper currency are taken care of, that also takes care of the country's credit resources and their allocation and distribution through the channels of investment banking; and the work is carried on by the same personnel, at the same time, through the same channels, and by use of a solvency resting on the same assets. The creative use of credit in generating and floating corporation securities is, after all, no more than another branch of that business of issuing, endorsing, and transferring fiduciary paper, that has to do with bank-notes and commercial banking. The transactions are of the same general kind. The banker's incentive in both cases is also the same margin of gain to be got for letting someone else go to work, whether it takes the form of a bonus or commission for the flotation of corporation securities, or a rediscount, or an excess of note-issues over the legal reserve; the method of earning this margin of profits is the same trading on the confidence of clients and customers; and the ulterior effect of the traffic is the same expansion of money-values through depreciation of the unit of purchasing-power.— Cf. H. L. Reed, *The Development of Federal Reserve Policy.*

interests, and in the nature of the case their custody takes effect in the way of an absentee control over that business and industry out of which the gains of these absentee owners arise. In effect, absentee ownership is a claim on free income to be drawn from the property owned; so that the property is necessarily of the nature of assets, in so far as it is held in absentee ownership; and "assets" is a financial category. Also in the nature of the case, the resulting absentee government of current business and industry, which so is vested in these custodians of credit, is in the nature of a fiscal administration, a strategic regimentation of assets, essentially a running allocation of credit allowances; which can take effect only by way of withholding needed credit extensions from doubtful and undesirable enterprises,—doubtful or undesirable in their bearing on the "income stream" that goes to the bankers and their clients. So that the powers and sanctions commanded by these custodians are of a permissive sort. That is to say, their strategy and administration are necessarily of a negative, quiescent, sedative character, something in the way of a provisional veto power, a contingent check on untoward undertakings and excursions, a fiscal disallowance of such projects in business and industry as do not manifestly promote the advantage of those absentee interests that are taken care of by the given investment banker or group of bankers, in effect a species of fiscal sabotage.

Crudely and in general terms the working-out of this absentee government of business and industry by this general staff of solvency may be described as follows. It works by way of an allocation of credit allowances among the clients of these custodians of solvency, preferentially and particularly among those corporate concerns that are clients of those larger captains of solvency who are effective members of the general staff,—concerns which are bound to these captains by a community interest of a businesslike sort. The credit resources of the country, the main body and dominant mass of which are under the hands of this general staff of solvency, may be, and by pressure of ordinary businesslike cupidity they will be, employed productively in the creation of new wealth, in the way of intangible assets, after the fashion already explained in an earlier passage. In ordinary times this expansive creation of intangible wealth goes forward in a cumulative fashion, by routine; it is part of the ordinary day's work of the banking community. This newly, progressively, created wealth is in the nature of capitalised overhead charges on current business and industry.

In practical effect, the rate at which such new assets will be created is determined by two main factors: (a) the volume of credit obligations already outstanding and assimilated into the routine of business ratings and transactions, and (b) what may be called the tensile strength of the business community's temper as regards new commitments in the way of liabilities and capitalisation. The latter is often spoken of loosely as "public confidence." Neither of these two factors which condition the rate of output of intangible wealth is a constant quantity; as one might say, neither has a constant coefficient of efficiency. And neither can be measured and reduced to a quite satisfactory statistical statement in objective terms. They are, therefore, not fully amenable to control by statistical computation or by an apparatus of bookkeeping. Accordingly the rate of production of intangibles and overhead charges is not a constant one, nor can it or its fluctuations be quite safely calculated beforehand. There is still in all this traffic a substantial margin of contingencies, which leaves a certain elbowroom for the personal equation of the captains, for sagacity and rule-of-thumb. The personal equation of these captains runs to "safety first"; at least so they say. Accordingly that element of uncertainty and hazard which still enters into the case will greatly further a faithful collusion among the sound captains of solvency.

When all due allowance has been made, therefore, the rate of production of intangibles will still be a rate which may be estimated with a very fair degree of approximation by those persons who are conversant with the credit business and its resources. And barring accident, this ordinary rate of production of intangibles should evidently rise progressively higher as the outstanding and "digested" mass of obligations on which it is conditioned grows progressively larger; so that under ordinary circumstances the rate of output of these capitalised liabilities will be subject to a cumulative acceleration, although no definite coefficient of acceleration can be assigned.[14]

[14] The standard manuals of economic theory make no reference to any such cumulative acceleration in the ordinary rate of output of capitalisation of liabilities, as a factor in the economic system with which their speculations are occupied, although writers on corporation finance have called attention to the practice from time to time. Economists habitully have seen the whole matter in another light. Economic theories have habitually been standardised in forms which would meet the requirements of that earlier "cash economy" that has been falling out of the scheme of things in recent times. Under the old order the use of credit was a matter of "deferred payments," rather than an instrumentality of absentee ownership. So economists have not been in the habit of looking to the volume of outstanding obligation and intangibles—capitalised overhead charges—as a creative factor in the continued expansion of liabilities and capitalisation; particularly not the certified economists of the ancient line. (Cf., e. g., J. Laurence Laughlin, *The Principles of Money*, chapters on Credit and on the Refined System of Barter). Their perspective has been somewhat faithfully foreshortened to fit the

Credit is extended by the keepers of the credit resources in the form of current credit-accounts—typically "deposits"—as well as in the flotation of new securities; it is extended to such business concerns of a sizable magnitude as prove themselves worthy. Those are eligible who can be depended on duly to pay over to their creditors such fixed charges as are borne by the credit instruments so created. They are worthy, of course, because and in the measure in which they continue to yield a secure net income to the dispensers of credit and to the absentee owners whose guardians the dispensers are. Directly or indirectly, the resulting credit instruments go to swell the volume of collateral on which the fabric of credit is erected and on which further extensions are negotiated. These credit extensions in this way enable the concerns in question to trade on a thinner equity. That is to say, such business concerns are thereby enabled to enter into

legal formalities of incorporation and the stipulations of economic doctrine as drawn up in the middle nineteenth century; at a time when it was still passably true in practice, or at least in the established tradition, that any extension of credit would be presumed to be secured by tangible assets available as collateral, in the case of negotiable securities, or by an available reserve of specie in the case of paper money. That was under the old order of business practice and the still older order of legal and theoretical conceptions. There is no call to take exception, or to call ungraceful attention to that ever-widening fringe of intangibles which was by that time progressively enveloping the nineteenth-century fabric of cash assets, and which eventually has overrun and surmounted it.

All that was under the old order, or under the rigorous tradition of it; while the slow-dying presumption still held its ground, that "assets" means "tangible property"; that corporate capital is measured by the initial cash cost of the corporation's plant; and that intangibles can be capitalised only by subreption, by making believe that they are transferable objects of use and have a ratable cost of production—as, e. g., patented processes and contrivances—and so entering them on the books along with the tangible properties and writing them into the capitalised assets at a make-believe purchase price. Except *de jure,* all that

larger commitments and undertake outlays that are more largely in excess of their tangible assets than before; to go into the market with a purchasing-power expanded by that much—or a little something more—beyond their available possessions, tangible and intangible. Which goes to enlarge the effective purchasing-power in the market without enlarging the supply of vendible goods in the market; which will act to raise or maintain the level of prices, and will therefore enlarge the total of the community's wealth as rated in money-values, independently of any increase of tangible possessions; all of which is "good for trade."

Any business concern which is in this way enabled to trade on a thinner equity will, by so much, be placed at an advantage as against the rest, provided that the rest do not come in for a similar advantage by a similar recourse to credit. Any advantage so gained is of a competitive or

has changed and passed, progressively with the passage of time and the accumulation of new usages and conceptions. In effect, assets are now capitalised on their earning-capacity regardless of cost or tangibility; the corporation is rated and capitalised at its value as a business concern, and among its valued and ratable possessions is its ability to borrow. An industrial corporation is necessarily rated on the sales-capacity of its industrial plant; that is to say, the prime factor in capitalisation is now in the nature of an intangible. Things have taken such a turn.

In the further course of capitalisation the capitalised intangibles, duly covered with negotiable securities, serve as collateral on which to secure an extension of credit, to be capitalised and covered with securities, which will be acceptable collateral so soon as they are "digested," etc. There is no question of the main fact; it is only a question of the rate of cumulative progression. It should also be noted that such liabilities may also serve as a creative factor in the progressive expansion of credit values without being formally capitalised in the shape of corporation securities conveying title to alleged assets. This is well shown by the case of government bonds or treasury notes and certificates, which are quite unexceptionable collateral at the same time that they neither represent tangible assets nor enter into the capital account of a corporation.

differential character, in that it presupposes that the rest will not make use of the same expedient, and it will immediately be offset and neutralised if and in so far as the like recourse to credit is adopted by the rest. From which it follows that all those who are to be saved, in the business sense, will go and do likewise. The practical outcome, as all men know, has been that the generality of such business concerns will habitually make such use of their borrowing capacity as they can, on pain of failure. From which it follows that such recourse to credit brings no net advantage to them, either as a differential or in the aggregate.

But it also follows that by this competitive recourse to credit these business concerns, commercial and industrial, all and several become clients of the dispensers of credit, and are loaded approximately to capacity with suitable overhead charges payable to the absentee holders of their paper, whether in the form of commercial credits or of corporation debentures. Whereby the business community at large, being made up of such business concerns doing business on such a credit basis, comes to be dependent on these dispensers of credit for the means of commercial subsistence and salvation,—in the degree in which this "credit economy" prevails.[15]

[15] This outcome follows in so far as business comes to be conducted on a credit basis. It is the working-out of a progressively improved stability of credits and improved facilities for their expeditious negotiation. The greater the ease with which credit extensions are negotiated, and the greater the security of outstanding obligations, the more will the use of credit become an everyday necessity and the more urgent will be the inducement to make full use of one's borrowing capacity; and the larger will be the volume of outstanding obligations and the resultant aggregate of overhead charges falling on business and industry. And evidently no net gain accrues from this traffic, except what

To commercial and industrial business as a whole no net aggregate gain accrues from this traffic in credits. But to the lenders there accrues a differential gain which is offset by a corresponding loss to the rest of the community; a net aggregate gain equal to the aggregate overhead charges borne by the resulting obligations, less the cost of carrying on the traffic in credits.[16] Therefore, the fuller the utilisation of credit and the greater its stability, the thinner will be the equity on which business is carried on; the larger will be the aggregate of overhead charges to be paid over to the trustees and owners of the credit resources; and the closer will the conduct of business and industry be bound up with the measures taken, for their own profit, by those captains of solvency who command the credit resources of the country.

Such would be the upshot of the matter, "other things remaining the same." And if such were the whole of the case the futility of it should presently become patent even to the business men who are immersed in this expansive credit and who (proximately) pay the cost. But other things do not remain the same, and among these other things is the price-level; which rises and continues to rise to meet the rising volume of purchasing-power that is thrown loose on the market at large by the current ubiquitous recourse to credit.

goes to the dispensers of credit; which is evidently of the nature of a differential gain at the cost of the business community at large.

[16] What amount is to be deducted as net eventual loss on the score of this cost of operation may be estimated, with a degree of approximation, from the total cost of carrying on the country's banking business, which is chiefly occupied with just this work; a reasonable allowance being made for other services rendered by the banks. What then remains of the sum of the cost of the traffic may be set down as paid to the bankers and

And like other persons, the business men are creatures of habit. By unbroken habit, prices are the substance of things in the working conceptions of the business men. Therefore their habitual frame of mind enables them to believe, or effectually to make believe, that they are gainers by as much as the prices advance; because they are enabled to foot up their assets and their net receipts in so much larger a number of smaller units of value. Such is the force of habit. The business man faithfully views the dollar *sub specie æternitatis,* even when he knows better. In extenuation of this businesslike imbecility it should also be noted that the men who do business are kept from reflecting on this state of the case by the fact that the cost of it all does not fall on them, finally and visibly, but on that underlying population with whom they deal, also called "the ultimate consumer."

As a further consequence, which is more immediately to the point here, by force of this endless network of credit that ties up the business concerns of the country in an interdependence of fiscal give and take, they are at the same time, each in his degree, large and small, tied in under the paramount fiscal jurisdiction of these keepers of the country's credit resources, as clients whose fortunes are forever in the balance and whose continued good fortune is conditioned on their continuing to be lucrative clients.

The key industries, it is true, occupy a special position in this regard, and the argument will return to their case presently. Smaller and outlying industrial and commercial concerns may be touched only at the second remove, by the outer ramifications of the fiscal organisation, but

their creditor clients for having enabled the country's business concerns, one with another, to inflate the figures of their receipts and disbursements.

they are all caught in the network of credit which serves the workday needs of all those who do business. And inasmuch as the country's industry is in the hands of the business men and is carried on as a business enterprise, it follows also that any question of industrial employment and of the rate and volume of production is likewise and perforce referred back to the same fiscal grounds and incentives, at any point that involves a question of initiative or eventual control. So that the industrial system, too, the productive use of the country's man-power and industrial plant, likewise waits on the collusive fiscal strategy of the same custodians of absentee credit. Whereby the livelihood of the underlying population becomes, in the language of mathematics, a function of the state of mind of the investment bankers, whose abiding precept is: When in doubt, don't.

Progressively, indeed at a cumulative rate, as the credit resources have been drawn together under a wide-reaching routine of profitable give and take, under the responsible surveillance of half-a-dozen massive credit institutions at the financial metropolis, the whole business of making credits and regulating them has gained in expedition and security; so that it has now reached an admirable footing of stability and swift execution. Stability, greater security from unforeseen or undesigned contingencies, will enable trading in credits and capitalisation on a thinner equity; which signifies a larger volume of fixed charges payable to the makers of credit, on the resultant increased volume of outstanding obligations; which means that the custodians of credit are enabled to take over the assets of the business community with increasingly greater expedition; which in turn will increase the stability of the business as well as the measure of control exercised by the keepers of credit over the conduct of business and industry at large. Eventually, therefore, the country's assets should, at a progressively accelerated rate, gravitate into the ownership, or at least into the control, of the banking community at large; and within the banking community ownership and control should gravitate into the hands of the massive credit institution that stand at the fiscal center of all things.

The stability of this fabric of credit, as well as the facility and effect with which its control of business and industry will be brought to bear, is greatly promoted by the inner concatenations of the system; particularly by the working arrangements and the bonds of common interest that gather about the nucleus of credit institutions at the fiscal center. These concatenations are of such a nature that, in great part, the chief banking-houses and their chief clients are now identical in point of their business interest; to a very appreciable extent identical in point of ownership. So that the same "Interest"—that is to say the same group of absentee owners working together as a team in pursuit of gain—will not infrequently be found to be the dominant owners on both the debit and the credit side of a given account; both within a given financial banking-house or group of affiliated banks and in the greater ones of the corporations whose credit and securities are taken care of by the given banking-house and its affiliated banks.[17]

---

[17] So, e. g., the same "Interest" which dominates the corporate business and industry in oil will at the same time dominate the leading banking establishment with which this oil business has to do, as well as its extensive retinue of affiliated banks. Among those business men who do business in oil it is a matter of course that the very extensive network of affiliated banks that are dominated by the Standard Oil Interest will faithfully serve that Interest in its endeavours to engross the oil resources of the

Such an arrangement will conduce in a marked degree to the stability of all suitable credit-extensions, capitalisations, and flotations; suitable, i. e., for the purposes of those who make up the general staff of solvency. At the same time it affords a ready means of discountenancing or disallowing ill-advised and adventurous projects, such as do not lend themselves to profitable capitalisation under the same auspices. Such, in effect, is the lie of the land in the domain of credit.

Any given one of these massive Interests will be the dominant factor in a number of corporate enterprises of the larger sort, each of which will do a large credit business with several of the greater banking-houses and their affiliated banks. It is a matter of common notoriety, if not of record, that the great Interests have been gaining ground of this sort at a progressively accelerated rate; gaining both in point of mass and financial consequence and in the reach and variety of the ramifications of their ownership throughout the business community. And it is fairly to be expected that their progress will continue unabated on somewhat the same lines in the calculable future. There results an intimate linking-up of client and custodian, a community interest between creditor and debtor, such as should virtually preclude any consequential derangement of the equilibrium of debits and credits except by mutual consent. In practical effect, the outcome is a pooling of credits and debits, within the financial sweep of the Interests. In practical effect, therefore, the preponderant mass of outstanding obligations and intangibles has come to rest in stable equilibrium, not to be upset except by choice of the interested parties, in pur-

country. Much the same disposition of forces is to be found in steel and railroads, of course. It is in no way obnoxious, either to the law or to business ethics.

suit of their joint gain, at the cost of the rest of the business community.[18]

This assured stability of the general fabric of credit serves greatly to augment the tensile strength of the business men's endurance in the face of new commitments. So that their goodwill and tolerance becomes available for capitalisation in behalf of the investment bankers at a higher coefficient than before. Whereby the output of new credit extensions and new capitalisations is enabled safely to expand at an unexampled rate.

So far, the argument has run to the effect that this American "credit economy," [19] organised in this way, will work unremittingly to draw the assets of the business community in under the ownership of those massive Interests whose captains constitute the general staff of solvency, in the manner already described. Such is doubtless the main drift of the forces engaged. But if the

[18] It is always conceivable, of course, that this American pool of solvency, or some one or more of the major Interests comprised in it, may under urgent pressure enter into hazardously extensive commitments toward the outside,—e. g., toward insolvent European clients. This may give rise to contingencies of so grave a nature as would eventually leave the pool at loose ends, derange the team-work of the Interests, and precipitate an unadvised and unmanaged liquidation. In view of the known European commitments of certain American Interests, it has been believed by apprehensive persons that the current situation in Europe is likely to contain the elements of such an eventuality. It is known that there is such an element of hazard for the American Interests in the case, but no person outside the American General Staff of Solvency, as already spoken of before, is in a position to hold a reasoned opinion on the complexion and magnitude of that hazard; and those persons who so are in a position to speak are maintaining a large and salutary reticence.

[19] As students will recognise, this term is borrowed from Knies and Hildebrand, who brought it into use in a somewhat wider application.

proposition were left standing in this unqualified form it would be too bald to serve as a sufficient description of what is actually taking place or of what is immediately in prospect. The main drift and its convolutions do not make so simple a tableau. It is necessary to note that the Interests and their captains and custodians do not appear to drive at all consistently and with a single mind toward such an undivided ownership of the assets engaged; nor does such an outcome habitually follow from their management of affairs, as a formal outcome, *de jure*.

It appears that, at least for the present and in great part, what is actually sought and obtained by their manœuvres is an effectual usufruct of these resources, rather than a formal acquisition and tenure of them in strict ownership. For many of the purposes of continued gain, such an effectual usufruct of the country's resources will serve as well as their formal ownership, at the same time that it can be administered quite as readily and profitably under the existing forms of law, and is less likely to irritate the public sensibilities. In effect, through the due working of this traffic in credit and capitalisation, the Interests and their custodians come in for the formal ownership of a progressively increasing share of these assets; and at the same time and by force of the same traffic they also come in for a progressively larger and more secure usufruct in the assets which still continue formally in the ownership of those concerns that have become their clients and that are dependent on their continued good will for indispensable credits by means of which to do business.

The case of the common run of these business concerns—that is to say, of the business community at large—as it is taking shape during these last years under the perfected credit economy, has a notable and instructive parallel and analogue in the plight of the prairie farmers, who have fallen into a state of something like effectual clientship and usufruct at the call of the implement makers, commission men, warehouse men, millers, packers, and railways. *De facto,* by drift of circumstances and sound business methods, these large business concerns which deal with the farmers and deal in their produce and their supplies have now come in for a reasonably secure and inclusive usufruct in the work and output of this farm population. The country bankers and country merchants, of course, also come in for their equitable share. Throughout this farming community there is a fairly steady drift of ownership into the hands of these business concerns with which the farm population does business; which takes effect in great part through the use of credit in the way of book accounts and deferred payments. But apart from absentee ownership of tenant farms and a certain, quite appreciable, volume of farm indebtedness, there is habitually no formal title of ownership, actual or contingent, covering the farmers or their work and output and vesting in the usufructuaries. The more substantial and more profitable source of gain to these concerns and Interests that make up the farmer's markets is doubtless their *de facto* vested right to do business with the farm population on their own terms.[20]

[20] To avoid dispute and exception, it may be as well to admit and note that such rights of usufruct have doubtless been capitalised in the capitalisation of these concerns that do business with the farm population, and that so they have been covered with corporation securities and incorporated in the assets of the corporations in question. In this way they doubtless make a very substantial mass of capitalised intangibles in the aggregate, and constitute a valuable body of assets; in the case of many such business concerns presumably these are the chief elements in their capitalisation. In so far, of course, this relation of usufruct has been given a formally legal existence, being capitalised and covered with negotiable corporation securities.

The current relation of usufruct between the packers, millers, warehouse men, and railroads, on the one side, e. g., and their underlying farm population on the other side, has no existence *de jure*, of course; the principles of jurisprudence which touch these matters being of an earlier date and not covering these features. It is only that as a practical matter of fact these Interests are in a position to make the terms on which the prairie farmers will go on with their work, if any; all the while that the farmers are left quite free to take or leave the terms offered, but with the reservation that their livelihood is contingent on their taking them. By this businesslike arrangement the farm population comes in for a very tolerable subsistence, to be had for steady work; while the railroads, packers, millers, etc., come in for a capitalised usufruct of the farm population and its work and for a steady run of earnings,—such a run of earnings as the traffic will bear.

In much the same fashion those major Interests on the financial plane, whose custodians are in command of the credit resources of the country at large, are enabled, informally and by a standard routine of management, to take over a reasonably complete usufruct in the run of business carried on by the business community at large. All the while this arrangement need involve no formal tenure of ownership of the underlying business traffic on their part. It may quite practically be done, as it is being done and as the circumstances entail that it must be done, by informal concert of action among those major Interests which are massive enough to make their pretensions good, and by a disciplinary "rationing" of the lesser business units in the allowance of credits with which to carry on their business. The packers, millers, etc., who do business with the farm population on a footing of usufruct may be entitled to rank among these major Interests that serve as custodians of the country's solvency, or they may belong among the lesser order of clients through whom the income-stream runs;—all that is a question of detail and personalities, which does not materially touch the general sweep and balance of the credit system and its appointed work.

Its appointed work, appointed by the drift of circumstances, is the due tutelage of the business concerns of the country and the governance of their conduct of the country's business and industry, with an eye single to the largest procurable net gains for those aggregations of absentee ownership that are spoken of as the Interests.

The procurable net gain in which the Interests are interested is counted in terms of the money-unit, of course; and it is invariably rated, received, accumulated, carried forward, disbursed, and accounted for, by way of a credit-instrument of some sort, book-account or transferable paper. Material wealth, metallic money, does not pass from hand to hand in this business traffic, except in transactions so small as to call for the use of what the economists call "token-money"; which is, in effect, another form of credit-instrument. The nearest approach to the material realities in the handling of these elements of income and disbursement is the use of banknotes; which is in the main confined to minor transactions. In ordinary times banknotes are presumed to outrun their specie basis by something over 500 per cent.; of late years they have fluctuated within an interval of perhaps twice that amplitude. It is in units of this fiduciary currency that the gains of business are valued and accounted for, and that the earning-capacity of any given business concern will be capitalised.

The increasing centralisation and coöperative spirit of the banking community, helped out by the good offices of the Federal Reserve, have been adding materially to the security of the outstanding note-issues.   So that this increased volume of paper money commands an increased measure of public confidence.   That is to say, the paper-money business is enabled to trade on a thinner equity. The note-issues have been enabled to depart somewhat more widely from the specie basis on which they are, at least ostensibly, hypothecated.   In effect, these credit-instruments which serve as the habitual measure of values are less exposed to the hazard of being called to account, at the same time that they are more widely detached from any material base.

It is this fiduciary currency that serves as the workday ground of reality in the pursuit of business, transactions being concluded in its terms and gains being "realised" in its units.   Evidently, this fiduciary currency is of the nature of certified make-believe, in the main; being a volume of intangibles hypothecated on the sound sense of the banking community and the Federal Reserve Board. The tutelage and governance exercised by these custodians of solvency over the conduct of business, therefore, has come to rest on this groundwork of outstanding liabilities which so are shielded from any ordinary hazard of liquidation, and their manœuvres of guidance and management are confined to a give and take between credit-instruments of one description and another.   The work is carried on by a systematic rationing of credit allowances.

The purpose and end of the traffic so carried on by the keepers of solvency is the up-keep and enlargement of the run of gains that will be credited to the party of the first part.   As has already been noted in an earlier passage, the gains which so are to be credited to the creditors are drawn from the receipts of the underlying business traffic, as an overhead charge on the working assets engaged in business. To enable such an augmented overhead charge to be carried by the underlying business traffic—and to be carried at a net profit—the gross receipts of this business traffic must also be enlarged by the same move and in a corresponding measure. The safe and sane procedure by which to bring receipts up to a practical maximum in any business enterprise is to limit the supply of vendible goods or services out of the sale-price of which the receipts arise, and thereby to advance the price per unit of supply up to the limit of what the traffic will bear, as has also been explained already. In ordinary times the supply and the sale-price will already have been adjusted, within reason, to what the traffic will bear, regard being had to the current level of prices and the available volume of purchasing-power. Therefore, to enlarge the receipts of the underlying business traffic and so enable it to carry an enlarged overhead charge, it will be necessary to raise the limit of what the traffic will bear; which is accomplished automatically by the increase of purchasing-power that is thrown on the market in the creation of the new credits which impose this new overhead charge, in that the new purchasing-power granted in these credits will go to raise the price per unit of vendible things and so will go to swell the aggregate price-receipts of the traffic by that much.

As a proposition in business and accountancy the outcome of these manœuvres is quite admirable; as a proposition in industry and livelihood it will stand somewhat different. It brings an increase of aggregate wealth and income as counted in money-values, independently of any increase of tangible possessions. But as a business proposition that is just as good, if not better. Such creation of new credits has much the same effect as the production of new gold used to have under the old dispensation;[21] but with the difference that the expansion of prices created by credit rests on the tensile strength of the popular credulity instead of the output of gold. Yet this later ground of price-inflation is presumably quite as secure as the earlier, more particularly by grace of the Federal Reserve Board's vigilant stabilisation of note-issues and commercial rediscounts.

It will be seen that the argument on this head runs on a progressive, automatic, and presumably interminable inflation of money-values; or on a continued depreciation of the effectual money-unit; according as one may choose to view it. Under the old dispensation of unconcerted banking, in so far as the money-unit was eventually accountable to an impersonal specie basis, such an inflation would be riding for an eventual fall, whereof there were repeated demonstrations. But under the new dispensation, since and so far as the price-level has become accountable to the sound business sense of the Federal Reserve Board and the keepers of the credit resources, no such sinister eventuality need be apprehended. The general staff of solvency have the situation in hand, and their interest in its maintenance may be counted on to endure.

The secure upward trend of the price-level, and its buoyant endurance under difficulties during the last few years, should sufficiently demonstrate the superior stability of a price-inflation which rests on constituted authority and businesslike common sense. Provided that the price-level continues to rise at a reasonable rate, such a tem-

[21] See chapter vii, Section iv.

perate rate as will not greatly jar the popular credulity and such as the sound business principles of its guardians may reasonably be counted on to dictate, then there should be no reason to apprehend that this price-level may not safely be advanced indefinitely, to the continued gain of those who stand to gain by it.

To any footloose observer it will be evident that the general price-level has been rising, without serious break or abatement, during the past quarter-century. The new gold has had something to do with this movement, more particularly during the earlier part of this period, and the new credit facilities have had more to do with it, particularly in later years. In a very appreciable degree this movement of price-inflation has been masked by the continued advance in the industrial arts, which has run along without abatement over the same period and has greatly increased the productive capacity of the country's industry, and which so has acted powerfully and unremittingly to lower the cost of production of the output, and thereby to depress prices of vendible goods and services.

In the face of a steadfast resistance from the side of safe and sane business, particularly from the financial section of the business community, the continued new growth of the technology of physics and chemistry has continued to insinuate a progressively heightened productive efficiency into the industrial system, cumulatively and ubiquitously, and with a particularly stubborn drive along the lines of quantity production; such as to depress the costs and enlarge the scope and rate in the quantity production of vendible goods and services. If these improvements in the ways and means of industry had been given a free run through this period, and if prices had not at the same time been inflated by use of credit, the higher potential of production at which these technological improvements have enabled the industrial system to do its work should in the course of this period have lowered production-costs at large to such a level as would have brought general prices down to an inconspicuous fraction of the current figures.

But such a free run of production, such as the technicians would be ready to set afoot if they were given a free hand, would mean a full employment of the available forces of industry, regardless of what the traffic would bear in point of net profit from sales; it would bring on such an inordinate output of vendible goods and services as to glut the market and precipitate an irretrievable decline of the price-level, and consequently also a fatal decline of earnings and a default and liquidation of capitalised earning-capacity,—a disastrous liquidation of capitalised intangibles. Therefore such a free run of production has not been had nor aimed at; nor is it at all expedient, as a business proposition, that anything of the kind should be allowed.

Still, under all that handicap of cautious businesslike retardation which sound business principles have entailed, the continued growth of the mechanical technology has taken effect in cheapened production in so large a measure as to have greatly masked that progressive inflation of prices which the larger use of credit has brought on and carried forward during the same interval. With the partial exception of the crude products of the soil, there is no one of the major lines of production that has not been gravely affected by it. From time to time the technological advance has even been able to give the progressive inflation of prices the appearance of being no more than a stabilisation and maintenance of the price-level; although in the long run the cumulative expansion of credit, reënforced with a resolute businesslike restriction of output all along the line, has proved to be the stronger, and has proved to be the determining factor in that parallelogram of economic forces the resultant of which has been a sustained upward trend of general prices and a cumulative capitalisation of intangibles.

Apart from scattered speculative gains which may come to shrewd outsiders here and there, those who stand to gain by this long run of expansion in money-values are the constituent members of the One Big Union of financial Interests. Between them they make up the party of the first part in that advancing press of credit transactions by which the expansion is made and maintained.[22] This One Big Union is not precisely a trade-union of bankers; although it is on the ground of investment banking and by use of transactions in credit and capitalisation that the One Big Union's tutelage and regulation of business and industry goes into effect. It is essentially a union of Interests, not of persons; at least not in a personal bearing; although it is through measures taken by those

[22] *De jure* there is no such One Big Union of the Interests, of course. It is perhaps needless to say so. This descriptive phrase applies only *de facto*. And even *de facto* the One Big Union of the Interests appears, hitherto, scarcely to have had a settled local habitation and a name. Only in respect of the One Big Union's surveillance of note issues and rediscounts can it be said the Federal Reserve has given its membership a "Central" —if one may take a metaphor from the usage of the telephone. The One Big Union, hitherto, has no corporate existence. It foots up to a concert of action and policy enforced by the drift of circumstances, rather than by deliberation and a reasoned plan looking to the long run. But by drift of circumstances—the drift of sound business principles and a common solicitude—their several movements result, in effect, in such a convergence of forces and such a concert of policy and action as to merit the name.

persons who are the appointed custodians of these Interests that those business principles by which they live have come to regulate these large matters, in point of tactics, scope and policy, not in point of detail manœuvres. There has been, hitherto, no such degree of organised responsibility and control as would permit this General Staff of custodians to dictate specific manœuvres to their clients, except it be at a critical juncture, when the common good of the Interests is in the balance or when the fabric of credit and capitalisations is exposed to some imminent hazard. If the name be employed in such a loosely descriptive fashion, the One Big Union of the Interests will come to much the same thing as what is covered by the colloquial phrase, "Big Business," but with a particular reference to that community-interest and that solidarity of principles which is entailed by the common responsibilities and the common benefits of the larger absentee ownership.

These Interests which so are drawn together, by force of circumstances, into this inchoate One Big Union of absentee ownership are many and various; but they have at least one distinctive trait in common, viz. large absentee ownership. It is also a characteristic fact that the Interests, or their assets, are quite generally if not invariably engaged in two or more lines of business at the same time, and that each of these distinct lines of business engages these assets to their full amount. Two such lines of business carried on in this way simultaneously for the same Interest and by the use of the same assets will touch and mutually reënforce one another in respect of their solvency, although they will be quite distinct in respect of their corporate identity and the technical character of the business traffic carried on by each.

The one line will be financial, in the nature of investment banking, occupied with the creative use of credit resources, capitalisations and flotations; while the other line will be commercial or industrial business of the corporate sort, perhaps more frequently the latter, occupied with the output and sale of vendible goods or services. Few if any of these Interests, or blocks of absentee ownership, are not to be counted with in both of these bearings; particularly such of them as rise into a position of dominance in the business community. The type-form would be that which is shown by those well-known dominating Interests whose force of ownership is to be counted with equally in the banking community at the fiscal metropolis and in one or another of the key industries, as, e. g., steel, coal, oil, or railways. But of much the same value and effect, for the purpose of the present argument, are those other notable Interests which combine a metropolitan enterprise in solvency and capitalisations with large industrial undertakings that are not commonly classed as key industries; as, e. g., sugar-refining, meat-packing, flour-milling, the manufacture of explosives, or trolley lines. Illustrative instances will readily come to mind.

This characteristic bifurcation, or spread, of the Interests, or, if one prefers the expression, this conjugation of industrial and fiscal enterprises under the same block of absentee ownership, is by no means a casual or fortuitous occurrence. It is of the essence of the case and lies at the root of the current situation. It is not in any conclusive sense an effect of personal choice and inclination, for it is contained in that drift of circumstances out of which the whole situation arises, and which no personal bias or caprice can turn aside or defeat. The underlying and conclusive fact of the matter is that such procedure is profitable; which is conclusive for the pursuit of business.

Such double use of the available assets will yield double earnings; indeed, ordinarily something more. Sufficiently large assets engaged as corporate capital, say in one of the key industries, will at the same time and to their full amount, and without prejudice to their earning-capacity as corporation assets serve also to their full amount as assets of solvency in the fiscal enterprise of the metropolitan investment banking, provided always that the assets are held in sufficiently large blocks. Indeed, the more fully and profitably such assets are employed in such industrial business, especially if they are engaged on a large and dominant scale, the better will be their rating in the business community and the more securely and fully will they serve as the substance of that solvency on which the traffic in credit extensions and capitalisations is carried on. The larger the success, in point of earnings, and the more assured the prospective earning-capacity of any such block of assets, the larger and more assured will be its solvency and its funded carrying-power as a factor in the business of investment banking, and the more effectually, therefore, can it be mobilised for the creation of new credit extensions and new intangibles. Its effectual capital-value is enlarged by so much.[23] For what they are worth, industrial assets of the larger sort

[23] Such enlargement of effectual capital-value of given assets by the proven earning-capacity of an industrial business concern is well shown, e. g., in the case of the Standard Oil securities that were outstanding some years ago; when the market value, and the consequent value as collateral, of the common stock advanced by steady growth of earnings till it reached some 700 per cent. over its face value. As an element of solvency and a credit-bearing asset that parcel of securities then counted at their market value, of course, not at their face value; as was also seen and turned to account presently in the issuance of stock dividends of some 700 per cent. Substantially the same operation has been repeated by the various Standard Oil properties during the past year (1922).

have, therefore, such a secondary—or perhaps rather a primary—service to render their owners, or their constituted custodians, under the conditions inaugurated by this new order of business enterprise that runs on funded credits. The whole fabric of business is built on and about this double use of asserts, and its movements are regulated by the circumstances which.govern this double use.

Sound business principles—the principles of the main chance—will not allow the benefits of such double service of assets to be overlooked, nor will they let this fruitful duplication of earning-capacity go to waste. To lend itself most profitably to such double service, the parcel of assets in question should be of reasonably massive proportions, such as to place its owner or manager on a footing of some strategic independence and initiative among those large absentee owners on whose assets the country's credit system is erected and with whom he will have to negotiate for whatever share is coming to him out of the proceeds of that business. All the while it is also true, and it lies in the collusive nature of the fiscal system and its work, that many businesslike owners who command only relatively small and inconsequential parcels of assets will elbow their way into participation in the traffic, to come in for whatever margin of supernumerary profits they can touch while serving as outliers of the system and subsidiaries of the larger captains of duplication.

This is one of the prime considerations on the strength of which their banking operations are carried on by that multitude of minor and outlying banking concerns that do business as branches, subsidiaries, and correspondents, immediately or remotely dependent on the favorable attitude of the major concerns at the metropolitan center of solvency. These outliers are bound into the working system of credit by a bond of profitable compliance with the tactical dispositions made by its masters.   On this ground do the ramifications of the system run.   Without this faithful docility which characterises these outlying correspondents, the efficiency of the system as a generator of intangibles and incomes would be greatly curtailed, if indeed it could come to anything substantially lucrative at all in that case.   By this double use of assets, and by help of this all-pervading give and take of profitable margins and commissions, the assets which are so employed are made to pay their way both going and coming, as one might say.   The organisation is in the nature of a contrivance for killing two birds with one stone, or for making two overhead charges grow where one grew before, if one should prefer that form of the adage.

In the nature of the case, those massive aggregations of absentee ownership that are elected by circumstance to make up the One Big Union of the Interests, and to share in its counsels, revenues and perquisites, will necessarily take on such a duplex working formation; whatever may have been the underlying sources from which their assets have once been derived, or the employments in which they may once have been engaged during their growth and maturation.   The earning-capacities which enter into their composition as assets, and the personnel which administers them as Interests, may be of one derivation or another; they may, e. g., have come out of oil or out of commercial banking.   But whether a given Interest has in its initial phase been identified with industrial business or with financial undertakings, its destiny under the circumstances which establish and regulate the new order of things in business will be to throw the full weight of its assets and prestige into both lines alike, so soon as it reaches the due measure of maturity in mass and in years of discretion.[24]

In respect of their financial commitments and their share in the guidance of the country's financial policy at large, these several Interests and their several custodians stand together on reasonably common ground; but the like is not to be said of their strategy and tactics as concerns engaged in industrial business. As financial Interests they are drawn together in team-work for their common good and are able to take measures in common, looking to their joint advantage and particularly to their mutual security, to the security of their several commitments and the maintenance of the level of capitalisation. Whereas in their capacity of industrial business Interests they are habitually somewhat at odds, if not at cross purposes; being in the position of rival salesmen in a limited market. As industrial Interests, that is to say as business concerns which do business in an output of vendible products, they all are in some degree in the position of rivals in trade, sellers of alternative goods in a closed market, in which one tradesman misses what another takes of the available purchasing-power. In this bearing the most amicable contact which the circumstances of the case and the ethics of trade will admit among them is the watchful courtesy of a negotiated peace,—a peace negotiated for their mutual relief from "cutthroat competition" and for the common gain of the same Interests in their ca-

[24] Consider, e. g., two such typical credit institutions of the first rank as J. Pierpont Morgan & Co. and the National City Bank, which have come into the business from widely different beginnings and antecedents, but which now count at their full weight both in industrial enterprise and as banking houses. It is also interesting to note that the dates from which the two take their departure as prime-movers in this twofold pursuit of gain, coincide in a loose way with the period out of which the new order of credit and capitalisation took its rise.

pacity of credit-brokers, investment bankers, creators of capitalised intangibles. It is, therefore, as massive parcels of funded solvency and formidable strategists in capitalisation that they come together as constituents of the One Big Union of the Interests; and it is as such that they safeguard that peace of moderation and mutual concessions that broods over the traffic of industrial business.

All the while, of course, it is the same Interests, the same parcels of assets and administered by the same responsible personnel, moved by the same incentive of net aggregate gain in terms of price, that do business in both connections. It is incumbent on these custodians and strategists of the Interests, collectively and severally, to regulate and administer affairs in a large way both in the traffic of industrial business and in the marketplace of credit and capital. But the seat of executive power as well as the high court of judicature, touching all the major issues of business traffic of whatever complexion, under this new order, are to be found on the financial ground, in the bailiwick of the high magistrates of solvency. Circumstances have taken such a turn.[25]

[25] There is a singular, but presumably idle, coincidence of dates and characteristics between this *de facto* magistracy of solvency, its scope and powers, on the one side, and the rise and scope of the Injunction as applied in American court practice on the other side. Both are unprecedented, both have grown out of inconspicuous beginnings and have come to their present sovereign powers within the same general period of time; the same period during which the large-scale industrial business and the free capitalisation of credits have also come into bearing, and have in time come to dominate the country's industrial system and its scheme of life. Both serve the ends of the larger absentee ownership, in the main and *de facto*. Both combine judiciary with executive powers, and the powers of both are of an inhibitory sort; essentially powers of retardation and inertia, powers which take effect by way of penalising activities that are not otherwise obnoxious to law or morals. It appears also that, in

Chief among the circumstances which have given this turn to the pursuit of business, and which so have given rise to the new order of things and the sovereign powers of the larger credit, has been the circumstance that a businesslike competition in production and marketing was running loose among the major industries in the late nineties, at such an unguarded rate as to be a menace to the traffic; such as threatened to entail a grievous retrenchment of the outstanding capitalisations and jeopardise the fixed charges payable on outstanding debentures. The discord in the industrial business was rising to an intolerable pitch and volume, such as to threaten the continued earning-capacity of the business corporations that were caught in it. The new order of things has emerged from the remedial measures which that state of affairs invited, as has been explained in an earlier passage in describing the rise of the investment bankers. It lies in the nature of this industrial business, as conducted in a closed market by competitive business concerns, to breed dissension, distrust and cross purposes among the Interests engaged in the traffic.[26]

practical effect, the two mutually befriend and sustain one another.

[26] This description of the case, as necessarily running to distrust, cross purposes, and sharp practice, applies to the conduct of the business, not to the mechanics of production. It is a proposition concerning business principles and practice, not concerning the technique of industry. It remains true all the while, of course, that in point of workmanship, in point of efficient tangible performance, as contrasted with the strategy of salesmanship, the industries are always and everywhere best served by a cordial and calculated coöperation between the various industrial units that make up the industrial system. The maximum net production is to be reached only along that line. But business enterprise is a pursuit of maximum net gain in terms of price, not of maximum production in terms of goods. It is an enterprise in salesmanship, whether the trading is done in material goods or in the credit instruments.

In due time, so soon as the corporate interests that were contending for the traffic had grown to formidable proportions and their market was closing in, this unhappy state of affairs became intolerable. So, under the spur of desperation, there has presently emerged the new order of collusive moderation under the administrative guidance of the One Big Union of the Interests. Concert and mutual accommodation in the conduct of this industrial business is effectually dictated not by the technical requirements of industry but by considerations of finance, with a view to mutual financial benefits, by financial concessions and alliances, under pressure of financial necessity.

Financial peace and stability is a matter of the first consequence to the Interests, and to all those who are concerned in the business of capitalised credits. The fabric of credit and capitalisation is essentially a fabric of concerted make-believe resting on the routine credulity of the business community at large. It is therefore conditioned on the continued preservation of this prevalent credulity in a state of unimpaired tensile strength, which calls for eternal vigilance on the part of its keepers. The fabric, therefore, is always in a state of unstable equilibrium, liable to derangement and extensive disintegration in case of an appreciable disturbance at any critical point, with unhappy consequences for the business of capitalisa-

In the technological respect, as a proposition in workmanship and tangible performance, the industries of the country are bound together in an orderly network of interlocking processes of production; but in respect of the business interests engaged, as a proposition in salesmanship and sales-profits, in their capacity of business concerns, these many parcels of industrial property are at cross purposes, being in the position of competing bidders for custom. The strategy of salesmanship and net gain brings with it into the industrial system the defects of its own qualities, and among these defects is an inveterate bias of distrust and sharp practice.

tion and overhead charges. Hence the eminently wise and unremitting exhortation to retain or restore confidence, and to return to "normalcy" in case the popular credulity has suffered a lapse. This care is incumbent on the Interests of the One Big Union. So that it is incumbent on them to stand united and play safe, to avoid shock, to promote moderation and tranquillity throughout the world of credit and capitalisation; for it is after all a confidence game—in the blameless sense of the phrase—and is to be played according to the rules governing games of that psychological nature. To this end these major Interests, which in their financial entity make up the One Big Union, will use a reasonable degree of neighborly accommodation in pursuing their several advantages as special interests in the traffic of industrial and commercial business. And to the same salutary end the minor participants, subsidiaries, outliers and interlopers in the industrial business will be rationed in respect of their needful credit extensions, according to the same reasoned plan looking to the stability of price-levels and outstanding capitalisations.

The outcome of this régime of financial peace and stability is not that rivalry and sharp practice are eliminated from current industrial and commercial business, not even from industrial business of that larger sort which will generate a "Special Interest"; but only that the rivalry and competitive manœuvring runs within reasonable and salutary bounds; that is to say, reasonable and salutary for the purposes of profitable financiering, as touches outstanding credits and the level of capitalisation. Reason and security in this bearing have to do with the maintenance and enlargement of earnings, of income in terms of money, and of possessions in terms of price; not with the maintenance and enlargement of productive output or of livelihood. Competitive manœuvres in industrial business under this régime, therefore, may without hazard run free in so far as they will not tend to impair the price-level. It is on the price-level that the level of capitalisation rests, at the same time that the volume of capitalisation determines the price-level, in the main and in the long run.

Competitive manœuvres which will leave the price-level intact, or which will tend to raise it, will be manœuvres of competitive salesmanship, not of competitive production, of course. Now and again such manœuvres of salesmanship will involve an increased output of the line of goods or services to be sold, in case the manœuvres enlarge the volume of sales. As an incident of the business, in such a case efficient salesmanship may provoke an increased production of the given line of goods. In a closed market, that is to say in a market which runs on a provisionally fixed volume of purchasing-power, such increased production and sale in any one given line of goods will be balanced (approximately) by an equivalent curtailment of output and sales in other lines which come in competition, directly or indirectly; or otherwise the price-level will be deranged. In effect and in the main it is a question of alternative purchases.[27]

[27] So, e. g., increased sales of yeast-cakes, cosmetics, Red Cross doles, furs, or rubber tires—wares which have of late been selling in very notably increased quantities as a result of large and persistent advertising—will be offset by a shrinkage of sales in other, alternative lines, as, e. g., fruits, flannels, alcoholic beverages, savings-bank accounts, or butcher's-meats.
The current situation of this business community at large, which so does business in commercial and industrial traffic within the bounds appointed by the massive Interests of the One Big Union, is a situation of much the same complexion as that which has prevailed in the country towns of the Middle West, as already explained in an earlier chapter. The traffic

This state of the case leaves a fairly large scope for initiative and enterprise in salesmanship. And as is well known a very large and steadily increasing expenditure of talents, funds, and apparatus, has gone into this work in salesmanship in recent years. Even those major industrial Interests which would seem to be in a position to make their own terms, the terms on which they will buy their materials and on which they will dispose of their marketable output, have been going strong on this rivalry in salesmanship, as, e. g., the packers or the millers. They too are driving hard against these pliable but resilient barriers of competitive salesmanship in a closed market. The only ones among these industrial business enterprises which are passably exempt from the cares of salesmanlike rivalry are those which have to do immediately with one or another of the key industries. And even they are not wholly exempt, as may be seen, e. g., in the case of the oil business, whose sign-boards, advertisements, and decorated sales-booths are to be met at every turn; while their very reputable spokesmen continue to solicit the popular good-will with the most assiduously devout and humanitarian verbiage.

It is after all in the Key Industries—in coal, steel, oil, lumber, railways, waterpower—that the administrative center of this system of industrial business traffic lies; just

runs on the same general lines of reserved and evasive rivalry within and of sturdy solidarity toward the outside, toward the underlying population; very much as the local community of retailers carries on the business traffic of a typical country town. Except for its larger dimensions it is much the same thing over again, both as regards the manner and the degree in which the cost of it all falls on the underlying population. In both cases it is an enterprise in usufruct carried on under a loosely defined code of Live and Let Live, designed to safeguard the joint advantage of the usufructuaries.

as its executive center lies outside the industrial system proper, in the massive credit institutions of the fiscal metropolis. And it is on these key industries, in the main and primarily, that the dominant Interests of the One Big Union rest their weight of absentee ownership and pivot the sweep of their industrial dominion. The Key Industries are so called because the rest of the industrial system waits on their operations; so that they set the pace and govern the practicable rate and volume of employment and output for the industrial system at large,— practicable, that is, in point of business expediency.

The management of the key industries works out, in effect, as an administrative control of the industrial system at large; immediately in and through the mechanical industries, and indirectly also throughout the underlying industrial system. But all the while the management of the key industries is neither prompted nor guided by any such far-reaching administrative purpose, nor is it biassed by any sentiment of administrative responsibility in that connection. This guidance of industrial affairs is all, in a way, an undesigned and fortuitous by-product of the steadfast pursuit of their own advantage by those Interests that do business in the key industries. The measures taken by the Interests are directed to no such end. But such is the exacting balance and concatenation of the work and of its ways and means, under this mechanistic state of the industrial arts and under the price-system, that the operations of these key industries which turn out the primary output of coal, steel, oil, and transport, will unavoidably make the pace for the rest of the mechanical industries, whether by design or not.

As a matter of common sense and a fact of common notoriety, the key industries are managed on the businesslike principle of charging what the traffic will bear;

that is to say, what will bring the largest net gain to their owners and managers. It is a simple, though sometimes delicate, question of restricting the rate and volume of their output to such a figure as will yield the largest net return in terms of price, when the price is determined by this restriction of the output.[28]

Those other massive industrial undertakings that come into the same class with the key industries in respect of their dominant mass and reach and in the respect that they are concerned immediately with the prime necessities of life, stand on much the same footing in this matter as the key industries proper; as, e. g., meat-packing, flour-milling, or sugar-refining. The management of these has the initiative in industrial business; that is to say, the initiative rests finally with the financial management of these concerns. Therefore, the Interests which have the financial custody and direction of these key industries are in a position to make the terms on which industrial production will be carried on, and it is for the management of the underlying industries in the system to take or leave the terms which are offered them.

[28] The net aggregate price-return is a product of two variables; one of which—the output—varies at the discretion of the businesslike management, and the second of which—the price per unit—is a function of the first. "What the traffic will bear" is that volume of output which will give the largest product when multiplied into the price per unit. Hence the need of a vigilant restraint on production.

The principle of restraint which so comes to govern the business of what the traffic will bear has been spoken of as the "law of balanced return"; as being a principle which determines the expedient maximum of output in any given case, and which therefore also determines what will be the expedient size of an industrial business unit in any given line of production and sale. —Cf. A. S. Dewing, *The Financial Policy of Corporations,* vol. iv, ch. ii.

The business men in charge of these key industries are able to use this discretion with a passably free hand, inasmuch as these industries stand at the apex of the industrial system,—the apex of growth and of industrial strategy. Their management is vested with the initiative in industrial matters. Their administrative policy consequently falls into relatively simple lines, in its general application. In its elements, it comes to the broad question of how large an output of these prime ways and means of industry will yield the largest net aggregate price-return to the business men in charge and to their absentee owners. In its practical application this will foot up to a question of how far production had best be allowed to go, or how nearly full an employment of the available equipment and man-power will yield the largest net income, for the time being, to these owners and their managers; which may be restated as a question of how large a running margin of unemployment will best serve this purpose.

In ordinary times there is always such a running margin of unemployment, both in the key industries and in those underlying industries which depend on them for their necessary ways and means. And even in busy times few if any of these industries will ever come up to anything like the volume of production that would result from a free use of the same man-power and material resources under competent technical management with an eye single to production. Sound business considerations will not permit it. The businesslike duties of management turn constantly on a sagacious restriction of output at the point of "balanced return," and on the many exacting details of speeding-up and slowing-down, of laying-off and taking-on, of hiring and firing, which arise out of this necessary strategy of balanced unemployment. Balanced Return involves Balanced Unemployment.

The gains of business enterprise, whether in the key industries or in the underlying industries of the system, are money-values and they are derived from the margin of sales-price over the cost of the output. The aim of business is to widen this margin and to come in for as large a share of it as may be. The margin may be widened by raising the sales-price or by lowering the cost of the output. And any given business concern may increase its share in this margin by more efficient salesmanship. These are the points to be covered by the strategy of industrial business management.

As has already been explained above, the price-level at large will rise progressively in response to that progressively enlarged volume of purchasing-power which arises out of the progressive creation of credits in the ordinary course of investment, merchandising, and corporation finance. This expansion is self-propagating. Each successive advance of the price-level calls for a corresponding increment of the working-capital of all those concerns that do business within its scope; which includes virtually all of the business community. The needful increase of working-capital is got by a creation of new credits; which goes to increase the volume of purchasing-power; which goes to raise the general level of prices, etc. It is a matter of workday routine, and is, in effect, to be broken into only by such a general liquidation of credits as is no longer to be apprehended, since the Federal Reserve and the One Big Union of the Interests have taken over the stabilisation of credits on a reasoned plan.

The major financial transactions of investment-banking work out to the same effect, these being also in the nature of a creation of credits, capitalisations, and overhead charges. So that the progressive rise of the price-level goes forward in an orderly, and conservative, way, as a secondary but unavoidable outcome of business-as-usual. By so much, industrial business enterprise at large is assured of a reasonable and progressively widening margin of money-values over the cost of its merchantable output, provided always that the (money) cost of the output does not also advance in like measure.[29]

As has been explained in an earlier chapter, the business concerns of the underlying industrial system, the concerns that do business in commerce and manufactures, as these words are commonly understood, are engaged in competition among themselves for a share in the run of the market,—competitive management designed to increase each concern's share in the distribution of the available

[29] It will be seen that the current situation in this respect has much in common with the interval of prosperity, inflation, or speculative advance, that makes up the rising segment of such a business cycle as the experience of the nineteenth century and the discussions of the nineteenth-century economists have made familiar; but with a difference. There is in the current situation an element of sobriety and a factor of salutary reserve that were lacking in the nineteenth century. Prosperity ran somewhat headlong in those days, and came, in the ordinary course, to a headlong liquidation, ending in panic, crisis and depression. Under the conservative surveillance of the Federal Reserve and the One Big Union of the Interests in the twentieth century the prosperity of business—that is to say the inflation of capital and prices—does not run riot. It is an orderly advance, in the course of which the progressive creations of credit and capital are duly stabilised and "digested," distributed and consolidated under the aegis of the Interests, with such effect as to make them a secure ground on which to hypothecate further creations of the same character, in indefinite progression. And no undesigned liquidation need be apprehended in this case, since the major debits and credits are pooled, in effect, by being drawn in under the custody of these major Interests that informally make up the One Big Union. Both the need of credits and the progressive creation of them are indefinitely extensible.

purchasing-power. Their market is a closed one, in a large way, in that the volume of purchasing-power available for distribution among them at any given time is a fixed quantity. Under current conditions the volume of purchasing-power will expand by a more or less orderly progression in the course of time and with the continued expansion of the outstanding volume of credit. But for the time being it is limited within fairly definite though not inflexible bounds. Salesmanship may divert given items and fractions of this outstanding volume of purchasing-power from one line of sales to another, but it does not in any appreciable degree enlarge the total volume of sales at any given time.[30] Expenditure on sales-cost, taken as a whole, will therefore count as a deduction from the available margin of sales-price over cost of output. Yet continued and progressively increasing attention to salesmanship, and a continued and progressively increasing expenditure on sales-cost, are primary and essential to any reasonably large success in this field of business enterprise under the current conditions.[31]

[30] The "market" as here used is the volume of effective demand for things to be bought at the current level of prices, and it may be taken to mean the national market or the international market at large, according to the context of the argument. In either case it is a "closed market," in the sense that the available purchasing-power which constitutes the demand in this market falls short of the productive capacity of the industrial system, at the ruling level of prices. Hence attention and expenditure in this field of business enterprise has been converging on salesmanship rather than on increased production, with the result that total sales-costs have gained largely and progressively, at the same time that the rate and volume of output have remained relatively stationary on the whole.

[31] One of the secondary consequences of this imperative recourse to salesmanship and enhanced sales-cost is to be noted in this connection. In great part salesmanship takes effect by way of establishing a conventional need for articles which have previously been superfluities, shifting given articles of con-

Again, inasmuch as the gains of business, the earnings of enterprise and invested capital, are always eventually to be drawn from the margin of sales-price over production-cost, it is incumbent on all business management to curtail production-cost so far as may be. The earnings of invested capital are of the nature of overhead charges, for the sake of which the business is carried on, and any curtailment of which will therefore foot up to so much of a defeat of the purpose for which business is carried on. It follows that any curtailment of production-cost which shall be reasonable, within the logic of business enterprise, must be a curtailment in expenditures on those factors of production which are not capitalised or included among the rateable assets of the business community. Which comes to saying that the curtailment, if any, must take effect in those expenditures which go to the industrial man-power and the outlying farm population; these factors of the industrial system being not capitalised and, for the time being, not capitalisable, and so being not carried on the books as assets to which the business is bound over in the way of fixed charges.

In respect of their business interests, therefore, there results a division or cleavage of the people who live under this system of industrial business, whereby the business community, heading up in the Interests of the One

sumption from the footing of superfluities to that of necessary articles of livelihood, necessities by conviction of morals and decency rather than by requirement of subsistence or physical comfort. By so much the necessities of life for the consumers will be enlarged, and by so much the (moral) subsistence minimum to be provided for out of wages will be raised, without a corresponding increase in the workmanlike efficiency of the wage-earners; which acts in its degree to increase the labor-cost per unit of the marketable output of industry, and therefore also to narrow the margin of sales-price over production-cost. E. g., the moral necessity of consuming furs, cosmetics, or high heels.

Big Union, comes to stand over against the underlying population, which is taking articulate shape in the labor organisations and the sentimental swarming gyrations of the farmers. Quite generally these organisations and projected movements among the underlying population run true to the "action-pattern" of business-as-usual, in that their consistent aim is to come in for an increasing share in the margin of sales-price over production-cost. This they endeavor to accomplish by bargain and sale, enforced by a well-considered limitation of their marketable supply, quite in the spirit of that larger financial business enterprise that administers the affairs of the capitalised manufactures, and that governs the rate and volume of the industrial output by a conscientious withdrawal of efficiency, as dictated by the law of balanced return. In these endeavours the fortunes of the underlying population are subject to ebb and flow; but in the nature of the case it is mostly ebb. The underlying population, it is true, is caught in the business system; but it is after all not an executive factor in the system; only a creative factor, which is quite another matter. It comes into the strategy of business enterprise at large in a more passive way, as man-power to be employed at discretion in the pursuit of earnings on capitalised industry, according to the law of balanced return, and as a body of ultimate consumers to be supplied at discretion in the pursuit of commercial gains, according to the principle of what the traffic will bear.

As organised industrial man-power, particularly as mobilised in the shape of standard labor-unions, these elements of the underlying population are consistently endeavoring, with a fluctuating measure of success, to enforce an indefinitely extensible claim in the way of better pay. But in the nature of the case these endeavours if successful will ordinarily come to nothing more than a running process of catching up. The better pay is better in terms of price. But in the nature of the case the general level of prices continues to rise under current conditions of credit, capitalisation, and salesmanship. And since these progressively better-paid workmen are at the same time ultimate consumers of the goods whose prices continue progressively to advance, they continue to lose in the higher cost of living whatever they gain in the advance of wages. With a change of phrase the same proposition applies to the farm population. And it should be noted in the same connection, as applying without much distinction to all classes and conditions of ultimate consumers, that all the while the ever-increasing personnel and proficiency employed in salesmanship continues to convert additional articles of superfluous consumption into items of morally necessary use; at the same time that the increasing expenditure on sales-costs goes unremittingly to raise the price of living.

The organised industrial man-power endeavours, with a fluctuating measure of success, to make good its claim to an enlarged allowance of livelihood. The ways and means employed in these endeavours foot up, invariably, to a standardised conscientious withdrawal of efficiency, designed to bring the Interests to terms by a punitive restriction of the industrial output. In effect, this is the sole purpose for which the industrial man-power has been organised. So also the farmers are aspiring to make head against the Interests and to reinstate themselves as "Independent Farmers" after the good old fashion of the day before yesterday. The Independent Farmer is one of the lost arts of the nineteenth century. They are hop-

ing to contrive some sort of a businesslike plan of concerted action by which to put themselves collectively in
line as a practicable Interest that shall be able to make
terms and reshape the scheme of things nearer to the
bucolic heart's desire. By and large, the remedial aspirations of these farmers appear to fall under three several heads: restriction of output; restraint of trade; and
expansion of credits. Their great hope appears to center on an inflation of prices by a conscientious withdrawal
of productive efficiency and an inflation of purchasing-
power. By this means they hope to cover their outstanding liabilities and procure their needed working-capital.
Their aspirations, at least, are businesslike.

Meantime the Interests, the One Big Union of the
Major Interests and the network of minor concerns
through which the business of credit and capitalisation
runs, are engaged on a loosely collusive plan for bringing
the industrial man-power to reasonable—that is to say
profitable—terms by the punitive use of unemployment.
At the same time the volume of outstanding capitalisation
is being continuously augmented by a continued flow of
securities, in great part representing recapitalisations of
existing assets, and working-capital to be applied toward
increased sales-costs. By and large, or "in principle,"
the Interests and the Federal Reserve take a position of
prudent conservatism; in practical effect the drift of businesslike exigencies decides that, as a matter of transactions in detail, the continued issue of new capital-
securities runs well up in the hundreds of millions weekly;
while the physical aggregate of the capitalised assets appears on the whole to be declining in a moderate way,
through uncovered wear and tear. More particularly will
it be seen that the physical ways and means are falling
short when it is considered that both the numbers of the

population and the requirements per capita go on increasing, with no sensible net addition to the ways and means of life and production, while an increasing proportion of the available ways and means is spent on sales-costs.

CHAPTER XIII

The Secular Trend

As has been explained in earlier chapters, and as will readily be seen by any intelligent person who takes an interest in these matters, secular life among the peoples of Christendom is governed in recent times by three several systems of use and wont, sovereign action-patterns induced by the run of past habituation:—the mechanical system of industry; the price-system; and the national establishment. The existing industrial system is dominated by the technology of physics and chemistry, and is a product of recent times, a profoundly modified derivative of the handicraft industry. The current price-system is dominated by absentee ownership and is also a greatly altered outgrowth of the handicraft industry and its petty trade; its continued growth in recent times has, in effect, changed it into a credit-price system. The nation, considered as a habit of thought, is a residual form of the predatory dynastic State of early modern times, superficially altered by a suffusion of democratic and parliamentary institutions in recent times.

By continued growth of use and wont in recent times the price-system has in effect become a credit-price system; and driven by the same growth the system of ownership has to all intents and purposes become a system of absentee ownership, in all that concerns any effectual initiative and authority in the conduct of economic affairs. The effectual control of the economic situation, in business, industry, and civil life, rests on the control of credit. Therefore the effectual exercise of initiative, discretion, and authority is perforce vested in those massive aggregations of absentee ownership that make up the Interests. Within certain wide limits of tolerance, therefore, the rest of the community, the industrial system and the underlying population, are at the disposal of the Interests, as ways and means of business, to be managed in a temperate spirit of usufruct for the continued and cumulative benefit of the major Interests and their absentee owners. The nation, both as a habit of thought and as a governmental going concern, comes into the case, in effect and in the main, as an auxiliary agency the function of which is to safeguard, extend and facilitate this work of surveillance and usufruct which has by drift of circumstances become incumbent on the Interests.

Such appears to be the state of the case, in the large and in so far as the forces engaged have yet fallen into definite lines and groupings, in those respects which come in question here.

It will be seen, accordingly, that the current economic situation is drawn on lines of a two-sided division of its forces or elements:—the Interests; and the underlying population. Such is the situation, typically, in the case of America; and such is also the state of things in the other civilised countries, in much the same measure in which they are civilised according to the same pattern. The Interests, properly speaking, are made up of those blocks of absentee ownership which are sufficiently massive to come into the counsels of the One Big Union of the Interests. Associated with these in their work, as co-partners, auxiliaries, subsidiaries, extensions, purveyors of traffic, are the minor Interests and the business community at large; primarily the banking community. The work which they have in hand is to do business for a profit by use of the industrial system and the underlying population. For the purposes of business the underlying population has two uses:—as industrial man-power; and as ultimate consumers,—that is to say as ultimate purchasers, since the business interest does not extend beyond the ultimate sale of the goods.

To do a profitable business one should buy cheap and sell dear, as all reasonable men know. In its dealings with the underlying population the business community buys their man-power and sells them their livelihood. So it is incumbent on the business men in the case to buy the industrial man-power as cheap as may be, and to sell the means of living to the ultimate consumer as dear as may be. All of which is a platitudinous matter of course.

The source of profits is the margin of sales-price over production-cost (or purchase-cost). In earlier chapters it has already been explained how this margin is widened by raising the level of sales-prices; both by efficient salesmanship in the merchandising trades and by a continued expansion of the outstanding volume of purchasing-power through a continued creation of credits at the hands of the investment bankers and similar credit-establishments. In the same connection something has also been said of the service which the agencies of government render, in the way of enhancing prices by contributing to the security of this expanded volume of credit and so helping to make it indefinitely expansible without risk.

On the side of costs the underlying population comes into the case as being the industrial man-power that is to be bought, including the skill and technical knowledge that makes up the state of the industrial arts. On this side this population comes in as vendors of the ways and means of production. For the present purpose they may be classed loosely under two heads:—the industrial workmen; and the farmers. Also loosely and with a negligible fringe of exceptions it may be said that both of these groups of industrial man-power come into the negotiations on a businesslike footing, governed by the principles of the price-system and aiming to sell as dear as may be.

In these endeavours to sell dear the farmers have hitherto met with no measurable success, apparently for want of effectual collusion. In effect and in the common run the farm population and its work and livelihood are a species of natural resources which the business community holds in usufruct, in the nature of inert materials exposed to the drift of circumstances over which they have no control, somewhat after the analogy of bacteria employed in fermentation.

The case of the industrial man-power in the narrower sense is somewhat different, the case of the specialised workman engaged in the mechanical industries. In great part, and more or less effectually, these have been drawn together in craft-unions to do their bargaining on a collusive plan for the more profitable sale of their man-power. In the typical case these unions are businesslike coalitions endeavoring to drive a bargain and establish a vested interest, governed by the standard aims and methods of the price-system.[1] The unions habitually employ the standard methods of the merchandising business, endeavoring to sell their vendible output at the best price

[1] The American Federation of Labor may be taken as a type-form; although it goes perhaps to an extreme in its adherence to the principles and procedure of merchandising, in all its aims and negotiations, its constant aim being an exclusive market and a limitation of supply.

obtainable; their chief recourse in these negotiations being a limitation of the supply, a strategic withdrawal of efficiency by means of strikes, union rules, apprenticeship requirements, and devices for consuming time unproductively. The nature of the business does not admit the use of sales-publicity in this traffic in anything like the same measure in which that expedient is employed in ordinary merchandising. Hence the strategic stress of their salesmanship falls all the more insistently and effectually on the limitation of the vendible supply; a running balance of unemployment and orderly inefficiency under union rules, rising promptly to the proportions of an embargo on productive work in any emergency. The aim being a scarcity-price for work done, quite in the spirit of business-as-usual.

Meantime the continued flow of credits and capitalisations continues to expand the volume of purchasing-power in the market, and so continues to enhance the price-cost of living for the workmen, along with the rising level of general prices. Which provokes the organised workmen to a more assiduous bargaining for higher wages; which calls for a more exacting insistence on mediocrity and obstruction in the day's work and a more instant mobilisation in the way of strikes. On sound business principles, the organised workmen's remedy for scarcity of livelihood is a persistent curtailment of output.

As a secondary effect—which may presently, in the course of further habituation, turn out to be its gravest consequence—this struggle for existence by way of sabotage fosters a rising tide of hostility and distrust between the parties to the bargain. There would seem to be in prospect a progressively settled and malevolent hostility on the part of the embattled workmen over against their employers and the absentee owners for whose ease and gain they are employed; which should logically be counted on to rise in due course to that pitch of vivacity where it will stick at nothing. But in the mean time the logical recourse of the workmen in their negotiations for wages and livelihood, according to the logic of sound business under the price-system, is a strategic withdrawal of efficiency, of a passive sort, increasing in frequency and amplitude to keep pace with the increasing urgency of their case.

And the urgency of their case is increasing progressively, in the nature of things. The increasing stability of the credit system, such as it has attained during the past decade, enables the price-level to rise progressively, and thereby progressively to increase the price-cost of living. At the same time the business community, the absentee owners with whom the workmen are carrying on their acrimonious argument about wages and livelihood, are in a progressively stronger position and a progressively more determined frame of mind. They have learned to act in concert and have also learned that, in a business way, the industrial man-power is their common enemy, against which it is for them to make common cause, within reason,—that is to say within the bounds of profitable business.

While the business men are endeavoring to enhance the reasonable gains of business by expanding the volume of capital and lifting the level of prices, and so widening the margin of sales-prices over production-costs, the organised workmen are forever cutting in on the same margin by pushing up the labor-cost. And on this employers' side of the argument, as well as on the side of the embattled workmen, the standard and reasonable recourse by which to bring their opponents to reason is a strategic use of unemployment, a conscientious withdrawal of efficiency, carried to such a point as will bring an effectual degree of privation on the ultimate consumers, including the workmen, without reducing the net aggregate sales-price of the decreased output when sold at the resulting enhanced price per unit. In all these negotiations there is, on the employers' side also, relatively little effectual use to be made of salesmanlike publicity. The ordinary and effectual means employed is privation brought on by unemployment. So also, in these endeavors to economise on labor-cost as well as in the flotation of credits, capital-isations, and overhead charges, a more intelligent concert of action and a wider solidarity of interests on the side of the employers and owners is of great service; in that it enables the business of strategic unemployment to be carried out with a wider sweep and with increased confidence and security.[2]

At this point the national establishment, federal and local, comes into the case, by way of constituted authority exercising surveillance and punitive powers. In effect and ordinarily the intervention of governmental agencies in these negotiations between the owners and the workmen redounds to the benefit of the former. Such is necessarily the case in the nature of things. In the nature of things, as things go in any democratic community, these governmental agencies are administered by a businesslike personnel, imbued with the habitual bias of business principles,—the principles of ownership; that is to say, under current conditions, the rights, powers, and immunities of absentee ownership. In the nature of the case, the official personnel is drawn from the business community,—lawyers, bankers, merchants, contractors, etc.;

---

[2] As has appeared, e. g., in the wide-concerted campaign lately carried on for the suppression of the unions, spoken of by courtesy as a "campaign for the open shop."

in the main and ordinarily drawn from the country towns and the trading-centers; "practical men," whose preconceptions and convictions are such as will necessarily emerge from continued and successful experience in the conduct of business of that character. Lawyers and magistrates who have proved their fitness by their successful conduct of administrative duties and litigations turning on the legal niceties of ownership, and in whom the logic of ownership has become second nature.[3]

[3] There is no fault to be found with all this, of course; but it is necessary to note the fact. It is one of the substantial factors in the case, and it lies in the nature of things in any democratic community. Life and experience in these democratic communities is governed by the price-system. Efficiency, practical capacity, popular confidence, in these communities are rateable only in terms of price. "Practical" means "businesslike." Driven by this all-pervading bias of business principles in all that touches their practical concerns, no such democratic community is capable of entrusting the duties of responsible office to any other than business men. Hence, in increasing measure as the situation has moved forward and approached the current highly businesslike order of things, the incumbents of office are necessarily persons of businesslike antecedents, dominated by the logic of ownership, essentially absentee ownership. Legislators, executives, and judiciary are of the same derivation in respect of the bias which their habits of life have engendered and in respect of the drift to which their bias subjects them in their further conduct of affairs. There need of course be no question of the good faith or the intelligence of these responsible incumbents of office. It is to be presumed that in these respects they will commonly grade up to the general average, or something not far short of that point. But by force of the businesslike personal equation that is ingrained by habit in the official personnel, the growth of use and wont, of law and custom, of precedent and enactment, during recent times has fallen into lines drawn on considerations of expediency for business; it has followed that line of least resistance which the sound bias of legislators, executives, and judiciary has made easy and reasonable, at the same time that it has conformed to the logical bent of the substantial citizens. Doubtless in good faith and on sound principles, the ceaseless proliferation of statutes, decisions,

In the negotiations between owners and workmen there is little use for the ordinary blandishments of salesmanship. The two parties to the quarrel—for it is after all a quarrel—have learned to know what to count on. And the bargaining between them therefore settles down without much circumlocution into a competitive use of unemployment, privation, restriction of work and output, strikes, shut-downs and lockouts, espionage, pickets, and similar manœuvres of mutual derangement, with a large recourse to menacing language and threats of mutual sabotage. The colloquial word for it is "labor troubles." The business relations between the two parties are of the nature of hostilities, suspended or active, conducted in terms of mutual sabotage; which will on occasion shift from the footing of such obstruction and disallowance as is wholly within the law and custom of business, from the footing of legitimate sabotage in the way of passive resistance and withholding of efficiency, to that illegitimate phase of sabotage that runs into violent offenses against

precedents, and constitutional interpretations, has run, in the main and with increasing effect, on these lines that converge on the needs and merits of absentee ownership.

As a late and notable illustrative instance of this logical bias, it has been found on judicial consideration that such corporate income as is distributed under the absentee form of a stock-dividend is legally exempt from the income tax.

So again, in the main and ordinarily, the "injunction" which has lately come into extensive application in American practice is an expedient for the conservation and enforcement of the rights and immunities of absentee ownership in case of controversy between owners and workmen. The injunction has other uses, but in practical effect this is its main and ordinary use. Effectual recourse to the injunction to enforce the demands of the workmen is of rare occurrence and of doubtful legitimacy. In effectual scope and force the injunction has grown with the growth of the scope and range of absentee ownership and at the call of issues which have arisen out of its administration and safe-keeping.

persons and property. The negotiations have habitually and increasingly taken on this character of a businesslike dissension. So much so that they have come to be spoken of habitually in terms of conflict, armed forces, and war-like strategy. It is a conflict of hostile forces which is conducted on the avowed strategic principle that either party stands to gain at the cost of the other.[4]

[4] Many public spirited citizens, and many substantial citizens with an interest in business, deplore this spirit of division and cross purposes that pervades the ordinary relations between owners and workmen in the large industries. And in homilet-ical discourse bearing on this matter it is commonly insisted that such division of sentiment is uncalled for, at the same time that it works mischief to the common good, that "the interests of labor and capital are substantially identical," that dilatory and obstructionist tactics bring nothing better than privation and discontent to both parties in controversy, as well as damage and discomfort to the community at large.

Such homiletical discourse is commonly addressed to the workmen. It is a plain fact of common sense, embedded in im-memorial habit, that the business men who have the manage-ment of industrial production must be free to limit their output and restrain employment with a view to what the traffic will bear. That is a matter of sound business, authentic and meri-torious. Whereas unemployment brought to bear by collusion among the workmen in pursuit of their special advantage will interfere with the orderly earnings of business and thereby bring discouragement and adversity upon the business com-munity, and so will derange and retard the processes of in-dustry from which the earnings are drawn. As things go, be-cause the continued subsistence and material comforts of the community are contingent upon the continued profits of the business men in charge, prosperity is a function of earnings, not of wages; and the material fortunes of the community at large are in practical fact bound up with the continued peace of mind of the absentee owners of the industries, which in turn is bound up with the continued run of free income from the business. This is commonplace and familiar, an habitual fact of common sense, to which no sound man has a right or an inclination to take exception; for settled usage makes all things right. The workmen are not similarly within the familiar bounds of common sense in applying unemployment and restriction of output to en-

It is of the essence of the new order in business that the tactical units now run larger than before, in larger parcels and with a greater degree of compactness and solidarity in action. In industrial business this is exemplified in the growth of corporations and in the tactical grouping of corporations under the surveillance of those massive Interests that govern the pitch and volume of business activity. In effect, as tactical units in the conduct of industrial business, the corporations are associations of absentee owners who are working together on a

force their notions of what the traffic will bear in the way of wages. Their assumption of a business standing in an argument with their employers and owners violates common sense; that is to say it is not their right according to the precedents of use and wont, however securely it may be within the statutory formalities. It is not sound common sense, because it has not been ingrained by workday habituation into the action-pattern of the community. By use and wont hitherto the workmen have in practical effect been free to take or leave the terms offered by their owner-employers; and by use and wont the employer-owners have been free to offer such terms as the traffic would bear in the way of earnings. But increasingly for some time past the workmen have been drawing together on a businesslike plan of demanding all that the traffic will bear in the way of wages, and of enforcing their demands by the same businesslike recourse to unemployment and retardation that has long served the needs of the employer-owners in their dealings with the market and the livelihood of the ultimate consumers. In its character of industrial man-power, this organised fraction of the underlying population is endeavoring to negotiate for terms on the footing of a *de-facto* Business Interest. (The agricultural man-power, and the population at large as a body of consumers, have not yet made an effectual move of the kind.) And right lately the organisation, animus, and tactics of these industrial workmen have been brought to such a point of businesslike efficiency as to constitute a menace to reasonable earnings and to a reasonable balanced return on the outstanding capitalisation. Therefore, since prosperity depends on a continued free run of earnings on the outstanding capitalisation, the businesslike attitude and tactics of the organised workmen are also a menace to the prosperity of the community at large.

joint plan in a joint pursuit of gain. So that in effect such a corporation is a method of collusion and concerted action for the joint conduct of transactions designed to benefit the allied and associated owners at the cost of any whom it may concern. In effect, therefore, the joint-stock corporation is a conspiracy of owners; and as such it transgresses that principle of individual self-help that underlies the system of Natural Rights; in which democratic institutions as well as the powers and immunities of ownership are grounded. But the exigencies of business enterprise in recent times, as conditioned by the wide-reaching articulations of trade and industry, call for such large tactical units as will necessarily be composite in point of personnel and collusive in point of ownership.

And the official personnel of civil government, the constituted authorities who have had the making and surveillance of precedents and statutory regulations touching these matters in recent times, have necessarily been persons of businesslike antecedents, imbued with an inveterate businesslike bias, governed by business principles, if not also by business interests. Business exigencies, borne along on this habitual bent of the legislators and judiciary, and enforced by the workday needs of the substantial citizens, have decided that such collusion, conspiracy, or coalition as takes the form of (absentee) ownership is right and good, to be safeguarded in all the powers and immunities of ownership by the constituted authorities at any cost to the community at large. So that any strategic withdrawal of efficiency incident to the conduct of business by such an organisation of collusive ownership, any restriction of output to what the traffic will bear, any unemployment of equipment and man-power with a view to increased earnings on capital, has the countenance of the constituted authorities and will be defended by a suitable use of force in case of need.

It is otherwise, in a degree, with the collusive organisations of workmen. Being not grounded in ownership, their legal right of conspiracy in restraint of trade is doubtful at the best. It has also not the countenance of the substantial citizens [5] or of the minor business men, of the pulpit, or the public press. The effectual limits on strikes are somewhat narrower than on lockouts. Boycotts in support of strikes are illegal, and the more effectual methods of picketing are disallowed by courts and police, except in negligible cases. Since the striking workmen are not owners of the plant that is to be laid idle by their striking, they are excluded from the premises, and they are therefore unable to watch over the unemployment which they have precipitated, and to see to its unbroken continuance. This is a grave disability. The owners are more fortunate in this respect. The power to dispose of matters in the conduct of industry commonly attaches to ownership, and is not legally to be claimed on other grounds. The employer-owners are in a much better position to take care of any desired unemployment, as in case of a lockout. In the same connection it should be recalled that effectual collusion and concert of action is more a matter of routine and takes effect in a more compact and complete fashion on the side of the owners, who are already organised as a corporate unit. The block of ownership embodied in any ordinary business corporation of the larger sort covers a larger segment of the industrial processes involved in any given strike or lockout than does the body of industrial man-power with which the corporation is contending. This will more particularly be

[5] As has been remarked in an earlier passage, a "substantial citizen" is an absentee owner of much property.

the case where and in so far as the old-fashioned craft-unions have not been displaced by an industrial union. It comes to a conflict between a corporate whole on the side of the owners against a fragment of the working forces on the side of the workmen.

So again, in any eventual resort to force, the workmen are under a handicap as against the owners,—a handicap due to law and precedent as well as to the businesslike predilections that are habitual among the personnel of the constituted authorities. Labor troubles are disorders of business, and business is a matter of ownership, while work and livelihood are not. The presumption, in law and custom and official predilection, is against the use of force or the possession or disposal. of arms by persons or associations of persons who are not possessed of appreciable property. It is assumed, in effect, that the use of weapons is to protect property and guard its rights; and the assumption applies to the use of weapons by private persons as well as to the armed forces of government. Under the statutes regulating the possession and use of weapons, such, e. g., as the so-called "Sullivan Law" of New York, it will be found that permits to carry weapons are issued in the main to substantial citizens, corporations, and to those incorporations of mercenaries that are known by courtesy as detective agencies; these latter being in the nature of auxiliary forces employed on occasion by corporations which may be involved in strikes or lock-outs. All this is doubtless as it should be, and doubtless the intention of it is salutary. So also it will be found that the state constabularies, as well as any units of the National Guards that may be called out on occasion of labor troubles, are, quite habitually and as a matter of routine, employed in safeguarding corporation property and guarding against trespassers on the corporation's premises or interference with the corporation's employees.[6]

This is not to be construed as partisanship, but rather as defensive measures for the preservation of things as they are, or as they recently have been. But the effect is much the same, by and large. It signifies that other than peaceable methods are not effectually at the disposal of the organised workmen in the recurring quarrel with their owner-employers. Of late years the difficulties in the way of any recourse to forcible measures, or even of preparation for demonstrations in force on the part of the unions, have been appreciably increased by the judicial use of the injunction. The injunction has been applied with increasing frequency and an ampler sweep and scope, and its restraint has fallen on the organised workmen, as a rule, rather than on the owners. In effect, the use of the injunction as a means of creating an actionable "contempt of court" enables the authorities to penalise by anticipation; which has visibly turned the endeavours of the unions into channels of passive resistance in preference to anything in the way of overt action. There can be no question but that, in its bearing on the rights and immunities of absentee ownership, this freer use of the injunction has had a notably salutary effect. In one way and another the organised workmen are perforce and progressively reduced to tactics of passive resistance, to tactics of unemployment and retardation by a strategic withdrawal of efficiency, after the same general pattern of inconspicuous restriction and retardation which the owners of industry habitually employ in adjusting the rate and volume of output to what the traffic will bear. And such undivided attention to the strategy of inaction

[6] Cf. e. g., *Report on the Steel Strike of 1919*, by the Interchurch Movement, pp. 235–248.

on the part of the workmen is already giving them a visibly increasing proficiency, and is hastening the adoption of a standard routine of retardation. That is to say, the industrial man-power is by force of circumstances taking the same businesslike position as their owner-employers; prudently seeking their own advantage at the cost of any whom it may concern, unmoved by passion, except the passion for the main chance.

In so meeting their owner-employers on their own businesslike ground of graduated curtailment and abeyance the organised workmen are still somewhat at a disadvantage. They have not the countenance of popular sympathy in any unreserved way, inasmuch as they do not speak for a recognised businesslike vested interest. Morally the workmen are still in a precarious position, according to the common sense of a community which is by unbroken habit bound to rate all economic actions and claims in terms of price and ownership. The workmen are under a moral disability at this point, in that the industrial man-power has not been formally capitalised and written into an issue of corporation securities or similar credit-instruments bearing a fixed charge. It is not covered with negotiable paper, such as would invest it with a morally defensible claim to an undiminished income, and would therefore justify any conduct which may serve to make good such a claim. This ethical infirmity of the embattled workmen's case should logically be remedied in some measure by habituation; by their getting used to it and getting their fellow-citizens used to it. In a degree such an effect of habituation is already visible, in the greater tolerance with which the community puts up with the inconveniences that result from the obstructive tactics employed in labor troubles.

But whatever may be the relative strength of the two

parties to this controversy, present or prospective, the negotiations between them are visibly falling into more tangible and more standardised shape and are conducted on increasingly businesslike principles of what the traffic will bear, and on both sides alike the negotiations as to what the traffic will bear are carried on in terms of competitive unemployment, mutual defeat, designed to hold the work and output down to such a minimum as will yield the most profitable price per unit to one party or the other. In due consequence, as the contending forces achieve a more effectual mobilisation on a larger scale, and as these tactics of inaction and retardation take effect with greater alacrity and consistency, the practicable minimum of work and output should logically become the ordinary standard practice. So that in "ordinary times" the effectual volume of work and output should run at a minimum.

So soon as the contending forces achieve a sufficiently alert and inclusive mobilisation on both sides, and bring their strategy to a finished and consistent routine, this ordinary balanced minimum of work and output should logically fall somewhat short of the ordinary consumptive needs of the underlying population. The fluctuations should run under, as a general rule. It is reasonable to expect that any fluctuations in excess would be curbed with all due dispatch by a watchful businesslike application of unemployment on one side and the other. In effect, the contending forces are doing team-work in the strategic use of unemployment. Business principles worked out on conservative lines of "watchful waiting" and "safety first" may be counted on with some confidence to keep the run of current production temperately short of current consumptive needs, so soon as these businesslike dispositions have been completed,—in the absence of disturbing causes; and fluctuations in deficiency would come in as workday incidents of the tactical routine. This follows in the nature of the case. The conflict of interests in the case is a conflict of business interests, in which each of the contending parties endeavors to bring the other to terms by as unremitting a pressure of privation as the traffic will bear, leaving the benefit of the doubt quite consistently on the side of deficiency.

The manner in which this routine of deficiency is expected to work out, on business principles consistently applied, is shown in a concrete way in the situation of American industrial business as it has been running during the interval since the Armistice. The dispositions on both sides of the controversy have not yet been perfected, but the results already achieved are enough to serve as notice of what may eventually be looked for. Strategic unemployment of plant and man-power results in a depletion of stocks on hand; a deficiency of maintenance, repairs and replacements; resulting in an impairment of the means of production, a consequent lowering of the practicable level of production and output, and a correspondingly lowered base-line on which further tactics of competitive unemployment will run. The logic of the case, as well as the object-lessons of current experience, appears to say somewhat unequivocally that these mutual businesslike negotiations in unemployment will in all reason work out in so closely-shorn a withdrawal of productive efficiency as to yield but a scant margin for maintenance and necessary extensions and a still more dubious margin for necessary repairs and replacements.[7]

[7] An illustrative instance is that of the American railways, which have been suffering a shrinkage of physical assets for want of due repairs and replacements. The commitments of the railway corporations in the way of fixed charges hinder their

A further line of considerations runs to the same general effect. The several tactical units engaged in this business of strategic unemployment for a revenue, the concerns which do business in industry and its output as well as the associations of workmen that negotiate with them for a division of the proceeds, are, each and several, fractional segments of a larger composite industrial mechanism and of the industrial system at large. Each unit large or small, composite or single, pursues its own ends, negotiates for its own differential advantage at the cost of any whom it may concern, by a strategic retardation of the industrial process within that segment of the whole which is subject to its particular jurisdiction as a business concern, in detachment from the rest of the system or with slight and contingent regard for any ulterior consequences which its tactics of unemployment may have for the rest. Such is the nature of that system and canon of free competition which has stood over out of the eighteenth century as an axiomatic fact of Natural Right, and which still underlies the law and morals of business enterprise.

applying an adequate proportion of their earnings to repairs and replacements, at the same time that the rigidity of their outstanding capitalisation hinders their writing off the resulting depreciation and obsolescence of the plant; whereby they are driven to charging more than the traffic will bear in the way of freight and passenger rates as well as in the way of retrenchment on wages and dismissal of workmen. All of which works together cumulatively toward a progressive decline of efficiency and a more accentuated policy of strategic unemployment.

The remedy which is ordinarily applied in such a case is that universal solvent of business exigencies, the creation of new credit obligations, with which to provide needed working capital, and which are duly capitalised with the due complement of fixed charges, payable out of an advance of prices due to the resulting increased volume of outstanding purchasing-power helped out by a temperate limitation of output.

As business concerns, and therefore as tactical units in the management of industrial business, these several segments of the business community go about their business on a competitive basis, on the principle of "putting it over"; also called *caveat emptor*. But as industrial factors, and therefore as technological units engaged in the conduct of industrial production, they are members of a close-knit industrial system, bound in a comprehensive fabric of interlocking processes of work, in such a way that the continued working of any one member is conditioned on the due working of the rest. Technologically each member of the system, each of these tactical units, is bound to bear its due part in the ceaseless give and take of interlocking industrial processes. So that any retardation or suspension of the rate and volume of output at any point in the industrial system will check the work throughout a series of industrial plants and processes that go before and that follow after in the balanced sequence of operations, and it will therefore cripple the industrial system at large by that much.

Owing to this articulated character of industrial work as carried on by the methods of the mechanical industry, the ulterior (systemic) consequences of any strategic suspension or retardation of work at any point are likely to be more serious than the direct waste and loss incurred at the initial point, where the strategic unemployment is applied. This applies with especial force, of course, in the case of unemployment initiated in the key industries; but it will apply in only a lessening degree outward from the key industries throughout that fabric of "continuation industries" whose interlocking processes of work play into one another to maintain the due rate and volume of output; and it will apply with increasing urgency and effect as the industrial system takes on more of the character of the mechanical industry and is organised on the lines of quantity production.[8]

In recent times, and especially in recent years, the balance, articulation, and interdependence of industrial processes has been growing visibly greater, wider, more delicate, and more imperative. At the same time the facilities for instant and drastic suspension of work in the various mechanical industries are being greatly perfected; both in the way of a swift and resolute mobilisation of the workmen and in the way of loyal concert of action and standard methods of unemployment among the owner-employers and the governmental agencies of surveillance and enforcement.

The work of industrial confusion by recourse to unemployment in the pursuit of business has been greatly facilitated and abridged. The recourse to unemployment is readier and more sweeping, and the articulations of industry are growing progressively more extensive and more exacting, resulting in a wider and profounder effect in the way of derangement and deficiency due to suspension of work at any point. These two lines of improvement in methods—in business and in technology—converge and concur in such a way that the ceaseless, though fluctuating, application of unemployment entailed by the current exigencies of business will have presently—if not rather, has already—brought the industrial system to such a state of chronic, though fluctuating, derangement as will result in a chronic, though fluctuating, margin of deficiency; whereby the rate and volume of output of those goods and services that make up the livelihood of the

---

[8] The case has latterly been well illustrated by what happens in the way of ulterior consequences for industry at large when work is suspended or seriously abridged (for strategic purposes), in coal-mining, railroad transportation, or steel production.

community will fall short of current needs by a progressively widening margin of deficiency. The eventual outcome of such progressive disallowance of work, disability, and privation, can, of course, not be predicted; although it seems plain that there should be an eventual limit to its continuance.[9]

Over against this orderly drift into retardation and industrial paralysis there are, of course, other factors at work running to the contrary effect. There is a continued run of discoveries, inventions, adaptations, and short-cuts in the industrial arts, new ways and means and new uses of the old. With the result that the coefficient of productive capacity per unit of man-power continues to gain in a cumulative fashion. New processes,

[9] All the while there need, also of course, result no decline in the community's total wealth, as counted in money-values. Business should presumably continue on a conservatively prosperous footing, with fluctuating variations, and with an increasing devotion to salesmanship and overhead. Any shrinkage in physical possessions, in the current output of goods and services, or in the available means of subsistence and physical comfort, could and presumably would be offset, or more than offset, by a conservative creation and capitalisation of new credits, with new and valuable fixed charges. Such a running creation of capitalised wealth will be all the more imperatively called for, in that the progressively widening deficiency in the material supply, coupled with rising prices and rising costs, will entail an urgent and progressive need of additional funds to serve as working capital. It is perhaps unnecessary to note that such a view of these matters will not have the countenance of the certified economic experts. Those economists and public men who still faithfully construe the current situation in terms of the nineteenth century, as defined by formulas which have stood over from the eighteenth century, will scarcely see these matters in this light. By received preconception, credit is deferred payment, capital is assembled "production goods," business is the helper of productive industry, salesmanship is the facility of the "middleman," money is "the great wheel of circulation" employed in a "refined system of barter," and absentee ownership is a rhetorical solecism.

new materials from near and far, are continually being turned to account, and new methods of turning old materials to account and of coördinating known processes for the more efficient use of old resources, as well as for incorporating new resources into the routine of the day's work,—these improvements and accelerations in the industrial arts continue to insinuate themselves into the fabric of the industrial system, in spite of the uniformly conservative management on the part of the business community as touches all new projects and project-makers in the industrial field.

But all such advances in the mechanic arts bring new complications in the working structure of the industrial system; whether the innovations come by way of an increased scale of operation or by way of a new procedure in the mechanics of production and distribution; whether they draw into the complex of industry material and power-resources previously unknown or unused,—as, e. g., petroleum and the obscure industrial metals, or power transmission by electricity; or they facilitate and abridge the work in hand—as, e. g., the Bessemer and the basic processes in steel production, or the internal combustion engine for use in vehicles, or the synthetic production of drugs, dyes, and condiments. At every move the network of technological interrelations will be drawn to a finer mesh, a more close-knit and more widely inclusive web of give and take, within which the working balance of coördinations runs on a continually closer margin of tolerance. With the result that a disturbance, in the nature of retardation or deficiency at any critical point, will carry derangement and sabotage farther and faster than before through the main lines and into the intricate working details of production. With every further move along the lines on which the industrial arts are advancing, therefore, sabotage—that is to say strategic unemployment at the instance of the owner-employers or of the workmen —becomes a swifter and more widely corrosive agency of miscarriage and decay.

At the same time, and in great part by help of these same technical appliances and powers, the business community is able, also in a progressive fashion, to bring sound conservative business principles to bear on industry in a swifter and more comprehensive way and with a slighter margin of error. That is to say, novelties will be disallowed with a freer hand and the tactical manœuvres of unemployment will gain something in frequency and amplitude; measures to suppress or disable the organisations of workmen and malcontents will take on added scope, assurance, vigor, and despatch. And the organised workmen, too, are coming to realise the increasing need as well as the increasing facilities for meeting their owners on a business footing and carrying on their negotiations in strategic unemployment and retardation with a wider and more effectual coördination and manœuvres and a more provident attention to their needful financial resources.[10]

Under these circumstances it seems reasonable to expect that the systematic retardation and derangement of productive industry which is entailed by the current businesslike management will work out in a progressive abate-

[10] Right lately, since 1920, certain of the more businesslike unions have gone into banking with a view to financing their own affairs. So far the plan appears to be practicable. It is expected that by this means these unions will be able to extend, consolidate and standardise those measures of unemployment and retardation that are advisable in their business. It should greatly "facilitate and abridge the labor" of conscientiously withdrawing efficiency in those lines of work with which these unions have to do. The farmers, too, are looking hopefully, and desperately, in the same direction with a similar end in view.

ment of the margin of net output of the industrial system
at large; that this progressive abatement of the net industrial output will presently reach and pass the critical point
of no net return—as counted in physical units of livelihood; and that in the calculable future the industrial
system, so managed on sound business principles, will run
on lines of a progressively "diminishing return," converging to an eventual limit of tolerance in the way of a
reduced subsistence minimum; beyond which the situation
at large should apparently be liable to revision by an intrusion of some sort of "disturbing causes." [11]

It is conceivable that the civilised peoples might yet
save themselves alive out of this impasse, in spite of their
addiction to business, if it were not for their national integrity.

Business-as-usual, helped out by its later extensions and
facilities, may be counted on to hold the ordinary level
of employment and output down to the minimum of what

[11] All the while there is not, at least not for the time being,
any reason to apprehend that this progressive deficit of industrial production will cause a shrinkage in the country's aggregate
wealth—as counted in money-values; or even that the current
rate of increase of such wealth will fall off. All that is in the
main a question of capitalisation, and therefore it is a question
of the continued creation of credit and overhead charges. The
aggregate of possessions, as counted in terms of "production
goods" and livelihood, should presumably continue to fall off, as
during the past few years; but wealth, as counted in money-
values, should presumably continue to increase, perhaps at an
accelerated rate, as during the past years. And as a matter of
course the wealth in hand should continue, perhaps at an accelerated rate, to gravitate into progressively larger blocks of
absentee ownership.

Just now (1923) the appearances would seem to say that
the critical point of no net aggregate product has been reached
and passed within recent years, since the Armistice. Yet it is
quite possible that these appearances are transient and misleading.
There is no reasonable doubt but that the countries of Europe
have been running on a deficit, industrially speaking, during these

the traffic will bear, with a reasonable degree of consistency, and with something of a conservative downward trend to a lower minimum. Frequent and substantial oscillations below the ordinary level are to be looked for, due to repeated and inconclusive trials of endurance between the owners and the workmen, in their businesslike endeavors to bring one another to terms in a struggle of mutual discomfort. These persistent excursions below the ordinary level should have a cumulative effect and establish a downward trend in the average run, such as to depress the practicable minimum. Provided always that a partial failure, or abrupt recession, of the state of the industrial arts, due to curtailment of technological instruction and personnel at home or abroad, does not bring the whole case to a precipitate liquidation.

As is the current practice, these manœuvres of strategic deficiency will continue to be financed by a conservative but effectual creation of capitalised credits, in great part if

years; and indeed on a progressively widening margin of deficit.

In effect, these Europeans have also curtailed their technological personnel by uncovered consumption of technical manpower during the War; while the production and upkeep of technological personnel and facilities are now running short of current needs, in rate, volume and quality, due to the present state of Peace. So that the Europeans, and by consequence the Americans also, face a technological deficit, and therefore a foresumptive disintegration of their industrial system.

Nor need it be doubted that the Americans have also been running slightly short of a net balance in their industrial output, as counted in physical units. But a cautious appraisal would perhaps say that this net industrial deficiency may be a transient effect due to transient causes connected with the War and the inordinately businesslike terms of the Peace; and that so soon as the international bargaining between the Interests has been concluded, and so soon as the earnings of the "profiteers," past and prospective, shall have been duly stabilised and capitalised, this businesslike embargo on industry and livelihood will be lifted. Such appears to be the expectation of the statesmen. It is a point in doubt.

not in the main. Such is, in effect, the established practice on the side of the owners, and such is now beginning to be the recourse also of the organised workmen. By this means these recurring depressions of the ordinary level of employment and output will, in some measure and progressively, be incorporated in the routine and will progressively lower the minimum which the traffic will bear. Such will necessarily be the case, inasmuch as any deficiency brought about in this way in the physical output will not count as a deficiency in money-values and will therefore not disturb the course of the businesslike negotiations on which the whole matter turns. Money-values are the conclusive realities of business, and the outstanding money-values will not suffer so long as the price per unit is suitably enhanced by a limitation of the output and an enlargement of the outstanding volume of purchasing-power. The progressive reduction of output through unemployment will take effect in physical terms of goods and services, not in terms of price, as current experience goes to show; price being a function of scarcity and purchasing-power.

In the long run, so soon as the privation and chronic derangement which follows from this application of business principles has grown unduly irksome and becomes intolerable, there is due to come a sentimental revulsion and a muttering protest that "something will have to be done about it,"—as, e. g., in the case which has arisen in the coal industry. Thoughtful persons will then devise remedial measures. As a matter of course, in a community which is addicted to business principles, the remedial measures which are brought under advisement in such a case by responsible citizens and officials are bound to be of a businesslike nature; designed in all reason to safeguard the accomplished facts of absentee ownership in the natural resources involved and in the capitalised overhead charges which have been incorporated in the business. Necessarily so, for the community at large is addicted to business principles, and the official personnel is so addicted in an especial degree, in the nature of things.

Yet all the while there are certain loose ends in this fabric of business convictions which binds the mentality of these peoples. There is always the chance, more or less imminent, that in time, after due trial and error, on duly prolonged and intensified irritation, some sizable element of the underlying population, not intrinsically committed to absentee ownership, will forsake or forget their moral principles of business-as-usual, and will thereupon endeavor to take this businesslike arrangement to pieces and put the works together again on some other plan, for better or worse.

"Other things remaining the same," some such shifting of the economic base should be due to follow, eventually. Not because a better plan than the present businesslike one has been projected or is likely to be conceived; but because, "human nature being such as it is," the present businesslike management of the industrial system is incompetent, irrelevant, and not germane to the livelihood of the underlying population. It is not that absentee ownership is wrong, in principle. "The law allows it, and the court awards it." It is only that its concrete working-out is incompatible with the current state of the industrial arts, and that the material welfare of the civilised peoples is conditioned on the full and orderly operation of the industrial system in which this state of the arts is embodied.

This precarious state of the case is now beginning to

engage the attention of the substantial citizens and of their constituted authorities,—on whom it is incumbent, through good report and evil report, to guard the *status quo* of capitalised overhead charges. Being "practical men," they bend their energies to the preservation of an arrangement which will not work, lest a worse evil befall. The accomplished facts of absentee ownership must and shall be preserved; and it is for the authorities and the substantial citizens to take measures to that end. The national integrity of the civilised peoples comes into the case as a pivotal factor at this point.

Whatever will bear the appearance of being a national interest, of being bound up with the fortunes of the national establishment, will find a ready lodgment in the popular sentiment as an article of patriotic infatuation. Such things become right and good, and it becomes the dutiful privilege of all citizens to cherish these things and to devote their substance and energies to the furtherance of them, without scrutiny or afterthought. Indeed, further scrutiny of any article of belief or practice which has found lodgment in the community's habits of thought as a standard item of national aspiration or national pretension will be odious, to the point of presumptive criminality. So also, whatever can be made to bear the appearance of hindering or trifling with those aspirations that are covered by the habitual canons of national integrity in force at a given time and place are presumptively treasonable. Such treason is the gravest of crimes, —next after lèse majesté. Indeed, the spirit of national integrity touches the skirts of divinity and carries more than a trace of religious intolerance. So that the crime of treason comes near to the unique atrocity of sin against the Holy Ghost. In both cases there is the same dutiful renunciation of sobriety and reason in dealing with delinquents, and the same presumption of guilt in the accused.

Uncritical devotion to the national pretensions being a meritorious habit, it is also a useful article of camouflage, a shelter for gainful enterprises and transactions which might otherwise be open to doubt, a means of avoiding unfavorable notice and of procuring a profitable line of good-will. In this sense it has come to have a merchantable value, so that professions of such devotion have become a businesslike matter-of-course among those who follow "gainful pursuits." Which weeds out profitless argument and reflection in these premises and dispenses with any irritating afterthought. And men will commonly believe and live up to those things which they habitually profess. That is the meaning of autosuggestion. "Auto-intoxication" can not properly be applied in this connection, since the term has been assigned a specific meaning in medical usage.

What is yet more to the point is the secondary effect of these businesslike professions of national faith, in that the young are taught to believe what their elders profess to believe. This indoctrination of the young by undeviating habituation in word and deed, precept and example, is very much in the foreground of their schooling just now, and it should logically bring grave consequences in the way of an accentuated nationalist bias in the incoming generation. It is something like drill in the manual of arms, both in respect of the mental qualities involved and in respect of the automatic responses induced in persons subjected to it. The resulting action-pattern of national animation runs on much the same lines as the habitual use of the Paternoster and Rosary, and carries the like uncritical assurance of well-doing.

In an earlier chapter something has already been said of the salesmanlike piety that is habitually professed by those who do business in the country towns. They and all their folks and ways are given to blamelessly devout observances and professions, by routine of the day's work in pursuit of salesmanlike gains. There is no especial degree of hypocrisy and no appreciable mental strain involved in their so professing and acting on a belief in religious verities of which they neither have nor seek an understanding. It is all a foregone conclusion, a businesslike matter-of-course incident to their "gainful pursuit." But in this as in other matters men (and women) come to believe what they habitually profess, and with a jealous solicitude they train their offspring, by precept, example, and systematic schooling, into due conformity with these canons of salvation and profitable respectability. So also as regards the secular faith and observances of national integrity. And in an eminent sense the country towns have the making of the community's ideals and mentality, beyond any other one agency. In much the same measure they have also the making of the country's official personnel and their mentality. National integrity, religious intolerance, and business principles march together under the banners of the country town in a co-partnership of means and ends, for the Glory of God and the good of man.

In any democratic community, such as the American, the official personnel which is vested with jurisdiction and initiative will be, in the main, such as the country town has made them, by exacting habituation and by selective elimination of the unfit. Fitness for responsible office being, on the whole, tested by conformity to these three canonical articles: national integrity, devout observance, and business-as-usual. A democratic community addicted to business enterprise and devout observances will not tolerate an official personnel endowed with a different equipment of habitual predilections. Exceptions may occur, but they are sporadic and negligible, and they fall into abeyance at any juncture of national exigency. Such a community will trust no one but its substantial citizens; which is another way of saying the same thing. Anyone may assure himself of the truth of this statement, as a general proposition, by a cursory survey of the case as it presents itself at large or at any point.

These persons who make up this official personnel, and in whose hands is the power to act, locally, departmentally, and at large, will go into action as practical men, faithful to the joint governance of these settled habits of thought whose creatures they are. With a mentality compounded of national integrity and business principles they will devoutly follow out the drift of the two conjointly; to such effect that in the official apprehension the community's fortunes are bound up with the pursuit of its business enterprise; that is to say, with the continued gains of its absentee owners. It lies in the nature of democratic institutions that any such community will select its official personnel from among its absentee owners, that is to say its substantial citizens. And it lies in the nature of the substantial citizen-official to let business interests coalesce with the national integrity in such a way as to make the safe-keeping of business-as-usual the first and constant care of the official establishment. So that any conjunction of circumstances which may threaten to encroach on the accomplished facts of absentee ownership or of capitalised overhead charges at any point will forthwith be rated as a menace to the national integrity and a call for official measures of repression to guard the public's safety.

Business-as-usual and the national integrity are joint and integral factors in that complex of habits of thought that makes up the official mentality; so that any irritation of the official sensibilities along either line will unavoidably bring a response along the two together and indiscriminately. In that parallelogram of forces in which business principles and the sense of national integrity combine jointly to move and direct the democratic officials there is no distinguishing the two joint factors. The fact may also be worth noting, although it is essentially of secondary consequence, that since any given democratic official is also in effect a substantial citizen, his pecuniary interests as an owner in his own right will fall into line with his civic principles at large in this mattter, and will therefore coalesce with his civic virtue and give urgency and singleness of purpose; with the result that the weight of the official establishment, national and local, will in the nature of things be brought to bear on the side of ownership at any juncture of doubt or dissension.

The point of immediate interest here is not any merit or demerit that may attach to this run of the facts, but only the fact that such is the run of them.

So far as concerns the argument at this point, the upshot of this run of the facts is that the habit of thinking in terms of national solidarity and civic allegiance, ingrained in the community at large as well as in its official personnel, comes into the case as an effectual bar to any departure from the standard routine. Faithful adherence to business principles and to the businesslike management of industry is second nature to the substantial citizen. But by process of growth, such businesslike management of the industrial system has become incompatible with the current state of the industrial arts; so that the continued management of industry for business purposes results in an industrial stalemate.

In that intractable dissension which divides the owner-employers and the organised workmen, the resources and appliances of constituted authority are brought into action on the side of the employer-owners, in effect and in the main. That such should be the case lies in the nature of things; partly for reasons reflected in the last few paragraphs above. Also in great part this run of the facts is grounded in ancient and standard law and custom, as well as in current statute and precedent.

The rights, powers, and immunities of ownership, including the incidents of free contract, are grounded in principles of law and usage which are by ancient habit deeply embedded in the popular common sense as well as in the common law. This body of law and usage grew out of habituation to an earlier order of things, and has therefore stood over from some time before anything like the present system of industry and business had come into action; before ownership and its share in the management of industry had passed over into absentee ownership and engendered the current credit system. So that these ancient principles of law and of common sense, in which the rights, powers, and immunities of ownership are grounded, are by way of being holdovers. The material circumstances have moved out of their way. But all the while that the shift to absentee ownership and credit has been going forward, the ancient principles have been progressively construed, adapted, and amplified to meet the newly arisen exigencies; and the work of construction and amplification has been carried on by men whose immersion in business affairs has imbued them with a steadfast bias; to such effect that, as a matter of formal scope and authority, the ancient principles have been enabled to sanction whatever arrangements may be expedient for absentee ownership and its administration. In point of statutory provision and constructive precedent, the rights, powers, and immunities of absentee ownership and cap- italised overhead charges have all that sanction and sta- bility that belong to habits of thought which are embedded in immemorial common sense. They are right and good, in point of statutory provision and constructive prece- dent, before the law; indeed, the law and the lawgivers have been busy with their enforcement and reënforcement, for some time past.

But they are not equally secure in point of common sense; that is to say, the grounds of habitual morality are not similarly stable. The material exigencies of life and the habituation enforced by them have not been running on precisely the same lines as those exigencies of business which have given rise to these statutory provisions and constructive precedents. At any juncture where a discrep- ancy arises between law and common sense it is incum- bent on the constituted authorities to take precautionary measures and guard the provisions of law against inroads of common sense. Under the circumstances, therefore, it has become the prime and particular duty of the con- stituted authorities to safeguard the rights, powers, and immunities of absentee ownership, at any cost to the underlying population.

Under "the majestic equality of the law," the organ- ised workmen enjoy the same rights, powers, and im- munities of absentee ownership and capitalised over- head charges as their owner-employers with whom they are forever at odds. But their circumstances are differ- ent, and the incidence of these legal provisions is there- fore different in their case. They have, in effect, no enforceable absentee rights and powers, and they have been unable to capitalise their income into fixed overhead charges on industry, collectible *in absentia*. They and their claims and circumstances do not fit into the legal framework of business-as-usual conducted on the current plan; which is their misfortune, if not their fault. The legal validity of any of those demands and perquisites for which they contend is of a slight and dubious nature. Being not capitalised into a corporate entity with fixed charges and limited liability, as their absentee owners are, any concerted action on their part is likely to be obnoxious to the law which penalises conspiracy. A few hundred or a few thousand absentee owners acting in collusion as stockholders in a corporation, on the other side of the controversy, are not guilty of conspiracy in the eyes of the law. So also, since the workmen are not owners of the plant about the use or unemployment of which the controversy turns, they have no right of access to the premises and are therefore unable to supervise and enforce the unemployment of the works in support of their contention. It is otherwise with the employer-owners. By and large, the legitimate powers of the workmen in such a controversy extend no farther than to take or leave the terms offered them by the employer-owners. Even a boycott is obnoxious to the law.

In effect it is recognised as a matter of common sense that this right of individual and passive unemployment is scarcely adequate to serve the turn in their negotiations with their owner-employers. Quite visibly the substantial citizens and the constituted authorities are of that mind. Indeed they are animated with a lively apprehension on that score, and precautionary measures are taken to guard against anticipated excesses on the part of the workmen at this point. There is no similar apprehension and no similar precautions are taken as regards the owner-employers. It is quite plainly the persuasion of the substantial citizens and the official personnel that the organised workmen may, at any juncture, be provoked by these disabilities into exceeding the limits of sabotage countenanced by the law—the passive withdrawal of efficiency—and that they will be likely, on due provocation, to resort to such "direct action" as will jeopardise the rightful holdings and incomes of the absentee owners in the case. The substantial citizens and the official personnel are moved by no serious apprehension that precautionary measures are necessary to restrain the employer-owners within the law. The ordinary legal correctives and remedies are sufficient for that purpose. Whereas such precautionary measures of forcible repression to keep recalcitrant workmen within due bounds and to safeguard the interests of the owners belong in the standard routine of things to be done. No doubt, all this is as it should be, in view of the relevant facts.[12]

[12] It has been said, with a disquieting verisimilitude though perhaps with unwarranted breadth, that "The Intelligence Service of the Army has for its primary purpose" a surveillance of certain obnoxious civil organisations; and the organisations enumerated as obnoxious are organisations of workmen and farmers,—the list includes the American Federation of Labor. It is to be presumed that such an avowal will not be found formally correct. It is at least inexpedient; but there is a disquieting verisimilitude about it, in view of the known facts.

Apart from international intrigue and intimidation, almost wholly in pursuit of business interests, the workday use of the administration's military arm is to keep the domestic peace. In practical effect and in the common run, the enforcement of domestic peace works out in restraining unruly workmen and safeguarding the interests of property and business, in the recurrent cases of dispute between owners and employees. The like will apply generally to measures of "preparedness" in the way of armed force; whether under the auspices of the Federal administration or as carried on in the several states; whether they

By force of ancient law and custom and by the later drift of circumstances it has come about that the resources and apparatus of constituted authority, whether by administrative direction or permissively, will in the main serve the needs of the employer-owners in their controversial dealings with their industrial man-power. It will not be denied that this state of the case has a very appreciable dramatic and sentimental value; but the merits of the arrangement, whether as a question of public

come under the name of the National Guard, State Militia, State Constabulary, or Municipal Police,—although some substantial reservation is to be entered as regards the last mentioned. The like is also true of those private enterprises in preparedness, the so-called Detective Agencies, which make a business of supplying mercenaries and "under-cover men." These mercenary fighting men are used by the employer-owners, almost wholly, as against the workmen. This private traffic in mercenaries is presumably quite right and proper, being permitted by the authorities and approved by the substantial citizens; although with some demur from the side of the organised workmen.

To complete the sketch at this point it is necessary to note that in those states or municipalities where the carriage or possession of firearms is subject to "Permit," the prohibition of arms will chiefly affect the workmen and others who have no substantial standing as owners or custodians of property; the need of guarding valuable property rights being the usual ground on which such permits are issued. Whether by intention or not, this regulation has the effect of leaving the employer-owners and their retainers armed, while the workmen are not armed except by evasion of the law. In the same connection, and as a characteristic circumstance, it appears that the larger industrial corporations come somewhat habitually into the market for firearms and ammunition, as good and valuable customers. This corporate preparedness includes rifles and machine-guns; whereas there appears to be little demand on the part of the same concerns for guns of such calibre as would be at all properly called artillery, such as "quick-firers" and "trench-mortars."

What has just been said is no more than a *pro forma* recital of obvious facts, of course. It is a description of the state of the case at large, and is to be taken with such qualifications as may be called for in detail.

morals or of class interest, will not engage the argument at this point. What is of immediate interest is the objective consequences of the arrangement. One of these immediate consequences is an abiding sense of grievance and hostility on both sides of the negotiations, but more pronounced perhaps on the side of the workmen. Mutual distrust and sharp practice has come to be of the essence of the case; working out in a standard policy of mutual defeat.

By force of law and custom, as progressively construed and amplified by successive generations of businesslike officials, any manœuvres which violate or exceed the immunities and powers of ownership are disallowed in this strategy of mutual defeat by which the working of the industrial system is governed. This bears on the manœuvres of the workmen in a peculiarly drastic way, since they are vested with none of the powers and immunities of ownership,—except in that Pickwickian sense in which "the majestic equality of the law" deals impartially with rich and poor. In effect, their powers and immunities in these premises are wholly of a negative order, such as will enable them to do nothing, to withhold efficiency, to lie idle and to put in their working-time as wastefully and ineffectively as the circumstances will permit; in short to go in for that negative sabotage which is of the essence of business management in industry. So they concentrate their endeavors and ingenuity on this line. Bent on defeating their owner-employers by such ways and means as are at their disposal, they apply themselves with all diligence to delivering as nearly nothing as may be in return for such wages as their latest manœuvres in unemployment have enabled them to carry off, for the transient time being. So that by what foots up to a concerted policy of mutual defect the two parties in interest work together to pare the effectual work and output of industry down to whatever level of deficiency the traffic will bear in the short run.

In the short run, under the spur of tactical necessity, the traffic will bear and the exigencies will enjoin so effectual a disallowance of work and output as to leave a margin of livelihood and maintenance uncovered, and to entail a shrinkage of the available man-power and material equipment. Under the hands of a businesslike official personnel, supported by a like-minded body of substantial citizens, the vindication of property rights coalesces in principle with the vindication of the national integrity, to such effect that any proposal to disallow or abridge the sovereign rights of absentee ownership in the conduct of industry will be constructive sedition. So that the spur of tactical necessity will drive with an unmitigated incentive to the one line of strategy which this posture of things leaves open,—an alert and obstinate disallowance of work and output. Short runs of intensified strategic sabotage come therefore to predominate in the contest between employers and employees; succeeding one another with increasing urgency and decreasing intervals; so that the long run falls into shape as a discontinuous chain of deficits, with scant and vanishing internodes of recovery. This describes the present rather than the future. And since the several lines of productive industry are bound by the state of the industrial arts into an increasingly intricate and exacting network of give and take, they will each and several be subject to undesigned and unforseen stoppages induced by tactical stoppages in related lines of industry, with increasing frequency and amplitude as business principles take the upperhand and the spirit of salesmanship finally displaces workmanship in the conduct of industry. All the while any shrinkage in the rate and volume of output and any curtailment of the material factors engaged is to be covered over and made good on the books with a capitalisation of credits and a rising level of prices, due to an increased volume of purchasing-power thereby thrown on the market. A progressively increasing volume of working capital is required for the conduct of an increasingly stubborn campaign of labor troubles and an increasingly large and exacting expenditure on sales-publicity; which is to be covered with a running creation of credits, duly capitalised and thrown on the market as an addition to the outstanding purchasing-power.

In recent times, and in a progressively increasing measure, the national establishments and the spirit of national integrity among the peoples of Christendom have been an agency of dissension and distress, a means of curtailing and impairing the material conditions of life for the underlying population, and an arrangement for the increase and diffusion of ill-will among men. Such is their major and ordinary outcome. Coupled with this is commonly some slight differential advantage to some special Interest in whose service these agencies are employed. In recent times the differential gains which so accrue from this usufruct of national ill-will, inure in the main, to certain commercial and financial Interests sheltered under the national Flag.

The net aggregate amount of these differential gains which so accrue to these special Interests at the cost of such ill-will and distress to the common run will ordinarily foot up to no more than a vanishing percentage of their net aggregate cost to the underlying populations that are employed in the traffic. In the material respect these institutional holdovers work out in a formidable aggregate loss of life and livelihood; while in the spiritual respect their staple output is a tissue of dissension, distrust, dishonesty, servility, and bombast. The net product is mutual and collective defeat and grief.[13]

[13] As has been remarked in an earlier passage, this characterisation has nothing to say as regards the moral or æsthetic excellence of these institutional holdovers, as to the righteousness, goodness, or beauty of national integrity, patriotic intolerance, or political intrigue. These are questions of taste and fashion, about which there is no disputing. Nor do these questions touch the present argument, which has to do with the objective consequences of these institutional factors.

By derivation, in point of institutional pedigree, the democratic nations of Christendom are a "filial generation" of those dynastic and territorial monarchies which filled Europe with a muddle of war and politics in early modern times. And these national establishments, and the spirit of national integrity on which they trade, are still essentially warlike and political. That is to say, predation is still the essence of the thing. The ways and means of the traffic are still force and fraud, at home and abroad. The actualities of that "self-determination of nations" which has so profoundly engaged the sentiments of thoughtful persons, always foots up to a self-determination in respect of warlike adventures, political jobbery, and territorial aggrandisement. Witness the newly self-determining nations, Poland, Czechoslovakia, Jugoslavia.

There are, doubtless, many mitigating circumstances, and many fanciful card-houses of cultural and linguistic conceits erected in good faith by the apologists of Chauvinism. But in point of fact, "realpolitik" continues to make satisfactory use of the chauvinists in a pursuit of its own ends by force and fraud. So also the universal type-form of national solemnities, even when staged by the mildest mannered and most amiable curators of the spiritual antiquities, continues to be a worshipful magnification of past warlike adventures, backed with a staging of histrionic obsequies of war-heroes, with parade of guns, uniforms and battle standards. "Breathes there a man with soul so dead, Who never to himself hath said, 'This is my own, my native land,'" when the national anniversary is being magnified with warlike fireworks and bombast, while veterans, Red Cross nurses and Boy Scouts parade their uniforms to martial music under banners? In any one of these democratic commonwealths the acid test of sound and serviceable citizenship still is the good old

Apart from any glamor of national prowess, in the way of blood and wounds, the nations have also a certain sentimental value as standard containers, each of its distinctive cultural tincture, very precious to persons of cultivated tastes in these matters. So also, as a matter of history these national commonwealths, as well as the territorial states in their time, have served to alleviate local animosities, each within its jurisdiction, and to bring consistency and correlation into the process of industry and of civil life within their several territories. But all that is beside the point today. The work of correlation, standardisation, and concatenation of local units and of the processes of work and life has been taken over, irretrievably, by the industrial arts, which do not go by favor of nationalities. The industrial arts, and the industrial system in which they go into action, have no use for and no patience with local tinctures of culture and the obstructive routine of statecraft. The mechanistic system of industry is of a collective and coöperative nature, essentially and of necessity a joint enterprise of all the civilised peoples, in so far as their civilisation is of the occidental pattern; and there is substantially only one such pattern. This industrial system runs on a balanced specialisation of work among its working members; standardised quantity production, which is always and of necessity in excess of the local needs; free draught on a limitless range of material resources from far and near. No isolated industrial undertaking and no isolated cultural activity is self-sufficient within the sweep of this industrial system of Christendom. And any degree of wilful iso-

propensity to fight for the flag without protest or afterthought. There is no question but this is a meritorious frame of mind. It is also the frame of mind which is sedulously drilled into the incoming generation.

lation is straitway and automatically penalised by a corresponding degree of impotence, under the impassive run of the industrial system at large, which draws impartially on far and near. In this new industrial order of things the national establishments and their frontiers and functionaries come in as an extraneous apparatus of deflection and obstruction, employed to perpetuate animosities and generate lag, leak, and friction.

Of this nature are customs-duties, shipping-subsidies, trade-concessions, consular service, passport regulations, national protection and enforcement of claims in foreign parts. Much has been said in censure of these and the like contrivances of discrimination, and much more in the way of censure is doubtless merited. The closer the scrutiny of this apparatus and its working, the more deplorable it all proves to be, in its material consequences. But this notorious imbecility of it all does after all not immediately concern the argument at this point. It is of more immediate interest to note that in all these diplomatic, legislative, and administrative measures in restraint of trade and industry, the measures are taken for the benefit of business, to stabilise, fortify and enhance the gains of one and another among the special business Interests that are domiciled in the country; that the national establishment is in this way employed in the service of these business concerns, at the cost of the national community at large; that in this way the national interests have come to be identified with the gainful traffic of these business Interests; that the sense of national integrity is by habituation to this routine of subservience made to cover the maintenance of business-as-usual and the insurance of capitalised earnings. The subservience of the national establishment and the official personnel to the aims and manœuvres of business becomes a fact of prescriptive use and wont, passes into law and custom, and is embedded in the community's common sense as a matter of workday routine.

In the last analysis the nation remains a predatory organism, in practical effect an association of persons moved by a community interest in getting something for nothing by force and fraud. There is, doubtless, also much else of a more genial nature to be said for the nation as an institutional factor in recent times. The voluminous literature of patriotic encomium and apology has already said all that is needed on that head. But the irreducible core of national life, what remains when the non-essentials are deducted, still is of this nature; it continues to be self-determination in war and politics. Such is the institutional pedigree of the nation. It is a residual derivative of the predatory dynastic State, and as such it still continues to be, in the last resort, an establishment for the mobilisation of force and fraud as against the outside, and for a penalised subservience of its underlying population at home.

In recent times, owing to the latterday state of the industrial arts, this national pursuit of warlike and political ends has come to be a fairly single-minded chase after unearned income to be procured by intimidation and intrigue. It has been called Imperialism; it might also, in a colloquial phrasing, be called national graft. By and large, it takes the two typical forms of graft: official salaries (The White Man's Burden), as in the British crown colonies and the American dependencies; and of special concessions and advantageous bargains in the way of trade, credits and investments, as, e. g., the British interests in Africa and Mesopotamia or the American transactions in Nicaragua and Haiti. The official salaries which are levied by this means on the underlying population in foreign parts inure directly to the nation's kept classes, in their rôle of official personnel, being in the nature of perquisites of gentility and of political suction. The special benefits in the way of profitable trade and investment under national tutelage in foreign parts inure to those special Interests which are in close touch with the nation's official personnel and do business in foreign parts with their advice and consent.

All the while, of course, all this trading on the national integrity is carried on as inconspicuously as may be, quite legally and morally under democratic forms, by night and cloud, and is covered over with such decently voluble prevarication as the case may require, prevarication of a decently statesmanlike sort; such a volume and texture of prevarication as may serve to keep the national left hand from knowing what the right hand is doing, the left hand in these premises being the community at large, as contrasted with the Interests and the official personnel. In all such work of administrative prevarication and democratic camouflage the statesmen are greatly helped out by the newspapers and the approved agencies that gather and purvey such news as is fit to print for the purpose in hand. The pulpit, too, has its expedient uses as a publicity agency in furtherance of this gainful pursuit of national enterprise in foreign parts.

However, the present argument is not concerned with the main facts and material outcome of this imperial statecraft considered as a "gainful pursuit," but only with the ulterior and residual consequences of the traffic in the way of a heightened sense of national integrity and a closer coalescence of this national integrity with the gainful pursuits of all these dominant business Interests that engage the sympathies of the official personnel. By this means the national integrity becomes ever more closely identified, in the popular apprehension, with the security and continued enlargement of the capitalised overhead charges of those concerns which do business in foreign parts; whereby the principles of business and absentee ownership come in for an added sanction; so that the official personnel which has these matters in charge is enabled to give a more undivided attention and a more headlong support to any manœuvres of strategic sabotage on industrial production which the exigencies of gainful business may dictate, whether at home or abroad.

Statecraft as a gainful pursuit has always been a furtive enterprise. And in due proportion as the nation's statecraft is increasingly devoted to the gainful pursuit of international intrigue it will necessarily take on a more furtive character, and will conduct a larger proportion of its ordinary work by night and cloud. Which leads to a substitution of coercion in the place of consultation in the dealings of the official personnel with their underlying population, whether in domestic or foreign policy; and such coercion is increasingly accepted in a complaisant, if not a grateful, spirit by the underlying population, on a growing conviction that the national integrity is best provided for by night and cloud. So therefore it also follows that any overt expression of doubt as to the national expediency of any obscure transaction or line of transactions entered into by the official personnel in the course of this clandestine traffic in gainful politics, whether at home or abroad, will presumptively be seditious; and unseasonable inquiry into the furtive movements of the official personnel is by way of becoming an actionable offense; since it is to be presumed that, for the good of the nation, no one outside of the official personnel and the business Interests in collusion can bear any intelligent part in the management of these delicate negotiations, and any premature intimation of what is going on is likely to be "information which may be useful to the enemy." Any pronounced degree of skepticism touching the expediency of any of the accomplished facts of political intrigue or administrative control is due to be penalised as obnoxious to the common good. In the upshot of it all, the paramount rights, powers, aims, and immunities of ownership, or at least those of absentee ownership, come in for a closer identification with the foundations of the national establishment and are hedged about with a double conviction of well-doing.

In that strategy of businesslike curtailment of output, debilitation of industry, and capitalisation of overhead charges, which is entailed by the established system of ownership and bargaining, the constituted authorities in all the democratic nations may, therefore, be counted on to lend their unwavering support to all manœuvres of business-as-usual, and to disallow any transgression of or departure from business principles. Nor should there seem any probability that the effectual run of popular sentiment touching these matters will undergo any appreciable change in the calculable future. The drift of workday discipline, as well as of deliberate instruction, sets in the conservative direction. For the immediate future the prospect appears to offer a fuller confirmation in the faith that business principles answer all things. The outlook should accordingly be that the businesslike control of the industrial system in detail should presently reach, if it has not already reached, and should speedily pass beyond that critical point of chronic derangement in the aggregate beyond which a continued pursuit of the same strategy on the same businesslike principles will result in a progressively widening margin of deficiency in the aggregate material output and a progressive shrinkage of the available means of life.

THE END

Transaction Books by Thorstein Veblen

Absentee Ownership

The Engineers and the Price System

The Higher Learning in America

Imperial Germany and the Industrial Revolution

The Instinct of Workmanship and
the State of the Industrial Arts

The Place of Science in Modern Civilization

The Theory of Business Enterprise

The Theory of the Leisure Class

Absentee Ownership